URBAN
CHANGE
IN CHINA

Politics and Development in
Tsinan, Shantung, 1890-1949

David D. Buck

THE UNIVERSITY OF WISCONSIN PRESS

Published 1978

The University of Wisconsin Press
Box 1379, Madison, Wisconsin 53701

The University of Wisconsin Press, Ltd.
70 Great Russell Street, London

First printing

Printed in the United States of America

For LC CIP information see the colophon
ISBN 0-299-07110-3

Publication of this book
has been made possible in part
by a grant from the
Andrew W. Mellon Foundation

This book is affectionately dedicated

to my parents,

Douglas H. and Mildred M. Buck

Contents

1: Tsinan and the Question of the City in Modern Chinese History   3

2: Tsinan in the Late Nineteenth Century   16

    Shantung's Nineteenth-Century Trading Systems, 22
    Post-1850 Shifts in the Prevailing Economic System in Shantung, 23
    Political and Economic Power in Tsinan, 28
    Tsinan's Social Life and Social Classes, 34
    The Twin Shocks of the Sino-Japanese War and the Boxer Uprising, 38

3: Tsinan During the Late Ch'ing Reforms, 1901-1911   40

    Yüan Shih-k'ai's Dominance, 41
    Yüan Shih-k'ai's Policy against German Imperialism in Shantung, 44
    Officially Backed Innovation at Tsinan, 50
    The Foreign Community in Tsinan, 59
    The Rise of Reform-Minded Gentry, 60

4: Tsinan During the Early Republic, 1912-1916   72

    The Revolution of 1911 in Tsinan, 72
    The Struggle between Yüan Shih-k'ai and the Shantung Gentry, 78
    Foreign Influence in Shantung, 83
    The Revolutionary Party Uprising of May 1916, 87
    The Continuing Modernization of Tsinan, 91
    Summary, 96

5: Political Power in Tsinan During the Warlord Era, 1916-1927   98

    Dominance of the Peiyang Clique, 98
    Japanese Policy Involving Shantung, 1916-1919, 107
    Resistance in Tsinan to Japanese Imperialism, 114
    Return of Tsingtao and the Shantung Railroad to China, 120
    Weakness of the Shantung Provincial Leadership, 124
    The Dark Days of Warlordism: The Rule of Chang Tsung-ch'ang, 125

6: Economic and Social Life in Tsinan During the Warlord Era   130

    Tsinan's Economy in the Golden Age of Capitalism (1916-1923), 130
    Labor in Tsinan, 140
    Administration and Government, 144
    Social Life in Tsinan, 149
    Summary, 155

7: Tsinan in the Decade of Kuomintang Rule, 1927-1937   156
      The Tsinan Incident, May 1928, 157
      The Situation in Tsinan During 1928-1929, 164
      The Administration of Han Fu-ch'ü, 165
      Tsinan under Han Fu-ch'ü, 170
      Tsinan's Economy in the 1930s, 176
      The Fall of Han Fu-ch'ü, 181
      Summary, 186

8: Tsinan in War, 1938-1948   188
      The Japanese Administration in Tsinan, 1938-1945, 188
      Tsinan under Kuomintang Rule, 1945-1948, 194
      The Impact of the War Years on Tsinan, 199

9: Politics and Development in Tsinan, 1890-1949   202
      Tsinan's Development since 1949, 202
      The Failure to Modernize, 210

Appendix A: Tsinan's Industry, 1900-1936   219

Appendix B: Tsinan's Population, 1770-1975   226

Appendix C: Demands of the Shantung Provincial Assembly,
      November 1911   237

Notes   239

Selected Bibliography   265

Character List   283

Index   291

Illustrations

Tsinan city wall   18

Tsinan commercial street about 1905   20

Tsinan, about 1906   48

The Li-hsia Pavilion   58

New construction outside the P'u-li Gate in the 1920s   142

The walled area of Tsinan, southwestern portion   190

Tsinan's outer wall, northeastern corner   191

Former settlement district of Tsinan, 1974   206

Maps

1 Shantung in the 1890s   24

2 Tsinan in the 1920s   100

3 Tsinan and its immediate hinterland, about 1928   132

4 Shantung in the 1930s   158

5 Functional zones in Tsinan, 1974   204

Tables

3.1	Shantung Governors, 1901-1911	43
3.2	Educational Status of Shantung Assemblymen, 1909	64
4.1	Shantung Military Governors, 1911-1916	76
5.1	Shantung Military Governors, 1916-1928	102
5.2	Shantung Civil Governors, 1919-1925	103
6.1	Chief Shantungese Commercial Elements in Tsinan, Early 1920s	133
6.2	Modern Banks in Tsinan, 1923	134
6.3	Flour Mills in Tsinan, 1914-1925	139
6.4	Shantung Provincial Budget, 1922	146
7.1	Tsinan's Newspapers in the 1930s	175
A.1	Large Industrial Concerns in Tsinan, 1901-1911	220
A.2	Major Industrial Operations in Tsinan, 1914	221
A.3	Survey of Tsinan Industry, 1926	222
A.4	Survey of Tsinan Industry, 1933	224
B.1	Population of Tsinan, 1772	228
B.2	Population of Tsinan, 1837	229
B.3	Late Nineteenth-Century Estimates of Tsinan's Population	229
B.4	Population of Tsinan, 1914	230
B.5	Population of Tsinan, 1919	231
B.6	Population of Tsinan, 1933	231

B.7   Population of Tsinan, 1942   232

B.8   Shantung's Population, 1787-1970   233

B.9   Tsinan's Population as a Percentage of Shantung's

      Total Population   234

B.10 Population of Tsinan since 1949   235

Acknowledgments

The research for this book took place in a number of libraries and research facilities in East Asia, Europe, and the United States. The staffs of the East Asian Collection in the Hoover Institution at Stanford, the Institute of Modern History of the Academia Sinica in Taiwan, the Tōyō Bunko in Tokyo, the U.S. National Archives in Washington, D.C., the Public Record Office in London, and the Missionary Research Library in New York City all were unusually helpful in providing access to their valuable collections and supplying working facilities for periods of research. Some of this work was conducted while I was a graduate student at Stanford University and I gratefully acknowledge fellowship support received from the university and under the terms of the National Defense Education Act during those years.

The idea for this book grew out of an interest in Shantung nurtured by my teacher Chao Ming, as well as the encouragement of Frederic Wakeman. Lyman Van Slyke patiently guided the completion of an earlier version of the first portion of this book as a Ph.D. dissertation at Stanford. A number of friends and colleagues, including Guy Alitto, Jerome Cavanaugh, Chang P'eng-yuan, Edward Friedman, Susan Mann Jones, Li En-han, Timothy Ross, Richard Sorich, G. William Skinner, Wang Erh-min, C. Martin Wilbur, and Arthur Wolf suggested important source materials to me.

Ramon Myers and Rhoads Murphey generously read the manuscript and made valuable suggestions, many of which have been incorporated into the text. Craig Canning, General Frank Dorn and Janet Salaff added their insight on important points. The process of revision was greatly assisted by Autumn Stanley, who did a great deal to improve my awkward prose. Carolyn Dulka typed the manuscript in its several revisions. The responsibility for all remaining errors is my own.

The problems of illustrating this kind of historical work are legion, but I received much assistance. J. G. Bell at the Stanford University Press permitted the use of maps of Shantung originally published in the volume

The Chinese City Between Two Worlds. Donald Temple of the University of Wisconsin-Milwaukee's Cartographic Laboratory prepared maps and schematic drawings from my sketches. Trev Sue-a-Quan provided the 1974 photograph of Tsinan's busy streets. My brother, Bruce M. Buck, lent a hand by contributing drawings of Tsinan made from photographs that were too poor for reproduction. The aerial views of Tsinan were made available from the archives of the United States Defense Intelligence Agency. Ke-lien Chiu did the calligraphy for the Character List and Bibliography.

D. D. B.

Milwaukee, Wisconsin
July 20, 1976

Urban Change in China

1

Tsinan and the Question of the City in Modern Chinese History

THIS STUDY HAS TWO PURPOSES: to discover how one Chinese city grew and changed during the first half of the twentieth century, and to use that city's experience to help assess the role of cities in recent Chinese history. The city I examine is Tsinan, the provincial capital of Shantung and a third-level trading city of the late Ch'ing. During the period discussed here, Tsinan became a major railroad junction in North China and increased its political and administrative importance.

The question that preoccupies most students of Chinese cities in recent history is to what extent these cities fulfilled their putative role as centers of a new economy, a new society, and a new political system that would radiate change and transform China into a strong and modern nation. This image of the urban role, of course, is drawn from the nineteenth-century concept of the modernizing, progressive industrial city in the West; until 1949 it dominated the views not only of Westerners but of most Chinese who hoped to change China. Let us look at the Western model in some detail.

In nineteenth-century Europe and North America, urban life was transformed as the burgeoning industrial cities concentrated production, population, technology, and economic power in ways never before experienced. Beginning with the application of the new industrial technology to the production of goods, a chain of factors led to the establishment of large industrial production facilities in cities: the rapid expansion of existing means and the development of new means of transportation to connect industrial cities with their sources of supply and markets, and, as industrial production increased, a basic shift in national residence patterns. Migration to the cities soon concentrated many Western nations' populations in the cities. This process, still continuing in modified form in developed nations, is called urbanization.[1]

Urbanization in its classical nineteenth-century form encompassed both a detailed division of labor and an accompanying increase in specialization of labor. Specialization was part of the new overall complexity of industri-

3

alization that required more complicated forms of financing, distribution, and marketing than the world had previously known. Typically clustering in exclusive business districts adjacent to the chief transportation service areas, these operations became even more heavily concentrated in cities than industrial production.

As nineteenth-century cities grew, they quickly spilled out beyond their pre-industrial boundaries. Upper-, middle- and working-class residential areas appeared, less sharply distinguished, however, than in Western cities of the mid-twentieth century.[2] Working-class neighborhoods usually sprang up amidst the industrial sections. The poorest elements found inadequate housing on the least desirable land, often right beside the noisome transportation and industrial facilities.

The social order in the new industrial cities reflected their growing size and complexity. Class distinctions grew stronger, while class conflict became more structured through division of labor and residential patterns. Male and female roles, and the roles of children and older people, changed to fit industrial and urban requirements. Children felt the change dramatically when state-controlled schooling became the norm. Retirement with its sudden separation from a lifetime's work habits— unknown to previous rural generations—became the common experience of urban workers.

The scope and complexity of urban life also encouraged special attention to certain artistic and creative endeavors, frequently underwritten by the wealthy commercial and industrial magnates. The proliferation of potential interests and activities in the urban setting produced a more vital and complex cultural mode than was common in most pre-industrial cities. This new urban culture was also partly a response to the greater complexity of work and the increasing freedom from community pressures that accompanied migration to the cities.

Expansion of personal freedom was generally thought to be a benefit of the new era. Not all of the changes taking place, however, were so positive. The large industrial city also quickly became identified with such unfavorable social phenomena as poverty, overcrowding, disease, child labor, and crime.[3] In order to preserve basic social values in such an atmosphere, various movements of urban social reform arose, focused on significant issues such as child labor, medical problems, and housing. A host of regulatory and social-service institutions, including police and fire departments, orphanages, and charity homes, were formed to help cope with the social problems of industrial cities.

Some of these endeavors were private, but most began in public institutions run by urban government. City government expanded enormously during the industrial era. Paving and lighting the streets,

4

supplying water, disposing of sewage, and providing public transportation are only the most dramatic of the many responsibilities assumed by industrial cities. These services were expensive to finance and operate. Large amounts of capital had to be raised for initial construction; large staffs of skilled employees had to be recruited and thenceforth paid.

Partly because it was becoming obvious that urban living required services far exceeding anything necessary in rural areas, the cities were given considerable authority over taxation. Although no city since the Italian city-states has had complete fiscal and administrative autonomy, the nineteenth-century industrial city won the essential powers needed to conduct its own affairs. The European tradition of a degree of urban autonomy contributed considerably to this process in many places. By the end of the century the typical industrial city had a strong sense of its own identity. It was oriented toward promoting, expanding, and improving itself, and it had most of the administrative autonomy needed to accomplish these tasks.

Urban political power typically functioned through a series of formal and informal representative institutions that served to legitimize the various decisions of urban administration. The form and means of selection for these bodies varied, but usually they reflected the interests of the wealthy and well-born urban residents. Considerable fault has been found with nineteenth-century urban governments, especially the forms of political bossism common in United States cities, but a strong movement of liberal reform focused on making these governments both more representative and more efficient in serving the needs of the urban residents.

In the nineteenth-century mind the city became the locus of change and progress within the whole society. The heart of the city's new role was its increasing importance as a center of production. Cities became responsible for a growing portion of the gross national product and total employment in the nineteenth-century West. The cities were the chief growing points within the economy of Western nations. Rural areas appeared backward and slower to change. People believed that new developments in science, technology, learning, and other phases of human activity occurred exclusively in the cities, a belief that persists in our time. The city was and remains for most of us the nucleus of life, from which vital messages and influences go out into the rest of the society.

This brief sketch of the nineteenth-century industrial city is the standard against which I will be measuring the history of Tsinan. To the extent that Tsinan moved toward the qualities of an industrial city, I have concluded that this was "development." These conceptions of the role of nineteenth-century cities have been worked out and elaborated on both by scholars

5

and by popular writers of the twentieth century who commonly have assumed that the characteristics of the industrial city represented the future of all cities. Likewise, many Western experts continue to advise developing nations to create large urban centers with vigorous technical, economic, and political forms drawn from the West if they wish to modernize.

In fact, most Western-backed economic development plans of the post-World War II era have contained an implicit urban bias. The transportation networks and urban-centered public service infrastructures called for in these plans tend to centralize production and distribution, while further linking the developing economies more closely to the international economic order. Such plans almost always spell considerable urban growth.

In political development theory, Samuel Huntington maintains the urban bias by arguing that cities are always first to break through into modernization. Then several scenarios are possible as the countryside comes to accept modern values and control from the cities, but a gap always develops between city and countryside in the process of modernization.[4] This emphasis on urban development persists among Western economists, political scientists, and planners in spite of the ugly problems that have continued in Western urban life in recent decades.

The bias toward urban-centered change was even more pronounced before 1950 and shaped most ideas about the way in which China in particular should modernize. As Rhoads Murphey has concluded, "The foreign presence [in China] was almost exclusively urban, as was the kind of modernization the foreigners tried to promote."[5] European and North American nations in the nineteenth and twentieth centuries went to considerable lengths to transplant their forms of urban civilization into Asia, Africa, and Latin America. Inevitably the model of the industrial city played a large role in the thinking of many native reformers when they began to envision an era free from the domination of foreign governments. In China this model was central to both foreign and progressive Chinese conceptions of the path to a modern China. In the words of the American-trained liberal philosopher Hu Shih,

> It is true that not all these material transformations [in production and exchange of goods] have touched the vast hinterland of China; they have taken place only in the cities.
>
> The city is always the center of radiation of the forces of change and progress. Trade and industry and the facilities of education draw people from distant regions.[6]

At the same time Hu Shih felt uneasy about the effects of urban life on established social patterns: "the influence of urban civilization cannot be overestimated. It means the breaking up of old homes, the removal from family and clan ties, the change of living and working habits, contact with new forms of social organization, the entrance of women and children into factories, the reliance of the individual upon himself for good or evil, new temptations and new wants."[7] Hu Shih's concern about the possible undesirable results of the urban industrial era was typical of his time and is repeated in the writings of other Chinese intellectuals, such as Fung Yu-lan and Fei Hsiao-t'ung.[8]

The new world of urban life for Chinese was found first in the treaty ports, large trading cities along China's coasts and inland waterways. These cities collected, stored, processed, and distributed goods for the international trade that was their lifeblood. Initially founded on foreign-dominated sea-borne transportation, they expanded in the twentieth century with the construction of railroads, motorized riverine shipping, and motor roads. Most Chinese and foreigners alike agreed that the treaty ports were "the forcing houses of Western culture,"[9] which would bring about inevitable modernization. Similar coastal trading cities located in colonies of South and Southeast Asia frequently became the chief colonial administrative centers as well. Geographers have taken to referring to the largest and most influential of these as "primate cities"; Rangoon, Manila, and Saigon are excellent examples of such cities.[10]

China, of course, was never a European colony, but the treaty system created cities with some distinctly colonial attributes. Shanghai, Tientsin, Foochow, Wuhan, and China's several dozen other treaty ports were all molded in this treaty-port variant of the colonial city pattern. The essence of the Chinese treaty-port system was found in the functioning of the Imperial Maritime Customs administered by foreigners for the Ch'ing Empire. Under the treaty system the foreign importers paid low ad valorem import taxes and then, by purchase of transit passes, could exempt their goods from all further tax on inland movement, thus avoiding all the *likin* (internal transit taxes) and other local taxes that hampered Chinese inland trade.[11] Along with this economic basis went the principle of extraterritoriality, which permitted foreigners to establish their own courts, police, and civic administrations. The foreign powers' willingness to station and use their superior military force in these treaty ports was another important factor in the character of these cities. Shanghai was the largest and most important of the treaty ports. There the foreign districts had their own urban administrations with taxing powers and their own courts with jurisdiction in both criminal and civil matters. The rest of the city—with a population far outnumbering the foreign one—remained under Chinese jurisdiction.

Because treaty ports and colonial cities served foreign masters, they

7

have been completely reappraised since the end of the colonial era around 1950. Recent scholars writing about Southeast Asian and Latin American coastal cities have stressed their parasitic nature and have distinguished the kind of change that was occurring in them from true urbanization in the classical nineteenth-century sense.[12]

According to these scholars, demographic and economic factors tell the story. Unlike the nineteenth-century Western industrial city, the parasitic colonial city grew without an accompanying shift in the population from rural to urban residence. Consequently, huge urban centers emerged in the colonial world as part of a general pattern of population increase and without a dramatic shift in the national population distribution. In the non-Western world, the population remained primarily rural, and the economies of primate coastal cities, even after the end of the colonial era, continued to be founded on exploiting the city's hinterland for the economic interests of foreigners.

The view that a Western colonial presence does not produce an opportunity to modernize along the lines of the colonial power, but, rather, dooms the colony—or in China's case the semi-colony—to a subordinate existence in an exploitative system was most forcibly stated by Lenin in 1916 in his "Imperialism, The Highest Stage of Capitalism." Following Lenin's arguments, Mao Tse-tung and the Chinese Communist party concluded that even though cities contained an important small proletariat, the party could not center its work within these cities—both the treaty ports and the other large cities in China—because reactionary power was concentrated there. The criticism of cities reaches its highest pitch in the writings of Mao Tse-tung:

> Since China's key cities have long been occupied by the powerful imperialists and their reactionary Chinese allies, it is imperative for the revolutionary ranks to turn the backward villages into advanced, consolidated base areas, into great military, political, economic and cultural bastions of the revolution from which to fight their vicious enemies who are using the cities for attacks on rural districts. . . . Such being the case, victory in the Chinese revolution can be won first in the rural areas.[13]

Mao's discovery of class conflict in the countryside and his efforts to use this conflict as a motive force in the Chinese revolution need no elaboration here. The practical experience of the Chinese Communist party in the countryside continued to reinforce the antipathy derived from the logic of Lenin's theory of imperialism. In present-day China, the preference for many aspects of rural work and living patterns is apparent in Chinese development programs. Rather than using urbanization to change attitudes and customs, as has been the dominant mode in modernization elsewhere, Chinese planners have devised a wide range of techniques and

8

organizations designed to revolutionize people in their rural villages. These experiments include cooperative farms, rural cooperatives, communes, production brigades, small-scale rural industry, rural resettlement of urban youth, and the May Seventh cadre schools that provide rural work experience for urban administrators and professionals.

This does not mean that Chinese cities have stopped growing since 1949. The People's Republic of China (PRC) has permitted considerable growth in established cities and has deliberately fostered the growth of certain new urban areas. The great emphasis in PRC economic planning on self-reliance, however, has led to a complete realignment of the economy of Chinese cities, even Shanghai and Canton, away from anything resembling the parasitic semi-colonial system. The Chinese themselves make this difference in the character of cities explicit in all their materials concerning urban life. Cities of the pre-1949 period are called "consumer-oriented" because they drew wealth from the Chinese hinterland for consumption by Chinese and foreign residents, as well as for export. Post-liberation cities are intended to be "producer-oriented" to contribute to the growth of Chinese socialism as sources of production of industrial goods.[14] It also is obvious that the Chinese are trying to modernize without the degree of urbanization that occurred in Europe, North America, and Japan. The imposition of this markedly different developmental approach creates a convenient breaking point in the history of Tsinan and is the main reason for concluding this study in 1950.

For these reasons, scholars of China have paid much more attention to China's rural situation than to developments in the cities. The most notable exception is Rhoads Murphey, whose 1953 monograph, *Shanghai: Key to Modern China*, suggested, in its title at least, that the treaty ports represented the future for Chinese modernization. Murphey, along with most other writers about urban change in modern China, saw the treaty ports as the representatives of a new kind of Chinese urbanism. This generally is true, but Tsinan, the particular case discussed in this book, was, as it happens, not a treaty port, although developments there and in other Chinese-controlled cities were strongly influenced by the patterns of the treaty ports.

In the text of Murphey's book on Shanghai, he stopped short of declaring that Shanghai represented the future for urban China. Writing in the first years after the establishment of the People's Republic of China, Murphey concluded that "Shanghai is a place where two civilizations met and neither prevailed."[15] In a book published in 1974, Murphey returns to the question of what role the treaty ports played in the modernization of China as a whole and reinforces his earlier conclusion that the treaty ports represented a foreign world that was separate from the real China: "The

9

treaty ports represented a new and exclusively urban phenomenon on Western models, while the rest of China remained not only predominantly rural but characterized by urban models (where they existed) of a fundamentally different sort, and which also had a far closer symbiotic relationship with their rural hinterland."[16] To buttress his argument, Murphey gathers information about the large intra- and inter-regional trade of late traditional China and concludes that the treaty ports had little impact on this trade either through the addition of foreign demand to the total Chinese demand or through the diversion of established trade into treaty-port channels. Murphey also introduces the issue of divided and limited political authority in the treaty ports to show that these cities had no decisive effects on the disorderly politics of the late Ch'ing and the Republican eras.

Murphey does feel the treaty ports had an important influence through the new kinds of technology brought into these cities. He also recognizes that treaty ports purveyed new ideas and new cultural modes that profoundly challenged long-established Chinese ways. Yet, according to Murphey, even these challenges made little impact on the underlying verities of life for the Chinese masses, for "the life-style of the great majority of Chinese was unaffected, directly or indirectly."[17]

We have, then, three distinct views of the city in modern Chinese history. The first sees Western-style industrial cities as the way of the future; the second sees them as dangerous bastions of imperialism; the third sees them as essentially irrelevant, extraneous to the deep and steadily flowing currents that have determined modern China's fate. When I began this study several years ago, it seemed clear that additional investigation was needed before adopting any one of these interpretations or advancing a new theory.

On the basis of the research for this book, I concluded that Tsinan's ability to modernize successfully depended heavily on economic changes that occurred in the city. During the period from 1890 to 1949 Tsinan experienced greatly increased commercial activity and some industrialization, but the political situation contained elements, both foreign and native, that disrupted the city's commercial development for extended periods and blocked the realization of its full potential for economic expansion even during times of domestic tranquillity.

As this research progressed, I encountered studies that changed my conception of the nature of the Chinese economy prior to 1890: the Chinese economy in late imperial times was not an "underdeveloped" one, but rather a very well developed pre-industrial economy where production took place in the hands of millions of agricultural and handicraft workers, primarily rural in residence and outside any large or

10

specialized production units. As the work of G. William Skinner shows, these producers were linked to consumers through elaborate and sensitive systems of markets. Mark Elvin has characterized this economy as operating at a "high-level equilibrium." The Chinese economy was not without its problems, principally because it could not break out of the dominant modes of production and distribution when the needs of the rapidly growing population surpassed the maximum levels of production possible within these modes.[18] China began the race for development along Western lines, then, from a basis much different from that of many other places in the non-Western world.

Furthermore, specialists in economic development are now beginning to acknowledge in their theoretical works that there is not one simple pattern of modernization toward which all the nations of the world are converging.[19] In particular, some are questioning efforts to fit China into the single social convergence model based on the Western urban-industrial experience. Such questioning is almost inescapable in that since 1949 the Chinese have obviously been developing, but have failed to adopt, many of the key patterns of the Western urban-industrial model. The Chinese population remains primarily rural in residence and agricultural in occupation. Great attention is devoted to small- and medium-scale industry, both in the cities and in the countryside. The Chinese have clearly adopted a policy of limiting urban growth. They emphasize "self-reliance" for both urban and rural areas by involving individuals periodically in some kind of industrial or agricultural labor. These are only a few of the signs that a "modernized" China will look much different from anything previously imagined by theorists either past or present who have based their predictions about China's future on the Western urban-industrial experience.

The fact that China started out from a different basis from that of most other nonindustrial countries, and also is going a direction quite different from our own Western pattern, does not mean, however, that the Western experience is totally irrelevant. For, as the following chapters will clearly show, during the half-century in which the Western model was the dominant one in Chinese and foreign thinking about the future of China, it profoundly altered traditional Chinese urban life.

But why study the inland city of Tsinan? Since most people have seen the Western industrialized city exemplified primarily in the treaty ports, why not choose one of them? Why not study Shanghai, Tientsin, or even Tsingtao, the port city the Germans created on the Shantung peninsula? The answer is that, rather than looking for a representative Chinese city, I tried to find the one that had the best potential to fulfill the Western model of an industrial city. Tsinan initially suggested itself to me precisely

11

because it had never been designated as a treaty port nor had had a separate foreign-administered enclave. Political authority in Tsinan lay in the hands of the Chinese for most of the sixty-year period being considered here, and the plans for modernization were drawn up and implemented by the Chinese themselves. In addition, Tsinan had been a major administrative city prior to the twentieth century and so had a well-established character as a center of political action. The same could be said of only a few treaty ports, such as Foochow, Canton, and Ch'angsha. Thus Tsinan, unlike Shanghai, Tientsin, and most other treaty ports, represents a Chinese effort to manage a city along modern lines.

The further my research proceeded, the more I became convinced that Tsinan was probably the best possible place for Chinese-controlled urban development to have occurred. Before 1949 China boasted five cities of more than a million people: Shanghai, Peking, Tientsin, Canton, and Nanking. Of these only Peking, the national capital, had not been a treaty port. Outside northeastern China, which was under Japanese domination, in 1938 there were nineteen cities with populations between 200,000 and one million. Tsingtao, Hangchow, and Chungking had over 500,000; Tsinan, Ch'angsha, and Chengtu, over 400,000; Soochow, Foochow, and K'aifeng, over 300,000; and Nanch'ang, Wuhsi, Ningpo, Chanchiang, Wenchow, Sian, and Suchow, over 200,000.[20] Of these cities Tsinan was the one that best combined economic and political centrality with some foreign contact and freedom from direct foreign domination, a combination that should have permitted rapid industrial, commercial, political, and social development in the classical nineteenth-century pattern.

The following chapters deal with Tsinan's history in terms of six distinct periods: the late nineteenth century, the post-1900 decade of Ch'ing reform, the first five years of the Republic, the unhappy period of warlordism from 1916 to 1927, the Nanking decade, and a final period of international and civil war from 1938 through 1948. For each period I have attempted to present a portrait of the city which covers its political, economic, social, and cultural life. Also, I have related the changes which were occurring to the overall problem of how Tsinan was progressing toward the Western-derived model of urbanization.

Aside from the fact that Tsinan was located on the densely settled North China plain near the established interregional transportation lines between the large commercial cities and close to an extensive, but undeveloped, coal deposit, three additional factors were decisive in Tsinan's modernization: foreign influence, Chinese political leadership, and the general pattern of economic change. For each of the six periods in Tsinan's history, I have taken the most significant manifestations of these three

12

forces and have tried to analyze how each related to the overall issue of Tsinan's modernization. Wherever possible in the following chapters, I have sought to identify and characterize those individuals—primarily Chinese—who held political, economic, and social power, in Tsinan. This is the "politics" element in the title of the book. I hope in these descriptions to shed more light on the question of how power was used in China between 1890 and 1949, and especially how it was used differently from the way it was in the mid-nineteenth century. This issue goes to the heart of the long-standing debate about the nature of gentry power in recent Chinese history and the way the privileged classes were able to adapt their traditional power to the changing situation in China after 1850.

Also important in these questions of political power is the problem of the warlords. That issue has been the subject of considerable scholarship in recent years, much of which has dealt with the personalities of the warlords, their competing power relationships, and the political dynamics of warlordism.[21] While those important aspects of warlord power are described for the various militarist governors in Tsinan, in examining the city of Tsinan I have tried also to look closely at ways warlords used their power in Chinese cities and to relate the differences in their political interests with those of the other political groups in the city, especially the gentry and the merchants.

In the treatment of economic interests in Tsinan I have attempted, as much as is possible with available information, to clarify the social background of the investors. The overall pattern is one in which a number of different relationships existed between officials and private investors, both Chinese and foreign. The range extends from projects inspired by Yüan Shih-k'ai that obviously derive from the nineteenth-century pattern of official supervision and merchant management (*kuan-tu shang-pan*) to forms of state capitalism that occurred in the 1930s when the provincial administration took over unprofitable public service industries previously owned by private interests.

In this spectrum of economic forms, two types warrant special attention: comprador capitalism and bureaucratic capitalism. Both of these are familiarly cited as negative influences from the perspective of Chinese modern economic history. Comprador capitalism refers to the investments and economic activities of that special class of merchants who made their initial fortunes as agents or employees of foreign trading firms. Although the comprador class has its apologists, compradors generally have been viewed as bad influences in China's recent history, for both their patriotism and their motives for investment have been subject to great question. In Tsinan there were some early investments involving official cooperation or monopoly privileges which drew comprador capital.

13

Although there is evidence that comprador merchants were not in the fore-front of nationalistic reaction to the Japanese in the May Fourth period, there is still no reason to conclude they exercised a pernicious influence on Tsinan's economic development.

Bureaucratic capitalism is a much more vague and potentially misleading term which is most frequently used to typify the economic conditions prevailing under the Kuomintang in the 1930s and 1940s. According to the use of this term by Chinese Marxist historians, bureau-cratic capitalism had two stages.[22] In the first, the Kuomintang state at Nanking took over control of private Chinese capitalist endeavors. The favorite example is the state's increasing domination of private banking in the 1930s. This trend is seen as continuing during the anti-Japanese war (1937-1945) when the Kuomintang was forced by wartime exigency to turn more and more private productive facilities into state-owned enter-prises. According to Chinese Marxist historians, the pernicious nature of bureaucratic capitalism does not lie in this initial stage of state capitalism, for in Marxist theory that might just as well be the basis for the economy's future transformation to socialism. Instead, the problem in China was that a few large families dominated the Kuomintang state and thus made state capitalism serve private interests. The great evil of this special form of bureaucratic capitalism became obvious after 1945, according to these arguments, when the second stage arose in which state-owned capital—including recent acquisitions from the defeated Japanese—were sold off by bureaucrats to their own families or to favored elements in the Chekiang financial clique which was closely associated with the Kuomintang.

In the case of Tsinan, there is simply a lack of evidence to indicate that this particular form of bureaucratic capitalism ruined the city's economy. There is one important reason: the Tsinan economy never recovered sufficiently after 1945 for any interests to take advantage of the state-owned capital for their own private interests. Nevertheless, bureaucratic capitalism did play an important role in Tsinan, especially between 1916 and the early 1930s when men connected with the Peiyang clique, espe-cially the Anfu club, used their bureaucratic positions to enrich themselves through the promotion of industrial investments, often with the use of large amounts of official monies and Japanese capital. It is to this early phase of bureaucratic capitalism that most attention will be directed in this book.

As the ensuing chapters will make clear, not even Tsinan's unique ad-vantages produced the kind of development envisioned by the foreigners and Chinese leaders before 1949. At the same time, Tsinan and many other Chinese cities had become part of new railroad or motorized shipping transportation systems that diverted trade from old paths into new ones clearly derived from Western experience. Those cities also became centers of new culture and technology derived from Western urban-industrial society and accepted by an important and powerful stratum in Chinese society. Accepting and understanding these facts may help to clarify the whole question of urban change in early twentieth-century China. Let us begin by examining Tsinan in the late nineteenth century.

2

Tsinan in the Late Nineteenth Century

RUNNING THROUGH CHINESE HISTORY in the century from 1850 to 1950 are three great forces—economic change, increasing militarization, and expanding foreign influence—which are familiar to all students of modern China. Naturally, all three forces played major roles in the history of Tsinan. The pattern of economic change began most noticeably in commercial activities connected with the opening of the treaty ports and the expansion of foreign trade. However, the economic changes cannot be explained simply as a result of foreign influence, because Chinese trade was directed into new domestic channels and certain lines of domestic commerce expanded while others declined, with obvious effects on the lives of the people involved in producing and exchanging these goods. In this chapter on Tsinan in the late nineteenth century we shall see how the first wave of this economic change produced a considerable alteration in the hierarchy of economic central places in Shantung and ultimately worked to increase Tsinan's economic importance. At the same time, these economic changes produced a new set of wealthy merchant families who had little influence on events of the late nineteenth century but became quite important in the twentieth century.

The theme of increasing militarization keeps reappearing in Tsinan's history from 1850 onward to 1950. As the seat of the top provincial offices, the city reflected this trend toward militarization in its political life. From the time of the creation of the anti-Taiping and anti-Nien militia in the 1850s through the arrival of Yüan Shih-k'ai's military units in Tsinan in 1899 to curb the Boxer uprising, the element of militarization of power grew in late nineteenth century China and assumed an even more important role in the twentieth century.

In military matters foreign influence and presence became a significant factor in the Sino-Japanese war of 1894-1895 and the German invasion of Chiao-chou Bay in 1898, but the foreign military action is only part of a larger theme of foreign imperialism so important in modern Chinese history. In tracing Tsinan's history we shall repeatedly examine how the

16

foreigners imposed their ideas and ways on Tsinan's life and how some Chinese welcomed certain of these changes while other foreign influences drew various degrees of Chinese opposition.

In this chapter we shall look briefly at how these great forces began to work changes in Tsinan and Shantung in the late nineteenth century. A description of the province of Shantung and its major political and economic divisions will make more clear the relationship of Tsinan to its surrounding area, both in political and economic terms. Also we shall be looking closely at the physical and social dimensions of Tsinan, since it was a representative commercial and administrative city of late traditional China.

To the Victorian—and perhaps especially to the Western treaty-port resident, who typically looked on China as a vast untapped market or a land full of souls to be saved—Chinese cities were certainly not agents or centers of change. Quite the contrary, they were citadels of opposition where conservative forces resisted superior Western morality and tried to block the inevitable advance of Western industrialism and commercialism. As a missionary wrote of Tsinan, "Until the time of the Boxer disturbances, Tsinanfu was one of the most conservative cities in the empire, with a decided distaste for everything foreign. There was no intercourse between the foreigners and Chinese officials. . . while the attitude of the people was one of active hostility."[1]

At its best, the pre-industrial Chinese city was an attractive place. At the close of the nineteenth century a visitor recorded the charm and serenity of Tsinan:

> As I arrived on the north side of the city wall, I found at my feet the often-praised lake, which contained abundant and clear water, but which was overgrown with weeds. Charming temples, pagodas and tea houses—illuminated by the evening sun—stood on its banks and were reflected on the smooth surface. Small boats, with cheerful social gatherings here and there; on some banks isolated fishermen; herons in the shallow marshes watching for prey; wild ducks in the reeds, untroubled by the people in their proximity. On the north side is a very charming bath temple, more beautiful even than those I saw in Japan, built by the inhabitants in honor of their former governor.[2]

The city of Tsinan is set in one of several depressions that occur along the northern edge of Shantung's central mountains. Each of these depressions contains natural springs created by sandstone outcroppings carrying runoff water from the mountains. At Tsinan, the springs provide water for the city's moat and its famous Ta-ming Lake.* Many of them

---

*Such springs are also found in Po-shan, I-tu, Ch'ang-shan, and Chang-ch'iu districts. In some places they provide water to irrigate wet rice. Cultivation of rice so far north was somewhat unusual, but the crop was in high demand, both as tribute grain and on the regular commercial market as a special-quality rice.

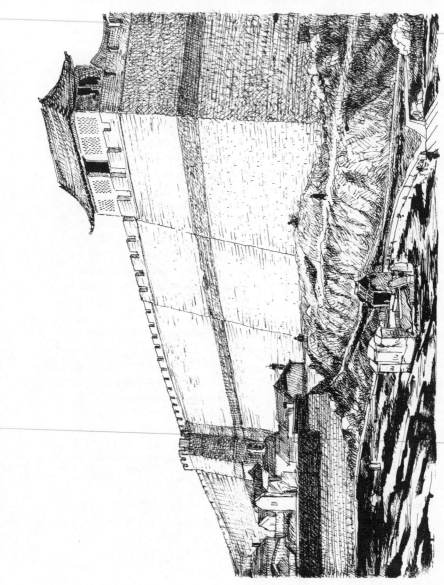

Figure 1. Tsinan city wall. The most imposing part of Tsinan (and of every other important Chinese city in its late traditional form) was the massive stone wall surrounding it. Tsinan's outer wall, shown here, was raised in the 1860s, in the days of the Nien rebels. (Sketch by Bruce M. Buck, from a photograph in *Sanō meisho shashinchō* [Photograph Album of Scenic Places in Shantung] [Ta-lien: Dairen bijitsu insatsusho, 1930].)

became scenic attractions. Tradition attributes seventy-two springs to Tsinan, but the geology of the city is such that any shallow excavation will produce a flow of water. By the late nineteenth century the list of seventy-two springs remained, but the locations of some of them had changed.[3]

The most famous of all was Leaping Springs (P'ao-t'u-ch'üan), so called because it spouted a bubbly column of water more than a meter above the surrounding pond. Located outside the southwest corner of the main wall, Leaping Springs was the site of a temple in the early Ch'ing and later became the location of an annual fair. The fair site developed into a periodic market that became the largest and most important in Tsinan by the late nineteenth century.

The dominant feature of the whole northern third of the city was Ta-ming Lake, created by damming part of the springs' runoff behind the northern city wall. This massive wall had been raised in the 1370s when Tsinan became the provincial capital of Shantung. In the late nineteenth century the wall was six and a half kilometers long, ten meters high, and over twenty meters thick at the base. With its many-tiered towers rising at the main gates, it was the most striking architectural feature of the city.

The city plan followed the standard Chinese design: a walled square enclosure oriented toward the south, one wall facing each of the cardinal directions. The main commercial streets in Tsinan were the east-west thoroughfares. The lake obviated the need for a northern gate, but a tower along the north wall marked the location of the Temple of the North Pole. The southern gate was ritually the most important gate, but its road ran only a short distance before stopping at the approach to Ch'ien-fo shan (Thousand Buddha Hill). The busiest gate was the Le-yuan (Source of the Le River) in the southwest corner, immediately adjacent to the temple and markets at Leaping Springs.

Through this gate and out to these markets ran the main commercial street of the city. Missionaries of the 1880s have left us descriptions of it. The portion of the street inside the Le-yuan Gate boasted the largest and best shops—one-story brick affairs with open fronts that the clerks boarded up each night—but the newer market area outside the gate was becoming increasingly active and prosperous. Inside the gate the first block contained twelve different establishments: the run-down official guardhouse, followed by a cake shop, a cash shop, and a large store selling foreign and domestic cottons and silks, among others. Beyond the first block the street widened and the shops became larger.

The main streets and the most important side streets in Tsinan were paved with large stone blocks, but after a heavy rain the accumulated dirt and dust turned to mud so thick that even the main streets were practically

19

Figure 2. Tsinan commercial street, about 1905. This narrow, crowded commercial area, inside the old walled city, lay adjacent to one of Tsinan's principal gates. Note the traditional styles of the men's dress and their queues. (Sketch by Bruce M. Buck, from a photograph in James Boyd Neal, "Tsinanfu, Capital of Shantung," *East of Asia Magazine* 5 [1906]: 328.)

impassable. Along each side of the street ran raised wooden walkways about a meter wide that were maintained by the shopkeepers.[4]

Temple yards in the southwest section of the city near the Le-yuan Gate contained the large specialized markets in grain, coal, cotton, salt, and other regionally traded commodities. The food markets serving the daily needs of Tsinan's inhabitants were scattered within the walled enclosure. Outside the gates the shops varied from peddlers' displays to substantial brick buildings. The increasing trade around Leaping Springs was reflected in the new buildings and bustling streets of that area. At the opposite end of the city a smaller commercial district had developed around the northeastern gate. All three main gates were clogged with traffic from six in the morning until noon. Traffic slackened during the afternoon hours, quickening again from four until the gates were locked for the night at dark.

Tsinan's economy was built on guild capitalism with groups of craftsmen organized to restrict competition, share the market, maintain craft standards, and regulate prices. Tsinan's finest craftsmen and shops served the luxury consumption by government officials and the wealthy gentry who maintained residences in the city. The city's commodity markets, also controlled by specialized merchant guilds, served both the city and a hinterland which was much smaller than the area served by Tsinan with the later development of canals and railroad lines. Merchants from Chang-ch'iu, especially those connected with native coal mining and banking, were especially important in nineteenth-century Tsinan.

Tsinan's chief function was as the administrative center of Shantung province, and the plan of the city reflected this quite clearly. At the center of the city lay the provincial governor's yamen, its extensive grounds surrounding one of the city's most beautiful springs. In addition to these offices, there were large separate enclosures with many buildings which served as yamens for the financial and judicial commissioners, the governor's chief subordinates. The offices of the Shantung branch of the salt monopoly, which had answered directly to the governor since the early nineteenth century, were also located in the central portion of the city.

Tsinan, like other major Chinese administrative cities, housed several levels of officials. The *tao-t'ai* of the northwestern circuit in Shantung kept offices in Tsinan. The prefect in charge of Tsinan *fu*, which consisted of sixteen districts, had his offices in Tsinan, as did the magistrate for Li-ch'eng *hsien*, the district immediately surrounding the city. So many officials conducted their business from the city, in fact, that Tsinan's yamens were said to be as numerous as its springs.

During the nineteenth century Tsinan's economic importance never matched its administrative position. Nevertheless, the city's economic

21

activity did increase, especially late in the century, after the decline of the Grand Canal and the increase of coastal and international shipping brought new prosperity to the eastern part of Shantung.

SHANTUNG'S NINETEENTH-CENTURY TRADING SYSTEMS

Some description of Shantung's economic geography in the nineteenth century will be helpful both for understanding the position of Tsinan and for reference with regard to political groupings that developed out of the major regions within the province. In the early nineteenth century Shantung was divided into four distinct trading systems with centers at the cities of Chi-ning, Lin-ch'ing, Tsinan, and Wei-hsien. These cities each had a population of more than 100,000 and were "third-level" cities.* Chi-ning lay 72 kilometers south of Tsinan along the Grand Canal and was the center of the southwestern region. Lin-ch'ing was a similar canal port and trading center in northwestern Shantung, only 55 kilometers from Tsinan, but the influence of Lin-ch'ing extended into southern Chihli and the eastern portions of Shansi. Wei-hsien, an unusually active trading center in the late nineteenth century, 125 kilometers east of Tsinan, had grown from a more modest level to become the center of commerce in the eastern portion of Shantung.

Tsinan served a large trading system in the north-central portion of the province, and qualified as a third-level city by virtue of its administrative

*In recent years scholars have attempted to classify the hierarchy of central places in late traditional China. In Gilbert Rozman's scheme the highest of a seven-level hierarchy is reserved for the national capital (Peking). The second level contains such centers of inter-regional commerce as Nanking, Wuhan, Canton, Sian, and Foochow. The third level of cities includes the provincial capitals or the intermediate port cities linking the national administrative center at Peking with the inter-regional commercial centers such as Nanking or Wuhan. Tsinan, Chi-ning, and Lin-ch'ing were all such third-level cities. Wei-hsien became a third-level city during the second half of the nineteenth century. Wei-hsien had previously been a fourth-level urban place, a local city with several markets which served a network composed of the last three levels, the central, standard, and intermediate marketing settlements. The two leading exponents of these hierarchies of urban places are Rozman and G. William Skinner; they disagree on each other's system of classification. Skinner's published work, "Marketing and Social Structure in Rural China," parts 1, 2, and 3, *Journal of Asian Studies* 24:1-3 (November 1964, February and May 1965), deals primarily with the lowest three levels. Rozman's book *Urban Networks in Ch'ing China and Tokugawa Japan* (Princeton: Princeton University Press, 1973) concentrates on the upper levels in the hierarchy and has been criticized by Skinner in a review, *Journal of Asian Studies* 35.1 (November 1975): 131-34. The realm of greatest disagreement involves the third, fourth, and fifth levels and their separation in terms of size and function. Unfortunately it is precisely those levels of urban places, which include the provincial capital down to the district seat, that are the most important in the study of Tsinan's history. For example, my description of the late traditional trading systems in Shantung does not fit exactly that of Rozman's, *Urban Networks,* pp. 204-13.

functions, its size, and the complexity of its trade. It lay near the main north-south official highway and was served early in the century by a navigable river known as the Ta-ch'ing. A small satellite town called Le-k'ou served as Tsinan's port. Tsinan's commercial sphere included the districts within its prefecture and some others in T'ai-an prefecture. This hinterland lay primarily on the broad North China plain where villagers kept livestock and grew wheat, kaoliang, and other grain crops. Cotton was extensively grown and traded; and sericulture prospered.

In the mountains south of Tsinan, the population was sparser, but considerable mining was done, especially for coal. The center of this mining lay in the Po-shan Valley. In Tsinan the commercial interests connected with mining at Chang-ch'iu *hsien*—located between Tsinan and Po-shan Valley in another coal-producing district—controlled the coal business. Tsinan also served as a major center in the salt trade, with much of this valuable commodity stored in warehouses in the city after shipment from the salt fields along the Gulf of Chihli.

Chi-ning and Lin-ch'ing were the chief port cities along the Grand Canal on its route through Shantung. Chi-ning dominated the commerce of all southwestern Shantung and some parts of northern Kiangsu and Honan. Lin-ch'ing, whose trade in the late nineteenth century rivaled Tientsin's in volume and complexity, was the dominant trading city in northwestern Shantung and southern Chihli. Prior to the great rebellions of the mid-nineteenth century, these inland areas of Shantung were the most populous and prosperous parts of the province.

The Grand Canal's annual summer movement of tribute rice and the secondary trade in grain, salt, and handicrafts carried on in private and official boats sustained the commercial prosperity of both cities. Maintaining and operating the Grand Canal itself required large government expenditures that stimulated the inland regions' economic activity. The districts adjacent to the canal were small and heavily populated. Wheat and cotton were the staple crops.

POST-1850 SHIFTS IN THE PREVAILING ECONOMIC SYSTEM IN SHANTUNG

Chinese history when examined closely, as in this account of Tsinan, never displays the unchanging qualities often attributed to it. This is especially true of the economic geography of Shantung, which underwent a marked reorientation in the late nineteenth century under the impact of the internal rebellions, the change in the Yellow River's main channel, the increase in coastal trade after the opening of the treaty ports, and the opening of Manchuria to Chinese immigration.

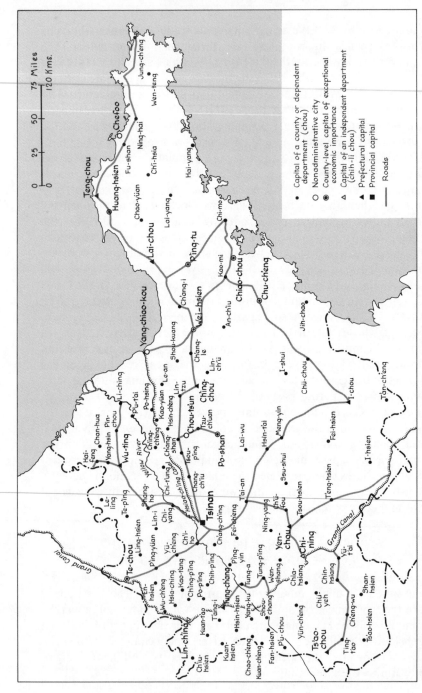

Map 1. Shantung in the 1890s. (Reprinted from "Educational Modernization in Tsinan, 1899-1937," by David D. Buck, in *The Chinese City Between Two Worlds*, edited by Mark Elvin and G. William Skinner, with the permission of the publishers, Stanford University Press. © 1974 by the Board of Trustees of the Leland Stanford Junior University.)

Ever since the uprising of Wang Lun in 1774 the northwestern section of the inland region had periodically seen disturbances connected with the heterodox White Lotus sect. The Eight Diagrams revolt of 1813-1814 also bore heavily on the western portions of the province.

The Lin-ch'ing section was especially hard hit by the mid-nineteenth-century uprisings. In late 1853 the Taiping Northern Expedition became stalled in Chihli province short of Peking. The next spring a relief column was dispatched from Nanking and while passing through Shantung took the city of Lin-ch'ing in April 1854. Troops of the Ch'ing dynasty retook the city ten days later, but the destruction in Lin-ch'ing was a major catastrophe in which thousands were killed. Then, from 1860 to 1863, Sung Ching-shih used the Lin-ch'ing trading system as a base for his revolt. The city and the surrounding districts never recovered from the combined effects of these uprisings and the great suffering caused by the change of the Yellow River's main channel.[5]

Chi-ning suffered less from the rebellions, even though Taiping and Nien forces operated in the city's hinterland for many years. Rebel forces threatened Chi-ning several times in the 1850s and 1860s, but a combination of imperial armies, local militia, and strengthened city fortifications proved sufficient to keep the city out of rebel hands.

The most serious blow the Taipings dealt Shantung was not the depredations of their armies but the closing of the Grand Canal to regular tribute grain shipments in 1853. Tens of thousands of Shantungese were thrown out of work, and many of the unemployed workmen turned to bandit activities to support themselves. These "turban bandits" (*fu-fei*) or "club bandits" (*kun-fei*) sometimes joined with the roving Nien bands. When the Nien were finally suppressed in 1867, the inland half of Shantung had been involved in an almost continuous struggle against various uprisings for nearly twenty years.

In 1855 the Grand Canal was further threatened, this time by natural forces. During the summer flood crest, the Yellow River broke its levees at T'ung-wa-hsiang in eastern Honan. Since 1342 this great river had flown south of the Shantung peninsula into the East China Sea. The dikes and floodwalls needed to control the river at flood time had been neglected in the heat of the dynasty's efforts against the Taipings. In 1855 the river broke loose and found a new course, meandering over the wheat and cotton fields of the North China plain until it reached Ch'ang-ch'un-chen in Shantung. There the river entered the channel of the Ta-ch'ing River and followed it northeastward past Tsinan to the Gulf of Chihli.[6]

The trouble and suffering caused by this change only began with the flooding and crop losses in the region east of the breach. The Ta-ch'ing levees had to be raised to protect against the heavy silt burden and annual flood potential of the Yellow River water. Smaller streams that had formerly emptied into the Ta-ch'ing were now blocked and created small floods outside the main levees. The water level in the Grand Canal dropped sharply between Chi-ning and Lin-ch'ing; and during most of the years after 1855 until 1950 the canal remained effectively blocked between these two cities.

In the last decades of the nineteenth century the northwestern region of Shantung fell into decline. Many of the most prominent and wealthy families moved away. Some of the peasants sent family members to Manchuria and later moved their entire families out of the northwest. The effects of this decline were quite noticeable in the first half of the twentieth century, when the northwest, unlike other sections of the province, failed to contribute any significant political leadership to provincial politics.

The Chi-ning region in the southwest fared much better. The challenge of the Taiping and Nien rebels was met by the effective organization of militia units (*t'uan-lien*) and the improvement of defensive works at Chi-ning and other walled cities. The loss in trade from the combined impact of the rebellions and the closing of the Grand Canal was considerable, but the canal stayed open south of Chi-ning and on into northern Kiangsu. The canal was still important in the regional salt and grain trades. The Chi-ning region included the birthplaces of both Confucius and Mencius. In the revival of traditional morality that followed the suppression of the rebels, the Chi-ning region especially took on a strong conservative tone. It was noticeably slower to accept Western practices and ideas than the eastern Shantung area centered at Wei-hsien. In provincial politics the Chi-ning region frequently was called "Lu," a reference to a state that had existed in the same general area during the Warring States period (481-221 B.C.). Political groupings in Shantung during the Republican period had a marked regional character. Individuals from the Lu region often claimed to act from Confucian principles and were clearly less willing than leaders from the other major region centered at Wei-hsien to accept new practices or to advocate nationalistic or democratic stands.

The Wei-hsien trading system lay to the east of Tsinan in a rich and fertile section of the North China plain. The region produced wheat, cotton, soybeans, coal, and silk. The handicrafts of the region were especially well developed. The embroidery was among the best made anywhere in nineteenth-century China. Other regional specialties included a kind of vermicelli made from beans and wheat, along with various straw goods plaited from wheat stalks. Ningpo traders and ships took Shantung bean cake from the traditional port at Chiao-chou to the Lower Yangtze Valley for use as fertilizer, developing a considerable intracoastal trade. Po-shan produced glass for ornamental use, mined small amounts of metals, and made coke from its coal. The coastal areas in the Wei-hsien region produced salt and fish that were widely traded.

In the late 1850s two decisions were made that markedly changed the economy of the Wei-hsien trading system. First, under the terms of the Treaty of Tientsin the port of Chefoo (Yen-t'ai) on the northern side of the Shantung peninsula was opened to foreigners as a treaty port. Foreigners did not take up regular residence there until 1862, but they soon began to stimulate the economy of the area with increased demand for traditional handicrafts such as straw braid, silk, and embroidery work adapted for Western markets. A more important result of the foreign presence, however, was the improved coastal transport, which stimulated the traditional lines of Wei-hsien regional production, such as vermicelli and bean cake fertilizer.[7]

Second, the Manchus began to encourage Chinese to settle in their homeland. The Ch'ing dynasty, fearful of the expansion of Russian influence into Manchuria, for the first time openly encouraged Chinese to emigrate into the northeast. Many of these Chinese settlers came from eastern Shantung through the ports at Chefoo and Lung-k'ou. After the opening of Chefoo and the development of Ta-lien (Dairen), the expanding volume of migration and trade from the Wei-hsien trading system was increasingly funneled through these ports. This flow of people had a seasonal aspect because many returned to Shantung to escape the harsh Manchurian winters or to pass the New Year's holidays at home. The opening of Manchuria also meant that for the first time during the Ch'ing dynasty the Gulf of Chihli became a thoroughfare of commerce and travel rather than a barrier to the outside world. This naturally had an impact on the activity in the peninsular and eastern portions of Shantung.[8]

The Wei-hsien trading system was to continue its late-nineteenth-century prosperity well into the twentieth century. The region lay roughly in the area of the Warring States kingdom of Ch'i, and consequently the Wei-hsien interests were commonly referred to as "Ch'i" elements in twentieth-century provincial politics.

The division of Shantung political groups along the Lu and the Ch'i regional lines was a continuing factor in Shantung politics and underlies many of the political squabbles and weaknesses that mark the efforts of Shantungese elements to control their own province in the twentieth century. Ch'i was more progressive than the Lu region in a number of ways. Ch'i people were closely involved in the Chinese migration to Manchuria and many men gained entrepreneurial, technical, and leadership skills there that they transferred back to Shantung in a host of commercial, industrial, educational, and political projects. In general, the Ch'i region was less closely tied to traditional Chinese philosophical principles than the Lu and more strongly in favor of republicanism, mass popular education, expanding commercialization, more industrialization, and even frank Westernization of China. These views are reflected in the city of Tsinan through the leadership of Ch'i individuals in much of the public service industry, newspapers, schools, and other western importations to Chinese urban life. These modernizing and Westernizing views associated with the Ch'i region flow from practical considerations, for from the late nineteenth century onward the Ch'i region—more than any other section of the province—underwent a process of development that included population migration, improved transportation, expansion of traditional commerce, and growth of new or modified lines of production for foreign trade.

The central Shantung mountains and the coastal region south of the peninsula were regions of little economic or political significance during either the nineteenth or the early twentieth centuries. The central mountain region, in particular, tended to be much less commercialized than that of the surrounding North China plains.

POLITICAL AND ECONOMIC POWER IN TSINAN

The prefectural seats and large trading communities were the chief arenas where political influence was exerted in the late nineteenth century. This meant that important men—both degree holders and individuals of wealth, property, and learning—would be as likely to seek the assistance of the local prefect on a major matter as they would be to journey all the way to the provincial capital to seek official redress from the governor or other high provincial officials. In the nineteenth century Tsinan itself was spoken of colloquially as "Tsinanfu" meaning literally, Tsinan prefecture, as was common with other prefectural seats in North China. This standard usage of the nineteenth century reflects how much of the practical decision-making capacity lay in the hands of magistrates, prefects, and intendants, and not the top provincial officials. In the Ch'ing period men of substance from various parts of the province could ordinarily protect their interests by cementing their relationships with these lower-level officials and did not need to take their business into Tsinan to see the governor or the provincial treasurer. As we shall see, this situation changed after 1900, with Tsinan becoming the center of political power and influence for the whole province of Shantung and consequently drawing the political interests away from the prefecture, which disappeared as a separate level of government after 1911. This atrophy of the lower centers of political power and the increasing importance of Tsinan as the center of political power, or as political scientists like to say, "interest articulation," is a major strand of the city's history and one which will require us to examine much about the history of the whole province of Shantung as the history of its capital city unfolds.

In the nineteenth century "Tsinanfu" was, however, something more than another prefecture, and the powerful men in the city can be divided into two groups on the basis of their sources of power. One group consisted of the government officials, whose influence arose from the offices they held. That group, from provinces other than Shantung, was enlarged by secretaries and experts the officials appointed to assist them. The second group was composed of local men, many of whom had experience in official posts in other provinces but whose power in Tsinan derived from their status and wealth within Tsinan's trading system. In contrast to the twentieth-century patterns, however, Tsinan did not commonly become the place of residence for wealthy and powerful men from Chi-ning, Lin-ch'ing or Wei-hsien, who normally would reside within their own trading system, usually close to their particular prefectural seat.

These outsiders serving in official capacities and the men of local power and wealth were natural allies. Their interests, and often their careers and private affairs, were closely connected. In Tsinan, the rebellions and the problems associated with the Yellow River after 1850 had brought them even closer together than usual. By the latter part of the nineteenth century, leaders connected with subduing the rebellions and controlling the Yellow River dominated both official and gentry circles in Tsinan.

Nine of the ten new public monuments erected in Tsinan between 1875 and the fall of the Ch'ing dynasty honored those connected with suppressing the Nien and Taiping rebellions. Obviously, the victorious antirebel campaigns left a strong political legacy that became the chief rallying point of political power in Tsinan until 1900.[9]

Several of the individuals honored by monuments were governors of the antirebel period, such as Yen Ching-ming, Ting Pao-chen, and Chang Yao. These officials in turn were associated in some way with either Li Hung-chang or Tso Tsung-t'ang, two strong Chinese officials at the metropolitan level during the last twenty-five years of the nineteenth century. After the rebels were suppressed, Li Hung-chang generally controlled appointments in Shantung, and he arranged for the posting of men loyal to him with experience in the province. As a group the Shantung governors tended to be more conservative than Li and his most liberal officials, but they worked well with the local Shantung gentry.

The local powerholders in Tsinan were as closely associated with the antirebel forces as the officials were. Tu O, a *chin-shih* from the Tsinan trading system, was appointed head of the Shantung provincial militia

29

in the 1850s and remained an important force in local politics until his death. In the Tsinan prefecture, as elsewhere in China, these militia units were led by local men who left their official posts to return to the Li-ch'eng district and organize its defenses. Some of the militia organizers later returned to official careers, but they contined to be strong forces in Tsinan politics during the 1870s. By the 1880s they clearly exercised real control.

In addition to forming military units to defend against the rebel threat, the officials and community leaders also built a second Tsinan city wall, creating a double enclosure. The new wall was about twelve kilometers in circumference and increased the city's compass on three sides (marshes lay beyond the northern wall, so no extension was made in that direction). The new wall was irregular, bulging in the southwestern corner to take in the Leaping Springs temples and market area which had developed beyond the original city wall. Another bulge at the northeastern corner took in the commercial quarter at that location. The wall began as earthwork construction in the early 1860s, and received a brick and stone facing in 1865-1867. Initially much of the newly enclosed area was vacant land, but in 1867, during a phase of Li Hung-chang's anti-Nien campaign, the wisdom of undertaking such a large and expensive project was justified when the entire walled area was temporarily filled with refugees from the countryside. A third earthwork rampart had been constructed well beyond the city walls as Tsinan's first line of defense.[10]

The character of political leadership in Tsinan during the late nineteenth century is best typified by the support given to Chang Yao, the highly popular governor portrayed so favorably by Liu E in his famous novel *Lao-ts'an yu-chi* (The Travels of Lao Ts'an). Chang Yao began his career in Shantung as military commander, and as governor acted as patron to former militia leaders. Shortly after Chang Yao became governor, he sanctioned the establishment in Tsinan of a new Confucian philanthropic association called the Benevolence Bureau (*Kuang-jen shan-chü*) modeled on a similar bureau in Tientsin. Many of the Benevolence Bureau's directors were former militia leaders, and the Bureau was a highly prestigious and visible link between the conservative but activist approach to China's problems favored by Chang Yao and the Tsinan prefectural elite. Under the joint management of the local gentry and the Chi-nan prefect, Te-chun, the Benevolence Bureau supported orphanages, hospitals, and schools. The largest contributor was Ch'en Ju-heng, scion of a prominent and wealthy Tsinan family. Ch'en was too young to have fought against the Nien, but the board of directors of the Benevolence Bureau was controlled by men who had been militia leaders in the 1860s.[11]

Early Protestant missionaries in Tsinan identified the Benevolence Bureau as a sorce of strong local opposition to their efforts in the 1880s. The missionaries believed the Bureau was responsible for their inability to rent quarters in Tsinan.[12] The Benevolence Bureau remained a strong official-and-gentry-managed institution until after 1900, participating actively during the 1890s in school construction and flood relief in addition to its regular charity works. In the late Ch'ing reforms prior to the 1911 revolution, most of the orphanages and workshops run by the Benevolence Bureau were taken over by newly created government offices.

Another key to understanding Tsinan's political character in the late nineteenth century can be found in the unhappy history of efforts to control the Yellow River. After 1885 the new path of the Yellow River caused considerable economic hardship in Tsinan and farther downstream. The port of Le-k'ou declined sharply because of the heavier, swifter flow of the Yellow River, and at the mouth of the river the port of Li-ching, the former breakpoint between riverine and coastal shipping, was closed. This situation was hardest on the salt merchants who had depended on riverine shipping for transporting salt from the Gulf of Chihli to inland portions of North China.

In the 1870s much money and labor were invested in building strong dikes and levees along the course of the Yellow River in Shantung. One walled district town, Ch'i-tung, was even moved to a new location on the south bank. By 1876, Shantung officials felt the river-control works were complete, but in the 1880s serious flooding occurred again. Tsinan and some of the areas downstream near the Gulf of Chihli were hardest hit. In 1885, Governor Ch'en Shih-chieh proposed that Shantung establish a river control bureau (*ho-fang chü*) at Tsinan to coordinate the flood-protection work. Around Tsinan the water inundated much agricultural land in the districts of Li-ch'eng, Ch'i-ho, Chi-yang, and Ch'i-tung, but never touched the city itself. Consequently, Tsinan had to provide for a great many flood refugees during the 1880s.[13]

The economic disruption and the expense of reconstruction efforts consumed huge amounts of both government and private capital in Shantung during the 1880s and 1890s. Officials usually worked hard to secure tax remissions or special flood-control funds for Tsinan. The local gentry took the leadership in relief work for refugees. Both from the accounts of foreign missionaries and from the biographies of gentry donors to flood relief, there is every reason to believe these flood-relief projects created a reservoir of good will for the gentry leaders in the Tsinan area. In this instance at least, the picture of the gentry as wholly exploitative of the peasantry, providing no social investment in return, is clearly wrong.[14]

31

In the late nineteenth century the salt merchants retained their position as the leading commercial interests in Tsinan. Along the coast, especially at treaty ports such as Tientsin and Chefoo, the dominance of the salt merchants was being challenged by Chinese commercial interests involved in expanded lines of the coastal trade or new lines for foreign trade. At Tsinan, however, these new influences became more significant in the 1890s and soon thereafter displaced the salt merchants.[15]

The absence of strong extra-provincial groups was a distinguishing characteristic of Shantung commerce in the late nineteenth century, and most internal trade in the Tsinan trading system, as elsewhere in Shantung, lay in the hands of local merchants. Still, several provincial associations (*hui-kuan*) figured in Tsinan's economic and political life. The chief commercial association in Tsinan was the Shansi-Shensi *hui-kuan*, which was involved in the extensive salt, grain, coal, and iron goods trade between those provinces and Shantung. A Chekiang-Fukien association represented the interests of those involved in the important coastal trade out of eastern Shantung. A banking guild dominated by Shansi interests was another feature of Tsinan's commercial life in the late nineteenth century.*

The Grand Canal had long been the principal commercial artery in Shantung, and consequently Tsinan's extra-provincial ties had remained oriented toward Tientsin until the 1890s, when the opening of the Hsiao-ch'ing Canal began to break that pattern. After 1900 the opening of the Tsingtao-Tsinan railroad markedly increased Shanghai's influence in Tsinan's trade.

The salt merchants, general merchants, and officials all joined forces in a project to dredge the Hsiao-ch'ing River to make it navigable from Tsinan eastward to the Gulf of Chihli. The canal began at Tsinan and ran through the Ch'i region to the Gulf of Chihli. The project was talked about in the 1880s under Chang Yao and was actually begun later in the 1890s with the support of Sheng Hsuan-huai, who was serving as the *tao-t'ai* at Chefoo during some of those years, and Li Hung-chang. The work went slowly and was interrupted by some flooding along the lower reaches of the Yellow River. Most of the funds apparently came from flood-protection sources. The improvement of the stream boosted trade in eastern Shantung and helped the Tsinan-based salt merchants. Yang-chiao-kou, at the mouth of Hsiao-ch'ing Canal, became a regular port of call for steamers of the China Merchants Steam Navigation Company. The canal was soon to be replaced by the German-built Tsingtao-Tsinan railway, but

*Certain of these, such as the Anhwei *hui-kuan*, were more official, rather than commercial, in character because of their ties with the important officeholders and their staffs in Tsinan.

is noteworthy as a successful joint effort of innovative and traditional interests in North China to improve commercial conditions for Chinese business interests in the late nineteenth century.[16]

From the pattern of public projects undertaken in Tsinan after 1850, it is plain that the internal problems of the region were more important than any foreign influences in shaping the politics and policies of the officials and important gentry. Several academies (*shu-yuan*) were improved during those years, but there was no effort to incorporate any foreign learning. The improvements were financed and managed by men—often the same militia leaders and wealthy individuals important in the Benevolence Bureau—who were interested in preserving traditional Chinese learning.

Foreign influence began to appear at Tsinan most noticeably in the large Catholic church established in 1865 as the seat of a vicarate staffed by Franciscans. The Catholics had been active in Shantung before they were expelled in the eighteenth century and quickly reoccupied Tsinan after treaty provisions permitted it. The Catholics were also very active at Hung-chia-lou, a village a few kilometers to the east of the city. Hung-chia-lou eventually became the site of the Catholic cathedral and the bishop's residence.[17]

The Protestant missionaries were less obvious but still quite active. As noted above, the Benevolence Bureau tried to keep Protestant missionaries out of the city as regular residents, but the missionaries nevertheless succeeded in establishing medical clinics and small churches during the late 1880s. Before that time only itinerant missionaries, who distributed literature or spoke from street corners, had represented the Protestants in Tsinan.[18]

Foreign goods also became available in some of Tsinan's stores. Matches, kerosene, pots and pans, clocks, and some machine-woven cotton and woolen cloth were the most important items. The trade in foreign goods, however, was only a luxury trade, and traditional Chinese products suffered only minor displacement by foreign goods before 1900.

Officially sponsored modernization was limited to military projects. In 1875 Governor Ting Pao-chen had built an arsenal at Le-k'ou. The arsenal manufactured small-arms ammunition for the various official military units in the province, which included Manchu Banner troops, the Green Standard forces, elements of the Huai Army, and some Shantung militia forces. The Le-k'ou arsenal was refitted in 1895 under Governor Li Ping-heng, but remained a munitions assembly plant and warehouse.[19]

The first major telegraph line in China was opened in 1882 to connect Tientsin and Shanghai. The line followed the Grand Canal and bypassed Tsinan. In 1885 Tsinan was brought into the system when, at the suggestion of Governor Ch'en Shih-chieh, a branch line was built from Chi-ning through Tsinan and Wei-hsien and on to Chefoo. The construction of both lines was justified on military grounds, and travelers' stories verify that the line had little commercial or private use.[20]

TSINAN'S SOCIAL LIFE AND SOCIAL CLASSES

Tsinan also was a major regional cultural center in the late nineteenth century. The examination halls for the triennial *chü-jen* examinations stood on the south bank of Ta-ming Lake, along with separate examination halls for the *hsien*-level examinations. Four academies were located in the city. All four were distinguished and received the patronage of wealthy and powerful men.[21] The most famous was the Le-yuan Academy inside the West Gate, which was headed during this period by several noted scholars.

Tsinan also boasted a special kind of regional theatre performing "Drum Stories" (*ta-ku shu*), a genre which remained extremely popular in Tsinan during the 1920s and 1930s. The stories were ordinarily sung by young women who were accompanied by drums and sometimes other instruments. Liu E describes the pleasure of this kind of theatre in his novel *Lao-ts'an yu-chi*:

> Then she took up the drumstick, lightly struck the drum twice, lifted her head, and cast one glance at the audience. When those two eyes, like autumn water, like winter stars, like pearls, like two beads of black in quicksilver, glanced left and right, even the men sitting in the most distant corners felt: Little Jade Wang is looking at me! As to those sitting nearer, nothing need be said. It was just one glance, but the whole theatre was hushed, quieter than when the Emperor comes forth. Even a needle dropped on the ground could have been heard.[22]

Tsinan was filled with temples, archways, and pavilions dedicated to famous and worthy people. There was, of course, a full complement of Literary Temples, City God Temples, and special local temples. Some of these public buildings were used for cultural purposes, but several had become sites for markets in commodities such as fuel and rice.

Tsinan had been a city of 50,000 in the late eighteenth century. By 1840, on the eve of the great rebellions, the city had more than doubled in population. On the basis of the *pao-chia* registers of 1837, Tsinan's population numbered 128,000. Unfortunately, no official estimates or figures for the city's population are available from the latter half of the nineteenth century, but the reports and estimates of foreign observers, along with evidence from the building of the new wall and other construction, indicate that Tsinan grew at a fairly steady rate during this period (see Appendix B). In the early twentieth century Tsinan was a city of 250,000.

34

Tsinan, like many other Chinese cities, experienced large temporary influxes of people during times of war and natural calamity. The Nien threats of the 1860s and the floods and famines of the 1870s and 1880s all brought large numbers of temporary inhabitants to Tsinan. In 1894-1895 the defeat of China by Japanese forces, and the landings and assaults of Japanese forces along the Shantung peninsula, brought a sudden influx of wealthy refugees. Most of the people in these various waves of refugees, both the rich and the poor, returned to their homes after the disasters were over, but some chose to stay on in the safer and more active life of the city.

Although the cities provided protection against rebellion and banditry, they had serious drawbacks. As in pre-industrial cities in other parts of the world, the health problems in China's cities were often serious. Tsinan's spring-fed water, drained through sandstone from the Shantung mountains, was normally free of waterborne diseases such as typhoid and typhus. During flood periods, however, these diseases ravaged not only the city's refugees but its regular populace. A more constant threat was fire. Fire struck without respect to social class, but most often in the heavily built-up area inside the main city wall. The worst fire of the late nineteenth century, in 1891, burned out an important street leading to the provincial treasurer's yamen.[23]

The categories of employment in Tsinan follow the pattern of other North China cities during that period, but it is difficult to judge what proportion of the total population drew its livelihood from the various kinds of employment available. Most of the people inside the main walled city were employed in official capacities of some sort, ranging from the few appointed men of the civil service elite, all the way down to the clerks and yamen runners. The second largest group was that involved in commerce; it included the wealthy merchants in the salt trade and a variety of others, down to the warehousemen and casual transport worker. Chinese cities had no real patterns of residential segregation, but the inner walled city held large yamens, which also served as residences for high officials, along with many of the largest private residences. More humble dwellings, however, were crowded into the inner city's many small alleyways. The outer walled area held the same mixture of social classes, in newer buildings, along with a few peasants who tended fields near the city wall. Outside the walls, the villages tended to be close together and supported probably as many workmen and petty merchants as cultivators who tilled commercial plots growing vegetables or highly prized wet rice, or raised fowl or freshwater fish.[24] A few kilometers away from the city, the countryside took on a completely different aspect. The 1840 prefectural gazetteer gave this description:

The people of Li-ch'eng *hsien* are all farmers or vegetable gardeners. The poor are fuel gathers or hired labor. In the slack period they [the people of Li-ch'eng *hsien*] are merchants, but those who travel far are few. In the village the women-folk work at spinning. The men are idle in the winter. They tend the children, warm themselves in the sun, and make certain the women do not neglect their spinning. In the hills south of Tsinan there are people who die without knowing what proper clothing is.[25]

Thus the sparsely populated hilly southern reaches of Li-ch'eng district only a few kilometers from Tsinan contained some of the most isolated and backward villages in all Shantung.

Fortunately, a careful foreign observer has left a description of Tsinan's social classes which, although it does not make all the distinctions present-day sociologists would desire, does help in understanding the people of Tsinan. In the 1880s Alexander Armstrong classified the population of Tsinan city into seven categories: 1) acting officials, 2) retired or expectant officials, 3) wealthy gentry, 4) a middle class composed of doctors, teachers, priests, and merchants, 5) skilled workmen, 6) servants, soldiers, and laborers, and 7) beggars. The first three categories obviously are composed of the elite.

The household of a very wealthy Tsinan resident, Chang Shan-ma, represented the lifestyle of the most affluent individuals in the elite group. Chang's household was made up of a wife, two concubines, "several" children, thirty retainers, and four women servants. The house itself consisted of several buildings in a courtyard near the Governor's yamen in the center of the city. The layout of the residence was typical of North China elite homes. The house lay within a walled enclosure, with a main gate serving as the entrance from the street. Inside the enclosure a series of interconnected buildings created several courtyards, with the lesser rooms in front and along the sides. Various formal rooms for family living or receiving different kinds of guests occupied the central axis of the walled enclosure, with more intimate—thus more prestigious—rooms in the rear of the enclosure. This formality paralleled the arrangements of an official's yamen. Such elite households must have been quite numerous in Tsinan, for in 1897 the expectant officials alone numbered more than two thousand.[26]

Although not always members of the elite, the wealthy residents of Tsinan increased their numbers during the nineteenth century. More and more wealthy families chose to live in the cities, entrusting their rural lands to bursars and relatives who remained behind in the countryside. These urban residents were likely to put part of their capital into urban real estate or commerce after taking up residence in a city like Tsinan.[27]

Armstrong provides almost no information about his so-called middle class, but this group included large numbers of businessmen, as well as teachers and the educated staff of official offices. Since the priesthood attracted few men in the nineteenth century, that category would necessarily have been rather small. The skilled artisans in Tsinan worked primarily to fill the needs of the city's own trading system; Tsinan was not noted for any special handicrafts that were widely distributed in North China. We do not know what guilds (hang) flourished among these artisans, but various associations based on common origin are known from the records. In some places on Tsinan's back streets, craftsmen in the same line clustered together, but along the principal commercial thoroughfares, shops were mixed.

Armstrong's sixth category—servants, soldiers, and laborers—was certainly a large one in Tsinan. Not only the elite but also the middle classes usually had servants. There were not many soldiers in the late nineteenth century, but garrisons were assigned to the city. Crowded out of their quarters inside the main city wall, the soldiers had encamped in the outer walled area. The thousands of laborers in Tsinan included salt coolies, carters and barrowmen, apprentices and hired laborers in the shops, warehouses, and official offices; the main thoroughfares of the city were usually filled with barrows and carts.

A beggar contingent organized under a leader was a regular feature of Chinese cities; Tsinan was probably no exception. Armstrong's beggar category may also have included some of the refugees from famine and flood who were more seasonal than the established beggar groups. Armstrong did not mention Tsinan's other déclassé elements, the prostitutes and entertainers who lived in the northeastern part of the city near Ta-ming Lake. Prostitution flourished at examination time, when thousands of prospective young graduates and their parties filled the city's inns. On one occasion the provincial judge became so upset at the behavior of the candidates after the examinations that he arrested all the prostitutes he could find in the city and sold them to peasants as wives by weight at the market price of pork that day.[28]

The only identifiable minority groups in Tsinan were religious. An estimated eight thousand Moslems lived in one district outside the main city wall and east of Le-yuan Temple. They built a large mosque which was refurbished in the 1880s. They were said to be quite clannish, to practice circumcision, and to marry only within their faith. At other places in Shantung the Moslems were connected with mining, but it is not known what lines of work they followed in Tsinan, although they apparently took some less desirable and more menial jobs, including peddling and operating small food stalls.[29]

The Christian community in Tsinan in the late nineteenth century appears to have been quite small. The Catholics numbered their flocks in terms of a few hundred, whereas the Protestants counted in tens. The missionaries employed many converts in their orphanages, hospitals, and other projects.

THE TWIN SHOCKS OF THE SINO-JAPANESE WAR
AND THE BOXER UPRISING

The stability that Tsinan had experienced in the post-rebellion decades came to an abrupt end in the winter of 1894-1895 with China's crushing defeat by the Japanese. The sea and land engagements of that brief war touched Shantung, especially the peninsular areas, and sent tens of thousands in flight to the safety of the larger inland cities like Tsinan. The war brought the downfall of Li Hung-chang and cut the whole of the northern China adrift from his firm direction and control for the first time in a quarter-century.

At Peking the defeat set off shock waves that produced the abortive 1898 plan to restore governmental leadership to the Kuang-hsu Emperor and eventually resulted in the antiforeign Boxer uprising of 1899-1900. The first stages of the Boxer movement occurred in Shantung. Among officials who sanctioned the movement were the governors Li Ping-heng and Yü-hsien, both conservatives with long experience in official posts in Shantung and other parts of North China. Adrift after the disintegration of the conservative revival, these officials and some like-minded gentry hoped to quiet peasant unrest by reviving the militia tradition that had saved the Ch'ing a generation earlier. This time, though, the militia movement became more aggressive than defensive. Local units attacked the communities of foreign missionaries and their converts. The Empress Dowager at first endorsed the militia revival, but when the movement failed to win support throughout the empire, she withdrew her favor, abandoning the hapless Boxers to the harsh foreign reaction against their excesses.[30]

In December 1899 Yüan Shih-k'ai, a rising star in the dimming galaxy of Ch'ing authority, took over the governorship from Yü-hsien. Most of the foreign missionaries had already left the interior for the safety of the coastal treaty ports. Yüan could not immediately eradicate the Boxers, but he did stop the spread of antiforeign attacks. Specifically, he managed to confine the most serious aspects of Boxer activities to the northwestern section of the province, the area around Lin-ch'ing that had been deteriorating both economically and socially in spite of the revival that had occurred in the other areas of the province.

The Boxer uprising was the last instance of the conservative policy determined by the generation of the antirebel leaders. It failed miserably and completely discredited their leadership. A new kind of leader emerged in Yüan Shih-k'ai. Although inherently conservative on almost all basic political, economic, and social questions, he envisioned more contact with foreigners and sanctioned the careful adaptation of foreign ways while preserving the basic values of Chinese civilization. Yüan Shih-k'ai dominated Shantung from 1900 until his death in 1916; the history of that period is discussed in the following chapter.

3

Tsinan During the Late Ch'ing Reforms, 1901-1911

IN THE WAKE of the disastrous Boxer uprising, Yüan Shih-k'ai emerged as a major powerholder in the highest levels of the Ch'ing bureaucracy. Yüan's influence lay in North China and encompassed all of Shantung province. He exercised decisive and continuing control in the affairs of both Tsinan and the province of Shantung until his death in 1916. This period produced a series of major innovations in Tsinan's political, social, and economic life. Yüan Shih-k'ai and his supporters, however, had to contend with two other strong groups for control of Tsinan and Shantung. These were the foreigners, primarily the Germans before 1914, and the Shantung gentry; both of these groups had different ideas about how the city and the province should develop. This chapter traces the roles of these elements in Tsinan down to the 1911 revolution.

The main force for change in Tsinan stemmed at first from German imperialism, which sought more power, both direct and indirect, in Shantung. The initial Chinese resistance to the Germans was led by Yüan Shih-k'ai and other officials. Certain foreign powers, especially Great Britain and Japan, joined Yüan in his effort to check German dominance in Shantung.

Yüan Shih-k'ai's reform policies in North China not only checked the Germans but also helped consolidate his own power in that region. The reform program centered around the military but included educational and industrial development and had the effect of further centralizing the economy and politics of the province during the decade from 1901 to 1911. Yüan's policies then placed considerable emphasis on the modernization of Tsinan, and officially backed projects were the main source of change in the city.

Although the spectre of imperialism served as a goad both to official and gentry endeavors, foreigners actually played only an indirect role in Tsinan's modernization. In most of the changes introduced in Tsinan during these years the model was Western but the implementation was entirely Chinese. This fact sets Tsinan apart from the treaty ports, where foreigners, through special legal and quasi-governmental powers, often planned and carried out the Westernization of the city.

The third group to become involved in changing traditional life in Tsinan was the gentry class. Following the pattern of bureaucratic reorganization and reform set in motion by the Ch'ing dynasty, in the wake of the Boxer uprising the gentry realized a great opportunity was available to play an increasingly important role in the administration of the province. Education and the organs of representative government were the chief arenas for this new role, but the gentry also influenced commercial and, to a lesser extent, industrial development. Thus Yüan's program of officially sponsored innovation also fostered growing gentry power, and the gentry became increasingly drawn into Tsinan because that city had become a main arena of Yüan's efforts as well as the seat of political influence and power.

YÜAN SHIH-K'AI'S DOMINANCE

While the foreign units garrisoned Peking, and the Imperial Court remained in refuge at Sian, an imperial decree announced a new Manchu approach toward reform. The decree declared a willingness to "adopt the strong points of foreign countries in order to make up for China's shortcomings."[1] Although these words may have been intended to moderate the foreigners' demands during the Boxer settlement negotiations, they also permitted those officials—including Yüan Shih-k'ai—who had been urging various reform schemes on the dynasty to move ahead with their plans.

In the post-Boxer days, Yüan Shih-k'ai for the first time became a major figure in Peking politics. In December 1901 he left the Shantung governorship to become the governor-general of Chihli. He retained his power in Shantung, however, by leaving soldiers behind there and by controlling appointments to the top posts in the Shantung administration. The military unit involved had been known as the Right Division of the Imperial Guards (*Wu-wei yu-chün*) when Yüan brought it to Shantung in July 1899. It was part of a new modern-trained elite force Yüan had organized in Chihli after the Sino-Japanese War with the support of several Manchu nobles. Renamed the Fifth Division of the Peiyang Army, it stayed in Shantung—with its chief garrison at Tsinan—until the mid-1920s. It was a key element in Yüan's control and proved to be an unwelcome legacy after his death.[2]

Over the sixteen years of his dominance, Yüan's policies in Shantung hewed consistently to three principles: resistance to foreign imperialism, development of Chinese capacities as a counterweight to foreign pressures, and control of all policies and projects by government officials.

Credit for China's success in checking German imperialism in Shantung until 1914 must go primarily to Yüan Shih-k'ai and to the government officials in Tsinan who followed his policy directions.*

Yüan's policies consisted primarily of checking Germany's imperialist gains of the years 1897-1901 with a set of countermeasures which would block or limit Germany's plans in Shantung. This contest between German policy and Chinese countermeasures frequently focused on the city of Tsinan and in particular added the function of modern transportation hub to the city's already established importance as an administrative and commercial center. An important technique Yüan used to offset foreign power was to encourage gentry and popular activity against the foreigners, but he wanted responsible gentry control of this activity to avoid another Boxer episode. The gentry and popular forces Yüan encouraged soon found a common cause in the movement for representative politics in China. Thus the gentry, originally encouraged by Yüan, came to confront his steadfast adherence to the Confucian principle that the governance of the people was the responsibility of government officials. The clash between Yüan and the forces favoring representative government has its conception in the pre-1911 years but it surfaces as a critical issue only after the founding of the new Republic, and so will be discussed in detail in the next chapter.

In 1901 as the situation began to return to normal in Shantung after the Boxer uprising, Yüan began almost immediately to enact a reform program. In April he called the recently returned Christian missionaries of Tsinan to his yamen to discuss his plans. A missionary reported afterwards, "It rejoices the heart of those of us who have lived for some years in quiet old Chinanfu [Tsinan] to hear of these plans to make this ancient city wake from its long sleep and take its part in the renewed life of the Empire, which we all hope is about to begin."[3] Yüan outlined plans for modern schools, including a military school and a college-level institution. He also planned a daily newspaper, a government bank, a handicraft bureau, and a modern police force for Tsinan.

---

*John E. Schrecker has discussed this conflict at length in *Imperialism and Chinese Nationalism: Germany in Shantung* (Cambridge: Harvard University Press, 1971), concluding, "it was the development of a new and nationalistic foreign policy which proved decisive in containing the German threat" (p. 250). Yüan was the chief architect of this policy of nationalistic resistance to foreign imperialism in Shantung exactly in the same way that he was the principal opponent to the Japanese Twenty-One Demands in 1914-1915. The question is not merely an academic one, for many of Yüan's contemporaries applauded this quality in him, and his successors from the Peiyang clique claimed, usually without any grounds, to be following similar policies. In 1919 in the May Fourth demonstrations this issue of the Peiyang clique's patriotism, and by implication the patriotism of Yüan (the then-deceased head of the Peiyang elements), became a major political issue and has remained a hotly contested matter ever since.

Yüan did not stay in Shantung long enough to carry out his program personally, but he managed to have a series of friendly officials appointed to the governership. The first was Chou Fu, who had served with Yüan earlier in Korea and who succeeded Yüan within a few months. Chou Fu, like Yüan, had been a protégé of Li Hung-chang, and in Shantung he worked smoothly to carry out Yüan's policies. Together with Yüan he submitted a number of reform proposals to the throne, including many embodying the plans Yüan first outlined to the missionaries. Chou Fu also was responsible for starting the new programs after imperial approval was received. Thus Chou Fu's two-year tenure (August 1902-November 1904) in Tsinan was a crucial factor in bringing about Yüan's reform movement.[4]

Table 3.1
Shantung Governors, 1901-1911

Name	Tenure	Duration
Yüan Shih-k'ai	December 1899— December 1901	24 months
Chang Jen-chun	January 1902— August 1902	8 months
Chou Fu	August 1902— November 1904	28 months
Hu T'ing-kan	November 1904— December 1904	2 months
Shang Ch'i-heng	January 1905— February 1905	2 months
Yang Shih-hsiang	March 1905— September 1907	30 months
Yüan Shu-hsun	October 1907— July 1909	22 months
Sun Pao-ch'i	July 1909— February 1912	31 months

Source: Sun Pao-t'ien, comp., *Shan-tung t'ung-chih* (1915), ch. 51.

In March 1905 the governorship passed to Yang Shih-hsiang, a man both personally and professionally connected to Yüan. Yang had served as Yüan's subordinate in the post of Chihli provincial treasurer. His brother, Yang Shih-ch'i, was a close personal assistant to Yüan Shih-k'ai, and Yang Shih-hsiang's son married one of Yüan's daughters. Thus it is no surprise that Yang followed Yüan's policy of asserting Chinese rights against foreigners and supporting efforts to create commercial forces to counterbalance foreign interests. A measure of Yang's success was his promotion to the post of governor-general in Chihli when Yüan vacated that post in October 1907.[5]

Yüan Shu-hsun, a former *tao-t'ai* in Shanghai, succeeded Yang Shih-hsiang as governor of Shantung. Yüan knew Tsinan because he had

43

recently been consulted on the establishment of a Chinese-controlled commercial district there (see pp. 51-53). Yüan Shu-hsun emphasized fiscal retrenchment during his nearly two years in office, thus angering many minor officials whom he dismissed. His stringent policies slowed the pace of reform programs in Shantung, but still he did much to modernize the city of Tsinan. He appointed a new police commissioner, who paved the streets in the old city, began regular refuse collection, and planned a new set of city gates for better traffic patterns. From his experience in Shanghai, Yüan Shu-hsun brought knowledge of China's most modern city to bear on Tsinan's problems, and his tenure saw the adoption of many practices common to the foreign style of China's largest treaty port.[6]

Sun Pao-ch'i replaced Yüan Shu-hsun in July 1909 and stayed on through the troubled times of the 1911 revolution. When Sun came into office, Yüan Shih-k'ai was living in forced political retirement in Chihli because the Manchus dominating the court feared his power. Sun had served as minister to Germany and, like Yüan, wanted to check German power in Shantung. He also was an ardent modernizer. Thus, although not so close to Yüan as previous governors, Sun had policy aims closely parallel to Yüan's. Sun followed Yüan's directions in the critical stages of the 1911 revolution and during the new Republic became important among Yüan's supporters.[7]

YÜAN SHIH-K'AI'S POLICY AGAINST
GERMAN IMPERIALISM IN SHANTUNG

Section Two of the Sino-German Convention of 1898 began, "The Chinese Government sanctions the construction by Germany of two lines of railway in Shantung."[8] One line was to connect Tsingtao with Tsinan, the second to link Tsingtao with I-chou, in southern Shantung near the Grand Canal.* The convention also provided that these railways be constructed and operated by a joint Sino-German company. In June 1899 the railroad company, Schantung Eisenbahn Gesellschaft (SEG), received a charter in Berlin. The company was capitalized at 54 million marks (U.S. $13,500,000, circa 1905). In March 1900 Yüan Shih-k'ai and H. Hildebrand, a royal inspector of the Prussian Railways, signed a set of operating regulations that permitted construction to begin. The first article provided that, although the company itself was a joint Sino-German enterprise, "the Company for the present shall be exclusively under German management." According to the terms, Chinese participation would begin when the Chinese investment totaled more than 100,000 taels of stock. As in

*The second line was never begun because of a combination of Chinese resistance and declining German interest.

44

most other instances where China had an opportunity to invest in rail-roads, wealthy Chinese chose not to put their capital into these foreign-dominated joint stock companies. As a consequence the Sino-German character of the railroad remained a legal fiction, and the Germans made no attempt to hide their complete domination over the railroad in actual practice.[9]

This lack of interest in purchasing the shares of the SEG, which consti-tuted a new investment medium as well as a new foreign technology, is typical of the early twentieth century. The inability of railroads to attract gentry and merchant capital is a major element in the history of Chinese railroads, and, whatever the reason, it is an indication of the unwillingness of Chinese investors in Tsinan and elsewhere to shift their capital from commerce into investments in Western-style industrial enterprises.

The Tsingtao-Tsinan railway generally followed the former highway between Chiao-chou and Tsinan, deviating from the old road for commercial, mining, or engineering considerations. The resulting route passed through *hsien* seats at Chiao-chou, Kao-mi, Wei *hsien*, Ch'ang-le, and I-tu (Ch'ing-chou *fu*). It passed near the coal fields at Fang-tzu and the commercial town of Chou-ts'un. Construction began in 1900, but the Boxer uprising and the lack of adequate port facilities at Tsingtao delayed the first stages of the work. The survey and construction crews encoun-tered some local resistance, especially in Kao-mi *hsien*, in the summer of 1900. After the Boxer settlement, construction went on rapidly and faced little open resistance along the line. At Tung-ch'ang, in northwestern Shantung, however, demonstrations broke out because people correctly feared that the new railroad would further reduce commerce along the Grand Canal.[10]

At the annual meeting of the SEG held in Berlin in August 1903, man-agement reported that 34 million of the authorized 54 million marks of capital had been paid up. Stock of the railroad issued at 100 in 1899 sold at 103. Chou Fu, the Shantung governor, owned some three hundred shares, but he was the only Chinese stockholder. SEG's stock never became widely traded, but the company did become a moderately profitable operation.[11]

The city of Tsinan felt the economic impact of the railroad soon after service was opened in 1904, when a 60 percent decrease in coal prices at Tsinan foretold a general increase in the level and variety of trade. A Japanese report summed up the impact of the Shantung railroad on Tsinan in the 1904-1912 period:

> Prior to the establishment of the Tsingtao-Tsinan railway, Tsinan trade was dominated by Tientsin. The organizations and shops had close ties with Tientsin trade circles. When the Germans took over Shantung and built a port with a rail-road, a great change occurred. Chinese merchants from Shanghai moved to

Tsingtao, as did Chinese merchants from Chefoo. The development of Tsingtao had a directly beneficial influence on Tsinan. As the Grand Canal failed, the grip of Tientsin merchants on Shantung was loosened and new Shanghai influences pulled more and more trade into Tsinan. Foreign influence had the same effect. Germany used Tsinan as a forward base to expand trade. Some specialty items of trade, however, have not yet been broken away from Tientsin hands.[12]

In 1898, after the creation of a German sphere of interest in Shantung, representatives of German and British financial interests agreed jointly to finance and construct a long-discussed trunk line running from the Peking region across East China to the Lower Yangtze Valley. This project eventually became the Tientsin-Pukow railroad. The 1898 arrangement divided the line into two sections; the British would build and run the part lying within Kiangsu province, while the Germans would build and run the part lying within Shantung and Chihli. Later the same year, the Anglo-German group reached an agreement with the Ch'ing dynasty to construct the north-south railroad. Again the Boxer uprising upset railroad construction schedules, but in this case both sides wanted to renegotiate the agreements in 1902.

In the post-Boxer years while the 1898 agreements were under review, wealthy Kiangsu interests sought assistance for a nationalization scheme under which the Chinese hoped to preclude foreign control of the railroad. Wang Mao-k'un, a prominent retired official living in Tsinan, who had once served as *hsien* magistrate at Shanghai, headed the project in Shantung to raise Chinese capital for building the north-south railroad. He failed to gather any significant support from the Shantungese.

The Ch'ing dynasty and the Anglo-German group did not reach a new agreement until 1908. Under its terms the title to the railroad remained in Chinese hands, but foreign interests would build the line and control accounting and operations when the railway went into service.[13]

The Tientsin-Pukow railroad paralleled an old imperial highway over most of its length. The most difficult part of the construction work lay in crossing the Yellow River near Tsinan. Work on a bridge began in the fall of 1908. Long before the bridge was completed, the rest of the line entered operation. In October 1910 trains ran from Pukow, on the northern bank of the Yangtze River, into the city of Tsinan. Ferries provided service across the river at Tsinan, where the railroad continued north to Tientsin. The Yellow River bridge was finished in November 1912, to complete the project.[14]

Although the Tsingtao-Tsinan and Tientsin-Pukow rails lay within a few meters of each other in Tsinan, no provisions existed for switching equipment between the lines until the mid-1920s, when both railways were under Chinese management. Earlier, the Chinese, fearing a German

46

military thrust at Peking, had wished to keep the roads separate in order to forestall a surprise strike at Peking.

The Tientsin-Pukow railroad had much less visible impact on Tsinan than the Shantung railway eight years before. Foreign technology, foreign cultural forms, and a larger foreign community had already arrived with the earlier line. At the same time it must be remembered that the Tientsin-Pukow railroad had been planned since the early 1890s, before the first Tsingtao-Tsinan railroad schemes were broached. Knowledge that a major north-south link would pass through or near Tsinan gave increased impetus to all plans for that city after 1900. Once the Tientsin-Pukow railroad entered full service in 1912, it greatly enhanced Tsinan's role as a transportation center and contributed considerably to the city's commercial and industrial growth during the early Republican period.

Yüan Shih-k'ai and his successors in the governor's offices at Tsinan never tried to thwart the plans for foreign railroads. Instead, they worked—successfully—to keep the Germans from using their railroad as an arm of imperialist expansion into the interior of Shantung. The third section of the 1898 convention gave Germany an exclusive right to engineer and construct all manner of development within the province: "The Chinese government binds itself in all cases where foreign assistance in persons, capital, or material may be needed for any purpose whatever within the province of Shantung, to offer the said work of supplying of materials in the first instance to German manufacturers and merchants engaged in undertakings of the kind in question."[15] In fact, the Chinese officials in Shantung ignored this provision and frequently contracted with British, American, and Japanese firms for foreign assistance. The issue of German mining rights can help illustrate how Yüan Shih-kai and his successors operated.

In 1899 at the same time that the SEG was chartered, and closely resembling it, the mining firm Schantung Bergbau Gesellschaft (SBG) was created. Capitalized at 6 million marks (U.S. $1,300,000, circa 1905), the SBG was also a Sino-German joint enterprise in theory. Chinese officials and gentry showed even less interest, if possible, in investing in the mining company that they did in the railroad. According to the German text of an agreement signed between Yüan Shih-k'ai and representatives of SBG at Tsinan in 1900, Germany had the exclusive right to use modern mining machinery within the thirty-*li* (eighteen-kilometer) corridor alongside the Tsingtao-Tsinan railroad. The Chinese text omitted this proviso, and consequently the Chinese officials resisted German claims, first by denying that the German privilege existed, then by refusing to cause native producers to stop production and by not intervening against Chinese who employed Western mining technology.[16]

Figure 3. Tsinan, about 1906. Taken from a pavilion in Ta-ming Lake on the north side of the walled city, the photograph looks toward the south across the reeds growing in the lake; in the middle distance is the center of the walled city with its many low government offices and private residences, and beyond that the hills south of the city. The hill in the center is Ch'ien-fo shan. The new railway station and the settlement district lie outside the field of the photograph, to the right. (Photographed by an unidentified Chinese. From Ernst Boerschmann, *Picturesque China: Architecture and Landscape*. New York: Brentano's, n.d.)

48

At first SBG operations concentrated at the Fang-tzu coal field in Wei *hsien*. But the commercial quality of the Fang-tzu coal disappointed the SBG management, and after the Boxer uprising the firm shifted its attention to the Po-shan Valley, where Chinese had mined coal with traditional methods for centuries. Near the *hsien* seat at Tzu-ch'uan, in the Po-shan Valley, SBG tests located an excellent site. A large colliery was established there, about six kilometers from the walled town of Tzu-ch'uan. A spur from the Po-shan branch line of the Shantung railway was run out to the pithead of what became the most important mine of the SBG.[17]

Once this Tzu-ch'uan colliery was opened, German diplomats at Tsingtao, Tsinan, and Peking used its existence as the basis of an SBG claim to exclusive modern-mining rights in the portions of the coal-rich Po-shan Valley that fell within the thirty-*li* zone. The Chinese officials at all levels refused to recognize this claim, for to do so would put thousands of miners working in traditional mines out of work, as well as harm the investments of many wealthy merchants and mine owners. The SBG never got rid of its Chinese competition.[18] The preferential freight rates and the railroad services provided by SEG, however, should have given SBG coal a considerable commercial advantage over its Chinese competitors.

In spite of this, the Chinese producers apparently prospered, whereas the SBG never could make a profit. There were many Chinese coal merchants in Tsinan in 1914, and nearly all of them located in the newly developed section of the city, indicating the recent expansion of this kind of commerce. In addition, the names of some coal yards can be linked with the important Shantung merchant groups (*pang*) in Po-shan, Chou-ts'un, and Chang-ch'iu.[19] These merchant groups were small but powerful local trade associations involved in the grain-and-silk trade, banking, and general commerce, as well as coal. These merchants had no reason to continue in any line of business where they faced ruinous foreign competition, because they could profit from several other lines of commercial endeavor. Thus, it seems reasonable that they profited from the coal trade as they did from other lines and expanded their activities in the coal trade as well as in other lines of commerce as the new railroads increased commercial opportunities. The Chinese merchants maintained discriminatory pricing or other restrictive arrangements that reduced the market for SBG coal in the interior of the province, limiting the German company more or less to the China coast. Nonetheless, the ability of the Chinese commercial elements to compete successfully against foreign interests in established commercial lines in the Shantung domestic economy reflects the fundamental strengths of the Chinese commercial

49

interests, just as the failure to attract their monies to investment in the railroads illustrates their weaknesses.

The SBG, unable to halt Chinese mining operations, then requested German diplomatic intervention to constrain Chinese competition in coal sales. This, too, failed. The German company simply never became a profitable commercial operation and in 1913 was sold to SEG for railway stock worth about half the SBG investment in Shantung.[20]

In political terms, the struggle between German and Chinese mining interests served to concentrate more Chinese economic power in the provincial capital. Before the railroad came, the chief coal merchants in Tsinan had included powerful Chinese mining interests from Shansi. These interests were squeezed out by the development of the various new operations—both foreign and Chinese—in Shantung. In the days before 1900, when officials sought to tax the Chinese coal trade rather than use it to thwart German influence, coal mining interests had little reason to make Tsinan a center of their operations. They much preferred to try to stay out of sight and so avoid the attentions and exactions of high officials. But after 1900, because the officials, led by Yüan Shih-k'ai, took positions against the Germans which were favorable to Chinese mining interests, Shantung coal interests were drawn to Tsinan to seek political protection for their mining operations. Thus, politics as well as commercial advantages drew Chinese commercial interests into Tsinan in these years. This pattern of official protection for Chinese commercial interests in order to achieve political goals represented an important new mode of official and merchant relations. In most such cases the officials derived no obvious personal benefits from such policies, while the merchants did not receive monopoly license privileges, the common mode of official and merchant relationship in the Ch'ing.

OFFICIALLY BACKED INNOVATION AT TSINAN

Creating a Chinese-sponsored and administered commercial settlement (*shang-pu*) at Tsinan was a key element in Yüan Shih-k'ai's policy of blocking German imperialism. In October 1904 Yüan joined with Chou Fu to propose that the Chinese themselves create a special commercial district outside the Tsinan city walls where foreigners could live. The amenities and privileges provided would be the same as in the treaty ports, except that the administration of the settlement would remain under the full control of Chinese officials. In his memorial, Yüan argued,

> Since the Germans leased Chiao-chou Bay in 1899, port facilities and a railroad have been constructed. The railroad already extends to Tsinan. At the same time work has begun on the Tientsin-to-Chinkiang railroad [eventually the Tientsin-Pukow line] that will link up with the Shantung line. Tsinan originally was a port

50

for the Yellow River and the Hsiao-ch'ing canal. Now it will also be the meeting place for two railroads. That means it will become extremely advantageous for commerce and transportation. . . . [Therefore,] outside of Tsinan city we would open a commercial port. Within a short time the profits enjoyed by the foreign merchants will extend into the provincial capital itself.[21]

The memorial went on to suggest that similar commercial districts be created at Chou-ts'un and Wei-hsien, two important commercial cities on the Shantung railroad. The newly created Board of Foreign Affairs (*Wai-wu pu*) concurred and the throne endorsed these proposals.[22]

By creating a special foreign settlement area, Yüan answered in advance, and on China's terms, the inevitable German demand for suitable facilities for German merchants in the Shantung interior. At the same time, the settlement plan provided a way for the city of Tsinan to cope with the wave of foreign influence that would certainly accompany the arrival of the railroad.

One of the strongest tools Yüan could use to restrict German influence in Shantung, as he clearly saw, was the desire shared by other foreign governments to keep Germany from becoming too powerful in this area. Governor Yang Shih-hsiang invited the Japanese to establish a consulate and promised them a free site to build it on. In addition he set aside a choice location for future use by the important Japanese Mitsui trading firm. The British also established a consular office in Tsinan.[23]

The settlement was laid out west of the old city and south of the terminus of the Shantung railroad. The site lay on higher ground outside the geological depression that gave the old city its springs and lake. Streets formed a grid pattern. A special park area marked the center of the settlement.

The British wanted to help check German designs, but they feared that Yüan's ideas might limit the rights of foreigners in China. The Chinese, well aware of foreign sensitivities about treaty rights, did everything possible to make their new commercial settlement in Tsinan acceptable. Yüan Shih-k'ai enlisted Yüan Shu-hsun, the former *tao-t'ai* at Shanghai, to oversee the establishment of the settlement administration. The laws and regulations of Shanghai served as models for the new settlement.*

The formal opening of the Tsinan settlement came in January 1906 in ceremonies presided over by Yang Shih-hsiang and attended by two hun-

---

*This use of Shanghai practices as a model for modern urban administration in China is an important aspect of Shanghai's influence. In the years after the 1911 revolution, Chinese urban administration experts began to draw directly upon the examples of European and American city administration, but as long as treaty rights were a central issue for foreigners living in China, the treaty-port standards served as the chief guide. Another example contemporary with the Tsinan case was the opening of Ch'angsha as an ordinary treaty port in the summer of 1904. There, too, Shanghai practice served as the model. See *North China Herald*, 15 July 1904, p. 137.

dred invited guests, including seventy foreigners. In his speech Governor Yang stated, "The idea of commercial settlements is a step in the right direction. This one is our starting point and will serve as a pattern for all others in the interior."[24] As the name implied, the settlement was intended to serve as a commercial, as distinct from an industrial, center. This commercial character reflects a realistic appraisal by Yüan's officials of the impact of the railroad on the city, for it was trade that would increase most dramatically in the first years after the railroads reached the city. Tsinan's potential for progress toward the urban-industrial model had to begin with increased commercial activity, and Yüan's commercial settlement provided the basis on which further economic development could be built.

The chief authority of the foreign settlement at Tsinan was placed in the hands of the Commercial District General Bureau (*shang-pu tsung-chü*). The *tao-t'ai* for the northwestern part of Shantung became the concurrent head of the bureau. A powerful engineering office (*kung-ch'eng-ch'u*) approved land leases and building projects, and arranged all other matters concerning land usage and sanitation. A separate foreign-style police force maintained order. Petty cases arising within settlement boundaries went to a separate judge at the Tsinan courthouse. A whole series of special arrangements existed to ensure that settlement district police would not violate foreigners' treaty privileges. Foreign consuls' duties included participation in decisions on police matters and on land-usage cases.[25]

The administration of the settlement districts remained completely separate, both in legal form and in fact, from the administration of Tsinan city. The walled-city administration continued as before to be the technical responsibility of the Li-ch'eng *hsien* magistrate. However, in a fashion typical of traditional Chinese cities, the governor, the provincial judge, the provincial treasurer, the *tao-t'ai*, the Chi-nan prefect, and the Li-ch'eng *hsien* magistrate all shared overlapping practical responsibilities for administering Tsinan city. Consequently, the settlement provided an opportunity to compare Western and Chinese styles of municipal administration. In the first few years of its existence, the settlement administration had little impact on Tsinan city administration, but increasingly after 1911 the old city adopted techniques and forms from the settlement. Paradoxically, because the Chinese controlled the settlement, its impact was greater.

In a commercial sense the chief difference between Tsinan and a treaty port was that Tsinan had no Imperial Maritime Customs Office. Consequently, instead of paying only the low customs duties, as they would have in a treaty port, foreign traders had to buy transit certificates by which they paid half the ordinary internal transit taxes (*likin*) levied by provincial authorities. This made the price of goods traded through Tsinan somewhat higher than those traded at interior treaty ports such as Ch'angsha. But because no competing treaty ports existed in Tsinan's area, and because the foreign traders could transport their goods with a tax advantage over their Chinese competitors, who had to pay full transit taxes, the regulations worked to the foreign traders' advantage.[26]

The Chinese hoped the settlement regulations would induce all the foreigners in Tsinan to live in the settlement, but since treaty rights permitted them to reside anywhere in the interior, many decided to remain in the old walled city. Most missionaries declined to move for fear of jeopardizing their work, and many Japanese shopkeepers who did business in the old city also refused to go.

The settlement district served the expanding foreign influence in Tsinan, and reveals Tsinan's increasingly important role as an inland commercial center. Large foreign firms, new foreign residents, and most people with consular duties preferred the new settlement. In 1911 a survey revealed that one-sixth of the settlement's 3500 *mou* (583 acres) were already in use. There were seven kilometers of paved roads. The Deutsch-Asiatische Bank built the largest commercial building in 1907. The bank, however, lacked sufficient business to cover its mortgage and operating expenses. Other German businesses included a hotel, some commercial firms, and a number of shopkeepers, including a grocer, a butcher, and a baker. The British-associated Asiatic Petroleum Company and the British-American Tobacco Company had offices in the settlement. Building sites were under development by the Yokohama Specie Bank and the Mitsui Trading Company. Many Chinese also moved their businesses or residences to the district because the conveniences of transportation and public services were much better than those within Tsinan's walls. Also many of the new Chinese commercial establishments preferred the settlement to the overcrowded quarters available in the old city. Aside from small shops, the most common Chinese businesses were inns (34) and brothels (106). In addition, traditional theatres as well as a new motion picture theatre opened in the settlement. A majority of the settlement population was Chinese.[27]

The Ch'ing officials also played a key role in bringing all kinds of modern technology and public services to Tsinan. For example, although telegraph and official postal services had existed in Tsinan before 1900, it was only under Yüan Shih-k'ai in 1901 that the first regular branch of the Chinese Post Office was established. In 1905 the postal facilities were expanded, probably in part to check the growth of the Imperial German Postal Administration in Shantung. By 1909 the city's rail connections brought a new centralization of Chinese postal business to Tsinan. Three foreign postal inspectors were assigned to Tsinan and the city was made the central distribution point for all of Shantung.[28]

Official initiative was also responsible for the first telephone and electric services in Tsinan. In 1902 a special telephone system was installed to link the governor's yamen with the yamens of the provincial treasurer and the provincial judge; this system was later expanded to include other official offices. In 1905 Governor Yang Shih-hsiang arranged for technicians attached to the Le-k'ou arsenal to help install and operate a small electric generator he had purchased from the Germans.[29]

Within a few years, these official experiments were superseded by private business endeavors. Tsinan's electric service became the monopoly of the Tsinan China Merchants Electric Company (*Chi-nan Hua-shang tien-tung kung-ssu*) in 1906. The firm, with over 200,000 taels of capital, purchased used equipment from the Germans in Tsingtao and began service in 1906.[30] The Tsinan electric generating facility was one of a dozen such Chinese-owned municipal electric power companies that opened in the 1901-1906 period. This kind of public service industry in Chinese cities was one of the first to attract Chinese capital, perhaps because there was less foreign competition than in shipping, mining, and railroads.

The head of the Tsinan firm was Liu En-chu, a Shantungese business-man from the Chefoo region who also controlled Chefoo's electric company. Liu En-chu's background is obscure, but his initial career in a treaty port and his willingness to invest in modern technology both there and in Tsinan suggests that he was probably a representative of the com-prador class, although I have not been able to determine his exact business connections in Chefoo. The China Merchants Electric Company was a merchant-controlled (*shang-pan*) enterprise in which official protection played an extremely important role. Official initiative had been responsi-ble for the first experiments with generation of electricity in Tsinan, and the monopoly position granted to the firm was important in obtaining Liu En-chu's capital investment. This kind of merchant monopoly obviously derives from the late Ch'ing system of official supervision and merchant management (*kuan-tu shang-pan*) that was the dominant form of modern industrial development in China in the late nineteenth century.

These were small industrial undertakings, but their beginnings provided a clear foretaste of Tsinan's industrial development. The officials were really responsible for these innovations and they worked closely with private individuals to carry out their plans. This form of endeavor is best described as "bureaucratic capitalism" because the conditions for its operation required close cooperation, if not collusion, between officials and capitalists. In the future, as with these first few modern industries established in Tsinan, bureaucratic capitalism was the standard form of organization for large industry, while private Chinese wealthy interests, both gentry and commercial, stayed close to their established lines of economic activity.

Another area in which official initiative prodded private enterprise into activity was the newspaper business. Before 1900, a small daily gazette of official business was printed in Tsinan, but Yüan Shih-k'ai wanted to change it into a more general but still official newspaper. The result was the *Shan-tung kuan-pao* (Shantung Gazette), which began publication in 1907, and, under various names, continued to be published in Tsinan until 1938.[31]

Also active in promoting journalism were the missionaries, who saw newspapers as a means of spreading religious and social propaganda, and the Republicans. The first private daily newspaper in Tsinan was a missionary-backed operation, *Chien-pao* (The Synopticon), published each evening on two sheets of book-size paper. Political groups, most of which were associated with the Revolutionary Alliance (*T'ung-meng hui*), published several weekly and monthly papers, which were quickly suppressed by officials. In general, papers without official or foreign connections found it difficult to remain in business until after the 1911 revolution.[32]

The officials also served to promote modernization simply through their interest in foreign technology or foreign styles. The Shantung governors' taste for foreign furniture and touring automobiles fell into this category; whatever the reason for their interest, the officials were often responsible for importing the more expensive foreign gadgetry into Tsinan.

The thrust of education policy in Shantung typified Yüan's modernization efforts. The plan was broad and sweeping, but it enlisted active local participation, and official leadership remained dominant. In 1901 Yüan arranged for the most prestigious of Tsinan's academies, Le-yuan, to become a modern school at the university level. He hired foreigners, first Protestant missionaries from Teng-chou, and then Japanese, to teach in the school, and built a set of modern buildings in Tsinan. Yüan planned this provincial university (*ta-hsüeh*) to be the capstone of a hierarchical system of government schools in all the prefectures and *hsien* of Shantung.[33]

Unlike the growing numbers of Chinese who believed that education should be linked with the development of representative government in China, Yüan wanted modern education for the traditional purpose of training better officials to serve the dynasty. Thus, Yüan's educational

55

reforms were as conservative in intent as his other reforms and were consistent with his view of the good official as the principal source of a well-regulated polity.[34]

As part of Yüan's educational plan for Shantung, Chou Fu oversaw the transformation of traditional academies (shu-yuan) in seventy-one hsien into primary and secondary schools in 1903. Obviously a change in name alone did not produce a modern school where a traditional institution had stood. The plan included a changed curriculum that would draw on Japanese and Western examples while not totally abandoning the established Chinese ways.

Yüan's overall policy reveals a clear intent to bring about a rapid yet well-grounded change in the school system. His plans favored Tsinan as a location for new schools, thereby centralizing the new educational resources in Tsinan to a much greater extent than had previously been the case. In 1911 there were seven government schools at the secondary level and above in Tsinan, more than in any other place in the province. Most of the fifteen hundred students were taught by young men who had received modern educational training in the larger treaty ports or in Japan.[35] The teachers and students favored a kind of constitutionalism much more liberal than Yüan Shih-k'ai could support, but the schools owed their existence to Yüan's vision.

The Fifth Division of the Peiyang Army, based in Tsinan, also played a significant role in modernizing Tsinan through introducing many new technological and foreign influences into the city. Chang Huai-chih, a native of Shantung and loyal to Yüan Shih-k'ai, served as commanding general. Division headquarters occupied part of some Western-style buildings near the settlement district. The main encampment of the Fifth Division was farther west of the city, near the village of Hsin-chuang, about five kilometers from the center of Tsinan. The camp followed contemporary Western military practice with regimental units grouped around individual drill fields and separate buildings for barracks, mess halls, and latrines. The policy of enrolling recruits only from Shantung continued. Weapons, drill, uniforms, and general organization drew on Western practices. A British military attaché who visited the camp in 1908 described it as the best then in existence in China. He also had high praise for the quality of the Fifth Division itself.[36]

Attached to the division were a series of schools for the training of officers and men. Most important was the Army Preparatory School, which provided cadet training for boys destined to be Peiyang Army officers. According to the recollections of one student at the school, the classes there were demanding and the discipline strict. Yüan Shih-k'ai's younger brother, Yüan Shih-tun, served as commandant of the school

56

after 1903. Graduates went on to the Peiyang Schools at Hsiao-chan in Chihli for further military education.[37]

An arsenal, first put into operation in the 1870s, formed part of the military establishment at Tsinan. The arsenal never became a center of military engineering but remained a small munitions factory producing rifle cartridges. Personnel assigned to the arsenal did, however, provide technical assistance to the officially sponsored electric light and telephone systems that were especially installed in the 1902-1906 period for use by high provincial officials.[38]

The schools and the military establishment constituted two chief institutions capable of producing men with the kinds of technical skills needed if any shift toward industrial technology was to have occurred in Tsinan. Such a shift would have to occur if Tsinan were to move beyond fulfilling its increasing commercial importance and change into a significant center of industry. The schools, both civil and military in Tsinan, however, produced very few technicians and instead trained young men and women in the more genteel skills compatible with both the traditional Chinese bias toward scholarly education and the bourgeois character of the Western educational influences.

In early 1907 the Manchu noblemen who had cooperated with Yüan since 1898 began to turn away from him. As a result of this change, Yüan lost his direct control over the Peiyang Army. The Fifth Division and three other units were taken away from Yüan's control and placed in the hands of Manchus. A Manchu general, Feng-shan, who was closely associated with the move against Yüan, became the new commander of the Fifth Division. The unit retained its relatively high standing among other Chinese military units of the day, but Feng-shan cut back on the military schools and did not rehire the foreign advisors. Chang Huai-chih, involuntarily retired, moved to Tientsin.[39]

The Manchus were not able to replace the entire officer corps of the division, more and more of whom showed sympathy for anti-Manchu revolutionary ideas after Feng-shan assumed command. The Fifth Division in 1908 became heavily infiltrated with sympathizers of the Revolutionary Alliance (*T'ung-meng hui*). An informant estimated that a third of the 7200 men in the Fifth Division at Tsinan were active in the anti-Manchu movement in the years just before the 1911 revolution.[40] Thus the new modern army, in Shantung as elsewhere in China, became increasingly radical during the final years of Manchu rule. The combination of the revolutionary bent on the Fifth Division and the already strong modernizing influences of its organization, technology, and education made the unit a potent force for modernization within Tsinan.

Figure 4. The Li-hsia Pavilion, a famous and beautiful spot in Ta-ming Lake. (Photographed by an unidentified Chinese about 1906. From Ernst Boerschmann, *Picturesque China: Architecture and Landscape*, New York: Brentano's, n.d.)

THE FOREIGN COMMUNITY IN TSINAN

In 1900 the foreign community in Tsinan numbered no more than fifty, including children. Most were European or American missionaries, but some were connected with commercial interests. As the core of the foreign community, the missionaries congregated in one of the city's better residential areas. The Protestant missionaries had chapels, schools, and residences clustered in the southern portion of the outer walled area. Outside the city the Catholic village of Hung-chia-lou, east of Tsinan, was the other primary center of foreign influence in Li-ch'eng *hsien*.[41]

The missionaries undertook many modernizing efforts in Tsinan, including hospitals and schools. Their operations contributed in some degree to Tsinan's modernization, but more as a model against which the Chinese could gauge their efforts than anything else. Missionary efforts never were decisive in setting the course of modernization in the city.

As noted in Chapter 2, medical missionaries had been active in Tsinan since the 1880s. In 1901 the Presbyterian mission expanded its medical facility first into a hospital and then, in 1906, into a medical college to train Chinese physicians. In 1908 a separate site for the medical college was obtained and a new building was constructed. In addition to American funds, there were donations from Shantung provincial officials. In 1910 the first regular class was admitted. The site of the medical school later developed into the campus of Shantung Christian University (Cheeloo). Even in medicine the Chinese did not rely entirely on foreigners, however, for in 1911 a Chinese-operated modern hospital with some Japanese staff opened in Tsinan.[42]

Perhaps the most unusual foreign addition to Tsinan's culture was the Whitewright Museum. Founded in 1905 by an English missionary named Whitewright, the museum became a locally renowned attraction. The museum building, located in the southern part of the city favored by the missionaries, featured displays ranging from stuffed fish to models of recent international exposition grounds in Europe. Both the collections and the reputation of the museum were to grow over the next few decades.[43]

Once the Shantung railroad reached Tsinan and the settlement district was opened, the numbers of foreigners rapidly increased. To the missionary community was added a leaven of consular families, international traders, and a lesser number of small businessmen. Before 1914 most of the foreign traders and shopkeepers were German, although the British, Americans, and Japanese were also represented. The presence of consular offices gave individual national communities a focal point, but there were numerous social and business dealings across national lines. The Japanese, however, were isolated from the Caucasian community.

It is difficult to assign to these various foreign residents a central role in the modernization of Tsinan. The administration of the settlement was always in Chinese hands, and Chinese initiative was required for most substantial civic improvements. Quite often, officials or Chinese private interests, favoring some new measure in Tsinan, would argue that such a change was required by the Westerners' presence, but the initiative in most matters remained with the Chinese.

Foreign shopkeepers in Tsinan had considerable competition from Chinese merchants at first. In fact, the Chinese merchants in the old city had carried foreign goods for some time and had opened the first stores that catered especially to foreign buyers. But these Chinese shops steadily lost ground, especially after the opening of the settlement district. With the railroad there also arrived an influx of small Japanese merchants who specialized in trading new foreign consumer items for the Chinese market. Japanese merchants dealt in machine-milled flour, machine-woven cotton cloth and machine-spun thread, drugs, and Western gadgets and furniture.[44] Foreign merchants were free from most taxes and exactions on Chinese businessmen—especially local levies—and this was to give them an increasing advantage after 1916.

THE RISE OF REFORM-MINDED GENTRY

The appearance of reform-minded gentry is the key to understanding Tsinan's development in the early twentieth century, surpassing in importance the foreign influence and even the official influence exerted under Yüan Shih-k'ai. These men, through their commercial interests, their organizations, and their access to power, built upon the early official impetus toward reform and made the movement a servant of their own interests. As early as 1908, Bertram Giles* mentioned a "Shantung reform party" that was pressuring the provincial administration to speed up implementation of imperial reform plans, calling for representative government.[45] In the course of working in reform programs initiated by the Ch'ing officials, gentry leaders formulated goals distinct from those of the Chinese bureaucrats serving the Ch'ing dynasty. The goals of these gentry leaders, it should be noted, were not always those of the dynasty.

This new orientation of the Shantung gentry originated in China's humiliation during the Sino-Japanese war of 1894-1895. Finding all their basic assumptions about their country shaken, many young men, some of whom had already begun their progress up the examination ladder, abandoned their traditional studies for the modern education offered at

*Bertram Giles was an unusually knowledgeable officer in the British consular service who served in Tsinan on two separate tours, first between 1905 and 1908 as acting consul and again in 1921 to 1923 as consul. He was the brother of Lionel Giles, the first holder of the chair of Chinese literature at Oxford.

Western-style schools in China or in Japan. Initially only a trickle of Shantung students were among them, but as reform proposals began to be advanced, between 1902 and 1905, more and more of them realized that at the very least the examination system would soon include some Western learning. Consequently more of those who were planning on traditional careers as government officials began to add foreign studies to their preparation.

By the time the decision to abandon the examination system was announced in November 1905, the gentry in Shantung had already begun to support modern schools. Especially in the eastern Ch'i region of Shantung, gentry leaders formed societies to study modern approaches to education, such as the Society for the Study of Mass Education in Wei hsien (*Chih-ch'ün hsüeh-hui*). According to the local gazetteer, the Society was formed, "in the late Ch'ing (1903) by some local scholars who were devoted to reform and knew that without teaching there can be no reason, and without cooperation with the masses there can be no strength. If you want to unite with the masses you must first nourish the people's virtue. If you want to nourish the people's virtue you must first increase their knowledge." [46]

Tsinan quickly became the center for this new gentry interest in modern schools. This was natural, because Tsinan was the traditional center of higher education in the province and also the center of Yüan Shih-k'ai's officially sponsored modern education programs. Nine private Chinese-run secondary schools were established by gentry in Tsinan between 1904 and 1911. The most significant was the Shantung Inland Public School (*Shan-tso kung-hsüeh*) established in 1905. Liu Kuan-san, a member of the Revolutionary Alliance from Kao-mi *hsien* in the Ch'i region, headed the new school, located at Pei-yang-chia village about two kilometers north of the city wall. Liu obtained support from many prominent Shantung gentrymen for his school, which demonstrated how these Tsinan schools drew support from other sections of the province. Among those contributing funds to the new institution was the Society for the Study of Mass Education in Wei-*hsien*. [47]

The Shantung Inland Public School became a center of revolutionary activity in Shantung. The staff consisted primarily of young men who had studied in Japan and had come under the influence of revolutionary ideas during their studies. Even though revolutionary activity was limited to teaching about republicanism and some military drill, the Shantung provincial education department forced the school to close in 1907.*

---

*Liu Kuan-san left Tsinan for Tsingtao, where he started another school and a revolutionary newspaper. Chinese authorities persuaded the German officials at Tsingtao to close Liu's operations there, too.

Many of the teachers and students from the Shantung Inland Public School remained in Tsinan, where they taught or studied at the official schools. At these schools, physical education periods became the cover for military drill sessions, undertaken in order to prepare for overthrowing the Manchus. Even in the military schools, students were swept up in the growing spirit of anti-Manchu nationalism: in the Shantung Military Preparatory School, the students all cut off their queues in 1910 as a gesture of anti-Manchu defiance. The commandant made the students sew the queues back onto their caps for parade purposes but did not take serious disciplinary action against them.[48]

Schools and newspapers remained the primary activities of the Revolutionary Alliance in Shantung. There was talk of some terrorist activities during 1911, but these plans never materialized. The Alliance in Shantung was generally a much more moderate group than the branches in the Yangtze Valley and South China.[49]

The great interest the Alliance showed in schools and education reveals much, both of the Alliance's character and of the Shantung adherents' vision of how China could be changed. Schools were seen as bases where a revolutionary army of the sort Tsou Jung advocated could be trained and, at the same time, as places where a corps of political leaders could be educated. The modern orientation of the Alliance schools reflected the changing ideas in education during the years when the examination system was being revised and then abandoned. Clearly the Alliance program in Shantung could never have operated without gentry support. Yet in lending their support the gentry were for the most part merely following the long-established tradition of gentry financial responsibility for education. It seems possible that the revolutionary message of young Alliance-associated teachers went beyond what the gentry supporters of the schools would have knowingly sanctioned.

The Manchu reform program had abolished old bureaucratic posts and created many new ones. Some of these new posts were open to residents of the province, and those with modern educational qualifications were frequently appointed. The overall impact was to increase the power of the provincial level of administration and to attract more talent to provincial capitals like Tsinan.[50]

The most important new post was that of educational commissioner (*t'i-hsüeh shih*). The new commissioner had responsibilities that ranged far beyond those of proclaiming the "Sacred Edicts" and conducting examinations. In addition to his provincial responsibilities, he supervised a new kind of *hsien* educational promotion office (*ch'üan-hsüeh so*), which was responsible for "coordinating all educational work within the borders of the district."[51] Its members were local men interested in educational matters.

These *hsien* educational promotion offices became the center of reform activity in the districts of Shantung in the years from 1905 to 1909. They were natural focal points for reform for three reasons. First, the gentry had a tradition of interest in educational endeavors. Second, both reform and revolutionary elements looked to education as a means of changing China. Finally, the educational promotion offices, with their provisions for formal advisory roles to be played by the local gentry, were forerunners of the representative assemblies promised by the Ch'ing reform program.

The schools lost their place as the center of reform interest in 1908 when the throne announced its intention to conduct elections in 1909 for provincial assemblies.*

In late 1908, more than three hundred people interested in the pending elections attended a meeting in Tsinan to listen to speakers, who included several high-ranking provincial officials. Shen T'ung-fang, a *chin-shih* who had received some education in Japan and was then living in Tsinan, made the most important speech. Shen constrasted the excellent administration of the treaty ports with the conditions in Tsinan and argued that in order to bring Tsinan up to treaty-port standards it was necessary to adopt representative forms of government.[52] From this meeting grew a plan to create a special training school to familiarize eligible voters with electoral procedures and the duties of representatives. The first such institute was held in Tsinan, and various branch courses were later held at *hsien* throughout the province. Graduates from the course in Tsinan usually organized and taught the courses at other locations.

In 1909 no one knew what power the provincial assembly might exercise, for the whole concept of elected representative government was untried in China. After 1913, when Yüan Shih-k'ai consolidated his power, the assemblies seemed weak and powerless. In the short span from 1909 through 1913, however, these bodies or their elected successors exercised considerable influence on the chief issues of the time, including overthrowing the Manchu dynasty, sanctioning the new Republic, and

---

*The franchise for the election was limited to males above twenty-five years of age who had experience in teaching above the primary level, who had a *kung-sheng* degree or higher, who had held official posts higher than the seventh rank in the civil list or the fifth rank in military positions, or who had any business valued at over 5,000 *yuan*—excepting those rendered ineligible by reason of individual or family wrongdoing or by illiteracy. Candidates for the assembly had to meet the same qualifications as voters but had to be at least thirty years of age (Chang P'eng-yuan, "The Constitutionalists," in Mary C. Wright, ed., *China in Revolution: The First Phase, 1900-1913* [New Haven: Yale University Press, 1968], p. 146).

enabling Yüan Shih-k'ai to become president. Within their own provinces, the assemblies controlled financial matters in the first two years of the Republic.

The elections held in the summer of 1909 chose one hundred assemblymen on a province-wide ballot. The Manchu banner forces residing in Shantung received three additional seats. Extensive background information is available on only thirty members, but twenty-eight of them had previously held posts in the reformed government education system—either in the new educational promotion offices, as advisors, or as teachers.[53] This information underscores the importance of education in the development of representative politics during the last years of the Ch'ing dynasty.

Table 3.2 gives the educational background for the members of the 1909 Shantung assembly. Half of the assemblymen (50) held *chin-shih, chü-jen,* or *kung-sheng* degrees. Even more interesting is the fact that forty-eight held the non-degree status of *sheng-yüan*, or government student. According to franchise regulations for the 1909 election, *sheng-yüan* would be

Table 3.2

Educational Status of Shantung Assemblymen, 1909

Degree of Education		Numbers
Chin-shih		6
Chü-jen		18
Kung-sheng		26
Regular (acquired by examination)	*17*	
Irregular (acquired by purchase from top two ranks of sheng-yüan)	*9*	
Sheng-yüan		48
Ling-sheng (upper)	*22*	
Tseng-sheng (middle)	*5*	
Fu-sheng (lower)	*21*	
Modern school		1
Without other qualifications	*1*	
Combined with traditional examination status[a]	*(3)*	
No educational qualifications		1
Total		100[b]

Sources: *Tung-fang tsa-chih* (Eastern Miscellany), 20 July 1909, pp. 347-51. Information on traditional degree status was drawn from Chang Chung-li, *The Chinese Gentry: Studies on Their Role in Nineteenth Century Chinese Society* (Seattle: University of Washington Press, 1955), pp. 3-20, 115-37; and Ho Ping-ti, *The Ladder of Success in Imperial China: Aspects of Social Mobility, 1368-1911* (New York: Columbia University Press, 1962), pp. 17-52.

[a]Not included in totals because already included above.

[b]The total does not include the three Manchu banner representatives who qualified on terms different from those for the Chinese.

64

eligible for office only by virtue of teaching experience, bureaucratic experience, or wealth. There is no way of knowing exactly how these *sheng-yüan* qualified, but it was probably by means of educational experience and wealth.

The majority of the 1909 Shantung assembly (57) were irregular *kung-sheng* or *sheng-yüan* and therefore were not among the group usually classified as upper gentry.* This indicates that the provincial assemblies opened a new avenue to power and status for the lower gentry, men who had been debarred from formal positions of leadership in Shantung before 1900. Clearly they profited greatly in terms of status and power from the opening of these new assemblies. Obviously, however, the lower gentry were still underrepresented in proportion to their numerical strength. Constituting perhaps 94 or 95 percent of the entire gentry class, they had only 57 percent of the seats.

The upper gentry saw in the new legislative bodies not only an avenue to power in general but an official voice in their home provinces. The upper gentry had never before had such local power, because they were restricted by the rules of avoidance, which sought to make it impossible for a man to serve in his own home area and build a power base which combined official power and local kinship ties. Constituting perhaps 5 or 6 percent of the gentry group, the upper gentry received forty-three of the hundred seats in the first assembly. And of course they had posts that had been dominated for centuries by the upper gentry. In sum, then, their access to power was also increased by the establishment of the provincial assemblies.

The Japanese scholar Ichiko Chūzō has advanced a hypothesis about the role of the gentry in the late Ch'ing and early Republican periods.

*The question of the proper line between the "upper" and "lower" gentry is one that has been argued by students of Chinese society for several years, with most scholars agreeing that some kind of distinction is possible, but disagreeing about where to draw the line. The upper gentry are always the smaller group, about 5-6 percent of the whole gentry class by one estimate. These upper gentry monopolized official positions and retained great influence in their home areas even when they lived somewhere else. The lower gentry can be characterized as the bulk of the gentry class whose interests and power were rather more narrowly defined within their home district. Sometimes lower gentry power was felt within their *hsien* or prefecture or may have extended to other areas through family or business connections. The lower gentry seldom advanced far enough in the educational status system to achieve power through official appointments, but their status on the lower rungs of the examination system was an important determinant of their right to exercise leadership in their communities.

The debate over the proper point at which to divide the upper from the lower gentry is extremely complex, but any definition that places *sheng-yüan* in the lower gentry indicates that the new assemblies opened access to both upper and lower gentry. The two most important contributions to this issue are Ho Ping-ti, *The Ladder of Success in Imperial China* (New York: Columbia University Press, 1962) and Chang Chung-li, *The Chinese Gentry: Studies on Their Role in Nineteenth-Century Chinese Society* (Seattle: University of Washington Press, 1955).

Ichiko argues that the gentry class always became more powerful and prominent during the last stages of any dynastic cycle. The late Ch'ing was no exception but differed from earlier cases in that the gentry for the first time had to contend with the forces of modernization. According to Ichiko, the gentry moved carefully to match their actions to the dominant political moods in the last days of the Ch'ing and then

> virtually took the lead in modernizing China, and for several years after the birth of the Republic their influence was at its peak. They could not disguise themselves forever and continue to increase their influence after the First World War, but they did maintain it, even under the control of the Kuomintang, until the emergence of the People's Republic of China in 1949. The tenacious strength of the gentry's influence was deeply rooted in traditional Chinese society. Modernization should have destroyed them, but instead it gave them a chance to expand their influence.[54]

Ichiko has not tried to divide the gentry into lower and upper groups, but he provides a clear explanation of the pattern of growing gentry power in the late Ch'ing period.

Most students of late traditional Chinese society have asserted that wealth became increasingly important in determining social status after the Taiping rebellion.[55] The information available on members of the 1909 Shantung assembly indicates that most assemblymen were probably men of considerable means, but no actual information on the size of family holdings or the extent of individual wealth is available. Certainly wealth was not a requirement for becoming an educated man or an assemblyman, but it provided the means for obtaining an education and the free time needed for taking a leading role in local community affairs—hallmarks of gentry power in late traditional China.

An interesting aspect of gentry wealth is the supposed division between landowning and commercial interests among the gentry class. Clearly, the younger men associated with the Revolutionary Alliance showed no aversion to commerce or industry and involved themselves with newspapers, machine shops, coal mines, and banks in Shantung and Manchuria.[56] Even those assemblymen who qualified as upper gentry did not oppose commerce on the basis of a narrow Confucian antimercantilism. An excellent example is the assemblyman from Li-ch'eng *hsien*, Wang Mao-k'un, mentioned earlier as the organizer of gentry investment in the Tientsin-Pukow railway. Wang was one of the six *chin-shih* in the assembly. His service as *hsien* magistrate at Shanghai from 1900 to 1906 had given him extensive experience in dealing with foreigners and with Chinese commercial interests. He was in office in Shanghai during the first large-scale boycotts against American and Japanese goods, and was well liked by the Chinese merchant community there. In Tsinan he served as president of the Shantung General Chamber of Commerce (*Shan-tung shang-wu tsung-hui*) after 1906. In his work in the assembly he was also closely allied with commercial interests.[57]

Wang Chih-hsiang, a representative from Huang *hsien*, an agriculturally rich district on the northern side of the Shantung peninsula that also boasted important trading and banking interests, illustrates the type of progressive lower gentrymen elected to the 1909 assembly. Wang is described in the local history of the 1911 revolution:

> [After the Sino-Japanese War] Wang Chih-hsiang founded a reforestation society (*fou-lin hui-she*) and the forestry industry prospered. When the examination system was abolished, Wang headed up educational affairs. He established the First and Second K'ai-ch'eng primary schools, the Feng-shan normal school, and the educational association. In 1909 he was elected to the provincial assembly. . . . When the assembly convened, Wang proposed the dredging of the Hsiao-ch'ing Canal, the chartering of a savings bank, the restoration of China's rights, and the rapid completion of the assembly's business.[58]

All of these high-sounding measures were very favorable to Huang *hsien* commercial interests, including even "restoration of China's rights," which would have returned tariff control to the Chinese government.

Once the provincial assembly was established, powerful men such as Wang Mao-k'un and Wang Chih-hsiang were drawn into Tsinan and away from the prefectural- and district-level cities where they more typically would have centered their activities. In 1910 a matter came before the assembly that clearly revealed that body's bias toward gentry-interests. In the peninsular district of Lai-yang a dispute had developed between peasants and the district magistrate over special taxes and levies (*chu*) that the magistrate had imposed on commercial transactions and official business. The merchants passed these new costs on to the peasants, who vented much of their anger on the large merchants in Lai-yang because they felt the merchants were profiting unduly in the collection of these new levies. Large crowds of angry peasants attacked and burned the rural residences of two leading Lai-yang merchants who had banking and commercial interests. At the magistrate's request, troops were brought in to suppress the disorders. One of the merchants who had lost his country home traveled to Tsinan to lay his case before the governor and the provincial assembly. A huge majority of the assemblymen backed the merchant's cause.[59] The Lai-yang case was then settled in favor of the magistrate and the merchants. The incident shows the bond between gentry and commercial interests, as well as the bonds between the gentry and the officials, in the face of peasant demands. It also supports Ichiko's theory of increasing gentry power in the late Ch'ing.

The commercial importance of Tsinan increased rapidly after

67

completion of the Shantung railway. In this facet of Tsinan's life, Yüan Shih-k'ai's group also followed a policy of encouraging Chinese competition against the foreigners. The salt and grain merchants had long dominated Tsinan's trade. Coal, cotton, wine, ironware, fish, and lumber were other major lines of trade. In the first decade of the twentieth century the power of the salt merchants slipped, and many new names entered the old established lines of commerce. Straw braid, peanuts, and soy beans became the big new export items; cigarettes, candles, kerosene, matches, and foreign ironware were the principal new imports. Long-established regional specialties, such as Chou-ts'un silk and embroidery, underwent changes to meet the tastes of export markets. Tsingtao became the center of this trade.[60] These changes permitted new merchants and new trade relationships to gain influence in Tsinan at the expense of older interests.

The traditional provincial associations (*hui-kuan*) began to lose some commercial functions to more modern institutions. The credit, transportation, brokerage, and agency functions of the commercially oriented provincial associations were being taken over by banks, railroads, and modern trading houses.

In addition to the expanding trade that accompanied Tsinan's growth as a transportation center, the increasing favor the Shantung official bureaucracy showered upon commercial interests—especially as a counter to German designs—also drew merchants to Tsinan. No longer was official attention a thing to be avoided. Official support for handicraft industry, urban public services, and Chinese commercial interests instead of foreign ones, all served to make Tsinan a political and economic center that Shantung merchants could not afford to ignore. Silk merchants from Chou-ts'un, coal merchants from Po-shan, lumber merchants from Chefoo, and many others from all over the province began to congregate in Tsinan.[61]

The most important form of organization among these merchants was the *pang* or group, a commercial association of merchants from the same locality within a province. At Tsinan these local Shantung merchant groups *(pang)* represented the interests of *hsien*-based merchants and were a variant of the common-place-of-origin associations typified by the *hui-kuan* representing extra-provincial interests.* The main interests of a *pang* might be in the specialty items of a certain *hsien* but their concerns usually extended to several lines of commerce. For example, the Chou-

---

*The extra-provincial common-place-of-origin societies (*hui-kuan*) also were frequently less commercial in their beginnings than the local ones (*pang*). For example, officials and bureaucrats from Anhwei province had filled many posts in Shantung ever since the days of the anti-Nien campaigns, and consequently the Anhwei *hui-kuan* in Tsinan had a bureaucratic rather than a commercial character.

ts'un *pang* at Tsinan was involved in banking, grain milling, and coal marketing, in addition to the silk trade.[62] These groups came to play an even larger role in Tsinan after the 1911 revolution. Even though Shantung commerce had never been dominated by extra-provincial interests, these Shantungese groups increased their power in Tsinan while the power of the extra-provincial groups began to decline.

The growth of these strong local commercial groups and the large number of new commercial operations not connected with foreign trade indicate the continued growth of Tsinan as a center of Shantung intra-regional commerce. Available trade figures which are oriented toward foreign trade interests do not reveal the full extent of this increase, so it must be deduced from the prosperity of the Chinese businessmen dealing in the chief domestic lines of commerce such as coal, grain, cotton, construction materials, and the native banking enterprises. All of these various businesses flourished in Tsinan as a part of the city's increased importance in Shantung's internal trade, which itself was a product of the centralizing influences of the Hsiao-ch'ing Canal and the two railroads.

The changes occurring in Tsinan's commercial life can be seen best in the banking business. Modern banking institutions, created by official and foreign interests, offered serious competition to the established Chinese native banks. Chinese banking interests made some effort to start new modern-style banks. Yet in the first days of increased commerce after the opening of the railroad, the Chinese banking circles remained conservative in their forms of organization and operation.

The sequence of development of modern banking operations in Tsinan follows very closely the general pattern underlying most of the events in these years: first, Chinese official banks were created, then foreign banking operations appeared, and finally local Chinese-controlled private banking interests were established.

The first modern bank in Tsinan was the Shantung Official Bank (*Shantung kuan yin-hang*) created by Yüan Shih-k'ai in 1901 from an earlier provincial innovation (1896) known as the "official exchange bureau" (*kuan ch'ien-chü*). The Shantung Official Bank issued notes of deposit, notes of exchange, and cash notes. The first foreign bank in Tsinan was the Deutsch-Asiatische Bank, which established a branch in Tsinan in 1907. The main Chinese office of the bank had been created by German interests in Shanghai, in 1889, and there were five other branch offices.[63]

When these new-style banks first appeared, the Chinese banking world in Tsinan was dominated by the Fu-te guild, a Shansi-controlled organization with important connections in Tientsin. Local banking interests, however, were in the hands of men from Chang-ch'iu *hsien*. Chang-ch'iu had long been a commercial center because it produced the highly prized Shantung wet rice in several depressions similar to the one in which Tsinan was located; in addition there was a well-established native coal-mining industry which had long served Tsinan. It was said that no native bank in Tsinan could operate without employing some men from Chang-ch'iu. When native banking interests at Tsinan began to adopt modern banking practices in their handling of deposits, credit, and transfers, sometime between 1905 and 1910, two banks from Chang-ch'iu led the movement. One was a long-established member of the Fu-te guild with its headquarters in the old city; the other was a newly organized firm in the settlement district.[64]

In 1910 the new national banks, such as the Ta-ch'ing Bank (after 1911, the Bank of China) and the Bank of Communications, established offices in Tsinan. At about the same time, private Chinese banking interests from Shanghai and Tientsin, as well as from Huang *hsien* from the Ch'i region and other areas in Shantung, began to move into Tsinan. However, several years passed before these new interests could challenge the long-established Chang-ch'iu domination of the banking business.

Industry, like banking, is a key element in Tsinan's modernization, and we shall return several times to review the progress in these two parts of Tsinan's life. The new industrial undertakings in Tsinan reflect both the late Ch'ing style of bureaucratic capitalism and the official promotion of industry that accompanied modernizing efforts after 1900 (see Appendix A). The most unusual departures from previous undertakings, such as the Le-yuan Paper Mill, drew on a combination of official and merchant capital. A clear division existed between the larger Chinese investors such as Liu En-chu and the smaller merchant and industrial enterprises associated with regional interests. The large, more technologically complex industries were beholden to official monopoly privileges and subject to bureaucratic regulations and exactions. These interests naturally supported Yüan Shih-k'ai's policies as long as he lived and in the post-1916 period continued to be closely aligned to official policy. Before 1911 the smaller merchant and industrial interests prospered partly because of official encouragement, but their operations were generally free from direct official involvement. The merchants operating without official involvement may have introduced some modern machines into traditional lines such as wine-making, grain milling, and other food-processing operations, but such changes did not attract attention before 1911. Overall, the introduction of modern machinery into goods production, as distinct from the official-merchant interest in public service industries, had no real impact until after the 1911 revolution. The smaller merchant projects derived from regional Shantung groups and were more closely associated with various factions within the Shantung gentry which

70

were seeking to create locally controlled representative government. These combinations follow the same general alignments during the post-1911 period, with the smaller merchants and industrialists being more liberal politically and more progressive commercially than the holders of official monopolies.

In summary, then, the last decade of Ch'ing rule enabled Yüan Shih-k'ai to consolidate his power in North China and to bring Tsinan into his influence. Yüan favored modernization, and his policies gave firm direction to Tsinan, which by virtue of the railroad construction plans was forced to abandon its old ways and become a more modern city. Yüan's policies proved adequate to check German imperialism. At the same time, his program encouraged new initiatives from Shantung gentry. Let us turn now to the 1911 revolution and follow the interplay among Yüan's official clique, the foreigners, and the Shantung gentry to see how their contest for political power affected Tsinan's progress.

4

Tsinan During the Early Republic, 1912-1916

THE END OF THE MANCHU DYNASTY and the beginning of the Chinese Republic marked a major turning point in Tsinan. There, as in other places, groups that had been increasing their role in politics during the last years of Manchu rule now strongly asserted their power. As the seat of provincial administration, the site of provincial assembly meetings, and the main base of the Fifth Division, Tsinan served as the main arena for political action, but the events in that city were closely connected with the stirrings of republicanism in various parts of the province. In this chapter we will disucss how the gentry and commercial interests joined in the Republican revolution only to discover that the president of the new Republic, Yüan Shih-k'ai, was a staunch anti-Republican.

Most of this chapter deals with political events because these reveal so clearly the differences among Yüan Shih-k'ai, the Shantung gentry and commercial interests drawn into Tsinan, and the new Japanese presence in Shantung. These events created political alignments which strongly affected the ways in which modernization came to Tsinan. In particular, the central question of this study of the ways Chinese interests attempted to modernize Tsinan cannot be understood without a clear grasp of the political situation. These political differences kept the various Chinese interests from cooperating with each other against foreign imperialism and also prevented a broadly based support for Chinese cooperation with foreigners to bring about Tsinan's modernization.

THE REVOLUTION OF 1911 IN TSINAN
In the weeks immediately following the Wu-ch'ang uprising, Tsinan and Chefoo became the two centers of political activity in Shantung.* In

*Chefoo was the outpost of militant republicanism, where military men, police, the chamber of commerce, and newspapermen all favored the Republican cause. An atmosphere of political innovation and freedom, common to the treaty ports, flourished in Shantung at Chefoo rather than in the more rigid German colonial setting of Tsingtao. Once Yüan Shih-k'ai was directing the dynasty's affairs, Chefoo opposed not only the Manchus, but Yüan as well. See copy of *Po-hai jih-pao*, 4 November 1911, Great Britain, Colonial Office 873/327, Revolution in China, 1911, Chefoo Situation.

Tsinan the officials, the provincial assembly, and the army took the chief parts in the short but tangled drama ending the Ch'ing dynasty. News of the anti-Manchu mutiny at Wu-ch'ang on 11 October did not reach Tsinan until the fourteenth. The effects of revolution were felt first in the marketplace. On 21 October, holders of paper currency drove the price of silver up with large conversions at the Shantung Provincial Bank and native banks.[1]

As the situation in the Yangtze Valley region became more unfavorable for the dynasty, the regent recalled Yüan Shih-k'ai on Yüan's own terms. On 7 November, Yüan was appointed prime minister with full powers over policy. But even though Yüan was trying to consolidate his power in order to subdue the revolutionaries, Shantung turned toward the Republican cause.

The initiative to declare Shantung independent of Peking came in Tsinan during the first week of November. The moderate supporters of the Revolutionary Alliance led the effort—Ting Shih-i, Chou Shu-piao, and Wang Na. In addition to being adherents to the cause of creating a constitutional republic for China, all three were involved in promoting Tsinan's modern secondary schools. Ting and Chou were assemblymen known as supporters of the peasants in the Lai-yang case of 1910. As in earlier political matters, the leadership in the independence activity was drawn from eastern Shantung, the Ch'i region.*

*Ting Shih-i was from Huang *hsien*; Chou Shu-piao and Wang Na came from An-ch'iu *hsien*. Other prominent leaders in the independence movement came from Huang *hsien*, Shou-kuang, Ch'i-hsia, and Chü *hsien*, all in eastern Shantung. One element in the Shantung Revolutionary Alliance leadership did not accept the idea of working through the provincial assembly. This more radical group was led by Liu Kuan-san, Hsü Chung-hsin, and Ting Wei-fen. These men had been plotting—through a maze of political and merchant support involving Peking, Manchuria, Tsingtao, and Shanghai—for an armed uprising in Shantung. After 11 October, they were drawn to Shanghai, where Alliance forces gathered. This group was not a key element either in the independence movement at Chefoo or in the provincial assembly independence actions in Tsinan, but close association with the Revolutionary Alliance made these men important as Shantung representatives in the central councils of the revolutionaries. This radical group was not in real opposition to other leaders; it was simply that moderate leaders in the provincial assembly like Ting Shih-i, Chou Shu-piao, and Wang Na did not recognize the radicals as their superiors in policy matters. The radicals managed to keep alive their webs of contacts which were revived in 1915-1916 for the Japanese-backed assault on Yüan Shih-k'ai in Shantung (see pp. 87-91). (see pp. 87-91)

Much of the history of the period from 1900 to 1930 was written during the 1930s, when these radicals (frequently less radical then than in their youth) were important men in the Nationalist party (*Kuo-min-tang*). Consequently the attention their actions received in the various gazetteers and histories compiled in the 1930s is out of proportion to the actual leadership they exercised in 1911 and afterwards. Probably the best example of this is *Huang-hsien ko-ming shih-shih*, which does not even include a biography of Ting Shih-i, the leading Huang *hsien* personality in the provincial independence movement of late 1911.

These men started a rumor that the Peking government was seeking an emergency loan from Germany in which Shantung territory was to be put up as collateral. This rumor naturally aroused the gentry, merchants, and students in Tsinan, and on 5 November some three thousand people gathered at the provincial assembly to demand that Shantung stand up against this mortgaging of the province to the foreigners. Under the forceful advocacy of Ting Shih-i and Wang Mao-k'un, the assembly stopped short of a resolution declaring independence but instead presented a list of eight demands to Peking (see Appendix C). Ting and Wang wanted the government at Peking to grant their demands rather than to place them in the position of having to defend Shantung's independence against the central government. If these eight demands were not met within three days, Shantung would declare its independence.[2]

The first of the eight points dealt with the loan rumor by demanding that Peking not borrow foreign monies to conduct military operations against fellow Chinese. The second demand placed Shantung squarely in the Republican camp by insisting that Peking accept whatever terms the Republican forces at Wu-ch'ang proposed. The next six articles dealt with Shantungese self-rule and revealed the intent to build provincial power at the expense of the central government. The Fifth Division was to be kept in the province, and tax revenues were also to be retained. Moreover, the new constitution of China must take a federal form. Finally the assembly demanded that all matters concerning land tax rates, official appointments, the right to maintain a provincial army, and the regulations governing the provincial assembly be the prerogative of the provincial government rather than the central government.

The Peking government replied on 8 November. Not only did it reject the key second item concerning acceptance of the Republican terms, but it hedged its assurances of provincial autonomy in financial and military matters. Rejection in hand, the moderate republican leadership proceeded to organize a Security Committee (*pao-an-hui*). The committee was chaired by Hsia Chi-ch'üan, the president of the Shantung Provincial Assembly.* In fact, the Security Committee was the provincial assembly under a new name.[3]

---

*Hsia Chi-ch'üan was from a wealthy family in western Shantung. He had connections with the Revolutionary Alliance and served in a number of important Shantung provincial posts from 1912 through 1922 (Gaimushō Jōhōbu, *Gendai Chūka minkoku Manshū teikoku jinmeikan* [Tokyo: Gaimushō, 1937], p. 77). The vice-chairman of the Security Committee was Yü P'u-yuan, who was from the Ch'i region and also had close connections with the Revolutionary Alliance in the 1905-1911 period, but who dropped out of active politics after Yüan Shih-k'ai came to power in 1912 (Liu Tung-hou, comp., *Wei-hsien chih* [1937], ch. 30/41b-42a). These two men both were acquainted with a Japanese teacher named Fukuda at the Tsinan Normal School, who is the only foriegner mentioned as a friend of the revolutionaries.

74

On 12 November, a mass meeting was held in Tsinan under the Security Committee's auspices. Ting Shih-i was the leading spokesman for independence at the meeting. At his urging the meeting adopted a resolution that Sun Pao-ch'i should be declared governor (*tu-tu*) and General Chia Ping-ch'ing, the commander of the Fifth Division, lieutenant-governor (*fu tu-tu*) in a newly independent Shantung. The Security Committee also adopted three principles to guide Shantung's new independence: 1) complete severance from the Ch'ing dynasty, 2) support for the Yangtze Valley revolutionaries, and 3) a Republican form of government in Shantung.[4]

But independence was short-lived. The revolutionaries for unknown reasons had approved for key posts two individuals, Sun Pao-ch'i and Chia Ping-ch'ing, who were not loyal Republicans. This proved to be a fatal error in the actions taken by the Security Committee. Sun Pao-ch'i continued to maintain contact with Yüan Shih-k'ai and the Peking bureaucracy after the announcement of independence. In November, Yüan Shih-k'ai sent Chang Kuang-chien and Wu Ping-hsiang to Tsinan to serve as Shantung provincial treasurer and police *tao-t'ai* respectively.* Sun Pao-ch'i turned effective control of the provincial administration over to these subordinates of Yüan Shih-k'ai. On 30 November, the day after Yüan announced a cease-fire at Wu-ch'ang, Sun Pao-ch'i renounced Shantung's declaration of independence. Sun justified his action on the basis that the revolutionaries did not have the support of the Fifth Division.[5] In fact, the Fifth Division had never been an ardent supporter of the Republican cause, but had simply been anti-Manchu.

When Chang Kuang-chien and Wu Ping-hsiang arrived in Tsinan, they began to make Yüan Shih-k'ai's wishes clear to the officers of the Fifth Division, most of whom had been trained in the schools of the Peiyang Army. As the Army shifted to active support of Yüan's position, Yüan's subordinates were able to overturn the independence of Shantung and bring that province securely into his camp by the end of November.

*Chang was from Ho-fei *hsien*, Anhwei province. He had previous service in Shantung in connection with railroad and telegraph affairs. He became acting governor in January 1912. In March, when Chou Tzu-ch'i arrived, he went back to Peking and subsequently served in a number of posts in Kansu, including a term as governor from 1916 to 1921 (H. G. H. Woodhead, ed., *China Yearbook 1924* [London and Tientsin: Tientsin Times, 1912-39], p. 976). Wu Ping-hsiang also was from Ho-fei *hsien* and had served in Shantung with the forerunner of the Fifth Division in 1900. He later headed Yüan Shih-k'ai's secretariat at Peking and was a leading member of Tuan Ch'i-jui's clique (Gaimushō Jōhōbu, *Chūka minkoku manshūkoku jinmeikan* [Tokyo: Gaimushō, 1933] pp. 116-17). During the governorships of Chou Fu (1902-1905) and Yang Shih-hsiang (1905-1907), both from Anhwei, large numbers of Anhwei men, especially from Li Hung-chang's home district, Ho-fei *hsien*, found civil and military positions in Shantung, revealing a continuation of Li's influence on politics through a legacy of officials whom Yüan Shih-k'ai inherited.

Table 4.1

Shantung Military Governors, 1911-1916

Name	Home	Term of Office	Duration	Cause of Removal
Sun Pao-ch'i	Hang-chou *hsien* Chekiang	5 November 1911— 22 December 1911	1 + month	Mishandling of the Republican revolution in Shantung during October-November 1911
Hu Chien-ch'ü	Ho-fei *hsien* Anhwei	23 December 1911— 23 January 1912	1 month	Acting governor only
Chang Kuang-ch'ien	Ho-fei *hsien* Anhwei	23 January 1912— 28 March 1912	2 months	Acting governor only; sent to reestablish Yüan's control
Chou Tzu-ch'i	Shan *hsien* Shantung	28 March 1912— 18 August 1913	17 months	Assigned as field commander commander in Second Revolution, June-July 1913
Chin Yun-p'eng	Chi-ning *hsien* Shantung	18 August 1913— 30 May 1916	32 months	Followed Feng Kuo-chang's lead in not giving Yüan full support during anti-monarchical uprising
Chang Huai-chih	Tung-a *hsien* Shantung	30 May 1916— 25 February 1918	23 months	Remained in office after Yüan's death

Source: Kao Yin-tsu, comp., *Chung-hua min-kuo ta-shih chi* (Chronology of the Republican Period) (Taipei: Shih-chieh she, 1957), pp. 4, 23, 37.

76

The leadership of the independence movement then had either to flee or to face arrest. Some men, such as Wang Na, went south to Nanking, where they served as the Shantung representatives in the new Republican government formed there in January 1912. Several younger teachers associated with the Alliance were arrested in Tsinan.[6]

Most of the Alliance adherents, however, merely returned to their home districts, where they began to organize local military forces against Yüan Shih-k'ai. Chefoo remained a center of republicanism in Shantung. In January the Chefoo Republican forces, which had held the city under their armed control since November 1911, were further reinforced with rebellious Chinese troops and cruisers from Manchuria and took Teng-chou while advancing into Huang *hsien*. In the latter part of the month, three battalions of the Fifth Division came eastward to oppose the Republicans.[7]

The military struggle in eastern Shantung continued while Yüan Shih-k'ai was coming to terms with the provisional government at Nanking. Reinforcements for the Fifth Division took Teng-chou on 11 February, ending armed opposition in eastern Shantung. The province was then under the effective control of Yüan Shih-k'ai and his newly appointed governor, Chou Tzu-ch'i.

Yüan had made temporary peace with republicanism when he accepted the presidency of the new Chinese Republic. In that post he undertook the creation of a new Republican administration complete with provincial assemblies and a national parliament. Many of the Shantungese Republican supporters agreed to join this new government, in spite of their recent opposition to Yüan. The brief episode of armed opposition was significant, however, for it established both sympathy and a precedent for the Republican forces in eastern Shantung to act with the Yangtze Valley anti-Yüan leadership. On another occasion—the antimonarchical movement of 1915-1916—the Ch'i region Republican leadership would again take up arms against Yüan Shih-k'ai.

The finale of the revolution in Tsinan consisted of an uprising by a unit of the former Ch'ing armies. The governor's guards (*hsün-fang-ying*) had not received their pay regularly since October 1911 and faced disbandment. On the night of 13-14 June 1912, the men of that unit broke into the old city during the early morning hours and looted shops on West Gate Road. More than fifty large shops were destroyed by fire. The Fifth Division remained loyal and drove the rioting soldiers out of the city. Rain put out the fires.[8]

The riot reveals a great deal about the policies followed in the early months of the Republic. Old obligations of the Ch'ing system, such as those to a special governor's guard unit, were being abandoned; in their place appeared an administration headed by local generals, staffed by Shantungese bureaucrats and guided by the Shantung assembly, which placed gentry and local concerns above military or central administration concerns.

THE STRUGGLE BETWEEN YÜAN SHIH-K'AI
AND THE SHANTUNG GENTRY

Since 1900, Yüan Shih-k'ai's leadership had played a key role in the modernization of Shantung. Through Yüan's own policies and those of succeeding Shantung governors, the late Ch'ing reform program in Shantung had won broad support among the Shantung gentry. During the four years of Yüan's domination of the young Chinese Republic (1912-1916), the tables were turned. Yüan found himself struggling against the local interests whose power he had been encouraging a few years earlier.

For practical financial reasons and because of his own antidemocratic bent, Yüan began trying in 1913 to decrease the power given to gentry interests in the form of the new institutions introduced during the Ch'ing reforms: the provincial and district assemblies, the school boards, and the chambers of commerce. At the national level, the struggle centered in the Peking parliament; in Shantung province, it centered in Tsinan. Chefoo and other locations in eastern Shantung counted as sites of some of the more daring military attempts to resist Yüan Shih-k'ai's power, but Tsinan was the seat of the provincial assembly and the high provincial officials appointed by Yüan.

The groups competing for power in Shantung also remained fairly stable from 1912 to 1916. Under Yüan's direction, the interests of the central government officials and the Peiyang Army naturally merged. In the months after October 1911, gentry power found additional opportunities to broaden and diversify; Shantung gentry secured most of the high bureaucratic posts within the province. This was in addition to the new gentry power represented by the assemblies at the *hsien*, province, and national levels. The merchants also found more important roles open to them.

Yüan Shih-k'ai was aware of this growing gentry power. In 1912 he had adopted a general policy of permitting men to hold high office in their own provinces. In Shantung he appointed one of his followers, Chou Tzu-ch'i, a registered Shantung native, as governor. After his appointment as governor, Chou sought and received the cooperation of Hsia Chi-ch'üan, president of the assembly. Chou later rewarded Hsia by appointing him to the intendency of northwest Shantung.[9]

Chou Tzu-ch'i reconvened the 1909 provincial assembly in March 1912 so that it might select Shantung's representatives to the Peking provisional parliament (*lin-shih ts'an-i yüan*).* In addition Chou appointed a civil administration dominated by Shantungese. The provincial treasurer, the provincial judge, the educational commissioner, the police *tao-t'ai*, and the commercial commissioner all hailed from Shantung.

Local power was further entrenched by the election of a new provincial assembly (*sheng-i-hui*) in December 1912. The composition of the new assembly was not much different from that of the 1909 body, but it was free of the taint of the ousted Manchus.[10] Unfortunately for the progress of republican institutions in Shantung, however, the new assembly was drawn into the struggle between Yüan Shih-k'ai, with his highly conservative approach to constitutional government, and the more radical Republicans. The most dramatic part of the struggle involved political parties and representative institutions.

It was not until the Peking provisional parliament began meeting in April 1912 that definite parties began to take shape. These parties began as parliamentary groups and had no popular base.[11] Nevertheless, the Peking groups had close ties with provincial assemblies. The Peking parties had several offshoots in Tsinan in the spring of 1912. The Revolutionary Alliance appeared as a public body with its own clubroom in the old city for a few months in 1912. The Republican party (*Kung-ho-tang*), classified as moderate constitutionalists, had a Shantung branch which is identified as composed of "the Hanlin academy members, *chin-shih*, old officials and bureaucrats."[12] In 1913 shortly after the assassination of Nationalist party (*Kuo-min-tang*) leader Sun Chiao-jen, the rival Republican party in Peking joined with several other more conservative groups, including Yüan Shih-k'ai's supporters, to form the Progressive party (*Chin-pu-tang*). In Shantung, the Republican party drew wide support both from representatives to the new National Parliament (*Kuo-hui*) and in the Shantung provincial assembly, indicating a strong conservative feeling in the province.

In November 1913, as opposition to his policies mounted in the National Parliament, Yüan Shih-k'ai ordered all Nationalist party members dismissed from the National Parliament. Chou Tzu-ch'i did the same in the provincial assembly in Shantung, and sixty assemblymen lost their seats. This left the National Parliament and the Shantung provincial assembly under the control of the Progressive party. Still, these bodies

*There were two provisional parliaments created in 1912. The first met at Nanking, the second at Peking. According to the membership lists of Ku Tun-jou, there were two Shantung representatives in the Nanking parliament and five in the Peking body (Ku Tun-jou, *Chung-kuo i-hui shih* [1931] [T'ai-chung: Tung-hai ta-hsüeh, 1962], pp. 288-89).

were not pliable enough to suit Yüan, and in January 1914 he dissolved the National Parliament. The next month he did away with all self-governing bodies in China. By these moves against representative government, Yüan planned to gain political and fiscal control over the new Republic. Yüan's measures against the Nationalist party had been so high-handed, however, that many Progressive party members abandoned the party in early 1914. In Shantung many of these former representatives from all parties returned to private life, where they found posts in educational work or in *hsien* and provincial administrations. Some also went into business. [13]

One political party still remained in Tsinan. This was a Citizens' party (*Kung-min-tang*), composed of people from the old Nationalist and Progressive parties, as well as several prominent Shantungese who had held office under Chou Tzu-ch'i. The president was Ch'ü Cho-hsin, a conservative constitutionalist from Chi-ning. Other members included Chang Chao-ch'uan, the powerful merchant from Chang-ch'iu *hsien*. The most radical figure was Chuang Kai-lan, an individual with close links to the Revolutionary Alliance but also with the credentials of a Hanlin scholar. [14] Significantly, the leadership of the Citizens' party included men from both Ch'i and Lu regions of Shantung. The existence of the Citizens' party reveals that even after the assemblies were dismissed, local interests would not always bend to Yüan's will. Gentry power might be checked, but not destroyed. Yüan's moves against representative bodies so alienated many Shantungese that they had difficulty accepting Yüan as an honest national leader when the Japanese invaded Tsingtao and made their Twenty-One Demands.

Money is the real key to all the political struggles in Shantung during the first years of the Republic. The central administration's control over provincial tax collections had declined all over China during the nineteenth century. With the advent of representative institutions in 1911, remittances from the provinces became even more difficult to collect. A general breakdown occurred in *hsien* remittances to provincial treasuries and from the provinces to the national treasury. For the fiscal year 1913 (July 1912 through June 1913), for example, Shantung was expected to remit $1,200,000 (6 percent of the total revenues due the central government from all provinces) but paid in little, if any, of that amount. [15]

Clearly, by the summer of 1913, the new Republic had a serious financial crisis on its hands. According to the *North China Herald*, "nothing but a succession of foreign loans will enable the government to carry on." [16] A large loan from a foreign consortium for the purpose of reorganizing China's administration, under discussion since the spring of 1912, finally materialized in the spring of 1913. Most historians have claimed that Yüan used this $250,000,000 to put down the Second Revolution of 1913 and for a number of unsavory purposes, including bribes and special allowances.[17] Although it is not possible to tie the loan monies directly to administrative reorganization, reports of the Shantung provincial administration make it clear, however, that Yüan did try to carry out a major reorganization of provincial government beginning in July 1913.

The most important goal of this reorganization policy was to reestablish control over provincial revenues. A new governor, Chin Yun-p'eng, assisted by a fellow Shantungese from the Lu region, P'an Fu, implemented this policy in Shantung.* On P'an Fu's advice, Chin created a new post—*hsien* financial secretary—to be appointed by the governor and not the *hsien* magistrate. Chin dispatched special officials to audit accounts of the tobacco and wine monopolies. In November 1913, Chin published a list of *hsien* magistrates who had defaulted in their remittances to the provincial treasury. The list contained the names of 188 men, 122 of whom had entered office after the 1911 revolution. One-fifth of the Shantung *hsien* magistrates then in office found their names on the list.[18]

The pressure placed on *hsien* magistrates was only one aspect of these new fiscal policies; provincial expenditures also had to be reduced. Yüan believed that the provincial legislature had gone too far with the expansion of public education. Many new government-supported schools were closed or combined in order to save funds.[19] All the old prefectures (*fu*) were abolished and the post of *tao-t'ai*, which included both territorially and functionally defined offices, was reorganized into a system of territorially defined offices filled with officials known as *tao-yin*.

Another major new fiscal policy adopted by Chin Yun-p'eng on the advice of P'an Fu consisted of increasing revenues by levying several new taxes, the most important of which were commercial taxes (*ya-shui*) on all kinds of business transactions. These taxes were farmed out to special tax collection firms (*ya-hang*) formed by groups of merchants, thereby ensuring that the reforms did not completely alienate commercial interests. These firms bought the right to collect the taxes in a given area,

---

*Chin was born in 1887 in Chi-ning. He attended military schools of the Peiyang Army and after graduation he served with Tuan Ch'i-jui, to whom he continued to be linked. Before becoming governor, Chin Yun-p'eng had served as commander of the Fifth Division. Chin was completely loyal follower of Yüan Shih-k'ai until Yüan announced his monarchical plans; then Chin supported Feng Kuo-chang in opposing Yüan. This switch cost him the governorship. Chin later became a major supporter of Tuan Ch'i-jui in the political fighting for control of the Peking government. Although Chin later fell out with Chou Tzu-ch'i and other members of the Communications clique, there appear to have been no major differences between them before Yüan's death. For the most complete information on Chin, see Howard L. Boorman, ed., *Biographical Dictionary of Republican China,* 4 vols. (New York: Columbia University Press, 1967-71), 1:382-84.

and promised the government a 2 percent return on retail sales. The Shantung provincial administration also declared a new property title tax, and all landowners were required to reregister their land titles and in the process to pay the new tax.[20]

Restructuring of the tax system for the benefit of the central government continued into 1914, when a new sub-provincial collection bureau (*cheng-shou chü*) was created to supervise the tax matters of ten *hsien*. The new programs began to show success, and in February 1914 the district magistrates who remitted the most funds received special decorations from the Shantung provincial authorities in Tsinan.

Although these administrative reforms have been discussed separately from the struggle against the political parties, the two were part of the same general policy. In fact the administrative reorganization was accompanied by a wholesale dismissal of officeholders associated with political parties and their replacement with men known as Yüan Shih-k'ai's pawns. For example, the civil governor of Shantung, T'ien Wen-lieh, an official greatly popular with the Shantung gentry, was replaced by Kao Ching-ch'i, a former tutor of Yüan Shih-k'ai.[21]

These new officials did not match the caliber of those they had replaced, but at least they had the central government's interest at heart. By June 1914, the financial situation in Shantung was well in hand, and regular remittances to Peking could start again. Between January and June 1914, Shantung sent nearly $3,000,000 to Peking.[22]

In summary, then Yüan was as successful at reorganization and tax reform as he had been at suppressing opposing parties and parliaments. These policies, however, cost Yüan a great deal of gentry support, a factor which affected him significantly during his final months as president and then emperor of China. But the forces of militarism, in Shantung as elsewhere, had won a major victory against the gentry and the gentry vision of a China governed through a federal constitution with local elements transferring their informal influence into formal control of the provincial and sub-provincial administrative levels.

Support for this vission of self-rule (*tzu-chih*) came both from the traditional gentry leadership with its combination of imperial degrees, education, and wealth, and from those Chinese interested in new commercial ventures, who, as we shall see, were appearing in Tsinan in important community leadership roles in the early Republic. The new commercial interests were to try to expand their influence and control in Tsinan over the next few decades, but their failure to best Yüan Shih-k'ai was a major loss in a string of setbacks that occurred up until 1949. We shall be looking more closely at these new commercial elements in Tsinan in later sections, for they represent an adaptation of the traditional gentry to the increasing commercialization in Shantung and Tsinan. Moreover, the kind of political, economic, and social goals they espoused come close to the kind of bourgeoise ideals that shaped the nineteenth-century Western city.

FOREIGN INFLUENCE IN SHANTUNG

The Germans in Shantung originally intended to turn their leasehold on Chiao-chou Bay into a colony modeled on Hong Kong. With a German port and city at Tsingtao on the southeast portion of the bay, German influence would radiate into Shantung from the railroad and mining concessions. The German foreign office, however, opposed these colonial dreams on the grounds that a distinct German sphere of influence would threaten the policy of cooperative imperialism followed by the major powers and ultimately would harm Germany's larger interests by causing her exclusion from other powers' territorial spheres in China. Consequently, the German colonial character of Tsingtao was diminished somewhat. The turning point in the internationalization of Tsingtao came in 1905 when the Tsingtao administration agreed to integrate Tsingtao fully into the Chinese Imperial Maritime Customs Service.[23]

In the two brief years of the Republic before the Germans lost control of Tsingtao to the Japanese, Germany, like the other Western nations, tried to continue its old policy of cooperative imperialism. Two indications of this are found in the German financial interests' involvement in the Reorganization loan of 1913 and in German support for Yüan Shih-k'ai, which meant that German influence was used to support Yüan and his appointees in Shantung.

Yet, the Germans, through their policy of cooperative imperialism, permitted a growing role to the Japanese, especially Japanese traders, who used Tsingtao as a base of commerce. The nation-by-nation totals for Tsingtao's trade in 1913 reveal that the Germans could not claim to dominate foreign trade in Shantung. As early as 1907, the Japanese handled approximately half the total dollar volume of Tsingtao's imports.[24] In light of Japan's later role in Shantung, this early indication of her commercial stake in the area is significant.

World War I brought a swift end to fifteen years of German presence in Shantung. In mid-August, Japan delivered an ultimatum to the Germans at Tsingtao, demanding that they turn the entire leasehold over to Japan and her British allies by 15 September 1914 or the Japanese would invade Tsingtao. The Germans refused. The Japanese, with the British as reluctant participants, invaded Shantung in early September. Although Tsingtao was administered by a military arm of the German government, the colony was not a fortress. The German defenders numbered only about five thousand, whereas the Anglo-Japanese force totaled more than twenty thousand. The Germans surrendered on 7 November.[25]

Japanese military units occupied the entire Tsingtao-Tsinan railroad system and established garrisons at all the major rail stops. In Wei-hsien they established military-run civil administration; in Tsinan they stationed a large garrison.[26] Not content with running Germany out of Shantung, the Japanese intended to extend their influence in Shantung far beyond anything the Germans had attempted.

The official Chinese response to the Japanese invasion was both tardy and inadequate. In the late summer of 1914, the Chinese had declared neutrality in the world war. The Japanese invasion at Tsingtao was the first test of this policy. When the invasion was only a threat, the Chinese foreign ministry thought China could maintain her policy of neutrality by not openly objecting to what was going on. Once Japanese troops were on Chinese soil, however, neutrality seemed a less practical policy to Peking.[27]

Fearing an invasion, Shantung's Governor Chin Yun-p'eng, with the concurrence of Peking, took certain defensive measures. As early as 13 August, before the Japanese ultimatum had run out, he dispatched troops to maintain order along the Shantung railway, and increased the Chinese garrisons at Teng-chou and Lai-chou on the Shantung peninsula. On 15 August, Chin ordered the Fifth Division to Wei-hsien and the Forty-seventh Mixed Brigade to Lai-chou. Additional artillery was dispatched from Tientsin to bolster the strength of Chin's positions. In mid-August, the Chinese central and Shantung provincial authorities were seeking to limit the effects of the European war in Shantung.[28]

Within a few days of the Japanese ultimatum of 15 August, rumors of two different plans to keep the Tsingtao-Tsinan railroad out of Japanese hands began to circulate in Tsinan. The first called for the SEG to turn over control of its operations to Chinese stockholders. Apparently the lack of substantial Chinese stock holdings, together with the fact that SEG was a German-registered company, blocked progress on this proposal. A second plan would have had the Chinese government railways purchase the Shantung railroad from SEG on terms similar to those be which the Tientsin-Pukow railroad was operated. That would have left the German investment intact but shifted the title to Chinese hands. Both these plans ran into strong Japanese diplomatic opposition and were unsuccessful.[29]

The Japanese expedition against Tsingtao became the first phase of a new Japanese policy toward the Republic of China. The new policy was the handiwork of Kato Komei, the foreign minister in the Okuma cabinet which had come to power in April 1914. As soon as he took up his new post, Kato set about reversing the direction of Japan's China policy. For the previous several years, Japan's policies in China had been shaped by Ijūin Hikokichi, Japanese minister in Peking, who was friendly with Yüan Shih-k'ai. Ijūin advocated that Japan, along with her British ally and the other imperialist powers, should adopt a friendly policy toward Yüan and the Chinese Republic. This policy was not acceptable to the Genrō, who looked to China to follow Japan's model and would therefore have preferred a constitutional monarch in China.[30]

Foreign Minister Kato dropped Ijūin and began to develop a more activist policy toward China. Kato had begun his career as a secretary of Okuma Shigenobu in the 1890s. As a member of Okuma's cabinet in 1914, Kato built his China policy around his mentor's ideas. The so-called "Okuma doctrine" proclaimed that because Japan had been the most successful of the Asian states in mastering the ways of the West, Japan should adopt a stewardship role in guiding other Asian states, especially China.

When placed in this light, the Japanese invasion of Shantung reveals a number of its significant features. First, in spite of a sizable established Japanese trade in Shantung and Tsinan, there is no evidence that pressure to take Shantung came from commercial or industrial quarters in Japan. In addition, Shantung had no strategic significance for Japan. Consequently, the Japanese presence in Shantung was guided by somewhat different considerations from those operating in Manchuria, where Japanese political and economic interests of practically every stripe were agreed that Japan must dominate Manchuria for her national safety and economic well-being.[31] The Japanese invasion of Tsingtao was, in fact, the opening move in Kato's plan to bring about Japanese domination of China. The next phase of Japanese plans involved the Twenty-One Demands.

These infamous demands developed from an effort by a Japanese military attaché in Peking to reconcile Japanese policy goals in Manchuria, Mongolia, and North China. Out of the attaché's drafts grew a document, approved by Foreign Minister Kato, containing five groups of demands transmitted to Yüan Shih-k'ai on 18 January 1915 by the Japanese envoy Hioki Eki.[32] Of the original five groups, the first group directly concerned Japanese rights in Shantung. The fifth group, which sought broad advisory, policy, military, and economic development privileges in all of China, was the most controversial.

Negotiations began in Peking on 2 February 1915 with Ambassador Hioki representing the Japanese, but the talks broke down in mid-April. The Japanese government removed the entire fifth group and resubmitted the demands in late April. By 1 May, the Chinese still refused to accept the revised demands. The Japanese replied with an ultimatum to Yüan Shih-k'ai, and on 9 May, the Chinese accepted the new Japanese position in principle. On 25 May, the formal agreements were signed.[33]

The first group of the original demands sought four points in regard to Shantung. First, China was to agree to any arrangements between Japan and Germany about the disposition of German interests in Shantung. Second, China was barred from permitting new foreign leaseholds or land grants in Shantung. Third, Japan was granted permission to build and operate a railway from Chefoo to Wei-hsien. Finally, the Chinese were required to open a number of other locations in Shantung as commercial areas. The exact locations of these areas were to be negotiated between the Japanese and the Chinese.[34]

The most important point was the first, for it handed Japan a position equal to Germany's before August 1914. The second article seems obviously intended to limit other foreigners' penetration of Shantung, yet the fourth article would theoretically benefit all foreigners. In addition, the third article appears to have been a sop to the British interests at Chefoo, who favored a rail link from that treaty port with the interior.

While negotiations on the Twenty-One Demands were under way in Peking, the situation in Tsinan was uneasy. The Japanese military units remained along the Tsingtao-Tsinan railway, and a detachment of 150 troops was specially established at Tsinan to protect the Japanese consulate and Japanese citizens. There were no riots or disturbances in Tsinan at any time during the negotiations over the demands. Newspaper coverage of the negotiations voiced only timid criticism because all news stories were censored by the provincial administration. Chin Yun-p'eng and the other provincial officials did everything possible to avoid conflict with the Japanese. The British consul in Tsinan described the officials' attitude toward the Japanese as "fawning."[35] The general populace remained concerned about the demands, but since they had neither accurate press coverage nor political leadership in their dissent, there never was any public outcry. The only other possible public forum was the provincial assembly, and that had been dismissed the previous fall.

In March 1915, when negotiations were beginning to drag, the Japanese increased their troop strength in Shantung by an additional seven thousand men. Three thousand of these were sent to Tsinan by rail between the twenty-second and the twenty-fifth of March. In Tsinan, Japanese units widened their patrols to cover many parts of the settlement district, but Chinese administration in the old city continued to function. The Fifth Division remained in its base west of the commercial settlement, careful not to challenge the Japanese.[36]

In early May when the crisis over the Japanese ultimatum to Yüan Shih-k'ai on the Twenty-One Demands was developing, the Japanese units at

86

Tsinan made moves that threatened a Japanese takeover. All Japanese residents of the old city moved into the settlement; women and children were sent by rail to Tsingtao. The three thousand Japanese troops built defense works around the railroad station and important Japanese buildings in the settlement. When the Chinese signed the revised demands, the sandbags and defense works were taken down.[37]

By mid-June 1915, most of the Japanese troops at Tsinan were withdrawn, and the Japanese set about the business of restoring trade and mining. The impact of the European war—both in the loss of overseas markets and the conduct of military operations in Shantung—had stopped most trade at Tsingtao and Tsinan in August 1914. It was not really until the fall of 1915 that trade picked up again. Even then the important straw braid, hairnet, and peanut trades were suffering from the disappearance of export markets.[38]

When trade revived at Tsingtao, the shortage of shipping proved a great hindrance. German and British shipping had abandoned East Asian waters, and the only available foreign ships were Japanese. But Japanese ships were busy in direct trade with Japan and had little free space to devote to the coasting trade. Consequently the important Shantung coasting trade had to depend on Chinese ships and firms. The Japanese presence reshaped the patterns of Shantung and Tsinan trade just as it was reshaping Chinese and Shantungese politics. Moreover, the Japanese military garrisoning of Tsinan during the negotiations over the Twenty-One Demands shows that foreign imperialism was going to have more decisive and direct influence in the city than it had had before 1914. Foreign military influence easily made itself felt in Tsinan in 1914, and similar occurrences of this kind of bold Japanese disregard of Shantungese military and civil authority were to occur at critical moments several times after 1914.

THE REVOLUTIONARY PARTY UPRISING OF MAY 1916

The 1913 uprising against Yüan Shih-k'ai, known as the Second Revolution, had had little impact in Shantung, where there was no great support for the Yangtze Valley rebels. The main effect was that Chou Tzu-ch'i and the Fifth Division were transferred to Kiangsu to help put down the rebellion. The story of the antimonarchical movement of 1915-1916 was, however, a completely different one.

Within a few weeks of accepting the revised Japanese demands, Yüan began to promote himself as consitutional monarch of China. After an appropriate series of political and legal maneuvers, Yüan accepted a bid to the throne on 12 December 1915. But as the scope of Yüan's ambition became known, a new coalition of anti-Yüan forces developed in China.

At the center of the anti-Yüan forces were the adherents of Sun Yat-sen's clandestine Revolutionary party (*ko-ming-tang*), formed in Japan in July 1914 after Yüan had destroyed the parliamentary Nationalist party. These anti-Yüan forces drew important support in southern and southwestern China in areas not controlled by stalwarts of the Peiyang Army. Even within Peiyang circles, there was growing dissatisfaction with Yüan's monarchical plans. Feng Kuo-chang was the most outspoken critic of Yüan. The Japanese found ways to support some of these various anti-Yüan movements.[39]

The Revolutionary party's first attempt at an armed uprising against Yüan was an effort by Ch'en Ch'i-mei to take over Shanghai in November 1915. The attempt failed and Yüan reestablished firm control in Shanghai for the next six months. In late December 1915, after Yüan's formal acceptance of the throne, a larger, more successful uprising took place in Szechuan, led by Ts'ai Ao and others. From this action a new National Protection Army (*Hu-kuo chün*) took shape. That anti-Yüan army began to extend its power into the Yangtze Valley provinces.

The successes of the National Protection Army were accompanied by growing dissatisfaction within the Peiyang ranks. In mid-March 1916, Yüan began to talk of renouncing his throne and by March 22 he had formally stepped down and declared his intention of reorganizing the Peking administration. But, as a result of new financial shortages and continuing disaffection among his closest supporters, Yüan's power in China was quickly slipping away. Physical collapse now paralleled political decline, and Yüan died on 6 June 1916.

In the midst of these final weeks, the Revolutionary party launched a new attack against Yüan in Shantung. The revolt was under the leadership of Chü Cheng, an old member of the Revolutionary Alliance from Hupei, who in 1914 had left political retirement in Japan to join with Sun in the new Revolutionary party. Chü Cheng was given responsibility for organizing the Northeast Army (*Tung-pei chün*) of the Chinese Revolutionary Army (*Chung-hua ko-ming chün*). Chü Cheng was supposed to have worked closely with Ch'en Ch'i-mei. After Ch'en's death in the wake of the abortive Shanghai uprising, Chü persisted in his part in the plan.[40]

Chü Cheng continued to work in Shanghai, Dairen, and Tsingtao to put together a Northeast Army. The Revolutionary party had many important supporters who had emigrated to Manchuria from Shantung and other parts of China. The Shantungese maintained contacts in their home districts and were ready to help make a revolution in Shantung. Among these Shantungese residing in Manchuria were many young men who had been supporters of the 1911 revolution. By 1916, their experience with

88

Yüan Shih-k'ai's brand of republicanism made them willing supporters of the anti-Yüan army.

Two of these leaders were Lü Tzu-jen and Chang Lu-ch'üan, Shantungese who had supported and joined the Revolutionary Alliance while attending school in Japan. After the 1911 revolution, Chang was elected to the National Parliament and became involved in a colonization project in Feng-t'ien province.[41] Lü Tzu-jen was neither a member of parliament nor an assemblyman but a small entrepreneur. Together with Liu Kuan-san, the founder of Shantung Inland School, he started a small weaving factory in Tsinan. Governor Chin Yun-p'eng forced Lü Tzu-jen to leave Tsinan. He went first to Tsingtao and then, in 1915, to Japan. In Japan he joined the new Revolutionary party. Later that year Lü was sent back to Tsingtao by Sun Yat-sen to plan for an uprising.[42]

In addition to educated young men with commercial interests, Chü Cheng also enrolled more martial types, like Wu Ta-chou. Wu had served as police chief at Yen-t'ai when the Republican rebels had held that city in the aftermath of the 1911 revolution. He was forced to emigrate to Manchuria in 1912 and there became closely associated with bandits.[43]*

The Japanese lent invaluable support to Chü Cheng and his followers. They permitted his organizing activities in Dairen and his frequent trips back and forth among Tsingtao, Dairen, and Shanghai. Japanese authorities played a role in providing transportation for Chü Cheng's forces from Dairen to Tsingtao and also sold arms and munitions to the Northeast Army. In the end, the Japanese let the rebels use the railroad to reach the towns they hoped to attack. The whole plot would never have been possible without a combination of support first from Japanese adventurers and later from the Japanese government.[44]

Early in May 1916, Chü Cheng gathered his forces at Wei-hsien and took the city from its defender Chang Shu-yuan. Chang, although a trusted Peiyang commander, put up little resistance. At the same time Lü Tzu-jen established himself with military units in his home district of Kao-mi, and Wu Ta-chou took Chou-ts'un.[45]

On 18 May, Chü Cheng's combined forces tried to take Tsinan, but Chin Yun-p'eng repulsed the attack. Chin also stopped two later assaults on the city, on 24 May and 4 June 1916. With the death of Yüan Shih-k'ai on 6 June, the Northeast Army ceased its attacks. Chü Cheng left his command to take a seat in the reconvened National Parliament at Peking. Many other leaders returned to their homes.[46]

*Another source of support for Chü Cheng's plans came from the surviving anti-Yuan elements in Shanghai. One of the Shanghai-based men who participated in the 1916 Shantung uprising was Chiang Kai-shek. Chiang came to Shantung to serve as a vice-commander under Chü Cheng in the final stage of the Shantung uprising, but returned to Shanghai soon after Yüan's death.

Wu Ta-chou, at Chou-ts'un, was in a different position. Wu's troops, composed largely of bandit elements, had demanded and received substantial sums of money from merchants at Chou-ts'un. When an impasse over continued financial support of the unit was reached in July 1916, Wu's troops set fire to the main commercial section of Chou-ts'un. These actions turned the initially friendly merchants of Shantung's Ch'i region against the Northeast Army and its political directors, the Revolutionary party.[47]

Wu Ta-chou continued negotiations with the Shantung authorities about the future of his units, and eventually, in October 1916, Chang Huai-chih, the new governor of the province, enrolled Wu's troops as a special unit. Within two months, however, Chang found an excuse to put down disturbances among Wu Ta-chou's troops; this "mutiny" marked the end of the unit's existence.[48]

The Revolutionary party uprising of 1916 had little to do with Yüan's fall from power, but it does reveal clearly the alignment of political forces in Shantung in that year. The Japanese opposed Yüan Shih-k'ai and supported Sun Yat-sen and the Revolutionary party. The Japanese experience with Yüan during the negotiations over the Twenty-One Demands had ended whatever good will toward Yüan was left over from the first days of the Republic. The Revolutionary party in Shantung was based primarily upon men who had been leaders in the Revolutionary Alliance; by 1915 many had drifted into commerce or industry in Manchuria, Tsingtao, and Shanghai. Most of these men came from the Ch'i area in eastern Shantung.

In 1916 the focus of anti-Japanese sentiment in Shantung lay not within the Revolutionary party, but within the Peiyang clique, whose spokesman in Shantung was Governor Chin Yun-p'eng. In addition to officials, the anti-Japanese group had the support of many gentry. P'an Fu, an entrepreneur and official from Chin Yun-p'eng's home district of Chi-ning, was the most prominent of the many gentry who were leaders in the nationalist movement against Japan.[49]

Prior to Yüan's death the anti-Japanese elements in Shantung had come primarily from the inland areas, with strong representation from the central and southern parts of the province. Thus, in 1916 there continued to be a major political difference between the Lu and Ch'i regions of Shantung. After 1916, when Chin Yun-p'eng and P'an Fu became stalwarts of the Anfu clique in Peking, their anti-Japanese nationalism faded and they became two of the principal backers of Japanese influence in Shantung. The Japanese, naturally, completely abandoned Sun Yat-sen after 1916 and shaped their policies around working with the Anfu clique. In this later period the Ch'i region commercial leaders emerged as the leaders of the anti-Japanese nationalist movement. These Lu and Ch'i orientations continued to be a major factor in shaping Shantung politics for many years.

The conduct of the Northeast Army, especially that of Wu Ta-chou's troops, won few friends in Shantung. The occupation of Wei-hsien, Wu's high-handed conduct at Chou-ts'un, and the attacks on Tsinan all had turned initial support for the uprising into sullen opposition in the Ch'i region.

The resentment of the eastern Shantung leaders, especially the merchants, increased when they saw that Japanese merchants did not suffer from the presence of Wu Ta-chou and his troops. As their businesses languished, Shantungese merchants began to turn against Sun and the Revolutionary party. Sun was to meet the same phenomenon again in Kwangtung during the 1920s; there, too, his cooperation with warlords turned local leaders against him.

After the 1916 uprising, Sun's support in Shantung disappeared almost completely. The few Shantungese who remained closely associated with Sun and his cause during the next decade nearly always operated outside their home province. The only activity of Sun's Revolutionary party and the later Nationalist party in Shantung was clandestine propaganda or organizing work. This remained the case until the Northern Expedition reached the Shantung countryside in 1927-1928. Even after that date, the legacy of Sun Yat-sen's cooperation with Japan continued to have a negative impact on the influence of the Nationalist party in Tsinan and elsewhere in Shantung.

THE CONTINUING MODERNIZATION OF TSINAN

In spite of the disruption to normal life that accompanied the 1911 revolution, the 1914 Japanese occupation, and the 1916 anti-Yüan uprising, the modernization of Tsinan continued to gain momentum. Each disruption temporarily slowed the growth of commerce and industry but also served to further unify the Shantungese political and economic interests that increasingly gathered in Tsinan. In the wake of the 1916 uprising, there emerged a coalition of these interests that opposed the Japanese and supported republicanism but preferred the Peiyang clique to Sun Yat-sen.

Administrative authority in Tsinan remained seriously divided between the Li-ch'eng *hsien* magistrate and a separate head of the Tsinan Settlement Bureau. The *tao-t'ai* for the northwest circuit in Shantung became the most important and powerful official in Tsinan because he had authority over both of them. Hsia Chi-ch'üan, former president of the Shantung provincial assembly, was *tao-t'ai* from 1912 until 1914. Hsia lost his office when Yüan Shih-k'ai installed his own supporters after reducing

91

the power of provincial assemblies and local leadership. A series of unimportant followers of Yüan occupied the post for two years.

With the legislatures no longer in session, the newspapers became the chief public voice at Tsinan. Their editorial positions constituted both a considerable influence on their readership, largely the better educated, and a check on the provincial administration. The influence of the press is also a reflection of Tsinan's modernization, for newspapers did not exist in the city before 1900. A closer look at the editorial policies and circulation of these papers tells much about the direction of political thinking in Tsinan.

The *Ta-tung jih-pao* (Great Eastern Daily), representing the Tsinan business community, had the most influence, with a daily circulation of about eight hundred.* Its operation reveals that the need for cooperation among Chinese businessmen could overcome the Ch'i-Lu split. The editor, Yeh Ch'un-ch'ih, was from a coastal district, but the paper cooperated fully with P'an Fu and other inland leaders in bringing the 1914 exposition to Tsinan (see pp. 93-94). Yeh founded the *Ta-tung jih-pao* in 1912 and editorially supported the Progressive party and Yüan Shih-k'ai until the summer of 1915. Then as Yüan's monarchical plans became clear, the paper opposed the monarchy but stopped short of openly endorsing the anti-Yüan uprising, for such a position would have brought a closure enforced by the governor.[50]

The other major daily paper was the *Shan-tung jih-pao* (Shantung Daily), a private newspaper published and edited by the same staff that issued the official *Shan-tung kung-pao* (Shantung Gazette). The latter paper contained only official announcements of the Shantung provincial administration. The two papers were apparently distributed together and had a circulation of about twelve hundred. The joint editor was Ma Kuan-ching, brother of Tsinan's most important capitalist, Ma Kuan-ho, who was involved in a number of large and officially favored industrial and commercial projects. The *Shan-tung jih-pao* generally supported the positions of the Shantung administration.[51]

The *Chien-pao* (Synopticon) published articles excerpted from other newspapers. *Chien-pao* had a circulation of about a thousand, but it took no independent editorial position. Beginning in 1915, a Japanese newspaper entitled the *Santō Shimbun* (Shantung News) was published in Tsinan, with a circulation of two hundred. There were another half-dozen Chinese papers with circulation of a few hundred each. These included special business and commercial sheets as well as papers with definite

---

*It should be kept in mind that circulation figures refer to subscribers. Because of the Chinese habit of posting and passing a newspaper from hand to hand, actual readership was probably much greater than indicated by the number of subscribers.

political alignments. Those with political views unwelcome to the Shantung warlord of the moment had a short life.[52]

The domestic upheavals of the early Republic had brought temporary stoppages of trade; World War I, however, produced a major reorientation. Within a few weeks of the outbreak of war, markets for Shantung silk, hairnets, and straw braid disappeared; foreign trading firms lost their members to enlistment in national armies; the removal of British and German coasting vessels ruined the coastal markets for perishable goods. Only Japanese ships and Japanese markets were left.

The influence of World War I continued to be felt in China until the early 1920s, for not until then were the Europeans and Americans able to return to China to reestablish their trading ventures. In the interim, Chinese capital could undertake all kinds of modern investments that never could have succeeded against foreign competition. Since most of these innovations came after Yüan's death, they will be discussed in the following chapter.

We have, however, an unusually complete portrait of Tsinan's economic life on the eve of World War I. In the summer of 1914, the First Shantung Exposition was held in Tsinan. The exposition was proposed by the provincial legislature, reflecting that body's commercial leanings, and had been undertaken by the Shantung administration in spite of the disbandment of the legislature. For this exposition, Yeh Ch'un-ch'ih of the *Ta-tung jih-pao* published a special handbook called *Chi-nan chih-nan* (Guide to Tsinan) which is an excellent source of information about Tsinan's economic and social life.

The park of the commercial settlement contained the exposition grounds, complete with temporary buildings and a special market area. Both Chinese shopkeepers and foreign traders set up booths in the market area; British and Japanese firms were well represented, but not the Germans. The main exposition hall was reserved for the display of Shantungese products.

The goods listed as on display in the exposition hall included some goods produced by modern industrial means, but demonstrated that most of Shantung's output consisted of traditional handicrafts and agricultural products. Outside of the small arms manufactured at the Tsinan arsenal, most of the modern industrial goods shown came from small Tsingtao and Tsinan metal-fabricating shops, mostly makers of pots and pans. Other manufactures included the pottery and glass from Po-shan—both traditional ornaments and the more utilitarian window glass produced by the Chinese-owned modern Po-shan glass factory. Chou-ts'un exhibited traditional handicrafts—candles, soap, and paper—all of which had been Chou-ts'un specialties for many generations.[53]

93

Handspun cotton thread and handwoven cotton cloth were major items of display in the main hall. The domestic cloth, known as "patriotic cloth" (*ai-kuo pu*), was produced on hand looms but passed through large dyeing works in Wei-hsien, Ch'ing-chou, Chi-ning, and Tsinan in the finishing process.

Agricultural products on display included many kinds of grain, raw cotton, braiding straw, peanuts, and bamboo. Trade figures from Tsinan for 1915 and 1916 reveal that wheat, peanuts, peanut oil, cotton, hides, and bean oil were the largest trade items ranked by tonnage. This reflects the growing commercialization in the Shantung economy that accompanied the development of railways.[54]

Handicraft workers of Chou-ts'un, Wei-hsien, and Chi-ning supplemented traditional lines, such as paper manufacture or cotton spinning, with new specialties for foreign markets, including straw braid and hairnets, but the older products were not totally displaced.

The location of the exposition itself is relevant to our theme of Tsinan's development. Dealers in agricultural and handicraft goods from all over the province wanted Tsinan to hold the fair because provincial monies could then support it and because Tsinan was growing in importance as a trading city. Located as it was at the intersection of the Tientsin-Pukow road and the Shantung line, Tsinan was becoming a new focal point of trade in Shantung, and consequently increasingly important as a center of intraregional trade. The character of the exhibition—containing as it did few exportable products but a great variety of goods produced by traditional means for Chinese consumption—shows that the canal, railroads, banks, and other modern facilities in Tsinan facilitated intraregional trade and made Tsinan more and more a commercial center.

The exposition guide also describes the social life of the city. According to the household registry figures reprinted in the guide, there were 245,990 people living in Tsinan in 1914. During the years 1912 to 1916, Tsinan's population remained relatively stable in spite of the increased economic and political importance of the city.

Rickshaws (*jen-la ch'e*), then a very utilitarian vehicle capable of carrying either passengers or cargo, had become common in Tsinan by 1911. Up until 1912 these vehicles used iron or iron-faced wheels; then rubber wheels began to appear and within two years were prevalent.[55] The older barrows and carts remained in service but commanded lower rates than the rickshaws. Of course, the carts, drawn either by men or animals, continued to be used to transport bulk items such as grain, coal, bricks, and cotton. There were a few automobiles owned by high provincial officials or foreigners. As of 1914, however, automobiles remained

94

essentially a luxury and played no significant role in the city's economic life.

With the coming of the railroad, the need for modern hotels and inns increased. The older inns in the walled portions of Tsinan provided limited accommodations and did not ordinarily serve meals. The extreme of Westernization in Tsinan was represented by Stein's Hotel in the settlement, run by a German hotelier and catering to German tastes. It served as a gathering place and social center for the foreign commercial community. The settlement also boasted twenty new Chinese inns that tried to provide the same kind of full hotel services as Western establishments. These inns could not match Stein's, but they did provide more furnishings and more services—including meals—than were ordinarily available at a Chinese inn. There also was a special inn at Tsinan run for Japanese travelers.[56]

The Japanese inn was but one sign of the considerable Japanese presence in Tsinan as of 1914. Three Japanese pharmacies, four Japanese trading firms (Mitsui among them), Japanese restaurants, and a Japanese-style barbershop also operated in Tsinan. In addition there was a Japanese consulate and an office of the Japanese official foreign trade bank, the Yokohama Specie Bank. The Japanese staffed and owned two private hospitals in the city. Thus, as already noted, even before World War I the Japanese presence was quite considerable beneath the veneer of German influence.[57]

The German administration at Tsingtao and the American missionaries both ran large hospitals in Tsinan, of about a hundred beds each. The Americans had also opened a medical school in Tsinan which later developed into Shantung Christian University (Cheloo).[58] There were thirty-two government-sponsored middle schools in the city and some forty primary schools. Many of the primary schools, however, were still organized as traditional gentry institutions and had no connection with the government's educational administration.[59]

The banking situation in Tsinan changed little in the first years of the Republic, although the large official banks changed their names to appropriate Republican names. Traditional Chinese banking institutions seem to have prospered in these early years of the Republic as a result of the larger role Shantungese were permitted in the administration of their own province. Pawnshops, not banks, served as institutions granting loans to ordinary people in China, and Tsinan supported nine such pawnshops: eight in the old city, and the ninth located near the Fifth Division camp.[60]

The old walled city of Tsinan increasingly became a site of official offices and schools, although cultural life was still centered there. West

Gate Road retained its important commercial character. There were ten bookstores and thirteen printing shops in Tsinan as of 1914. Four theatres, located within the old city on the banks of Ta-ming Lake, near the old examination halls, continued to present traditional operas. The halls themselves had been torn down and replaced by a new provincial assembly building and the Shantung provincial library. Near the theatre district was the old prostitutes' quarter. After the coming of the railroad most of the prostitutes were moved into the settlement district.[61]

The settlement district was an odd combination of consulates, foreign residences, Western-style business houses, Chinese hotels, and small, ugly shacks thrown up by poor Chinese. A new entertainment quarter developed in the settlement. There were three "tea gardens" (*ch'a-yuan*) where operas were put on and individual singers performed regularly. The city's only movie house was also located in the settlement district.[62]

The evidence of increasing business and political and cultural activity reveals that more and more wealthy and influential Shantungese were drawn into Tsinan. Some came to serve the new government and others came to take advantage of the new kinds of trade developing in the city. Still others came to attend the new schools. There was little, however, in terms of either new employment or other special opportunities, to draw ordinary men and their families into Tsinan. The new Shantungese elite flowing into Tsinan replaced many of the extraprovincial elite who had lived in the city while they held office or awaited appointment under the Ch'ing system.

SUMMARY

Two dramatic events marked the 1912-1916 period in Tsinan: the Republican revolution and the First World War. The full impact of the revolution on Tsinan and Shantung was clear by 1916. The full significance of the world war had not yet developed. The events of the early Republic clearly established Tsinan as the center of Chinese power in the province of Shantung. The city took on life as a new kind of political center different from the part it had played as the seat of provincial administration in the days of the Ch'ing empire. At the same time, other developments increased Tsinan's importance as a center of finance and trade far beyond any previous levels in the city's history.

The revolution in Shantung had been championed by moderate constitutionalists whose overriding political concern was to increase purely Shantungese political power and to establish a province free from central control. They accepted Yüan Shih-k'ai's leadership of the new Republic in the hope that he would permit the growth of provincial power. And so he did—for a short time—but in late 1913 he turned against the Republicans and their notions of provincial power. By 1914 he was able to check provincial independence, but not by reasserting the power of the central civil administration. Instead, Yüan relied upon the Peiyang Army to establish central control over the provinces. Once Yüan died, the Peiyang faction had no real central leadership, and the complex maneuvers among the Peiyang generals for control of Peking began. As we shall see, the Shantungese gentry and bourgeoisie never successfully challenged the military dominance of the provincial administrations.

World War I produced an immediate change in the balance of foreign power in Shantung: Japan replaced Germany as the most influential power, while British influence declined. The initial response to the Japanese presence in Shantung was remarkable calm, for one element of Shantungese leadership—the more radical Republicans associated with Sun Yat-sen, usually hailing from the Ch'i region within Shantung—welcomed Japanese opposition to Yüan Shih-k'ai. The failures of the 1916 anti-Yüan uprising destroyed this brief alliance between Shantungese political interests and the Japanese. After that fiasco, the Ch'i and Lu elements cooperated more closely in opposing the Japanese presence in Shantung. Within a few years Japanese imperialism had become the chief political and economic issue in Shantung. The economic impact of World War I was also not fully discernible in 1916. Initially the war had shut off export markets, but as we shall see in the next chapter, the war was also responsible for the development of capitalist industry in Tsinan.

5

Political Power in Tsinan During the Warlord Era, 1916-1927

THE ACCOUNTS of politics and social history in the preceding chapters will, I hope, have made clear the existence of a close relationship between political power and the direction of Tsinan's economic and social development down to Yüan Shih-k'ai's death. After 1916 the same three forces we have already examined—economic change, increasing militarization, and expanding foreign influence—continue to run through Tsinan's history. Following Yüan's death, however, both the political and social situations take on a new complexity which seems more readily understandable when dealt with in separate accounts. Consequently the present chapter is concerned with questions of political power and the following one with the social economic issues.

After Yüan's death the principal political contest in Shantung was that between Japanese efforts to dominate the province and Chinese efforts to stop the Japanese. The Japanese, on their side, shifted their efforts away from military adventurism to a combination of diplomatic and economic measures which sought to expand their control in Shantung. To this end they dealt both with the national government at Peking and with Shantung provincial political interests centered in Tsinan. The Japanese found that the Peking administration—successively dominated by various factions from Yüan's old military arm, the Peiyang Army—was frequently willing to compromise Shantungese interests to obtain funds from the Japanese. Some Shantung political leaders were tied into the Peiyang power elements which controlled Peking and the top administrative posts in the Shantung provincial administration. Other Shantungese, notably the new Shantungese commercial elements whose rise is traced in Chapter 6, appeared in Tsinan as leading opponents of the willingness of various Peking cliques to sacrifice local Shantung interests to their own ends.

DOMINANCE OF THE PEIYANG CLIQUE

After Yüan's death, his military and bureaucratic supporters in Peking, collectively called the Peiyang clique, soon split up into rival groups with

98

constantly shifting memberships, each struggling to succeed to Yüan's power. The politics of Tsinan and of all Shantung became entangled in these Peking struggles among generals, bureaucrats, and politicians. All the various officials who held power in Tsinan during this era followed a similar strategy. When appointed by a government in Peking to high office at Tsinan, they worked to serve the interests of that administration. Once the power situation in Peking shifted and a new cabinet was formed, the Tsinan appointee, hoping to continue in office, would start favoring increased provincial autonomy, a view that always attracted support from within the province. He would succeed for a short time but would ultimately be replaced by another figure aligned with a new power coalition in Peking.

It is possible, but not very edifying, to trace in detail each of these shifts and the factors that swung the balance in each instance. Table 5.1, Military Governors of Shantung, 1916-1928, and Table 5.2, Civil Governors of Shantung, 1919-1925, give some indication of the complexity of the situation. Eleven men held those two offices during this twelve-year period, and actual power was constantly shifting between the two posts, as well as from one man to another in the seemingly unending chain of new appointees.

The reason for these shifts is that Shantung was one of those north China provinces securely in the realm of the Peiyang Army's power. Tsinan was garrisoned by the Fifth Division, which continued to provide the practical means whereby the various Peking administrations manipulated the situation in Tsinan, in the same way Yüan had used the Fifth Division so effectively against local Shantung interests from 1911 to 1916. Thus the situation in Shantung depended ultimately upon the power-holders in Peking. Between 1916 and 1928 political power in Peking came into the hands of a series of second-rate leaders. Tuan Ch'i-jui, a former general under Yüan Shih-k'ai, stands out as the most active and influential figure among them. Tuan, however, became so involved in Peiyang squabbles and in Japanese machinations that by 1919 he had lost all hope of creating a united China, though he remained a major influence until 1922, through a coalition of bureaucrats and generals known as the Anfu clique.

Tuan distrusted the Shantung military governor, Chang Huai-chih,*

*Chang Huai-chih, who had won Yüan's confidence when he served as a member of Yüan's elite personal guard, had been posted in Tsinan between 1908 and 1910 as a brigade commander and was appointed military governor only one month before Yüan's death. He was roundly disliked by almost everyone in Tsinan. The British consul described him as "uneducated, uncouth in manner and untidy in dress," while among Shantungese he was called "the skinner" *(pa-p'i)* because of his extortionist tax policies (Liu Feng-han, *Hsin-chien lu-chün* [Taipei: Chung-yang yen-chiu yuan, chin-tai shih yen-chiu so, 1966], pp. 121-22; S. Wyatt-Smith, Tsinan Intelligence Reports, 4th Quarter 1917, F.O. 228/1938).

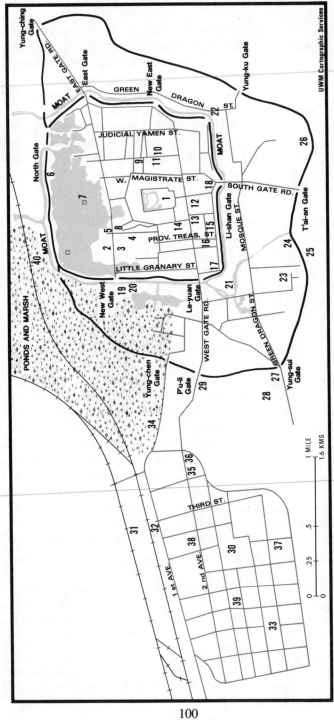

Map 2. Tsinan in the 1920s. (Based on Kogawa Heichi, ed., *Shina shōbetsu zenshi, Santō-shō* [Tokyo: Tōa dōbunkai, 1917] 4:50; Frederic de Garis, ed., *Guide to China*, 2d ed. [Tokyo: Japanese National Railways, 1923], p. 153.)

Key to Map 2

1. Governor's Yamen and Pearl Springs
2. Provincial Assembly
3. Civil Governor's Office
4. Circuit Intendent's Office
5. Provincial Library
6. Temple of the North Pole
7. Li-hsia Pavilion
8. Confucian Temple
9. District Magistrate's Office
10. 47th Mixed Brigade Headquarters
11. Police Department
12. Altars of Heaven and Earth
13. Bank of China
14. Provincial Normal School
15. Chamber of Commerce
16. Chung-chou hui-kuan
17. Telephone Company
18. Lu-feng Silk Filature
19. Le-yuan Paper Mill
20. Tsinan Electric Company
21. Leaping Springs
22. Black Tiger Springs
23. British Hospital
24. Whitewright Museum
25. Shantung Christian University
26. Military School and Barracks
27. Provincial School of Law and Politics
28. 5th Division Headquarters
29. Shantung and Tsinan Courts
30. Commercial Settlement Park
31. Tientsin-Pukow Railway Station
32. Tsingtao-Tsinan Railway Station
33. Tsinan Hospital
34. Po-li Flour Mill
35. Bank of Communications
36. Bank of Chosen
37. British Consulate
38. Mitsui Trading Company
39. Japanese Consulate
40. North Station

Table 5.1
Shantung Military Governors, 1916-1928

Name	Home	Term of Office	Duration	Cause of Removal
Chang Huai-chih	Tung-a *hsien* Shantung	June 1916— February 1918	21 months	Transferred out of Shantung because distrusted by Tuan Ch'i-jui
Chang Shu-yuan	Wu-ti *hsien* Shantung	February 1918— December 1919	22 months	Sacrificed because of supposed weakness toward nationalistic students and merchants in the May Fourth incident
T'ien Chung-yu	Lin-yu *hsien* Shantung	January 1920— October 1923	46 months	Removed because of foreign diplomatic pressure after kidnapping of foreigners in the Lin-ch'eng incident
Ch'eng Shih-ch'i	Ting-yuan *hsien* Anhwei	October 1923— May 1925	19 months	Removed as part of a compromise to recognize the increased power of Chang Tso-lin in North China
Chang Tsung-ch'ang	I *hsien* Shantung	May 1925— May 1928	37 months	Defeated by Northern Expedition of the Kuomintang

Sources: Liu Feng-han, *Hsin-chien lu-chün* (Taipei: Chung-yang yen-chiu yuan, chin-tai shih yen-chiu so, 1966), pp. 121 ff.; Howard L. Boorman, ed., *Biographical Dictionary of Republican China* (New York: Columbia University Press, 1967-71); Tsinan Intelligence Reports, 1916-1925, F.O. 228/3277.

Table 5.2
Shantung Civil Governors, 1919-1925

Name	Term of Office	Duration	Political Alignment
Ch'ü Ying-kuang[a]	August 1919— August 1920	13 months	Supporter of Chin Yun-p'eng
Ch'i Yao-shan	September 1920— October 1920	1 + month	Temporary appointee
T'ien Chung-yu[a]	November 1920— June 1922	20 months	Originally supporter of Chin Yun-p'eng; switched to Chihli faction. Concurrent military governor
Wang Hu	June 1922— September 1922	3 months	Temporary appointee
Hsiung Ping-ch'i[a]	September 1922— November 1924	25 months	Supporter of Wu P'ei-fu
Kung Chi-ping	February 1925— Fall 1925	9 + months	Unaligned bureaucrat ousted by Chang Tsung-ch'ang

Source: Tsinan Intelligence Reports, 1919-1925, F.O. 228/3277.
[a]Chief political power holders in Tsinan during their terms as civil governors.

and so, early in 1916, arranged for several of his own subordinates to receive key posts in Tsinan. Chang Shu-yuan became second-in-command of the Fifth Division, ensuring Tuan's control over the critical military unit; Ch'en Ming-hou became head of the province's civil administrative office, thus clinching Tuan's control over the provincial revenues and new bureaucratic appointments; T'ang Ko-san became Chi-nan circuit inten-dant (*tao-yin*); Ma Liang was appointed Tsinan's defense commissioner. The last two officials were the men primarily responsible for the administration of Tsinan. As Moslems, they were distrusted to a certain extent by many local people. Both of these men fit the model of narrow-minded military officers who had little to contribute to Tsinan's develop-ment, but, together with Tuan Ch'i-jui's other supporters in Shantung, they controlled the city firmly until the May Fourth period.

Two Shantungese from the Lu region, Chin Yun-p'eng and P'an Fu, were very important in both Peking and Shantung during these years.*

*Chin had risen in the Peiyang clique as a result of his service as the governor of Shantung (1913-1916) and his ties to Tuan Ch'i-jui. After Yüan's death, Chin emerged as a chief collaborator of Tuan Ch'i-jui's. Like Tuan, Chin developed close connections with the Japanese, but also had other loyalties to the Fifth Division and the Lu region of Shantung. Chin's career climaxed in his service as premier of the Peking government from September 1919 until December 1921, with but one short break. During that period Chin represented, but could not command, the remnants of Tuan Ch'i-jui's followers in the Peiyang clique. His policies clashed with Tuan's on the surface, though they really continued the main lines of antirepublicanism and double-sided relations with the Japanese followed by his former superior.

In this tale of shifting alliances, the two basic political interests Chin Yun-p'eng

Holding important cabinet or sub-cabinet posts at Peking, from 1917 onward, Chin and P'an Fu managed to channel considerable amounts of official monies into the Lu region, beginning with a $3,000,000 loan for improving the Grand Canal. In 1921 the Lu region projects centered on improving the city of Chi-ning. Planned were a new university, a special foreign trade market, and industrial development, to be financed by Chinese capital.[1]

Another loan for Shantung in which Chin Yun-p'eng played a major role was the Sino-Japanese Industrial Corporation Loan of September 1917. This loan, made directly to the Shantung provincial administration in the amount of $1,500,000, came concurrently with the Nishihara loans, but it is not known exactly how the monies were used. About the time the loan was completed, however, the Shantung provincial administration, dominated by Tuan's supporters, began avoiding anti-Japanese activities. The Sino-Japanese Industrial Corporation was formed to serve as a conduit for Japanese investments in exploiting Chinese natural resources in Shantung, apparently on the model of the SEG. It never fulfilled its role and this loan remained its most important interest in Shantung.[2]

Chin Yun-p'eng and P'an Fu represent the most successful of the Shantungese who turned connections with Peking into power within the province of Shantung. Naturally they used this power to bolster the interests of their home region of Lu. Chin Yun-p'eng's ability to reconcile loyalty to Shantung provincial interests with accommodation of Japanese imperialism in Shantung was typical of Chinese leaders of his time. Most of the important men in Shantung, like Chin, served their own self-interest and found it possible to maintain good relations with the Japanese while they promoted Chinese nationalism.

Chin Yun-p'eng and P'an Fu should be classified as bureaucratic capitalists, even though they were active more than a decade before the Kuomintang rule which usually is seen as the high period of bureaucratic capitalism. Both men came to wield important power as a result of appointments to major bureaucratic posts in Peking and then used their positions to enrich their own interests. Their dual role as bureaucrats and

---

represented proved also to be in deep conflict. On the one hand, Chin spoke for Lu region interests centered at his home city of Chi-ning. In national politics, on the other hand, Chin associated closely with the Japanese when he arranged loans, dampened anti-Japanese outcries, and became a partner in Sino-Japanese industrial enterprises. After he was ousted from the premiership in December 1921, Chin's power and influence declined sharply, and by the mid-1920s, he lived in retirement in Tientsin and had little influence in Shantung.

Chin's closest ally within Shantung was P'an Fu. Also from Chi-ning, P'an Fu brought expert financial and economic assistance to Chin Yun-p'eng on many occasions. For instance, P'an Fu played the major role in the 1914 financial reorganization of Shantung that had given Chin a reputation as an able administrator.

capitalists grew out of the precedents set by Chou Fu when he invested in the German-controlled SEG while serving as Shantung governor, as well as the kind of official initiative that was so important in starting the telephone and electric power services in Tsinan. For these bureaucratic capitalists from the Anfu clique—unlike their early counterparts—personal gain seems to have been the major motivating factor. As bureaucratic capitalists operating in Tsinan, they had fewer ties to the comprador elements than their predecessors had had under Yüan Shih-k'ai. The close ties of the bureaucratic capitalists to the Japanese meant, however, that they were not capable of protecting Chinese interests in their roles either as high government officials or as major private investors in business and industry. Consequently these bureaucratic capitalists played a much less patriotic role than the compradors.

The years after Yüan's death saw open competition between two groups of Shantungese in the city's economic life. Chin Yun-p'eng and P'an Fu's approach was that of the bureaucratic capitalists, and contrasts with the activities of the Shantung commercial elements to be described in detail in Chapter 6. It also happens that the dominant figures in the bureaucratic capitalist circles represented the Lu region, while most of the commercial interests in Tsinan derived from the Ch'i region. Thus a regional difference compounded the basic economic and political differences between the two groups.

These various elements constituted the political situation in Tsinan in the three years from 1916 to 1919, and together they form a pattern of the way in which political power was controlled and used in the warlord period. The strongest men in Tsinan in the years from 1916 to 1928 were all military officers who held one of the top two administrative posts—governor or civil governor—in the province, along with control over the Fifth Division. The style of these militarist administrators drew both on the Chinese official's traditional role and on the newer style of military bossism which originated in the mid-nineteenth century.

The warlord needed both a loyal army and some kind of sanction from Peking in order to maintain his position in Shantung. Although ties with Peking were not necessary in all regions of China, some connections with the alternating and progressively weaker Peking cabinets remained essential in North China. The warlords in Shantung—until the arrival of Chang Tsung-ch'ang—relied on their old Peiyang Army ties to link them to Peking and to control the Fifth Division.

As long as a particular general in Tsinan could keep on good terms with Peking and the Fifth Division, he could try to balance the other power elements in order to maintain his own power. To underpin his position he made certain that the key posts in the civil administration, the tax offices, the Tsinan area administration, the military hierarchy were held by trustworthy subordinates. His appointments had to take into account the pressures brought to bear on him by the Peking government, the Shantungese who were part of the Peking political power group—such as Chin Yun-p'eng and P'an Fu—the Japanese, and the Shantungese merchant and gentry elements which congregated at Tsinan. Naturally, it was not always possible for a warlord to keep all of these groups satisfied, and he had to face opposition from one or more of them. The warlord always tried to keep control over the provincial revenues and the Fifth Division, the two indispensable elements of continuing political power in Tsinan. In these situations the various military powerholders in Tsinan followed the patterns (described in the previous chapter) in which Yüan Shih-k'ai ensured his power in Shantung through control over the Fifth Division and the provincial revenues.

In February 1918, a member of Tuan Ch'i-jui's clique, Chang Shu-yuan, advanced to the position of Shantung military governor, replacing the uncouth and distrusted Chang Huai-chih. Chang Shu-yuan was almost the opposite of his predecessor. He had an excellent education for a Chinese military officer, and had been known as the best student in German at the Peiyang military academy. Later he received special schooling in Japan and was renowned for his good manners and fine military bearing. Chang Shu-yuan was remembered favorably by the Shantung gentry leaders because of his lukewarm support for Yüan Shih-k'ai, and on that basis he was taken as a friend of republicanism and of Shantung's provincial interests.[3] In the May Fourth crisis, Chang Shu-yuan proved weak in suppressing anti-Japanese activity and therefore lost control of the province and the city of Tsinan to more tractable officials who would carry out Tuan Ch'i-jui's policy of compromising with the Japanese.

Chang Shu-yuan's first eighteen months in office were remarkably calm. A new provincial legislature came into session at Tsinan, and none of the Peiyang squabbles intruded unduly into Tsinan's political life. The economy of Tsinan prospered and Chang Shu-yuan even had some success coping with the province's long-standing financial shortages. His efforts to stamp out the endemic banditry in southern Shantung were widely applauded. Chang Shu-yuan provided Shantung with the best administration it had between 1911 and 1931, but he was replaced during the turmoil of the May Fourth movement in Tsinan. Chin Yun-p'eng filled the post with a protégé and military officer, T'ien Chung-yu, who was to serve in Tsinan for almost four years.*

*T'ien maintained his position, however, only by withdrawing his support from Chin Yun-p'eng when Chin's cabinet in Peking was tottering in the autumn of 1921. T'ien's connections with Chin go back to T'ien's service as defense commissioner in the Lu region during Chin's military governorship in Shantung.

106

After Chin Yun-p'eng's fall, a new element in the Peiyang clique inherited power in Peking. Known as the Chihli faction, it was headed by Wu P'ei-fu and Ts'ao K'un. The Chihli faction seemed promising to local Shantungese interests because it was less pliable to the wishes of Japanese imperialism, but in fact its leaders were completely incompetent to govern in every other respect. Wu P'ei-fu, the chief military commander in the Chihli faction, was hopelessly inept at manipulating the military power-holders of the old Peiyang clique. A measure of his shortcoming is found in the continuation of T'ien Chung-yu as Shantung's military governor during part of Wu P'ei-fu's ascendancy in Peking. Wu, although a Shantungese himself, had so little support in the Fifth Division at Tsinan that he could not replace T'ien with a commander of his own choosing.

In truth, no one in Shantung or Peking followed Wu P'ei-fu's unclear and changeable aims. The Chihli faction by early 1925 had come more and more under the influence of the warlord of Manchuria, Chang Tso-lin. Chang Tso-lin lacked Wu P'ei-fu's scruples about interfering in Shantung politics. He secured the appointment of a Shantungese former subordinate, Chang Tsung-ch'ang, in May 1925. The results were to be disastrous for Tsinan and for the whole province.

The obstacle to modernization created by this succession of warlord regimes in Tsinan should be clear from this abbreviated account. Although we will return to this theme several times, it is important to notice from the outset how the warlords helped create an unstable economic situation in Tsinan. First, the warlord's control, though based on military power, was subject to a variety of external political influences, both from other warlords in Peking and from foreign governments. Second, the frequent sudden changes in warlords made any kind of economic prediction difficult. Thus Chinese capitalists—whether the bureaucratic-capitalist or the ordinary merchants—were hampered at every turn.

JAPANESE POLICY INVOLVING SHANTUNG, 1916-1919

After Yüan Shih-k'ai's death, Japan decided to stop supporting rebel elements in China. When General Terauchi Seiki formed his cabinet in October 1916, Japan's China policy took a new direction. One element in the Terauchi policy was to reestablish the cooperative atmosphere among the imperialist powers that had been the basic approach before the war in Europe. In a series of secret notes exchanged in February and March 1917, the British, French, Italian, and Russian czarist governments agreed to cooperate in support of Japan's claims in Shantung.[4]*

*The existence of the notes remained secret until the deliberations of the Versailles conference in 1919. At that time these agreements were brought forward as evidence prejuicing the title to the German holdings in Shantung in Japan's favor.

The other half of the Terauchi approach was to adopt a new stance of friendship toward the Peking government. Terauchi, who had previously served as governor-general of Korea, favored a program of economic development financed by Japanese-controlled banks as the most desirable form of Japanese influence in China.[5] To implement this program, Terauchi dispatched a close associate to Peking in February 1917 as his personal emissary. This emissary was Nishihara Kamezo, a name that would become infamous in China.

Tuan Ch'i-jui, the leading power in Peking, and in all North China, accepted the new Japanese offer of friendship, for he realized that he would need a great deal of money to achieve his goal of unifying China by force of arms. From January 1917 through September 1918, a series of Japanese loans were negotiated to help sustain the power of Tuan Ch'i-jui. Some took the form of the so-called Second Reorganization Loan of 1917 from the Yokohama Specie Bank to the Chinese government, while others composed parts of the so-called Nishihara loans contracted directly between Nishihara Kamezo and Ts'ao Ju-lin, Tuan Ch'i-jui's chief negotiator in Japanese policy matters.

The Nishihara loans involved six separate agreements signed in 1917 and 1918 and totaling ¥145,000,000 although only the sixth and final loan involved Shantung directly. Under the terms of that loan, the consortium of three Japanese-government-controlled banks lent ¥20,000,000 to Peking for the construction of railroads in Shantung from Kao-mi to Hsu-chou, and from Tsinan to Hsun-te. (See Map 4.) As in the other Nishihara loans, this agreement was negotiated directly between Nishihara and Ts'ao Ju-lin, without involving the Chinese and Japanese foreign ministries. According to the terms, the new railroad lines would belong to the Chinese government, but the railroad and all of its property would serve as security for the loans.[6]*

The collusion between Tuan and the Terauchi cabinet worked up to a point but not well enough for Tuan to achieve his planned military unification of China. The loan agreements themselves seriously compromised Tuan in the eyes of nationalistic opinion in China. Even within the Peiyang elements there was dissatisfaction with Tuan's cooperative attitude toward Japan. This was especially true in the Chihli faction led by Feng Kuo-chang, Ts'ao K'un and Wu P'ei-fu.

In September 1918 after the signing of the last Nishihara loan, the Chinese ambassador to Japan, Chang Tsung-hsiang, agreed to recognize

*Aside from the Second Reorganization and the Nishihara loans, other Japanese monies became available to China in 1917 and 1918 as part of the Terauchi policy. The previously mentioned September 1917 loan of $1,500,000 from the Sino-Japanese Industrial Corporation is an example. The Chinese directors of that firm include Chin Yun-p'eng (*Shina* 10.1 [January 1919]: 102-4).

Japan as the rightful claimant to Germany's leasehold rights in Shantung.[7] This agreement appeared to fulfill the goals of the Terauchi policy in China. However, by October 1918—only a month later—both Terauchi and Tuan Ch'i-jui were out of power, and when the issue of Japanese claims in Shantung arose again in the spring of 1919, the circumstances were vastly different.

The Japanese thinking about Shantung after 1914 can be demonstrated most easily by reference to Manchuria. Since the defeat of Russia in 1905, the Japanese in Manchuria had used industrial development, commercial exploitation, railroad construction, and military presence to dominate that region. They had found it neither necessary nor desirable to assume direct administrative control over all of Manchuria.

In Manchuria, a leasehold with a seaport served as the Japanese military, industrial, commercial, and cultural base. The South Manchurian railroad connected that base with the hinterland and played a major role in Japanese policy. Japanese heavy industry operated mines and processing plants at appropriate sites in the interior. Japanese commercial interests and, later, light industrial concerns were located in existing cities or at new rail junctions. Japanese military units garrisoned the chief depots, controlled certain telegraph and radio services, and established their own post offices. Japanese consular representatives, banks, and retail merchants completed the imperialistic web. This program had functioned in Manchuria for nearly a decade when the Japanese took over Shantung. The Manchurian approach was transferred, with only one important modification, to Shantung.[8]

Between 1905 and 1907, the Japanese Imperial Army acquired the controlling voice in deciding Japanese policy in Manchuria. Some Japanese politicians, together with the foreign office, had challenged this powerful role of the army. By 1917 this movement for civilian dominance had lost, for both the Okuma and the Terauchi cabinets enlarged upon the army's role in Manchuria.

In Shantung the hope was to avoid the differences between military and civilian interests that had plagued Japan's Manchurian endeavors. Terauchi's solution consisted of a policy that clearly gave the military control but at the same time appealed to civil interests. A military-dominated civil administration for Tsingtao formed the keystone of the Terauchi plan. To implement his policy, Terauchi appointed Akiyama Masanosuke, a former general and personal friend, to head this new civil administration in Tsingtao.[9]

The parallels to Manchuria are obvious: Tsingtao, like Dairen, was a Japanese-administered territory with a seaport; the Shantung railroad was the analogue of the South Manchurian railway. However, to avoid the problems that had arisen in Manchuria, the Shantung railroad was not granted the extensive powers that made the South Manchuria Railway Company the chief factor of Japanese civilian presence in Manchuria.[10] Tzu-ch'uan and Chin-ling-chen became the equivalents of the coal and iron mines in Manchuria. Po-shan was viewed as an industrial complex like An-shan. Light industry was centered at Tsingtao or Tsinan, with a few smaller enterprises scattered along the railway line at Wei-hsien and Chang-tien.

The Japanese took over and improved everything the Germans had built at Tsingtao. They began by enlarging the harbor and wharves; then they built more warehouses and a new section in the business district that quickly filled with Japanese banks and commercial offices. All the public service industries, including the telephone and electrical services, were expanded. In 1913 approximately 30,000 people, including about 1,000 Japanese lived in Tsingtao; by 1914, there were 55,000. According to available figures, the Japanese civilian population of Tsingtao remained less than 3,000 until 1916, when Terauchi announced his new policy. As a result of the more favorable policies toward Japanese civilians, the Akiyama administration of Tsingtao brought an additional 16,000 Japanese to reside in Tsingtao by 1918.[11]

In other ways Tsingtao became a Japanese city. Streets were given Japanese names; Japanese schools, for both Japanese and Chinese students, replaced German schools. The Japanese also took over the established German businesses in Tsingtao, such as the brewery and the large slaughterhouse. At this time the Japanese home islands could not produce enough food for the Japanese population, so that much of Tsingtao's development was directed toward export food processing. The Japanese expanded the salt pans along Chiao-chou Bay, built dried-egg-processing factories, a flour mill, and peanut oil mills, all for the export trade to Japan. Japanese commercial interests tried to promote sugar beet and tobacco cultivation in Shantung; they also bought North China cotton for export to Japan.[12]

In 1918 Japanese commerce in Shantung took a new direction. Civil administrator Akiyama began to encourage Japanese business interests to construct light industrial operations in Tsingtao to serve the Chinese market.[13] In 1918 the Nagai cotton mills started operation with twenty thousand spindles, using a combination of imported and Chinese long-staple cotton, and in 1921 a second Japanese-owned mill, the Dai Nihon Spinning Company, entered production. Japanese interests also owned match factories in Tsingtao that produced for the Chinese market.[14]

Initially the Imperial Army ran the Tsingtao-Tsinan railroad, but it

110

soon came under control of the Japanese National Railway Administration. Japanese crews and administrators held the most important positions. In 1921 the railroad employed 1,658 Japanese and 4,233 Chinese. The Japanese enlarged the German shops at Ssu-fang so that 1,700 workers could fabricate four to seven box cars there each month. They improved the Tsingtao-Tsinan line by adding heavier rails throughout and then imported new locomotives and freight and passenger cars.[15]

The railroad's business increased dramatically under Japanese management. By 1922 gross revenues had more than doubled over 1913 levels. Under the Japanese, the Tsingtao-Tsinan railroad operated at nominal profit levels comparable to those of German days, but because Japanese government shipments and coal from the Po-shan colliery were transported free, the real profits of the railway were much greater.[16]

The Japanese also took over the telegraph line paralleling the railroad and soon established radio transmitters at Tsingtao and Tsinan. Undersea cables connected Tsingtao with Dairen, Shanghai, and Kyushu. The Japanese set up nine post offices and five sub-stations outside the Chiao-chou leasehold area. Japanese money, in the form of silver notes of the Yokohama Specie Bank, circulated freely along the railroad line.[17]

The Japanese also inherited the German mining rights and turned their attention to getting the large Tzu-ch'uan mine in the Po-shan Valley back into production. The railroad operated that mine, but private Japanese mining operations also worked the Po-shan Valley. In some instances the Japanese operated independently, but especially after 1919 it was common for the Japanese to form firms with Chinese partners. By 1919 the railway administration brought an iron mine at Chin-ling-chen into operation to serve the Yawata works in Kyushu.[18]

Tsinan fit into the Manchurian model as an analogue to Shen-yang (Mukden). Both were existing Chinese administrative centers with some commercial functions and both became much more important through the addition of rail facilities. The difference, however, was that Mukden was a much faster growing city in a faster growing area.

After the Japanese took over the Shantung railroad, they left a permanent garrison of Japanese troops and railway police in the settlement district at Tsinan. These troops went into all sections of Tsinan bearing their arms, in spite of Chinese protests. Generally, after the first few weeks of 1914, the Japanese troops were well behaved. The only later incident in Tsinan was a 1916 riot in the settlement district during which Japanese troops destroyed twenty Chinese shops and injured several Chinese.[19]

Since the Japanese looked to North China as a source of food and cotton, they promoted some processing industry in Tsinan and Tsingtao. In 1916 the Japanese installed two cotton-baling machines at Tsinan to

111

reduce the number of freight cars needed to transport the cotton drawn from western Shantung and southern Hopei. Other Japanese-financed export processing operations in Tsinan included peanut oil mills and a dried-egg processing factory.[20]

Many Japanese trading firms kept offices in Tsinan. In addition to large houses such as Mitsui, branches of Tsingtao traders and some small independent trading firms established operations there to deal in cotton, wheat, peanuts, cattle, and hides, as well as straw braid, hairnets, and lace. The Japanese commercial people ordinarily located their homes and offices in the settlement district, where the Japanese community had its own chamber of commerce, a Japanese-language newspaper, and a small Japanese private bank. The Japanese colony numbered between two and three thousand from 1918 to 1924.[21]

In 1918 when Tsingtao began to develop industry that produced for Chinese markets, Tsinan underwent a similar but more modest development. Included in the Japanese-owned enterprises at Tsinan were two match factories and a flour mill. The largest and most expensive effort of Japanese enterprise turned out to be a failure when the Po-i beet sugar mill closed within two years of its opening. The sugar mill had hoped to process beets grown by Shantung farmers, but other crops proved more attractive, and the beet sugar mill never had an adequate supply of raw materials to operate profitably. The enterprise had been established shortly after the May Fourth incident, when Japanese control would have been a liability; thus, although financing and control were really Japanese, several prominent Chinese were brought in to make the operation appear Chinese.* This is a variant of the bureaucratic-capitalist pattern, in which Chinese officials cooperated with foreign interests and were well paid for providing a respectable Chinese component in what was basically a foreign investment. This type of collusion between officials and foreign interests became more common in Shantung after 1916 and probably reached its high point in the early 1920s, when the Sino-Japanese agreements on the Shantung question led many Japanese to seek Chinese to serve as front men in their continuing investments in Shantung.

Three Japanese-government-controlled banks—the Yokohama Specie Bank, the Bank of Chosen, and the Bank of Taiwan—all established branch offices in the Tsinan settlement. The Japanese consulate built a new, more spacious building in 1918. Other Japanese undertakings in Tsinan included a hundred-bed hospital for Chinese, which opened in

*Included were Ch'ien Nung-shun, a former premier at Peking, Ch'ü Ying-kuang, former Shantung civil governor, and Li Shih-wei of the Sino-Japanese Industrial Corporation (Bertram Giles, Tsinan Intelligence Reports, 4th Quarter 1921, 2d Quarter 1922, F.O. 228/3277; *Chinese Economic Bulletin* 1.7 [1 April 1921]: 6).

1918.[22] Japanese commercial and service establishments of all kinds appeared in the settlement. The Japanese influx was the chief cause of the settlement's dramatic growth during these years.

Direct Japanese penetration of Shantung did not extend beyond Tsinan, and few Japanese commercial or trading operations maintained regular offices in the southern or western parts of the province. The existing system of internal transit levies determined this residence pattern. Goods shipped on the Tientsin-Pukow railroad were subject to *likin* taxes at several barriers. Japanese merchants could avoid the *likin* by simply making Tsinan the center of their operations. They could depend on Chinese traders to bring the goods to Tsinan, and then the Japanese could ship directly to Tsingtao on the Tsingtao-Tsinan railroad without any further internal customs duties.[23]

The record of the Japanese in Shantung makes a revealing comparison with that of the Germans. The Germans had begun with the concept of turning Shantung into an exclusively German sphere of interest but eventually abandoned that scheme. The Japanese succeeded where the Germans failed, partly because the war in Europe diverted the attention of other foreigners from China, but partly because the Japanese economy could consume the agricultural products, the coal, the iron ore, and even the manufactures of Shantung much more readily than Germany could. In contrast, a full German sphere of influence in Shantung failed to develop, in part because the German home economy had little use for the exportable commodities of Shantung. Neither the Germans nor the Japanese had been able to bend Yüan Shih-k'ai to their policy, but the Anfu clique, including both Tuan Ch'i-jui and Chin Yun-p'eng, proved much more pliable. Japan proved effective at overcoming official resistance to her imperialistic policies; yet as the next section shows, Japan met opposition from another source.

Yüan Shih-k'ai's leadership had made the difference in determining that Shantung did not become a German sphere of interest. His official programs and the encouragement he initially gave to the gentry and the merchants helped build a strong base of local nationalistic resistance that was lacking in Manchuria. Consequently, when Japan took over the German leasehold and attempted to implement the Manchurian model for the exploitation of these new rights in Shantung, they found the Chinese commercial and political interests much stronger and more cohesive than their Manchurian counterparts had been. Nevertheless, within their short tenure in Tsingtao the Japanese made a vigorous start toward the subordination of the province to their imperialistic programs. The rise of the nationalistic spirit among China's educated population, especially in the nation's largest cities during the May Fourth period, and the focus of

113

that nationalism on the Shantung question stopped Japanese imperialism short of realizing its hopes for the "Manchurianization" of Shantung.

RESISTANCE IN TSINAN TO JAPANESE IMPERIALISM

When Japanese troops first landed in Shantung in 1914, several dozen incidents involving Japanese troops and Chinese civilians occurred. Soon, however, the number of such incidents dropped to very low levels.[24] Not until 1917 did the Chinese, led by their provincial assemblymen, begin to protest Japanese activities in Shantung. The assemblymen complained about the establishment of Japanese civil administration and post offices at various communities along the Tsingtao-Tsinan railway. They claimed that such practices encroached upon Chinese sovereignty and gave unfair advantages to Japanese commercial endeavors.[25] As the Japanese demand for exports for their homeland declined and Japanese investors began instead to compete with Chinese industry for Chinese markets, the complaints from Tsinan's business leaders grew.

In November 1917 a public meeting was held at Tsinan, over the Japanese consul's objection, to protest the Japanese civil administration at Fang-tzu in Wei *hsien*. The military governor, Chang Huai-chih, let it be privately known that he favored such anti-Japanese sentiments, but he also arranged for the meeting hall to be locked before the rally. Despite this action the meeting was held outside the locked hall and delegates were elected to take Shantung's case to Peking, but they received a poor hearing from Tuan Ch'i-jui's pro-Japanese administration. After this failure, the assembly and the people of Shantung did not attempt any significant anti-Japanese activities until 1919.[26]

In 1919, after the end of World War I, the Peking cabinet wanted German rights in Shantung to revert to China. As is well known, Chinese diplomats, along with much informed Chinese opinion, looked to Woodrow Wilson and the United States for help in their endeavor. The peace conference opened in January 1919. On 25 February a public meeting of several thousand people was held at the provincial assembly grounds in Tsinan to urge that Tsingtao and all other German interests be turned over to China. The provincial assembly and various other representative organizations, including the educational association, the chamber of commerce, and the farmer's association, sent telegrams to Paris urging the Versailles delegates to return Tsingtao to China.[27] This was more than two months before the May Fourth demonstrations.*

*Prominent signers of these telegrams included Chang Chao-ch'üan, president of the Shantung bank from Chang-ch'iu, Wang Hung-i, a gentry modernizer from Ts'ao-chou, and Chang Chih-lieh, former president of the Shantung assembly. These three men became the leading anti-Japanese spokesmen in Tsinan during 1919 and 1920.

Over the next nine weeks a series of meetings and demonstrations took place in Tsinan protesting the direction of the negotiations in France. The well-informed British consul in Tsinan, J. T. Pratt, summed up the pre-May Fourth situation:

> About the beginning of this year certain of the gentry of Chinan [Tsinan] began to realize that decisions taken at Paris which they were almost powerless to affect might consign Shantung to the same fate as Korea, and they initiated a campaign of public meetings, lectures and press articles throughout the province in order to educate public opinion into making a stand once and for all against Japanese aggression and against the still more insidious danger of traitors in high places who were selling their country to the foreigner.[28]

These Shantungese reactions, centered in Tsinan, began independently of the forces behind the May Fourth demonstrations in Peking. The leadership of this movement lay in the hands of the Shantung commercial elements, in cooperation with some of progressive Shantung gentry. It included neither the dominant Lu faction of the bureaucratic capitalists nor any significant influence from Sun Yat-sen's political followers and allies.

Once the May Fourth incident had occurred in Peking and the nationalistic response had begun to spread rapidly to other Chinese cities, the Tsinan protests became coordinated into the larger effort. The principal importance of Tsinan's earlier anti-Japanese activity in 1919 is not that it preceded the May Fourth incident, but that it was merchant and gentry led, whereas the May Fourth incident drew in the students and intellectuals in a new way, one that was to have profound impact on school life in all Chinese cities, including Tsinan.

The immediate impetus for the May Fourth demonstrations can be traced to a series of telegrams in April 1919 from the Chinese delegation at Versailles. In these telegrams the Chinese delegation, led by Lu Cheng-hsiang, advised the foreign ministry in Peking that public support within China for their position at the conference table would strengthen China's cause. Specifically mentioned were provincial assemblies, chambers of commerce, education societies, farmers' associations, and other public groups. The foreign ministry passed these instructions on to the various civil governors and provincial administrations, including Shantung's.[29] In mid-April 1919 the Shantung provincial assembly sent telegrams to the Big Four that followed the suggested pattern. One typical telegram began, "From the time the Japanese occupied Tsingtao and took over all German rights, our nation has opposed it. We do not recognize the Japanese right to succession [to Germany's treaty rights]."[30] The telegrams went on to state that the September 1918 diplomatic note of Chang Tsung-hsiang which the Japanese claimed gave them title to

115

Tsingtao had never been approved by the Chinese national parliament and consequently was not binding. The petition closed by asking that Tsingtao and the Shantung railroad be placed under Chinese control.

On 20 April some ten thousand people met in Tsinan to protest the Japanese claims. Wang Hung-i and Chang Chih-lieh were delegated to take the meeting's decisions to Peking, and on this occasion they found a more receptive audience in the capital.[31]

On 30 April the decision at Versailles to award full control of German rights in Shantung to Japan was announced. On 2 May, some three thousand people* demonstrated in Tsinan for the return of Tsingtao to Chinese control. On 4 May, the first large demonstration occurred in Peking. The following day demonstrations occurred again in Tsinan, and then, on 7 May, over one thousand students, workers, businessmen, and assemblymen met on the assembly grounds to protest the decision.[32] After the May Fourth incident in Peking, the anti-Japanese movement in Tsinan was subsumed into the general student strike and merchant boycott activities common in China's cities during this great nationalist movement.

In May and June 1919 the anti-Japanese movement in Tsinan copied such Peking practices as the "ten-man teams" (*shih-jen t'uan*) that students in the capital were using as an organizational aid. They began employing these teams to organize strikes and boycotts, with students from secondary schools and the missionary university at Tsinan supplying most of the demonstrators. Generally merchants honored the anti-Japanese boycott, and certain firms, especially branches of Shanghai stores, supplied food and money to the demonstrators. The heads of the two largest Chinese banks, the Shantung Bank and the Bank of China, publicly supported the boycott.

The boycott went into effect in Tsinan on 24 May. Student groups patrolled the streets in designated areas of the city, passing out anti-Japanese literature, haranguing crowds on street corners, and checking on goods displayed in shops. The merchants implemented the boycott through their own trade associations. Within each trade, arrangements of mutual supervision were established so that after Japanese stocks on hand were disposed of, no new Japanese items would be purchased.[33] During this phase of the movement—which lasted about a month—Pratt reported, "The movement shows moderation and self-restraint. Clashes between soldiers, police and students have been avoided by feelings of mutual good

*The crowd figures in the accounts contained in the special May Fourth issue of *Shan-tung sheng-chih tzu-liao* (Materials for the Shantung Gazetteer) have been quoted, even though such numbers appear, in comparison with the few hundred demonstrators in Peking on 4 May, to be exaggerations.

will and patriotism."[34] Included in the boycott at Tsinan was a rule against using the Japanese-owned Tsingtao-Tsinan railroad for any purpose.

The demonstrations upset the Japanese community at Tsinan. The consul protested to Chang Shu-yuan, the military governor, but did not threaten military intervention. Beginning in July, however, the Japanese began to react differently, under the leadership of a new Japanese commanding general at Tsingtao. Previously the Japanese had been content with publishing articles against the May Fourth movement in the Japanese-owned Chinese-language newspaper, *Chi-nan jih-pao* (Tsinan Daily). On 1 July, a Japanese railway police detachment arrested a Chinese student who had stopped Chinese barrowmen from transferring Japanese-owned grain into railway freight cars at Tsinan. When news of the arrest swept through the city, a large crowd gathered at the civil governor's yamen demanding the student's immediate release.[35]

The next several days were tense as Chinese at Tsinan continued to demonstrate. On 7 July a Chinese merchant who had been prominent in anti-Japanese activities had his shop vandalized. The same evening a group of Chinese attacked a Japanese community lantern festival parade in the settlement district. The situation remained uneasy. Then, on 20 July, a mob attacked and burned the offices of the *Ch'ang-yen pao* (The Plaindealer).

The *Ch'ang-yen pao*, which had just started publication in April 1919, was financed by Ai Ch'ing-yung, a prominent Shantungese and an ardent supporter of Tuan Ch'i-jui. Along with other newspapers in Tsinan, it had entered into the fight over the Shantung question in 1919. The *Ch'ang-yen pao*'s editorial stand strongly opposed the May Fourth movement and the anti-Japanese boycott. In a mass meeting held on 20 July, feeling ran high against the paper. Even though some speakers tried to dissuade the crowd, the mob surged out of the provincial assembly grounds and into the city's streets, where it smashed and burned the entire plant of the newspaper. Three days later the Shantung provincial administration announced a ban on all public demonstrations, and declared martial law on 31 July.[36]

At the same time, a shake-up in the Shantung administration occurred. Chang Shu-yuan, the weak military governor who had lost control of the situation in Tsinan, remained in office, but the civil governor and the Chi-nan circuit intendant were moved. In their places, the Tuan Ch'i-jui clique in Peking engineered the appointment of two pro-Japanese officials. Before the new appointees reached Tsinan, the Tsinan defense commissioner, Ma Liang, began a crackdown on the anti-Japanese movement. First, on 23 July 1919 three prominent Tsinanese Moslems were arrested on charges of promoting bolshevism. Then on 3 August

117

several hundred Tsinan students demonstrated against these arrests, in spite of the July decree prohibiting all demonstrations. Ma Liang's response was to arrest sixteen demonstrators and surround several hundred more on the grounds of the First Shantung Middle School. Prominent Chinese and foreign consuls intervened to free the students, but the three Moslems were executed, even though no proof of their supposed bolshevik ideas and actions was ever produced.[37]

When the new civil governor, Ch'ü Ying-kuang, arrived in Tsinan on 9 August, he upheld Ma Liang's unpopular actions. Before the 3 August demonstrations and arrests, J. T. Pratt had reported:

> The merchants are discovering that the boycott is a two-edged weapon. They refused to buy Japanese sugar, cotton yarn and any piece goods, but now that their stocks of these absolutely necessary articles are depleted they find that there is no other source from which they can obtain fresh supplies. Furthermore, they find that military men like the *tu-chun* [Chang Shu-yuan] and the military governor of Tsinan [Ma Liang] are not above embarking on trading ventures with the Japanese and reaping handsome profits. . . . It is freely rumored that some of the popular party leaders, one of whom in particular appeared above suspicion, have been bought over by the Anfu club [headed by Tuan Ch'i-jui and including Chin Yun-p'eng]. It is therefore highly probable that the boycott will collapse in a few days.[38]

On the contrary, Ma Liang's high-handed actions revived the boycott. For their own self-preservation, however, the merchants began to use the Tsingtao-Tsinan railroad to ship goods into Tsinan. Nevertheless, their boycott had a considerable impact on the railroad's business: during July and August 1919, freight returns on the railroad were only half of normal. Limited to Japanese goods, the boycott continued into the first months of 1920.[39]

So obvious was the collusion of the Anfu elements with the Japanese to suppress opposition in Tsinan and elsewhere in Shantung that anti-Japanese feeling remained intense for the remainder of 1919. As the anti-Japanese boycott wore on into the summer and fall of 1919, it produced ever bigger losses for the patriotic merchants and windfall profits for the pro-Japanese elements. In this situation, commercial support for the nationalistic boycott weakened and finally wilted. The merchants had not changed their minds about Japan, for the anti-Japanese movement was to revive in 1920 and later, though always taking the form of actions less damaging to the merchant's own interests than those used during the 1919 boycotts and strikes.

The public demonstrations, student interest, and citizen delegations associated with the May Fourth movement in Tsinan constituted new forms of political expression.* This activity eventually gave birth to anti-Confucian, anti-Christian, and Marxist groups in Tsinan, as it did elsewhere in China. These groups, however, were always small, and the power of both the Chinese provincial administration and the foreign community was arrayed against them.

In May 1920 Wang Hsiang-ch'ien, a minor administrator in a provincial school at Tsinan, organized a Marxist Research Society along the same lines as a society founded by Li Ta-chao in Peking. The Tsinan group began with only a few members and remained small, but one of its participants who later became a novelist has written a slightly fictionalized version of the society's activities.† Wang Chin-mei, a student at Shantung Normal School in Tsinan and a relative of Wang Hsiang-ch'ien, represented the Tsinan group at the first Chinese Communist party congress in Shanghai during July 1921. After the congress, the Tsinan activists, following the policies adopted in those meetings, concentrated on labor-organizing activities. Part of their program consisted of publishing a weekly paper, *Chi-nan lao-tung chou-k'an* (Tsinan Labor Weekly), which appeared as a supplement to the highly nationalistic daily, *Ta min-chu pao* (The Democrat).[40]

This publication program met with little success, for Bertram Giles, the British consul, reported that the paper "had come to an untimely end because of lack of support. The Shantung working class are exceedingly backward, even as compared with those of the Yangtze provinces, . . .organized industrialism, whatever its future may be, having as yet barely touched the fringe of this province."[41] Giles' judgment proved correct, for the work of the Communist party stopped sometime in 1922 and did not begin again until 1927 when the advance organizers for the Northern Expedition appeared in and around Tsinan.

The political leaders associated with the Nationalist party were closely connected to the Marxists. Wang Le-p'ing, the leading Nationalist party supporter in Tsinan at the time of the May Fourth movement, published a

*During this time John Dewey arrived in Tsinan, just before New Year's 1920, for a series of lectures. With Hu Shih serving as his interpreter, Dewey delivered lectures entitled, "The Child as a Living Organism," "The Social Values of Education," and "The Roots of Western Civilization." On 1 January 1920, following Dewey's last lecture, renewed rioting broke out in Tsinan when the civil governor attempted to prohibit students from using the student union (*North China Herald*, 10 January 1920, p. 67). For Dewey's reaction to the situation in Tsinan see "Shantung as Seen from Within," *New Republic* 22.274 (3 March 1920): 12-16.

†Wang I-chien (b. 1908), who writes under the name Chiang Kuei, was a nephew of Wang Hsiang-ch'ien, and the novel in question is entitled *Hsuan-feng* (Whirlwind). See Timothy Ross, *Chiang Kuei* (New York: Twayne, 1974), pp. 26-32; and Wang I-chien, "Feng-pao lang-ya," in *Wu-wei chi* (Taipei: Yu-shih wen-i ch'u-pan she, 1974), pp. 5-108.

119

newspaper, *Ch'i-lu jih-pao* (The Shantung Daily News) which was strongly Republican. Wang Le-p'ing, along with Wang Hsiang-ch'ien and Wang Chin-mei, were members of the wealthy Wang clan, centered in Kao-mi and Chu-cheng *hsien* in the Ch'i region.* Members of this clan played prominent roles in the 1911 revolution in their home area and had contacts with the Revolutionary Alliance. In addition to his newspaper, Wang Le-p'ing ran a bookstore that featured Sun Yat-sen's writings, other political tracts, and socialist publications. Wang Le-p'ing disappeared from active politics in Tsinan in the early 1920s about the same time the Communist party elements led by Wang Hsiang-ch'ien and Wang Chin-mei ceased their activities. The inability of either the Kuomintang or the Communist party to survive in Tsinan reveals the strength of the combination of foreign, warlord, and local opposition to these political parties and their views.[42]

The Caucasian community joined in the anti-Japanese spirit of the May Fourth movement very much on the side of Chinese nationalism; and the Japanese, in replying to criticism of their actions during these years, often blamed the British and American missionaries for stirring up the Chinese. Initially, Japanese criticism of the missionaries as cultural imperialists had little impact, but by 1924 the nationalist movement had turned against the missionaries and the Christian church. Anti-Christian demonstrations were more common. Missionaries were accused of abusing Chinese sovereignty and cultural sensibilities.[43]

RETURN OF TSINGTAO AND THE SHANTUNG RAILROAD TO CHINA

When the Versailles peace treaty was signed in May 1919, Japan seemed on the verge of consolidating her position in Shantung. The Chinese government, however, refused to sign that treaty. In hopes of changing the Chinese attitude, the Japanese delegation at Versailles made statements about returning the Chiao-chou leasehold at some unspecified date in the future. In August 1919, President Wilson and Foreign Minister Uchida revealed an understanding whereby Japan would return Chiao-chou and the Tsingtao-Tsinan railroad to China but retain the other economic interests granted to Germany.[44]

During the nearly four years from the signing of the Versailles treaty to the final withdrawal of Japanese troops from Shantung in 1923, a great deal of diplomatic activity went into making the Wilson-Uchida

*When Chiang Kuei went to school in Tsinan, Wang Le-p'ing served as his guarantor; at the same time, his paternal uncle, Hsiang-ch'ien, was living in Tsinan and soon influenced the young man to participate in his Marxist Research Society (Wang I-chien, "Feng-pao lang-ya," *Wu-wei chi*).

agreement a reality. Japanese policy during these years consistently followed the principle that Japan kept working to retain control—especially financial control—over the Tsingtao-Tsinan railroad, the Shantung mines, and all other enterprises in which Japanese capital, government or private, had been invested.[45] When Japanese troops finally left the province in 1923, these aims had been achieved, though some compromise with Chinese interests over the ownership of certain production facilities proved necessary.

Chinese interests were in the beginning and continued to be strongly suspicious of any Japanese-proposed initiatives on the Shantung question. Japanese spokesmen raised the prospect of direct negotiations with China as early as 1920, but nationalistic opinion in China immediately began to voice concern about a possible sellout by the Peking cabinet. Given the record of Tuan Ch'i-jui and Chin Yun-p'eng, such concern was well-grounded. In the spring of 1920, the anti-Japanese commercial and gentry interests in Tsinan began a telegram campaign to newspapers, educators, and other community leaders around China to gather support for postponing negotiations. In April opponents mounted demonstrations in Shanghai against direct negotiations. In Tsinan these demonstrations took place with promises of student strikes, renewed boycotts, and withholding of taxes unless the matter were postponed.[46]

The Shantung issue lay dormant over a year following the public outcry of early 1920, and then in September 1921 the Japanese government again took up the issue officially with the Chinese government at Peking. At that time Pemier Chin Yun-p'eng still felt compelled to refuse to discuss the matter because direct negotiations remained unacceptable to all shades of political opinion, except to those who were strongly pro-Japanese. The suggestion that the Shantung question might be discussed as part of the upcoming Washington disarmament conference was, however, acceptable to many Chinese, including the most vocal nationalistic leaders in Tsinan.[47] Finally in December 1921 the Chinese and Japanese delegations agreed to hold special sessions at Washington to settle the Shantung question. As the time for negotiations in the United States approached, renewed demonstrations occurred in Tsinan, but now the Chinese were split along radical and conservative lines, with the students and a part of the press opposed to any deals with Japan and the more moderate educators and businessmen favoring an agreement if one could be reached.

This was the period of greatest influence in Tsinan for Wang Chin-mei's Communist party elements and the Nationalist party group led by Wang Le-p'ing. Together with the *Ch'i-lu jih-pao* and the *Ta min-chu pao*, these two student groups supported all-out resistance to discussions with the Japanese. In Tsinan the students held large public meetings in December opposing the talks, and the boycott against Japanese goods was revived. Shops of merchants who refused to honor the boycott were smashed. The more moderate merchant group, speaking through the chamber of commerce, criticized the students and their tactics.[48]

The Chinese delegation to Washington included Shantungese known for their honesty and their opposition to Japanese imperialism. Since the United States was considered fairly trustworthy, moderate opinion thought the discussions should be judged by their results. When the official announcements from the Sino-Japanese talks were made public in January 1922, Tsinan accepted the settlement without either rejoicing or open disapproval. The student groups had by that time lost much of their support within the Chinese community by their adamant opposition; consequently both the Communist party and the Nationalist party elements began to decline quickly after the terms for settling the Shantung question were announced.[49]

The Washington discussions produced agreement on three major issues: 1) the return of the Chiao-chou leasehold to China, 2) the purchase of the Tsingtao-Tsinan railroad by China, and 3) disposition of the former German mines at Fang-tzu, Tzu-ch'uan, and Chin-ling-chen. Early in the discussions the Japanese agreed to relinquish administrative control over the entire Chiao-chou leasehold, including Tsingtao. They also agreed to turn over without charge, everything the Germans had left at Tsingtao, but insisted on payment for everything the Japanese government had improved. Because of extensive Japanese construction, this meant considerable expense for the Chinese.[50]

The disposition of Japanese private investments proved to be one of the most sensitive issues. Japanese firms, factories, and real estate owned by private interests remained unchanged, but the Chinese insisted upon buying back the extensive salt fields Japanese investors had developed around Chiao-chou Bay. The delegates agreed that a Sino-Japanese corporation, combining Chinese and Japanese capital equally, would be created to control the former German mines in Shantung. In August 1922 Japanese mining interests led by Takuma Dan, head of the Mitsui interests, met in Tokyo with Foreign Minister Uchida to implement these arrangements. Finally in December 1922 the Lu-ta Company (*Lu-ta kung-ssu*) was formed. The Chinese participants in the company included such prominent Shantungese as Chin Yun-p'eng, P'an Fu, and Chang Chao-ch'üan, head of the Shantung Bank and leader of the anti-Japanese commercial group in Tsinan. Still, in the Lu-ta Company the Japanese owned the majority of the stock and kept control in their own hands while sharing a small portion of the profits with a few select Shantungese and high officials.[51]

122

The railroad proved to be the most difficult question. The Chinese had hoped to be able to buy the road, but they found it impossible to raise enough money from either government or private sources. Feeling against an outright Japanese loan for the purpose ran high in Tsinan and elsewhere in China. In late January 1922 it was agreed, after long discussions, that Japan would take interest-bearing Chinese treasury notes in exchange for title to the railroad.[52]

After the Washington negotiations, additional exchanges took place in both Peking and Tokyo. In Tsinan, as elsewhere, it was feared that a sellout to the Japanese was still possible. Finally in December 1922 a large group of treaties, agreements, and incorporation documents were signed in Peking. By these terms the Chinese government paid $2,000,000 in cash and gave Japan, for Japanese improvements at Tsingtao, 6 percent notes that would mature in December 1937. The Lu-ta Company came into formal existence at this time, also. The railroad purchase was completed with Chinese treasury notes in the amount of ¥40,000,000 (gold), bearing 6 percent interest for a similar term of fifteen years. The notes were secured against the railroad revenues; in addition, a Japanese traffic manager and a chief accountant were retained.[53]

Although many observers both abroad and in China hailed the return of Tsingtao as a great diplomatic victory, a more realistic view appeared in the columns of the *North China Herald*: "She [China] has of course regained nominal sovereignty over her alienated territories and such national properties as the Tsingtao-Tsinanfu railway and the Kiaochow [Chiao-chou] salt fields, but to acquire these properties, she has had to pawn them to the Japanese on terms which make redemption look very remote."[54]

For Japan, the Shantung settlement represented a further retreat from the independent posture of World War I to the stance of cooperative economic imperialism favored by the United States. The Japanese government retained a major economic interest in Shantung in the form of the Chinese treasury notes, along with private investments in Shantung mines, factories, and businesses, including the Lu-ta Company. Japan no longer hoped to dominate Shantung militarily, but she still was the most influential foreign power in the province.

The settlement of the Shantung question influenced the later history of Shantung in two major ways. First, the large stake Japan retained there determined much of her future policy in regard to Shantung. Should anything happen to upset Japanese investment or to cause China to default on the railroad notes, Japan would sustain a large loss.[55] These factors figured importantly in determining Japan's support for Chang Tsung-ch'ang in 1925 and the concern of the Japanese over the prospect of a Kuomintang takeover in 1927 and 1928. In 1927 and 1928 the threat to Japanese interests in Shantung seemed so great that Japanese prime ministers dispatched expeditionary forces to Tsingtao and Tsinan.

The second major influence the Shantung settlement had in later years was related to Chinese internal politics. As China acquired the various forms of fiscal and administrative authority denied her during the period of humiliation, Chinese power groups rushed to claim control. The leading contenders in this rush (1922 and 1923) were Tuan Ch'i-jui and his Anfu group of supporters, the Chihli faction of the old Peiyang clique, and the important and wealthy Shantungese centered at Tsinan. Since the Chihli group appointed the officials controlling Tsingtao and the Tsingtao-Tsinan railroad with its considerable revenues, it should be no surprise that they obtained most of the new posts. The leaders of the Shantungese local elements at Tsinan, including the leaders of the moderate business and gentry interests, were furious. Bitter at the idea that the Peking bureaucrats, including many pro-Japanese, would reap the economic benefits of the five-year struggle against Japan, they struck out at all the Chinese officials responsible for implementing the agreements. The British consul at Tsinan claimed that they criticized everything "with little regard for hard facts" and opposed "any terms that might be arranged." The real question concerned not who would benefit from the new revenues produced by the returned properties, but rather how easily the Peking government's warlord elements had been able to control the situation. This episode revealed how weak the Tsinanese merchants and gentry were, compared to their domestic competition from Peking.

WEAKNESS OF THE SHANTUNG PROVINCIAL LEADERSHIP

The best gauge of the power of Shantungese political interests was the provincial assembly in Tsinan, which became progressively weaker and more corrupt after Yüan Shih-k'ai successfully suppressed the parliament and the assemblies in 1914. Large-scale fraud and open vote-buying marked both the 1918 and the 1921 elections. Once elected, neither assembly could enact any meaningful legislation. The assembly's only significant contribution at this time was to serve as a forum during the May Fourth period and to support the anti-Japanese movement in 1919 and 1920.[56]

A protracted struggle over the chairmanship of the new assembly followed the 1921 assembly election. The leading contender seemed to be Hsieh Hung-t'ao, who was closely associated with Chin Yun-p'eng and the Anfu clique. His rivals were Chang Chao-ch'üan, the powerful Tsinan banker, head of the Chang-ch'iu *pang*, and a representative of the Ch'i region, and Wang Hung-i, a gentry reformer and educator from Ts'ao-chou in southern Shantung. Prices for votes on the chairmanship ranged from $3,000 to $5,000. At one point in 1922, when it appeared that Hsieh might lose a roll-call vote, ruffians and soldiers sent in by the pro-Anfu clique governor created a riot in the assembly hall. After a year of indecision, the assembly rejected all three and compromised on Sung Ch'uan-tien, a Christian businessman from Ch'ing-chou.[57]

Hsieh was ruled out because of his pro-Japanese leanings. The opposition wanted to retain economic rights and opportunities for local commercial groups who would not sell out to the Japanese. Interestingly, Hsieh's opponents, who came from both the Ch'i and Lu areas, supported two different candidates, Chang Chao-ch'üan and Wang Hung-i, and could not get together on this matter for over a year. These ancient regional differences were still stronger than the drive for modern institutions. Thus divided, the local Shantung forces could scarcely hope to provide better leadership for the area than either the warlord cliques or the Japanese. And their defeat in the contest for control of Tsingtao was almost inevitable.

The new elite in Tsinan, the men who were leaders in banking, commerce, and industry, simply lost to the warlords and their bureaucratic allies. The Anfu elements could secure more funds to undertake larger industrial enterprises than the Shantungese interests could, while they somehow managed to sustain the precarious balance in Shantung's financial matters. The local elite could not overcome the divisions among themselves in order to challenge the Anfu clique's manipulation. Ever since 1914 the local elite had grown more numerous and powerful in economic matters, but their capacity to control Shantung politics did not show a similar improvement. A major test of their strength came at the time of Chiao-chou retrocession, but weakened by internal squabbles over the provincial assembly chairmanship and by competing intra-provincial loyalties, the local Shantung leadership was soundly defeated by a combination of Peking bureaucrats and Japanese interests.

The failure of the Ch'i and Lu elements to unite after 1916 reveals that Shantung was not sufficiently integrated, either economically or politically, to give the Shantungese a common outlook. Instead of a united provincial leadership that could hold its own against Peking and the Japanese, there existed regional, personal, and economic interests which crosscut and fragmented this leadership.

THE DARK DAYS OF WARLORDISM: THE RULE OF CHANG TSUNG-CH'ANG

Although Tsinan had lived under warlords since 1916, it was not until Chang Tsung-ch'ang became military governor in 1925 that the full force of warlordism descended upon the city. Chang Tsung-ch'ang had risen from obscurity in a checkered career as a military man. During the first Fengtien-Chihli war in 1922 he had joined forces with Chang Tso-lin, and one of his first assignments from the warlord of Manchuria was to attack Shantung. Chang Tsung-ch'ang and about four thousand troops landed on the Shantung peninsula, calling themselves the Shantung Home Rule Army (*Shan-tung tzu-chih chün*) in an attempt to appeal to that spirit of provincial autonomy which had become so important in Chinese politics after 1911. Chang claimed the backing of several prominent Shantung officials living in retirement in Tsingtao,* but the Fifth Division successfully contained his forces, and within a few weeks he had withdrawn to Manchuria.[58]

The next time Chang came to Shantung, he came to stay. The defection of Feng Yü-hsiang in early 1925 sapped the power of the Chihli faction while Chang Tso-lin became more and more powerful in Peking. From Manchuria, Chang Tso-lin sought to consolidate his new power by moving friendly forces into China's eastern coastal areas. As part of this plan, Chang Tsung-ch'ang moved to Kiangsu with Hsu-chou as his base. When Chang Tsung-ch'ang visited Tsinan in February 1925, rumors immediately began to circulate that he would soon be military governor.[59]

Chang Tsung-ch'ang's reputation for personal brutality and venery led provincial leaders to offer him $200,000 to leave the province, but the money only made him all the more eager to stay. The old military governor, Ch'eng Shih-ch'i, quietly retired, and Chang Tsung-ch'ang took his post on 7 May 1925, arriving with his harem and his feared White Russian soldiers. Making his presence felt at once, he declared martial law. Soon, because of his policies, the economic and social life of Tsinan was seriously disrupted. During the first six months of Chang's governorship, Tsinan's schools stood closed because they didn't have enough money to operate, even though Chang had established seven new commercial taxes. Commerce slowed because Chang closed the Tsingtao-Tsinan railroad to regular traffic in order to use it to deploy his troops around the province.[60]

Chang Tsung-ch'ang would not tolerate antiforeign activities and halted the anti-Japanese and anti-British demonstrations after the May Thirtieth incident in Shanghai by imposing heavy penalties on nationalist demonstrators. He also quickly installed his own appointees in the government offices in Tsinan.† Chang closed down the Shantung Bank run by

---

*Chang Shu-yuan, Ma Liang, and T'ang K'o-san, all associated with Tuan Ch'i-jui and the Anfu clique, lived in Tsingtao after being forced to leave Tsinan during the May Fourth period, and were often named in these plots.

†Chang naturally insisted that the Fifth Division take up duty outside Shantung. The transfer in May 1925 ended the influence of this military unit, founded by Yüan Shih-k'ai, that had played such an important role in the political and social history of Tsinan since 1899.

Chang Chao-ch'üan, opened his own Shantung Provincial Bank, and printed huge amounts of unsupported paper money. The ease and speed with which Chang Tsung-ch'ang dealt with the most powerful commercial institution in Tsinan is indicative of the relative power of the warlord and the Shantung commercial interests in the mid-1920s. And this was only the beginning.

By the winter of 1927-1928, conditions in Shantung had become appalling. A correspondent of the *North China Herald*, after surveying the recently flooded district of Lin-ch'ing, remarked, "Emigration to Manchuria seems to be the only remedy for the poverty stricken people of this province."[61] In addition to the floods in the northeast, military operations in the southern part of the province had ruined crops and interrupted harvests. Around Tsinan in the summer of 1927 there was a serious drought and a plague of locusts that extended northwest from the city across a large portion of Shantung and Chihli. The British consul in Tsinan estimated that in the spring of 1928 3.7 million people in Shantung had been left destitute by the winter famine.[62]

These conditions created an unusual winter migration to Manchuria. Instead of returning home from Manchuria, as many emigrants did annually, more peasants fled there. With seaports closed by ice and winter weather, most of the winter emigrants went by rail. Thousands flocked to Tsinan and other rail centers in Shantung, Honan, and Chihli, where they established squatters' villages outside the city or crowded into sheltered spaces along the city's walls while awaiting trains.

The British consul J. N. Affleck described the scene: "Everyday at the Tsinan railway station long queues of emigrants may be seen waiting at the ticket office—men, women, and children—struggling to get away from an impossible existence. A commotion was caused one morning when it was discovered that numbers of these wretched people had been supplied by some imposter with bogus railway tickets . . . ; the offender was, however, detected and shot."[63] It was estimated that over a million people left Shantung that winter for Manchuria.

By early 1928 most commerce and business in Tsinan had come to a halt, but this did not matter to Chang Tsung-ch'ang. With another season of campaigning ahead, he needed more money. He began to confiscate bank reserves outright, and a great many commercial interests simply closed their doors.

Chang's administration collected twenty-three different kinds of merchandise taxes in Tsinan, with ruinous effects on commerce. Even foreign companies like Asiatic Petroleum found it almost impossible to conduct trade in the city, while in the hinterlands Chang Tsung-ch'ang's troops raided large shipments of the British American Tobacco Company.

127

The exactions of soldiers and bandits had plagued the rural areas for several years, but in Tsinan in the winter of 1927-1928, robberies by off-duty soldiers became common.[64]

All of this was part of a pattern in which the warlord armies based in the cities not only destroyed urban commerce, but also broke the city's links with its hinterland, driving the peasants into the position of organizing their own self-defense units, resisting tax payments, fighting against conscription, and sometimes even establishing their own local administration as a defense against a warlord's rapacious rule from Tsinan.[65]

The history of Japanese imperialism in Shantung and the unhappy stories of warlord rule discussed in this chapter are much more than a recital of a dismal political history. The story of Japan's withdrawal from an open, armed imperialism of 1914 to the more subtle economic imperialism of the mid-1920s and the disruptive and debilitating rule of the warlords in Tsinan created a situation that clearly worked against any possibility of the city's ever achieving the Western form of urban industrial modernization. No matter how fast or how great the impetus to economic and social change in Tsinan, the forces of imperialism and militarism worked to undermine any gains that might be made. A major political goal for foreign governments—not only for Japan, but also for the other powers, including the United States—lay in retaining, and possibly expanding, their influence in the export trade, the internal transportation system, and the Chinese domestic trade in Shantung. Japan was the most significant power involved in these efforts, and this account has concentrated on showing how the Japanese efforts worked against control by the Chinese over trade and investment in their own country.

Warlord rule in Tsinan after Yüan Shih-k'ai was not only unpopular but also ineffective. Yüan at least had some claim to be a defender of Chinese nationalism against Japan and also possessed a vision of the direction in which China should develop. His successors lacked both his patriotism and his vision. Politicization of the Chinese people had not gone so far as to make it necessary for an administration to be both popular and effective. But lacking popular support, the series of warlord rulers in Tsinan also was marvelously ineffective. To a man they lacked any real conception of how Tsinan and Shantung should be ruled to protect the best interests of the populace. The only direction they possessed was protecting their own and their army's short-term political and financial well-being.

The next chapter takes a detailed look at the economic and social life of Tsinan in the 1916 to 1928 period. There the efforts of the Shantungese commercial and political leadership against both the warlords and the

Japanese will be the center of attention, but in this account of the political history we have already encountered key instances in which the Japanese and the warlords undermined the power of the progressive and modern-minded Shantungese who had prospered in both political and economic ways after 1900.

6

Economic and Social Life in Tsinan During the Warlord Era

BY 1916 THE COMBINED EFFORTS of foreign imperialists, Chinese officials, and Shantungese modernizers had already profoundly altered the economic and social life of Tsinan. Yet the city did not belong wholly to the modern world, even though it was no longer a typical high-walled city of late traditional China. A. G. Parker, an American professor of sociology at Shantung Christian University in Tsinan, tried to capture the unusual blend of old and new, Chinese and foreign, that characterized the city:

> In this city we find interwoven characteristics of ancient, medieval, and modern cities. The walls, the moat, and the narrow streets are characteristic of ancient and medieval cities; the trading center, the Guilds, and the family workshops are characteristic of medieval cities; and the railroads, the factories, the wider streets of the settlement, the schools, the lighting and telephone wires, and the settlement without a wall, are characteristic of the modern city.[1]

Class and cultural differences were present, but many diverse elements blended together to create the economic and social life of Tsinan. This hybrid life of Tsinan will now be examined in more detail.

TSINAN'S ECONOMY IN THE GOLDEN AGE OF CAPITALISM (1916-1923)

The brief flowering of Chinese capitalism during the First World War has often been assumed to be a product of the withdrawal of foreign competition.[2] For a few years from about 1916 through the early 1920s, Chinese industry and commerce did experience a period of great expansion and profitability that transformed many Chinese cities and towns, including Tsinan. In 1922 an American traveler passing through Tsinan observed, "The capital of Shantung Province announces itself by its smokestacks about the time the rumbling of the long German-built bridge across the Yellow River awakens the traveler to the fact that the day's ordeal is over. Flour-mills account for most of these spirals of smoke where ten or fifteen years ago little more than graves grew."[3]

It is true that the Europeans were forced to withdraw from many lines of the China trade because of their commitments to the European war, but it is still difficult to attribute the prosperity of Chinese business solely to this withdrawal. It is especially difficult in Shantung and in the city of Tsinan, where the degree of Japanese economic activity actually increased during the war years. The overseas trade in Shantung clearly did suffer from the war, but the chief lines of trade that prospered, including the flour mills mentioned in the comment quoted above, were closely connected to the domestic market. Consequently it seems reasonable to attribute the growth in Tsinan's economy more to the increased domestic trade, which continued to expand as a result of the railroad, rather than to any temporary competitive advantage the Chinese businessmen experienced because of the war.

In the case of the Japanese in Shantung, initially they were interested in exports from Shantung for the Japanese home economy and consequently did not compete seriously with Chinese entrepreneurial development, especially in products intended for the Chinese domestic market. After 1919, however, the Japanese in Tsingtao began to build factories intended to produce for the Chinese domestic market. At this point, Tsinan was badly hurt by Japanese competition.

In the mid-1920s the economic prosperity in China lost its bloom, and Chinese commercial and industrial interests encountered a host of unfavorable situations in the domestic and international economies. The events of the mid-1920s hit Tsinan especially hard. An economy already badly disrupted by Chang Tsung-ch'ang's rule was further weakened by the return of Tsingtao to Chinese administrative control. From 1900 until 1923, Chinese economic interests in Shantung preferred to do business in the Chinese-controlled seat of Chinese political power, Tsinan, rather than in foreign-controlled Tsingtao. When Tsingtao was free again, many Chinese firms, especially those from Tientsin and Shanghai, shifted their Shantung operations from Tsinan to the more convenient and more pleasant coastal city.[4]

From 1916 to 1925 Tsinan continued to collect and distribute commodities—chiefly food grains, cotton, and peanuts—for Shantung, southern Chihli, Shansi, and Honan. The secondary lines of trade included rural handicraft products such as silk, in all its semi-processed and finished forms, straw braid, and cotton cloth. Such traditional Shantung handicrafts as embroidery and lace work declined, largely as a result of changing Chinese fashions. Shifts in foreign taste also had a large impact on the handicraft market.[5]

Chinese merchants handled most of the trade in Tsinan. The foreign traders bought from these Chinese businessmen, often through agents sent from the foreign firm's headquarters in Tsingtao, Tientsin, or Shanghai. The Chinese merchants in Tsinan, as elsewhere in China, were organized into associations by place of origin. Shantungese merchants continued to dominate trade in Tsinan, and the most powerful Shantungese merchant associations—known as *pang* (clique or group)—represented various localities in the Ch'i region. Other kinds of guilds, both the *hui-kuan* associations of officials and merchants from outside Shantung, and common trade organizations (*hang*), also existed in Tsinan, but were much less important than the Shantungese *pang*. The older *hui-kuan*, such as the Shansi-Shensi or the Honan clubs, had declined markedly in power in the twentieth century. The important non-Shantung merchant elements in this

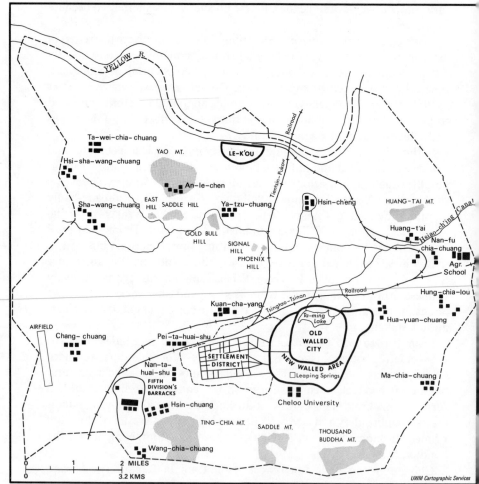

Map 3. Tsinan and its immediate hinterland, about 1928. (Based on Sun Pao-sheng, comp., *Li-ch'eng hsien hsiang-t'u tiao-ch'a lu* [Tsinan: Li-ch'eng hsien shih-yeh chu, 1928].)

period represented Shanghai, Tientsin, and Kwangtung, and those merchants also favored the more informal *pang* organization rather than the traditional and formally organized *hui-kuan* type of association.[6]

Within the Shantungese trading groups the four strongest had diversified interests. All four were involved in banking, the grain trade, and flour milling, three in various phases of the cloth trade, and two in the coal business. The activities of these four *pang* are summarized in Table 6.1. The home towns and cities of all four are located on the Hsiao-ch'ing Canal, the officially sponsored waterway built across the Ch'i region from the coast to Tsinan in the late 1890s. This suggests a relatively recent rise for these merchant groups, which apparently prospered with the expanding economy of the Ch'i region in the late nineteenth and early twentieth centuries.[7]

Banking has long been at the core of economic power, and banking in Tsinan was no exception. The banking business was still divided into modern and traditional forms, but the traditional Shansi banks which had handled interprovincial transfers had been largely replaced by the modern banks. Modern banks provided a full range of commercial banking services, including transfers of funds and commercial loans. Frequently these modern banks provided banking services to one branch of the provincial administration or another, and this business typically was essential to their existence in Tsinan. The traditional banking houses or *ch'ien-*

Table 6.1
Chief Shantungese Commercial Elements in Tsinan, Early 1920s

Trading Group	Business Interests[a]	Leaders
Chang-ch'iu	Banking, grain trade, coal mining and trade, flour milling, sericulture and silk embroidery, warehouses	Chang Chao-ch'üan
Li-ch'eng	Grain trade, public service industry, newspapers, banking, flour milling, cotton weaving	Ma Kuan-ho
Shou-kuang	Salt, banking, grain trade, coal trade, flour milling	Chang Lung-ts'ai
Huan-t'ai	Banking, grain trade, flour milling, cotton spinning (post-1930)	Miao Chi-ts'un and Mo Po-jen

Sources: Mishina Yoritada, *Kahoku minzoku kōgyō no hatten* (1942), quoted in Ch'en Chen, comp., *Chung-kuo chin-tai kung-yeh shih tzu-kiao* (Peking: San-lien shu-tien, 1958), 1:300-307; Oka Itaro, *Santō keizai jijō, Sainan o chu to shite* (Osaka, n.p., 1918), pp. 31-36; "New Industry at Tsinan," *Chinese Economic Monthly* 1.5 (May 1925): 12-17; Tsinan Intelligence Reports, 1919-1926, F.O. 228/3277.
[a]Listed in order of importance to the group in question.

133

chuang were much smaller-scale institutions which operated within a limited area—in Tsinan the *ch'ien chuang* represented primarily the Ch'i and the Tsinan's trading systems—with many fewer services than a modern commercial bank.[8]

The modern banks can be further subdivided into foreign banks, banks with official responsibilities, and private commercial banks (see Table

Table 6.2
Modern Banks in Tsinan, 1923

Bank	Rank by Volume of Business	Controlling Interest
Foreign banks		
Yokohama Specie Bank	—	Japanese government
Bank of Chosen	—	Japanese government
Bank of Taiwan	—	Japanese government
Bank of Tsinan	—	Japanese private interests
Official government banks		
National Government		
Bank of China	2	Communications clique
Bank of Communication	7	Communications clique
National Industrial Bank	6	Communications clique
Salt Industrial Bank	15	Salt administration
Frontier Bank	9	Tuan Ch'i-jui
Shantung Government		
Shantung Bank	1	Chang-ch'iu group
Commercial Bank of Shantung	5	Li-ch'eng group
Tung-lai Bank	3	Tsingtao group
Private commercial banks		
Shantung interests		
T'ung-hui Bank	4	Huan-t'ai group
Shantung Pawnbrokers Bank	10	Unknown
Shan-tso Bank	12	Huang *hsien* group
Tao-sun Bank	14	Shou-kuang group
T'ai-feng Bank	16	Huan-t'ai group
Chi-lu Bank	17	Li-ch'eng group (?)
Others		
Continental Bank	8	Tientsin
Shanghai Commerce &		Unknown
Savings Bank	11	
Sino-American Bank of Commerce	13	Unknown
Ming-hua Bank	18	Shanghai

Sources: "Banking and Currency in Tsinan," *Chinese Economic Monthy* 1.8 (August 1925): 23-28; Ho Ping-yin, ed., *Chung-kou shih-yeh chih, Shan-tung sheng* (Shanghai: Shih-yeh pu, kuo-chi mao-i chu, 1934), 8:1-8; Oka, *Santō keizai jijō*, p. 160; Sun Pao-sheng, comp., *Li-ch'eng hsiang-t'u tiao-ch'a lu* (Tsinan: Li-ch'eng hsien shih-yeh chu, 1928), pp. 160-61; H. G. H. Woodhead, ed., *China Yearbook 1921-1922* (London and Tientsin: Tientsin Times, 1912-39), pp. 317-19.

134

6.2). The Japanese had the only foreign banks in Tsinan after 1914; as mentioned in the previous chapter, the Yokohama Specie Bank (the official Japanese foreign trade bank), the Bank of Chosen, and the Bank of Taiwan (Japan's two main colonial banks) all had offices in the city. In addition there was a small Japanese-owned commercial bank, the Tsinan Bank (*Sainan ginkō*) that served the resident Japanese trading community.[9]

The Bank of China branch in Tsinan, the city's second largest bank, acted as the chief banking arm of the central government, and its managers became prominent as community leaders in Tsinan. The other official banks representing the central government did not have a large role in commercial business at Tsinan.*

The Shantung Bank had served as the official banking institution for the Shantung provincial administration since its founding in 1913. A product of the assertion of local power common in the first days of the new Republic, the Shantung Bank was a distinct departure from the traditional means of handling provincial finances. Chang Chao-ch'üan, the canny moderate business and political leader from Chang-ch'iu, controlled the bank from 1913 to 1925, when Chang Tsung-ch'ang forced it out of business. The Shantung Bank was extremely powerful within Shantung because it handled most of the province's ordinary tax remittances through a network of ten branch offices that included Tientsin and Shanghai. The bank's notes circulated widely in Tsinan and Shantung.[10]

Chang Chao-ch'üan was a representative leader of the new merchant power that was found in Tsinan in the early twentieth century. His presidency of the Shantung Bank was only one episode in a long and influential career in Tsinan. Chang was associated with the Chang-ch'iu trading group and maintained his ties with them by serving as chairman of the Native Bankers Association (*Ch'ien-yeh kung-hui*). This was a group of bankers, most of them from Shantung, who had broken away from the older native banking guild dominated by Shansi interests, the Fu-te *hui-kuan*. Chang Chao-ch'üan also served as president of the Tsinan and the Shantung chambers of commerce, as a provincial assemblyman, and as a member of the National Parliament. Appointed provincial finance commissioner in 1920-1921, he tried to cut spending and control graft in order to solve the serious financial problem then facing Shantung. He lost the commissionership in 1921 because of differences with the Chihli clique over tax policies. The warlords feared Chang's type of honest administra-

---

*Ch'ang Mien-chai, head of Tsinan branch during the May Fourth incident, was the leading business backer of the boycott (Chang Chih-lieh et al., "Kuan-yu Shan-tung hsüeh-sheng wu-ssu yun-tung ti-hui-i," *Shan-tung sheng-chih tzu-liao* 2 [1959]: 21). Yüan Ta-ch'i, manager in 1914, was a member of the *kung-min tang* group at Tsinan (Yeh Ch'un-ch'ih, ed., *Chi-nan chih-nan* [Tsinan: Ta-tung jih-pao, 1914], p. 44).

tion, for it would lessen their control over the province's revenues. The split between Chang Chao-ch'üan and T'ien Chung-yü, in this particular instance, is an important example of the deep differences between merchants and warlords that marked the years after Yüan Shih-k'ai's death, just as Yüan's opposition to the increasing power of local interests had characterized his sixteen years of power in Shantung. In spite of this defeat, Chang remained an important figure in Tsinan's political life. At the time of Tsingtao's retrocession he became an investor in the Sino-Japanese Lu-ta Company, which was to control the former German mining interests.[11]*

The type of local merchant interests represented by Chang Chao-chüan is distinct from the kind of official and comprador cooperation exemplified by Yüan Shih-k'ai and Liu En-chu in Tsinan, as well as quite different from the kind of bureaucratic capitalism represented by Chin Yun-p'eng and P'an Fu. These merchants as a group were seldom if ever in serious conflict with prevailing sentiments among the older gentry elements, but were still more progressive than the gentry. They shared with the gentry a hope that China would develop a strongly local representative polity which would place the government in their control and enable them to use it to advance their commercial and industrial interests. These local commercial interests were the heart of the Chinese bourgeoisie.

Another important bank with official connections was the Commercial Bank of Shantung (*Shan-tung shih-yeh yin-hang*), organized in 1915 by Ma Kuan-ho. Ma Kuan-ho, a leading entrepreneur from the eastern coastal district of Jih-chao, favored investment in franchised public service industries, including official newspapers, electric utilities, and telephone and bus companies. Although Ma's home was on the coast, he had close ties with the Li-ch'eng trading group. In the early 1920s he was reputed to be more powerful than most officials in Tsinan. Ma was less nationalistic than Chang Chao-ch'üan.[12]

The third official Shantung bank was the Tung-lai Bank, organized in Tsingtao in 1918. The bank remained a small operation until Tsingtao was returned to Chinese administration in 1923, at which time it became the principal bank handling Tsingtao taxes. The main office of the Tung-lai Bank was located at Tsingtao. The manager of the Tsinan branch, Yü Yüeh-hsi, became an important figure in the temporary administration of the city after the Tsinan incident of May 1928. The Tung-lai Bank had connections with Tientsin financial circles.[13]

*How deeply involved with the Japanese Chang Chao-ch'üan became I have not been able to discover, but throughout most of his career he hewed closely to nationalistic political positions, certainly much more so than any of the Shantung members of the Anfu clique.

Among the private commercial banks in operation in Tsinan, the T'ung-hui Bank warrants special comment. This bank was not particularly large but was controlled by Mo Po-jen and Miao Chi-ts'un, the leaders of the Huan-t'ai group in Tsinan. This trading group was the newest in Tsinan, appearing around 1914. Nothing is known about the Mo family, but the Miao family derived from a wealthy landowning clan in Huan-t'ai *hsien* at the market town of So-chen, the chief market of the district. At So-chen the Miao family had been engaged in the grain trade, oil pressing, and a Chinese apothecary shop. The family transferred part of its operation to Tsinan in the early Republic, and by the 1930s members of the family served as president of the Shantung chamber of commerce and as advisors to Han Fu-ch'ü.[14]

The traditionally organized sector of the Tsinan banking world remained quite powerful and important in the early 1920s. Some of these firms had as much capital as the small modern banks. In fact, the large traditional banks probably differed very little from the smaller modern banks. Finally, there was an association of merchants that engaged in banking as a sideline. These firms dealt primarily in grain and commodity trading, and had been drawn into banking through their credit arrangements.[15]

Until new laws were promulgated in 1923, the monetary situation in Tsinan was confused because all kinds of merchants could legally issue cash notes. Around 1920 over a thousand different varieties of notes circulated in Tsinan, the most widely accepted of which were those of the Yokohama Specie Bank and of the Shantung Bank.

The retail trade in Tsinan was still carried on by dozens of small outlets specializing in one or a few types of merchandise. For example, 261 shops dealt in Chinese handicraft cotton shoes, and 56 carried leather shoes. The 59 different printers in Tsinan managed to keep busy by publishing periodicals and books as well as printing all the different kinds of paper notes that circulated in the city.[16]

Tsinanese industry, like all Chinese industry, boomed between 1914 and 1921. A new cotton-spinning factory, new flour mills, a beet sugar mill, soap manufacturing, and other food-processing and household-necessity industries began operation (see Appendix A). Several features of the industrial scene deserve comment.

The story of Tsinan's Lu-feng cotton-spinning plant reveals a great deal about the locus of economic power in Tsinan. P'an Fu began promoting the plant as early as 1915 but could not organize it formally until 1917 when Chin Yun-p'eng and others associated with Tuan Ch'i-jui joined as backers. The plant, which used Japanese machinery, went into production

137

in 1919. To ensure the success of their operation, the backers obtained a franchise forbidding the establishment of any other cotton-spinning mills within a fifty-mile radius.[17]*

The cotton-spinning plant, the beet sugar plant and the paper mill accounted for more than 50 percent of the total capital invested in industry at this period. These operations all had several prominent political backers: backers of the beet sugar plant included Chin Yun-p'eng and P'an Fu, and among the backers of the paper factory was Ma Liang, the Tsinan defense commissioner. The obviously large role of bureaucratic capital in Tsinan[18] calls for some further explanation. In Republican China politically prominent men often lent their names to industrial and banking operations, and their reputations and influence helped establish the character of such projects. In most cases these men did not back their names with large capital commitments but in fact used such opportunities as means to build their own private fortunes. In these three cases, most of the officials (Chin Yun-p'eng, P'an Fu, Ma Liang) were so well known for their pro-Japanese sympathies that their involvement suggests that large sums of Japanese capital were involved in financing these projects. Since both their political and their economic interests were bound up in these operations, the official backers exercised considerable control over them. At the same time, some Chinese entrepreneurs who favored officially backed development (Ma Kuan-ho, Liu En-chu) also invested in this type of project. Unfortunately, it is seldom possible to get a clear picture of the intertwining of economics and politics, and Chinese and Japanese interests that lay behind the large industrial projects undertaken in Tsinan. Nonetheless, it is clear that the kind of capital we have been discussing—which I call "bureaucratic" because it obviously derives from the official-supervision, merchant-management (*kuan-tu shang-pan*) philosophy of late traditional China—dominated the sector of investment that would move in new directions.

Ordinary merchants typically kept their distance from such official involvements and concentrated on the lines of commerce most familiar to them. This characteristic is revealed clearly in the flour-milling industry in Tsinan. The city's ten flour mills represented 30 percent of the total industrial investment there and were the chief industrial undertaking of

---

*Such special monopoly production arrangements were common in Tsinan. The Yu-hsing dye manufacturing plant, owned by Tsung Liang-pi, who also owned Tsinan's match factory, had a similar arrangement. This device could not be used to restrict foreign competitors, who were free to ignore monopoly rights. Foreign companies, however, tried to gain monopoly privileges in order to exclude Chinese competition. As mentioned in Chapter 3, the German SBG had tried to stop Chinese miners from using modern machinery as early as 1903, and later the Japanese attempted to gain a monopoly on the sale of new grain-milling machinery during World War I.

the Shantungese commercial groups (*pang*). Table 6.3 lists the various mills that operated in Tsinan from 1914 through 1925. Most of the flour was consumed locally, but some also went to Japan, for from 1914 to 1921 China was a flour-exporting country.* During this period the mills regularly purchased new equipment to remain abreast of the competition.[19]

Table 6.3
Flour Mills in Tsinan, 1914-1925

Name	Capital (yuan)	Founded	Controlling Interests
Feng-nien	1,000,000	1913	Chang-ch'iu group
Chi-feng[a]	1,000,000	1916	Chi-ning group
Ch'eng-feng	1,000,000	1920	Huan-t'ai group; Miao family
Min-an	1,000,000	1920	Chi-ning group; Chang Huai-chih
Hui-feng	500,000	1917	Huan-t'ai group; Mo family
Hua-ch'ing	500,000	1920	Shou-kuang group
Hung-hsing	400,000	1920	Unknown
Mao-hsin	250,000	1916	Kiangsu interests
Cheng-li-hou	200,000	1920	Unknown
T'ung-feng	200,000	1923	Unknown

Sources: "New Industry at Tsinan," *Chinese Economic Monthly* 2.4 (January 1925): 13; Ho Ping-yin, ed., *Chung-kou shih-yeh chih, Shan-tung sheng* 4:421-40; Mishina, *Kahoku minzoku kōgyō no hatten*, in Ch'en Chen, comp., *Chung-kuo chin-tai kung-yeh shih tzu-liao* 1:301-5.

[a]Closed in 1925.

Price competition found little place in the Tsinan flour-milling business, however. When the Mao-hsing mill (backed by Kiangsu interests) first opened in Tsinan in 1916, it tried to sell its flour below the established prices in Tsinan. The other grain millers brought pressure on the newcomer, and soon its prices rose to accord with the administered prices of the other mills.[20]

The attraction of flour milling for Shantungese businessmen helps to explain the nature of the entrepreneurial interests in Tsinan. The mills' backers usually came from the powerful Shantung commercial groups (*pang*), all of which had close connections with the Tsinan grain market. Many members of these groups counted grain marketing among their primary interests, and they went into modern flour milling because they were involved in the traditional forms in this line of commerce. At the same time these wealthy people were very reluctant to risk their capital in unfamiliar new technological industries such as railroads and public utilities. In general these men also apparently shied away from officially

*Shantung province was exporting wheat even during the extensive famines in North China, 1919-1921.

sponsored projects, but it is not clear whether they feared the ineptness of politically influenced management or were just too conservative to enter into completely new fields.

Japanese industry concentrated at Tsingtao, but Tsinan did have some smaller Japanese-owned and operated factories. Two Japanese-owned match factories produced cheap matches of lower quality than those of Tsung Pi-hsing's Che-yeh factory; the Japanese-backed T'ung-feng Needle Company operated in Tsinan from 1920 to 1922. Other Japanese industrial interests were connected with export processing, as discussed in Chapter 5.[21]

LABOR IN TSINAN

Extensive recruitment of Shantungese for labor outside the province added a new aspect to the employment situation in Tsinan during the twentieth century. Emigration to Manchuria, recruitment for warlord armies, and the hiring of coolie battalions for foreign labor service had become regular features of the Shantung labor scene in the Republican era. Emigration to Manchuria had been under way on a large scale even in the late Ch'ing. This movement involved many Shantungese, especially from the peninsula, both as émigrés and as entrepreneurs promoting emigration. As late as 1923 Ch'i region representatives advanced a scheme in the provincial legislature to use several million *yuan* Shantungese tax monies to promote industry in Manchuria.[22] Accurate figures for the numbers of people who emigrated to Manchuria in these years do not exist, but probably more than ten million moved permanently in the years from 1900 to 1925.[23]

Recruitment for military service provided another outlet for young peasants with few prospects. At one time in 1921 eight different warlords and the Ministry of War in Peking were all recruiting within the province; enlistments were sometimes voluntary and sometimes forced. As noted earlier, these soldiers became a major problem in rural areas after their units disbanded and they tried to return to their home districts.[24]

Recruitment for overseas coolie service formed the third major outlet for Shantung labor in these years. With the passing of the Manchu dynasty, effective control over this outlet—often truly a kind of servitude—lessened. During World War I the British enrolled thousands of Shantungese for labor service in the European war. In one six-month period in 1917, 70,000 Shantungese left for Europe from along the Shantung railroad line.[25]

In 1924 Tsinan had a population of 300,000 (see Appendix B), with a work force numbering about 170,000 men, women, and children. Some of the women and children were employed in the factories but most worked in their homes, fashioning match boxes, weaving hairnets, or doing other kinds of work on the put-out system. Modern factories employed only about 10,000 of these workers, or about 5,600 men, 3,500 women, and 900 children. The Lu-feng Cotton Spinning Mill employed the most, with 3,000 workers, while the railroad repair facilities, the beet sugar factory, and the paper factory employed about 1,000 men each. Together, the flour mills gave work to 1,000 men. An estimated 30,000 people found employment in Tsinan's shops, while 15,000 worked as transport workers pulling rickshaws or carts—or, if they were well off, driving an animal-powered vehicle. Motor trucks were practically unknown.[26]

The majority of factory workers, including the men, lived at their place of work. The crowded and unsafe working and living conditions in the modern factories still were considerably better than prevailing standards for Chinese workers who worked in their homes in the city. Monthly factory wages varied from $2.00 for children to $20.00 for skilled men. In Tsinan during the mid-1920s, it cost $15.00 a month to support a family of five, or $7.50 for an adult living alone. The average factory wages ran about $7.50 per month. Rickshawmen or carters could earn from $10.00 to $18.00 a month in their exhausting work. Factory hours typically ranged from ten to fourteen hours a day, with fourteen by far the commoner figure. Those employed in their own homes and shops typically had to work even longer hours. Few shops closed even one day a week. Most employees, including the factory workers, received about fifteen holidays a year, following local custom for the chief celebrations of the Chinese calendar.[27]

The standards, both in terms of wages and working conditions, for the Chinese industrial labor force in Tsinan would be seen as highly exploitative from today's viewpoint. Yet the industrial laborers were less than 10 percent of Tsinan's total working force and their working conditions were usually superior both to those of the thousands of coolies and carters and to those of workers who did handicraft production in their own homes or small workshops. In addition, factory employees must have counted themselves lucky indeed when the rural poor converged on the city in the late winter months. Given the numbers of Tsinan's industrial labor force, the warlords' antipathy for any kind of popular organization, and the even more reactionary fears of most foreigners about "bolshevik" movements among Chinese workers, the attitudes of Chinese entrepreneurs who were even mildly understanding of Chinese working people's demands and problems must have seemed enlightened and benevolent by contrast. Certainly there is nothing to indicate that differences between capital and labor in any way checked the growth of Chinese industry in Tsinan.

141

Figure 5. New construction outside the P'u-li Gate in the 1920s. New two- and three-story buildings combined traditional and Western architectural styles. Rickshaws had joined the carts and occasional motor vehicles on Tsinan's streets. Compare this scene outside the walls with the old commercial street shown in Figure 2 and a street in the 1970s, shown in Figure 8. (Sketch by Bruce M. Buck, from a photograph in *Santō*

142

In Tsinan, the first signs of labor unrest were the result of organizing activities by the Marxist student groups who encouraged women match workers in the city's three factories (two Japanese-owned and one Chinese-owned) to strike for better working conditions and wages. The Chinese firm resumed operations rather quickly after meeting part of the women's demands. The strike against the Japanese firms proved more difficult, however, because the Japanese began hiring strikebreakers and eventually broke the workers' resistance. Boy workers in the Tsinan hairnet shops walked out in 1921 when their working hours were increased without additional pay. The Lu-feng Cotton Spinning Mill also was struck in early 1922, in a dispute that was settled by a sizable wage increase for the workers.[28] All of these signs of labor activity came during the height of student-fostered labor-organizing drives backed by both the Communist and the liberal student organizations. After the suppression of the Communist groups in particular, this impetus to worker's strikes slowed down. It should be noted, however, that, if Tsinan is typical, Chinese capitalists were more liberal toward their workers than were foreign employers, and that the first wave of strikes in 1921-1922 probably led Chinese employers to adopt still more liberal positions in order to undercut the labor unions.

Japanese interests in Shantung hated Chinese unionism of any sort. While the Japanese government controlled the Shantung railroad, they did not tolerate any kind of Chinese labor organization, and Japanese officials also defeated efforts to unionize the miners at the Tzu-ch'uan colliery in the Po-shan Valley.[29] Chinese officials also opposed the new-style unions, but looked more favorably upon associations of skilled laborers. In 1923 the masons and carpenters in Tsinan announced a 25 percent increase in their wages, and the provincial administration did not object. According to Chesneaux these "mixed associations" of masters and workers were typical of the years preceding the May Fourth period, but in Tsinan they continued to dominate labor organization through the 1920s. Such groups were encouraged precisely because their organizational principles blurred the class lines drawn by the labor unions and thus were more acceptable to all the powerful groups in Tsinan.[30]

The Shantung provincial administration suppressed labor-organizing activities among the workers on the Tientsin-Pukow railroad during the short period of intense organizing activity among Chinese railwaymen in 1922 and 1923. On the Tsingtao-Tsinan railroad, when the administration returned to Chinese hands, labor groups with names such as "Association of Worker Comrades" appeared. The first strike on the Tsingtao-Tsinan railroad developed out of labor rivalry between the Tsinanese and the Peking groups in 1923 over the issue of which city should supply workers on certain parts of the road and did not involve any economic issues. The strike issue challenged the Peking-appointed managers, and it produced a token change in management to include Tsinanese interests.[31] Consequently the strike represented a victory for local Tsinan solidarity between labor and management and shows how the proletarian, class-oriented organizing principles of the Marxist union movement had lost ground in that city.

ADMINISTRATION AND GOVERNMENT

Some of the most complete and revealing information on the history of Tsinan concerns the administration of the city, and from such data we can see rather clearly whose interests were best served by the prevailing system of government. The militarists, represented most often in Tsinan by the Anfu clique, occupied the top posts in the provincial, regional (*tao-yin* or circuit intendant), and local magistrate's offices. Although these militarists often assumed positions on political questions in opposition to the more patriotic Shantungese merchants, this latter group also derived great benefit from the pattern of administration in Tsinan, especially in the operation of the police, courts, schools, and philanthropy.

An organizational table of Tsinan's government would have showed the overlapping responsibilities characteristic of late traditional Chinese government, with new offices, sometimes carrying out significant modernizing programs, appearing at strange interstices in the already dense pattern of departments, bureaus, and offices. In the 1920s, aside from the administrative units of schools and the military, about fifty different official offices and yamens dotted the city. In general, the newer offices favored the settlement district, while the older ones remained inside the walled city. The public sector in Tsinan employed about 35,000 people, including those in the school system.[32]

The local offices of the national government in Peking constituted a significant modernizing influence in Tsinan. The Tientsin-Pukow railway was a government operation, with a staff of about a thousand skilled office personnel.* The Chinese post office was another large bureaucracy closely linked with Peking. Foreigners occupied the top administrative jobs in the postal system and at Tsinan administered the central postal facility for the entire province. The national salt administration and the Foreign Ministry also stationed representatives in Tsinan. Except in the foreign-administered post office, the central government usually appointed men to those offices who were acceptable to the military governors.

___

*The railway workers, as distinct from the administrative staff, were counted among the city's industrial labor force.

144

The military governor controlled the chief provincial offices—the civil governorship, and through that, the financial, educational, industrial, and police departments, the provincial procuratorship, and the provincial courts. He also controlled the positions of Chi-nan *tao-yin*, who supervised the affairs of eleven *hsien* in the Tsinan area, and Li-ch'eng *hsien* magistrate. Those two posts in turn controlled important offices connected with flood control, lower level courts, schools, and police in and around Tsinan. In addition, the military governor usually commanded the Fifth Division and appointed the Tsinan defense commissioner, who ordinarily was the commanding officer of a large brigade financed by the province. Both the Fifth Division, nominally a part of the central government's armies, and the Forty-seventh Mixed Brigade, the provincially financed unit, continued to be stationed at Tsinan, with a combined force of around 13,000 or 14,000 troops.[33]

The perennial problem of the provincial administration was money—keeping Shantung's finances patched together well enough so day-to-day operations could continue. Yüan Shih-k'ai's cutbacks of 1913 and 1914 had reduced spending, but after 1916 the warlord-dominated administration proved inept in financial management. Provincial budgets were a special kind of administrative fiction, for they rarely gave any figures for military expenditures and when they did, seriously understated the actual amounts the warlords spent on maintaining their military units. The announced 1922 provincial budget for Shantung (see Table 6.4) shows the same high dependency on land taxes and other land-derived income (81.3 percent) that had been characteristic of Ch'ing finances. Shantung continued to depend on land taxes into the 1930s when many other provinces had begun to depend somewhat more on commercial taxes.

Military expenditures probably amounted to two or three times those of the civil government, but accurate figures for military expenses seldom were announced. On the basis of the 1922 Shantung budget, the military would have had to support itself on 568,000 *yuan*, the 30 percent of the provincial revenues not committed to civil expenditures. In practice, however, this was only a small part of the total military expenses. The most important source of this money was the tax collected for the central government which the warlords could—and regularly did—simply keep. In addition, military expenditures were routinely concealed in the civil budget. In times of military crisis, when the warlords needed extra funds on short notice, they would openly appropriate civil budget monies to their own use and raise more by collecting taxes in advance and inventing extraordinary new taxes.[34]

The top officials in the various administrative levels in Tsinan do not measure up well as modernizers or even as enlightened representatives of

Table 6.4
Shantung Provincial Budget, 1922

	Amount (yuan)	Percentage
Receipts		
Land		
Land taxes	1,267,000	67.0
Rent	28,000	1.1
Land reclamation	199,000	10.6
Miscellaneous	48,000	2.6
	1,542,000	81.3
Consumer taxes and		
license fees	291,000	15.5
Other taxes	45,000	2.5
Extraordinary income	13,000	0.7
Total	1,891,000	100.0
Expenditures		
Administration	263,000	19.9
Finance	230,000	17.4
Education	741,000	56.0
Industry	89,000	6.7
Total	1,323,000	100.0
Surplus	568,000	

Source: Bertram Giles, Tsinan Intelligence Report, 3d Quarter 1921, F.O. 228/3277.

the traditional order. Most were minor military officers or bureaucrats connected with the Anfu clique, chosen more for their loyalties to Anfu interests than for intelligence, concern for public welfare, or administrative ability. Even if some had had ability, they probably could not have held their posts for very long, because the typical way of resolving any issue involving administration in Tsinan was to replace the administrator. At times the military governors sold the major offices for additional income. For example, during a period of financial stringency in 1921, the post of Chi-nan *tao-yin* was sold to a Kiangsu man for 50,000 *yuan*. [35]

Chin Kung, who held the post of Li-ch'eng *hsien* magistrate for five years from 1918 to 1923, became an exception to the rule of short-lived official appointees. Chin was the only important Tsinan official to survive the turmoil of the May Fourth period when the outburst of patriotic sentiment from students and merchants in Tsinan eventually toppled all the other important officials from the military governor on down. Chin managed to remain acceptable both to the Japanese and to the Shantungese community. Educated in Japan and married to a Japanese, Chin nevertheless earned the support of the Chinese business community because he favored Chinese business interests in any dispute involving foreigners. Chin's case clearly shows that support for the Chinese commercial interests in Tsinan could make a difference in a lower official's career.[36]

The areas in which the Shantungese commercial and landed interests had their greatest influence were education and philanthropy. Elsewhere I have discussed the development of education at length, pointing out how the educational system acquired an even stronger urban bias in these years, thereby pulling children and young people from all over the province to the city for their education.[37] In this maturation of a modern educational system in Tsinan, the old-style gentry control faded markedly around 1915 and was replaced by teachers trained in Western-style education schools and who demanded an increasingly strong voice in school administration by virtue of their professional and modern approach. These teachers followed educational trends set by the frankly modernizing national educational associations and their magazines. In the city's classroom the students studied a curriculum derived from Western educational practice, with strong doses of nationalism and liberal political philosophies, which contrasted sharply with the still largely traditional educational approach of rural schools.

Philanthropy shows the same changes. The gentry abandoned their traditional role as the financial supporters and managers of public institutions and turned over the financial backing of those operations to the government, while letting individuals with some claim to a modern or foreign approach assume administrative control of the city's poorhouses, widows' homes, and food kitchens. The Benevolence Association (*Kuang-jen shan-chü*), the powerful gentry society associated in the 1880s with anti-Christian activities, remained in existence in Tsinan after 1900. The society maintained and operated five public philanthropies: an orphanage, an old people's home, an assembly hall, a food kitchen, and a nursery. Various improvements were undertaken by the Benevolence Association in these operations after 1900; then, in 1917, the civil governor established a state-funded Office of Philanthropy that took over all the operations of the Benevolence Association.[38] This is only one of many cases in which the wealthy and powerful people in Tsinan and elsewhere were successful in having the Republican administration assume their traditional responsibilities.[39]

One of the most obvious ways in which Tsinan was accustomed to benefit was by spending more tax monies in the city than it contributed to the province's revenues. The combination of Anfu-clique militarists and Shantungese commercial and gentry elements cooperated to establish that practice as a regular feature of administration in Tsinan. A. G. Parker summed up the situation neatly:

There has been difficulty in discovering the sources of income for the government in Tsinan. Some of the taxes paid in the city are district or provincial taxes. The amount of money that is spent for the various government agencies in Tsinan is probably more than twice the amount that is collected in Tsinan, and the province has to support the city to that extent.[40]

The most fascinating new office in Tsinan was that of the police, who by the mid-1920s had evolved into the chief organ of urban administration. The police themselves drew support from the provincial, regional, *hsien*, and settlement district administrations, which all had some power to supervise police operations. With 1,750 men, the police in Tsinan handled the ordinary functions of several departments of urban administration. The organization and operation of Tsinan's police drew on Japanese models. The police issued building permits and inspected buildings, industries, street traffic, newspapers, theatres, amusements, markets, and slaughter houses. Thus, if any modern standards were to be followed in any of these areas, the police were responsible. A fire department of forty men came under the police, as did a health department that supervised street cleaning, nightsoil and garbage removal, and epidemic control. The police kept all vital statistics, including census records and household registers. In addition, they collected license fees for vehicles, boats, prostitutes, theatres, and amusements. Sixteen sub-stations located around the city coordinated all these functions in the individual neighborhoods.[41]

The structure of the schools, the police, the courts, even the tax system, favored the Chinese commercial interests in Tsinan. All of these features one would expect to find in a developing, bourgeois society. What is unusual about the situation is that more often than not the praetorian governors and the commercial interests found themselves in serious opposition. The need of the warlords to satisfy outside forces, both Chinese and foreign, was a major cause of these differences. Also important was the warlord's typically insatiable appetite for tax monies, which led them to undermine various cooperative schemes advanced by Chinese merchants interests in an effort to satisfy the warlords' needs without destroying the basis of commerce in the city. The warlords were always too badly in need of immediate funds, however, to undertake any longer range cooperative schemes. Moreover, these pressing demands often led the generals to impose highly unfavorable taxes on the Chinese merchants, which served only to further alienate them from warlord leadership.

In general it is clear that in the city of Tsinan in the post-1916 years there were many commercial interests—both the bureaucratic-capitalists and the more strictly commercial ones—who were willing to work with any

Chinese regime in Tsinan which would profit their own interests. The character of the warlords, however, caused this bourgeoisie to hold back from full support of the warlords, and in most cases the fears that generals would prove to be untrustworthy allies were more than justified.

The chief avenue by which the commercial and landed interests in Tsinan influenced the city's administration continued to be the representative institutions. By the late 1920s, formal elected bodies had disappeared and the chambers of commerce had become the most important of such representative bodies, even though they represented only the business community. The educational and agricultural associations and the provincial assembly had declined in importance after 1913. Indeed, the history of the assembly's failures in Tsinan, previously detailed, provides the best account of the difficulties besetting Shantungese politics in those years.

SOCIAL LIFE IN TSINAN

Tsinan had a population of about 300,000 in the mid-1920s. There was a marked increase in the density of population within the walled area and much building in the settlement district. Because Tsinan could offer safety from banditry, many rural people, and especially the wealthy, were moving into the city. The available population figures (see Appendix B) understate the city's growth, because its boundaries were redefined after 1900 to exclude many of the former suburbs. Information of population changes in the suburbs is not available, but because the poor could more readily find havens and support in these villages than in the city, it seems likely that the nearby rural population also increased rapidly during these years.

Unfortunately, Alexander Armstrong was not around in the 1920s to review the changes that had occurred in Tsinan's social structure since his characterization of the 1880s (see Chapter 2, pp. 36-37). Armstrong's categories, however, are useful in trying to understand the nature of social change in the city. Armstrong's first two categories, acting officials and retired or expectant officials, had undergone considerable modification, since no longer did Tsinan support large numbers of expectant officeholders from other provinces. Most of the officeholders were Shantungese or men who had had long careers of service in the city. Military men had become much more prominent, both in military and in general administrative roles, than in Armstrong's day. Retired officials, usually Shantungese, remained quite active. The category of expectant officials had disappeared, but the provincial assemblymen were their 1920s equivalent, for these elected representatives often advanced their careers by taking lucrative bureaucratic posts.

149

Armstrong's next three groups include the wealthy gentry, the middle class (consisting of doctors, teachers, priests, and merchants), and the skilled workmen. According to Marxist class analysis, these elements—the bourgeoisie and the petty bourgeoisie—are key factors in Republican China. In Mao Tse-tung's version of modern Chinese history, the flight of the wealthy gentry to the cities was a major cause of the proletariat's inability to organize there, for these feudal landlords, it is said, worked together with foreigners and with the Chinese bourgeoisie to suppress the proletariat.[42]

The fragmentary evidence on the location of wealthy Shantungese after 1900 seems to confirm Mao's conception of a gathering of wealth and power in the cities. These people came to the cities to conduct their increasingly commercial investments, obtain a modern education, or find a position suitable to their modern-style training. Cities like Tsinan were also safer than the countryside and offered comforts and diversions the villages lacked.

There is also evidence for a decline of gentry leadership in the countryside in the early 1920s. Officially sponsored schools there failed and in their place appeared schools that did not use the modern curriculum and therefore could not become part of the province's official school system, which was flourishing in Tsinan and other large cities. At the same time, disorder in the countryside was forcing villagers to band together for self-protection, not, however, as official militia but rather as groups with strong secret-society overtones. Inasmuch as the traditional gentry always sought official sanction for its activities, the absence of such connections for schools and for local police activities clearly reveals that the gentry was no longer as influential as it had formerly been.[43] Ramon Myers in his recent study of North China villages for this period concludes that beyond a point determined by the amount of available labor in the family, farm families invested any increase in wealth in commerce rather than in more agricultural land. As families advanced their fortunes, they came to concentrate their activities in market towns and administered their land on an absentee basis.[44]

The growth of Tsinan's commercial role drew large numbers of commercial men into the city. Leadership among these men did not remain in the hands of men who were originally from Tsinan, for all the powerful Shantung commercial figures represented groups (*pang*) from other parts of the province. Some of these merchants moved to Tsinan because of the relative safety of a larger city. For example, one small bank had originally been located in Chou-ts'un but had moved to Tsinan in 1916 after the depredations of the anti-Yüan army.[45]

150

Armstrong's doctor, teacher, and priest categories were still in evidence but had undergone a marked change. No longer were any of these lines dominate by men with traditional Chinese training and expertise. In the 1920s most of the city's teachers were products of the new normal schools, and more than a third of the licensed doctors had training in Western medicine.[46] These individuals represented a major shift in the cultural orientation of the city along the lines of Western-derived cultural forms and values.

Men belonging to Armstrong's classification of skilled workmen still remained, but the beginnings of industry had created an industrial working class separate from skilled craftsmen. The skilled craftsmen, especially where they still worked in shops with apprentices, maintained much of their traditional character and their traditional guild organizations. There were more than 3,500 shops in Tsinan, many of them businesses of skilled craftsmen.

Armstrong's final categories were servants, soldiers, laborers, and beggers. All had grown in absolute numbers in the intervening forty years. There are no available estimates on the numbers who fell into these categories, but the additional military units and the growth of transportation, commerce, and industry all required many new workers, so their relative importance in Tsinan's population probably increased somewhat.

Armstrong overlooked the petty bureaucrats and clerks in his original description. These functionaries remained at least as numerous in the 1920s as in the late nineteenth century. They were much less contented, though, for in the early Republican era they had suffered chronic financial shortages and arrears in salary payments.

Two significant elements of Tsinan's population appeared after 1900, and naturally are missing from Armstrong. One was the student class. The 12,000 primary school students were of course too young to play any political role, but the approximately 2,500 middle school students and the 1,200 students in institutions of higher learning were highly important.[47] Their activities in the May Fourth movement and afterwards made their impact much larger than their numbers. In marked contrast to the 1880s students who gathered in Tsinan only at examination time, the 1920s student class spent most of the year in the city and was a larger, more active, and strongly nationalistic force.

The other group that had increased rapidly were the foreigners. There were about 1,700 Japanese and 230 Europeans in Tsinan in the early 1920s. The missionaries, including their dependents, probably numbered about 150. In addition, foreign technical experts helped operate the railroads, the electric light company, and the telephone company. Like the students, they had far more influence on lifestyle, political power, and economic importance than their numbers would have indicated.[48]

The Americans had become the largest single group of Westerners in Tsinan, with seventy-five residents. A growing number of American missionaries came to Shantung during these years, both Protestants and Catholics, with the latter still headquartered in the village of Hung-chia-lou. The Protestant mission community developed a new center of activity in 1918 when Shantung Christian University (Cheloo) opened as a joint undertaking of twelve mission boards: five British, six American, and one Canadian. The school operated and granted degrees under a Canadian charter. Much of the money for the school's physical plant was given by Mrs. Cyrus H. McCormick, widow of the International Harvester Company's founder. R. G. Luce, the father of Henry Luce, was responsible for obtaining the McCormick gift. In 1924 Cheloo University had an annual operating budget of $315,000, and a staff of 51 foreign and 24 Chinese faculty members,[49] and 330 students. The school incorporated the pre-existing medical school and the Whitewright Museum. Another large Protestant program connected with students was the YMCA. The "Y" had opened in Tsinan in 1913 and moved to larger quarters in the settlement in 1924.[50]

In spite of the growing warlordism in China after Yüan Shih-k'ai's death, those years were remarkably free from armed violence in Tsinan. Until Chang Tsung-ch'ang's troops took over in May 1925, there had been few problems with the behavior of uniformed men in the city. While Tsinan lived in relative peace, banditry increased in the countryside. Many bandits were former soldiers who had been recruited by warlords and then returned to Shantung for disbandment without any prospects for work. These men operated in rural districts removed from the regular billets of Chinese or Japanese military units. Nevertheless, robberies, burglaries, and armed attacks occasionally occurred in the walled city and settlement areas.[51]

Tsinan was a favorite spot for bandit gangs to take their leisure—one notorious band came to town and took over a brothel for a few days of relaxation before returning to the countryside for more robbery and kidnapping. Bandits also came into Tsinan to buy arms, ammunition, and other supplies, and to get medical help when they needed it. Much of the trade with the bandits, in the hands of foreigners, could not be adequately controlled by the Chinese authorities.[52]

Not all lawbreakers visited Tsinan of their own volition, for the chief provincial courts there tried criminals from all over the province. Executions, held on a special field near police headquarters, continued to be a major public spectacle. Severed heads of criminals and pillories with offenders locked into them were still common sights near the inner wall's main gate.[53]

Life in Tsinan, of course, had its more genteel side. The foreign community, bolstered by the staff of the new missionary university, formed a literary society that presented lectures and concerts. This foreign culture remained separate from the tastes of many wealthy and educated Chinese who preferred traditional Chinese forms of poetry, history, gambling, and theatre.

The foreigners created a social organization called the Tsinanfu Club in the style of colonialist clubs elsewhere in Asia. In 1923 a Chinese club along the same lines was formed for wealthy and privileged Chinese of the city. The Chinese theatre, with its special Shantung forms of songs, continued to be a great popular entertainment. Chiang Ch'ing, the wife of Mao Tse-tung, is said to have begun her theatrical career in Tsinan. There were also several movie theatres in the city.[54]

The major civic problems in Tsinan were the control of opium and prostitution. Opium and its derivatives were a great social difficulty in the city. Although little opium was grown in Shantung (most of it came from Manchuria or other provinces), these drugs could be obtained and consumed on the premises of many hotels, houses, and bars operated by Chinese and foreigners alike. Up until 1918 the Japanese and Koreans were usually blamed for the spread of the opium trade; but when White Russian refugees appeared in the city, they acquired the same sort of reputation.[55]

Opium sales were difficult to control because foreigners involved in the trade could use extraterritoriality to avoid Chinese law. In addition, the police, usually five to six months behind in receiving their pay, were open to bribery; even judges and other court officials in Tsinan were involved in the opium trade as users or dealers. Several pharmacies in the city processed opium as a sideline.[56]

A. G. Parker found 1,080 prostitutes operating from 530 registered houses in 1923. Entertainers and prostitutes were subject to social stigma in the sense that they could rarely expect to marry respectable men or even become the concubines of wealthy or powerful figures. Yet, because most Chinese women lived highly restricted social lives in their own courtyards, the young women were a center of social activity among Tsinan's residents. The highest class of female entertainer was represented by singers in the Shantung *"ta-ku"* style. Typically one or two young women entertainers worked together under the supervision of an older woman. The more common prostitutes lived in groups in houses. Once opened, the settlement district became a favorite spot for such business. Girls were sold into prostitution by impoverished families. Drug usage was standard among prostitutes and their guests. In fact, brothels were a major source of drug sales, including the newly popular morphia introduced into Tsinan by the Japanese and Koreans.[57]

Flood and famine were major problems in Shantung during the early 1920s. In the fall of 1921 after the heaviest rains in forty years, thirty *hsien* reported flooding. The most seriously affected regions lay to the west of Tsinan where the Grand Canal joins the Yellow River, and to the east in Li-ching *hsien*. In Li-ching, near the Gulf of Chihli, a 6,000-foot break in the bank of the Yellow River left 200,000 people homeless, and the breach was not closed for a year. Although the water came to the top of the dikes where the Yellow River passed Tsinan, no serious flooding occurred inside the city.[58]

Serious conditions prevailed west of Tsinan in 1920-1922, the years of the great North China famine. Both Chinese and foreign relief groups undertook extensive relief measures. A common form of relief during these years was employment of people on public work projects, especially road construction, in return for food. Although there were some roads in the Tsinan area built as relief projects, much of the construction was done closer to famine areas in northwestern Shantung.[59]

Tsinan's variety of social problems demonstrates an intriguing continuity with the situation in the late nineteenth-century. Increased commercial activity and the introduction of a small industrial sector had not produced the new set of social problems typically associated with Western urban-industrial society. Tsinan's vices—opium and prostitution—were old vices, and its main problems—floods, famines, and refugees—old problems, familiar in traditional Chinese society.

Certain new social issues, associated with Western urban-industrial life, did surface in Tsinan, but these did not attract the interest that the more familiar problems did. For example, there were efforts at prison reform, improving women's rights, licensing physicians, and even at controlling child labor in factories. Predictably, these efforts produced meager results, while attention was focused, as before, on traditional social problems.

Only a few new public services in Tsinan started operation during these years. A public waterworks was discussed and a company was formed under Chang Chao-ch'üan, but the city continued to rely upon natural springs for its water until the 1930s. Long-distance telephone service connecting Tsinan with Tsingtao began in mid-1925. At Tsinan the telephone company had about three thousand subscribers in 1922 and kept purchasing more modern equipment.[60]

154

For a short while in 1921 airmail service from Peking and Shanghai was attempted, but it proved too costly, both in terms of planes and of pilots, to be continued. Less spectacular developments in postal services continued, including a large new main building, and the establishment of seven branch stations in the city. The post office building, constructed in 1920 with a 100-foot brick tower, its own electrical generator, and a steam heating plant, was the most modern building in the city.[61]

The entire commercial settlement grew rapidly during the war years, and by 1917 all available land in the original boundaries was in use. A new section, which added about one-third to the total settlement, was opened in 1919. The settlement had many two-story brick buildings and some three-story structures, the largest and most imposing of which were occupied by consulates, banks, and foreign trading firms.

Housing in the older section of the city featured cut stone in the lower sections of the walls and local brick at heights above a meter, with tile roofs. Poorer houses were constructed of sun-dried adobe brick with thatched roofs, and the poorest people resided in small lean-tos built in the city's alleyways.[62]

SUMMARY

The period from 1914 until the arrival of Chang Tsung-ch'ang in May 1925 represents the golden years of the emerging Chinese bourgeois urban culture in Tsinan. During these years, foreign influence proved especially strong, but still Tsinan's culture reflected a combination of foreign and traditional influences. The commercial interests, along with the professionals whose very careers derived from Western practices, set the tone of the new culture among the Chinese, but these groups always lacked the political power to shape the situation in Tsinan to their demands. Although they managed to resist the most compromising of the Japanese proposals for Shantung, they still proved unable to completely win back Shantung's economic rights for themselves and other Chinese business interests. The same Shantungese interests became deeply involved in provincial and national politics but lost out there to the Anfu clique; so the golden years were marked by political weakness for the Shantungese interests. Tsinan was to enter a third, markedly different era when the Kuomintang finally assumed power in the city. That story is taken up in the next chapter.

7

Tsinan in the Decade of Kuomintang Rule, 1927-1937

IN THE FALL OF 1927, elements of Chiang Kai-shek's armies entered southern Shantung and the flight of Chang Tsung-ch'ang appeared imminent. The internal differences within the Kuomintang between the Left Kuomintang government at Wuhan and the more conservative wing in the Lower Yangtze Valley under Chiang led to the postponement of the assault on Shantung. Thus, Chang Tsung-ch'ang received a short reprieve and his rule in Tsinan continued until May 1928. Tsinan and Shantung had already experienced two years of economic disruption and administrative chaos, and after 1927 three more years passed before Shantung once again enjoyed stable government and civil order. In the interim, Tsinan was to suffer more destruction than at any other time in the nineteenth and twentieth centuries. The situation in most of the other parts of Shantung was equally bad, what with widespread banditry, looting by troops, poor harvests, floods and famine—conditions reminiscent of the 1850s and 1860s.

The Kuomintang's difficulties in establishing control in Tsinan and Shantung after 1927 had two aspects, one a problem of internal rivalries in the Kuomintang coalition, the other, and more important one, a question of relations with Japan.* In the case of Tsinan, the important internal rivalries in the Kuomintang involve disputes between Chiang Kai-shek's followers and progressive warlords—especially Feng Yü-hsiang and Yen Hsi-shan—who supported Chiang Kai-shek's wing of the Northern Expedition in 1928 after he had broken with the Communists and the Left Kuomintang. First, let us turn to problems with Japan.

*Recent research on national integration under the Kuomintang blames internal politics for the failure to create a single unified nation. See T'ien Hung-mao, *Government and Politics in Kuomintang China, 1927-1937* (Stanford: Stanford University Press, 1972), and Robert A. Kapp, *Szechwan and the Chinese Republic: Provincial Militarism and Central Power, 1911-1938* (New Haven: Yale University Press, 1973). In the case of Shantung, however, relations with Japan outweigh the internal factors in the Kuomintang's limited capacity to integrate that province, as well as other parts of North China, into a single national federation under the firm control of a Kuomintang government at Nanking.

THE TSINAN INCIDENT, MAY 1928

When the Wakatsuki cabinet fell in April 1927 and Foreign Minister Shidehara lost his post, Japan's China policy changed. Shidehara's diplomacy combined economic imperialism with international cooperation. These ideas had formed the basis for the Japanese position at the Washington Conference and the subsequent return of Tsingtao to Chinese control. Shidehara had become identified with a China policy that would permit China to regain her sovereign rights, including tariff autonomy, in return for permission for Japanese interests to pursue trade, industry, and investment.

Many power elements in Japanese politics—including the army, some elder political figures, and certain business and intellectual circles—felt this approach unduly subordinated Japanese national interests to those of the Anglo-American partners. They insisted that Japan should assert special rights and interests in China and Manchuria, as she had done between 1914 and 1921.[1] The new cabinet in Tokyo, headed by Tanaka Giichi, was composed of Shidehara's opponents. Tanaka, himself an army general who deeply believed in traditional Japanese values, saw Shidehara's diplomacy as a betrayal of those values and proposed that Japan adopt a "positive policy" to protect her position in Asia. Tanaka considered Japan's special rights in Manchuria as the most basic of her interests.

The Tanaka policy toward China forms a critical chapter in modern Chinese history, for, in facing Japan's wishes in 1927-1929, Chiang Kai-shek had to deal for the first time with assertive Japanese military expansionism. Similar Japanese military adventurism was to produce the Manchurian incident in 1931 and the China incident of 1936. In all three cases Chiang proved unable to stop Japanese aggression.

Trouble between the Kuomintang and the Japanese surfaced in 1927 during the first campaign of the Northern Expedition when Kuomintang troops found several occasions to insult and injure foreigners in Chinese cities. In spite of these antiforeign incidents in Canton, Wuhan, Nanking, and elsewhere, Chiang Kai-shek himself clearly was associated with a policy which sought to combine an assertive political nationalism with a realistic course of accommodation with foreign economic interests. This was especially true after the split between Chiang Kai-shek and the Left Kuomintang government at Wuhan. By the spring of 1928 when Chiang resumed the Northern Expedition, the Kuomintang policy toward foreigners had been greatly moderated. In other words, Chiang plainly intended to avoid serious differences with the established economic interests of Great Britain, the United States, Japan and the rest of the foreign powers.

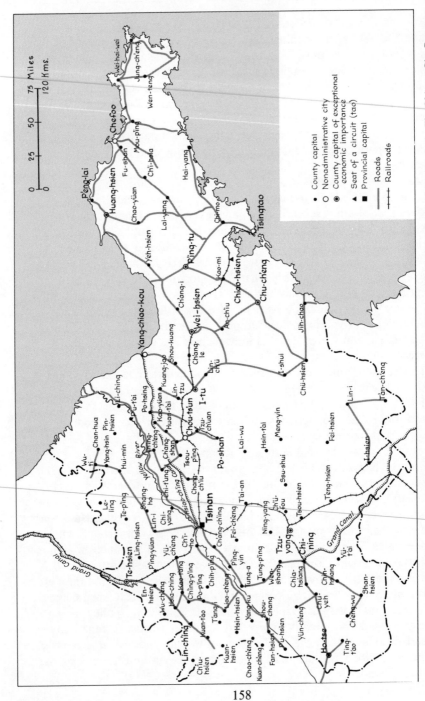

Map 4. Shantung in the 1930s. (Reprinted from "Educational Modernization in Tsinan, 1899-1937," by David D. Buck, in *The Chinese City Between Two Worlds*, edited by Mark Elvin and G. William Skinner, with the permission of the publishers, Stanford University Press. © 1974 by the Board of Trustees of the Leland Stanford Junior University.)

Legend:
- County capital
- Nonadministrative city
- County capital of exceptional economic importance
- Seat of a circuit (tao)
- Provincial capital
- Roads
- Railroads

Scale: 0 25 50 75 Miles / 0 120 Kms.

158

Chiang's approach would have worked with the Japanese if they had continued to follow the Shidehara policy toward China. The new Tanaka posture, however, clashed with Chiang's position, for Tanaka's "positive policy" was intolerant toward expressions of political nationalism by the new Kuomintang government and in particular was adamant that Manchuria should not be integrated into any Chinese state. All the foreign governments had diplomats who had many trying moments in the late 1920s accommodating themselves to this new assertive Chinese nationalism, but only the Japanese resisted so strenuously as to create serious military and diplomatic incidents.

In the fall of 1927 when the possibility of the Kuomintang armies reaching Tsinan was quite real, Tanaka sent Japanese troops to Tsingtao and Tsinan. The Kuomintang offensive halted, but the danger of conflict between Tokyo and the new Nanking government looked so serious that Chiang Kai-shek went to Japan to see Prime Minister Tanaka. Tanaka told Chiang that Japan's position in Manchuria must not be threatened by the military drive to unite China politically; Chiang insisted that all of China, including Manchuria, be politically unified under his rule.[2] Tanaka tried to convince Chiang that the Kuomintang government had enough power—and enough problems—in the Lower Yangtze Valley. Chiang rejected this attempt to territorially limit his regime just as he rebuffed other foreigners who later suggested something less than a "one-China" policy to him.

Behind Tanaka's policy lay a perception of the Kuomintang as a regional power; this view came to be the dominant Japanese conception of the Kuomintang in the 1930s. Much of Japanese thinking about China, especially that of military leaders, makes sense only when one accepts their conception that Chiang Kai-shek was merely the strongest warlord in a country not yet capable of national unity. This kind of thinking, which eventually produced the categorization of Shantung as part of a North China region, led Japan into a series of encroachments on Chinese territory in the 1930s.[3]

Failing to come to terms with Tanaka, Chiang returned to China to resume his military drive for unification. In February 1928 representatives of Chiang Kai-shek and his new allies—Feng Yü-hsiang and Yen Hsi-shan—met to plan their strategy against the northern warlord armies. Chiang's units planned to move northward along the Tientsin-Pukow railroad in March, while Feng Yü-hsiang's forces were to divide their efforts between Chihli and Shantung.[4]

The opposing northern armies, as the group of warlords under the leadership of the Manchurian warlord Chang Tso-lin are ordinarily called, also had undergone extensive reorganization during the winter of

1927-1928. Sun Ch'uan-fang assumed primary responsibility for the defense of Shantung, for his generalship and armies were superior to those of Chang Tsung-ch'ang. Chang's army listed 100,000 soldiers, but his troop roster was no more reliable than his paper money. Chang garrisoned Tsinan and protected the Tsingtao-Tsinan railroad while Sun Ch'uan-fang took up positions between Chi-ning and Hsu-chou against the coming Kuomintang offensive.[5]

According to plan, the Nanking government's forces began their expedition anew in March with a coordinated offensive of Chiang Kai-shek's and Feng Yü-hsiang's armies. On 21 April Chi-ning fell, and three days later the worried northern leaders held a conference at Tsinan. P'an Fu, the Shantungese premier of Chang Tso-lin's Peking government, attended the meeting. Afterwards, Sun Ch'uan-fang began to withdraw towards Tientsin along the Tientsin-Pukow railroad, while Chang Tsung-ch'ang made for the coast and flight to Manchuria along the Tsingtao-Tsinan railway.[6] Shantung was falling into the hands of the Kuomintang coalition, and the various armies were converging on Tsinan, the place where the Kuomintang armies could most quickly and conveniently cross the Yellow River and continue their pursuit northward toward Tientsin and Peking.*

At this juncture, Prime Minister Tanaka proceeded to act on his previously stated intention to send Japanese troops to Tsinan, as he had the previous year, if the situation demanded protection for Japanese lives and property. Tanaka had spoken frequently in the spring of 1928 of the need for Japan to act positively to protect her interests in China. In regard to Shantung, he had justified Japanese intervention there in January 1928 with a revealing statement about Japanese concerns in the province,† "It is

*Many accounts of the ensuing clash between the Japanese and Kuomintang troops at Tsinan suggest that the Kuomintang armies might have avoided Tsinan or even that Japanese Prime Minister Tanaka thought Chiang Kai-shek had agreed to bypass that city. This seems highly unlikely because bypassing Tsinan would have required the Kuomintang to exchange a quick and easy crossing to the Yellow River by means of the bridge at Tsinan for an inconvenient ferrying of the armies by boat. In addition, the Kuomintang pursuit along both main lines of communication, the Tientsin-Pukow and the Tsingtao-Tsinan railways, would have been slowed. Bypassing Tsinan also would have left the chief political and administrative center of the province in Japanese hands and would have required Chiang Kai-shek to abandon his position of nationalistic assertion of Chinese sovereignty at Japan's loud public request. All these reasons made it inevitable that Chiang Kai-shek's armies would take Tsinan. See Akira Iriye, *After Imperialism, The Search for a New Order in the Far East, 1921-1931* (Cambridge: Havard University Press, 1965), pp. 193-98.

†The occasion of Tanaka's speech was the dissolution of the Diet for a general election. Tanaka's party, the Seiyukai, was hoping to be returned, but the election looked close; therefore, Tanaka made an appeal to his opponent's constituency by emphasizing Japanese financial interests. Tanaka retained his premiership in the election and did not alter his China policy, although appeals to economic interest never again received such important emphasis in his remarks.

simply inevitable that *in the event of Chinese authorities disregarding their Treasury obligations* and giving inefficient protection to the lives and property of foreigners, we should take self-defense steps if necessary" (emphasis added).[7] This particular formulation of Japan's desires is interesting because it reveals Japanese concern over the Tsingtao-Tsinan railroad. Japan, it will be remembered, held ¥40,000,000 Treasury notes of the Peking government for the return of that railroad to Chinese control. Tanaka's reference to "Treasury obligations" was intended to indicate that Japan would not allow the new Nanking government to repudiate these obligations or other outstanding financial debts. Thus, although Tanaka publicly spoke of protecting Japanese lives, his actions came at a time when Japanese government financial interests might have been compromised by the new Kuomintang government.

On 19 April the Japanese government dispatched 300 men to Tsinan from the Japanese garrison at Tientsin and announced that they would be reinforced from Japan by a 5,000-man brigade to be sent from Japan via Tsingtao. The next day the Japanese Foreign Ministry sent a note to both the Nanking and Peking governments justifying Japan's actions on grounds of protecting Japanese lives and investments.[8] The first elements of troops from the Japanese home islands commanded by General Fukuda Hikosuke arrived at Tsingtao on 27 April. The general issued a circular that again reveals the importance of the Shantung railroad in Japanese policy,

> The Japanese government declares that the Tsingtao-Tsinan railway is essential to the [Japanese] economic enterprises in Shantung and therefore it is directly and closely related to the interests of the Japanese people in the province. If any party should cut off communication thereof, or do some other damage to it, Japanese troops would think it necessary to proceed immediately to take steps of prevention.[9]

As General Fukuda's units advanced toward Tsinan along the railroad from Tsingtao, he found that units of Kuomintang troops had cut the line in two places and blockaded it at two other points. These actions on the railway in defiance of Japan's stated position appear to be the trigger to the ensuing aggressive action taken by General Fukuda in Tsinan.[10]

On 30 April the last units of the retreating northern armies had dynamited the Yellow River bridge as they withdrew. The spans did not collapse, but train service was halted. Thousands of Nanking's advancing troops poured into Tsinan—including both units from the armies of Feng Yü-hsiang and Chiang Kai-shek. The condition of the bridge prevented further pursuit of the northern armies, and consequently there were more than forty thousand Chinese troops in Tsinan on the night of 2/3 May. Chiang Kai-shek himself arrived early in the morning of 2 May and made public statements against any disturbances by Kuomintang forces.[11] The purpose of these statements was to assure the Japanese that their publicly expressed concern for their citizens' safety was fully appreciated by Chiang and that Japanese troops were not necessary in Tsinan.

That same afternoon Chiang met with the Japanese consul Nishida Kōichi and the senior Japanese military officer—at that point a Colonel Koizumi who commanded the 300-man detachment from Tientsin which was the first Japanese military unit to arrive in Tsinan. Colonel Koizumi agreed to remove the barricades the Japanese had established in the commercial district. Chiang assumed full responsibility for maintaining law and order, but Japanese military units continued to guard Japanese offices and homes.[12]

Some hours after these agreements were reached, General Fukuda arrived from Tsingtao with some of his troops and became the senior Japanese officer present. Although the Chinese and Japanese generals and diplomats were in contact on the morning of 3 May when some looting by Chinese troops occurred around 9:30, General Fukuda did not consult with Chiang but took direct action.[13] Japanese troops began firing on the Kuomintang soldiers and the Tsinan incident had begun.

The ensuing first round of fighting lasted until 5 May. The Japanese resumed control of the commercial district, while the Kuomintang units retreated within the walled city. The Japanese suffered twenty-five casualties, while the Chinese estimated one thousand men lost during these three days of fighting. On 5 May General Fukuda and Chiang Kai-shek agreed to a cease-fire and the withdrawal of Kuomintang troops from Tsinan. On the morning of 6 May Chiang and his armies withdrew southward toward T'ai-an, where a new Kuomintang regime in Shantung was established.[14]

Although most of the Kuomintang troops withdrew from Tsinan, Chiang Kai-shek, in his own account given in a speech delivered at the Central Military Academy on the first anniversary of the incident, stated that he felt it was necessary to leave some troops in Tsinan in order to forestall the claims of the Japanese that their occupation was justified because the Kuomintang was incapable of maintaining order. Chiang left Tsinan realizing that General Fukuda would probably carry out additional attacks on the small Tsinan garrison, but he told the Kuomintang commanders that China's national honor had required these sacrifices.[15]

On 7 May, after two thousand fresh Japanese troops arrived in Tsinan, General Fukuda presented a surrender ultimatum to the Kuomintang units inside the city walls. Although General Fukuda claimed to have acted after Chinese provocations, there is no evidence to support this contention; in fact, he acted unilaterally without authorization from either military or civilian authorities in Japan for a second assault at Tsinan.[16] His was the first in a long chain of unauthorized attacks by Japanese military commanders in China.

162

The second phase of the Tsinan incident began on 8 May with heavy shelling of the walled city by Japanese artillery. The combination of aircraft, artillery, armored cars, and superior troop strength gave the Japanese total military dominance at Tsinan. In the next four days several gates of the city's two walls were destroyed. Damage to buildings, including both the main public service operations and many private residences, was extensive. Once the Japanese had attacked, Chiang Kai-shek gave his approval for withdrawal of the Kuomintang troops. On 10 May the Kuomintang commanders, Li Yen-nien and Su Tsung-ch'e, marched out of the city but were ambushed along their line of retreat by Japanese units. Finally on 11 May the local Tsinan chamber of commerce arranged a cease-fire. The Japanese announced 150 casualties in this second round of fighting, while the Chinese losses were put at 3,000 killed, with no indication of the numbers wounded.[17]

The Tsinan incident was a clear case of Japanese military provocation. The Kuomintang forces had nothing to gain by fighting with the Japanese at Tsinan, and all the evidence points toward the willingness of Chiang Kai-shek and his subordinates to make every possible compromise in order to keep the peace once they occupied Tsinan. Satisfactory arrangements for settling disputes between the Japanese and the Chinese existed on 3 May when the first round of fighting broke out, but General Fukuda simply ignored those procedures. The second round was an even more blatant example of Japanese military provocation. In spite of these Japanese actions at Tsinan, the Chinese received no real diplomatic recompense and, in fact, settled on terms quite favorable to the Japanese.

The cease-fire terms remained in effect for a year, from May 1928 to May 1929, and the Japanese retained control over the Tsingtao-Tsinan railroad and continued to occupy Tsinan. Japanese presence in the city delayed Chiang Kai-shek's efforts to drive the remnants of Chang Tsung-ch'ang's armies out of eastern Shantung. By the time an understanding was reached with Japan, Chiang had run into difficulties with Feng Yü-hsiang over who would control the Shantung province.*

*Nanking and Tokyo reached agreement on the chief issues in the Tsinan incident in February 1929 but delayed the signing of an agreement and the withdrawal of Japanese forces because of requests from the Nanking representatives. The full text of the Sino-Japanese agreement signed on 26 March 1929 involved Japanese withdrawal from Shantung and Chinese assumption of responsibility for the safety of Japanese nationals in Shantung. It has long been assumed that the same series of negotiations between C. T. Wang and Yoshizawa Kenichi, the Japanese Minister, involved basic understandings on tariff autonomy and the Japanese position in Manchuria. The Nanking position emerged in these discussions as a moderate nationalist one that could accommodate itself to continued Japanese domination in Manchuria.

Feng wanted to control Shantung as part of the personal satrapy in North China he felt was his due. The Nanking government hoped to include Shantung in the list of provinces that they controlled without relying on powerful military commanders. Consequently they asked the Japanese to leave slowly, to help Nanking buy time for more maneuvers against Feng.[18]

Faith in the Kuomintang and Chiang Kai-shek had not been high in Shantung since the 1916 anti-Yüan expedition in which Chiang had participated and which had received extensive Japanese assistance. In 1927-1929, Chiang had opposed the Japanese, but his leadership produced a situation that resulted in open warfare in Tsinan and completely disrupted the ordinary pattern of civil authority throughout the province, leaving a highly chaotic situation. In these circumstances the Kuomintang gained little new support in Shantung and Tsinan.

THE SITUATION IN TSINAN DURING 1928-1929

The Chinese chamber of commerce served as the chief liaison with the Japanese military units that garrisoned the city. After the chamber had arranged the cease-fire, the man who had served as police chief under Chang Tsung-ch'ang returned to his post in order to restore order in Tsinan. By the beginning of June, looting in the walled city had been stopped, and most businesses could reopen their doors.

The interruption of trade, however, had produced serious dislocations in Tsinan's trading area. Handicraft cotton weavers in northwestern Shantung had no cotton yarn to weave with and thus no cloth to sell. The Tientsin-Pukow railroad was out of commission north of Tsinan, both roadbed and rolling stock having suffered extensive damage during the campaign. A failure of the harvest in northern portions of the province produced a serious famine in the fall of 1929. In Tsinan's immediate area banditry was rife and many of the outlying market towns, including Chou-ts'un and Chang-ch'iu, were attacked by bandit units. In Tsinan itself many businesses failed, including both trading firms and retail merchants.[19]

The local Tsinan commercial community managed to administer both the walled city and the commercial district in Tsinan satisfactorily during the period from May 1928 until the departure of the Japanese in May 1929, but in doing so inevitably compromised itself as a tool of the Japanese in the eyes of the Kuomintang stalwarts who had formed an administration at T'ai-an. The stigma on the Tsinan business community was probably unwarranted, for their position was forced upon them by Nanking. Nevertheless, it did not help relations between the young nationalistic Kuomintang members who held important provincial posts in the 1930s and the established commercial leadership of the city.

164

Meanwhile the Kuomintang administration at T'ai-an was a disappointment to everyone. The *China Weekly Review* commented half a year after the Tsinan incident: "What the civil and military officials have done for Shantung [since establishing themselves at T'ai-an in May 1928] is rather a tale of what they have not done, a record of non-achievement that outstrips all records set by the former warlords who preceded them."[20]

THE ADMINISTRATION OF HAN FU-CH'Ü

As Japan prepared to withdraw from Shantung in the spring of 1929, Chiang Kai-shek and Feng Yü-hsiang quarreled over who should rule the province. Feng thought he should, and, in fact, one of Feng's subordinates, Sun Lien-chung, had held titular control of the province since the Tsinan incident. Sun's jurisdiction was limited, however, to the area west of the Tientsin-Pukow railroad. In the eastern and mountain sections, various commanders, local elements, and the Japanese exercised actual control.

By late April 1929 the differences between Chiang Kai-shek and Feng Yü-hsiang seemed to be so serious that a conflict between their armies was widely rumored. Just as a battle between Chiang and Feng appeared unavoidable, two of Feng's commanders—Han Fu-ch'ü and Shih Yu-san—defected to Nanking's side. Feng's biographer has remarked, "Observers then and since have unanimously ascribed these defections to bribery on an enormous scale . . . . These defections stunned Feng Yü-hsiang. Indeed, they might be considered the most important event in Feng's career."[21] On 10 September 1930 Han Fu-ch'ü was rewarded for his support by being appointed chairman of the Shantung provincial administration.[22]

Han's assumption of the chairmanship brought to an end two and a half years of political uncertainty that followed the Tsinan incident. Only under Han's leadership did the provincial administration begin to function again on a regular basis. Han proved to be a popular and effective governor throughout his six-year tenure, the longest period of coherent policy in Shantung since Yüan Shih-k'ai. He was, however, a staunchly independent man who had his own ideas on how to run Shantung and would not follow Kuomintang policies. His administration was staffed with military men loyal to him in key civil and military posts, together with a sprinkling of college-educated officials, and was marked by a stability of officeholders in Tsinan at the top ranks of the provincial government. Many of his appointees had been associates during Han's years with Feng Yü-hsiang; several relatives also received important jobs. However, at the lower levels of the Shantung administration—for example, *hsien* magistrate—a rapid turnover occurred.[23]

Han Fu-ch'ü held an unfavorable opinion of Sun Yat-sen, whom he believed to have been too strongly influenced by Western and Marxist thinking. Consequently he tried to limit the spread of Sun's ideas, even in the non-Marxist forms sanctified by the Kuomintang. Han only tolerated the Kuomintang and tried to undercut the party's authority wherever possible. The most outspoken Kuomintang activist in Tsinan in the 1930s was Chang Wei-ts'un, chairman of Kuomintang operations in Shantung. Chang was assassinated in Tsinan on 2 January 1935 and rumors implicated Han Fu-ch'ü.[24] Naturally, no place existed in Han's circle of advisors for military men associated with Chiang Kai-shek. Throughout his tenure in Shantung, Han acted as if he were essentially an equal of Chiang Kai-shek, only somewhat less powerful.

In a speech delivered in 1933, Han described his administration's approach: "Shantung is but a broken bowl which I am doing my best to mend. I shall always place the welfare of the people above everything else. If a thing is for the good of the people I will do it, otherwise I will not . . . even though planes and bombs are overhead."[25] Han's conception of how to mend the province of Shantung was influenced deeply by the traditional model of a good official. As chairman, Han regularly toured the province to review his subordinates' work. On these circuits he praised worthy magistrates and summarily punished backsliders. In Tsinan, Han made a practice of hearing personally some of the regular court cases. He cultivated a public image as a frugal, hardworking, morally upright individual.[26] The result was considerable popular support from representatives of various classes and regions within Shantung. Foreign visitors also were favorably impressed with Han's leadership. Henry Luce, after a meeting in Tsinan during 1933, termed Han a "rising star" in the Chinese political scene.[27]

One example of the conservative approach to reconstruction Han favored is found in the provincial financial administration. Shantung's finances had been in an almost continuous state of crisis since the first days of the Republic. Han changed that by appointing Wang Hsiang-jung, a subordinate who had been working with him for twenty years, to the post of financial commissioner. Wang proceeded to reestablish the pre-existing tax structure. Innovations were not important, and no new major sources of revenue were sought. The program cannot be described as a reform, because irregular collections at the local level—often important to the local officials and wealthy interests—were not prohibited. Wang also put off the issue of a new land survey, which might have apportioned the tax burden more equitably, with a greater share falling on the large landowners. Instead Wang, following traditional Chinese fiscal wisdom, concentrated simply on collecting and remitting the full amount of regular land taxes.[28]

Within a year of his assuming the chairmanship, Han resumed regular tax payments to Nanking and sustained them throughout his tenure. Within the province, the chaos of Chang Tsung-ch'ang's financial regime came to an end, and a new provincial bank with new currency was created to mark the change. By the mid-1930s Wang had established an efficient and regular tax system and financial administration. Of course, Shantung was more heavily dependent upon traditional tax collections from land taxes than any other province in China: 63.9 percent of the Shantung provincial revenues from 1930 to 1936 were derived from land taxes, as compared with an average for all provinces of 36 percent.[29] This dependence upon land tax by Han's administration was caused in part by Nanking's direct control over the province's two other good sources of revenue—the port of Tsingtao and the Tsingtao-Tsinan railroad. Under the arrangements established in the wake of the Tsinan incident, Nanking administered these two rich plums directly without any intervention from Han Fu-ch'ü.

In line with his conservative views, Han was deeply committed to reconstruction of social bonds in China's villages. While he was provincial chairman in Honan during 1929-1930, Han had begun a rural reconstruction program with the aid of Liang Sou-ming, a respected conservative Confucian thinker. Liang believed that revitalized traditional relationships in the countryside would permit the Chinese to resolve the great economic, political, and social problems they faced. When Han moved to Shantung, he continued to support Liang Sou-ming. He also urged Nanking to undertake such programs and frequently admonished the Shantung gentry to undertake a bold role in these projects.[30]

The main reconstruction efforts in Shantung centered at Tsou-p'ing *hsien*, in the Ch'i region, and at Ts'ao-chou in the Lu region. In both instances Liang sought to use traditional village leadership to begin new programs in literacy, school standardization, crop improvement, and equitable marketing arrangements. The programs succeeded reasonably well in those districts but especially well in Tsou-p'ing. Liang Sou-ming believed he had established a viable means to reform that should be applied on a wider scale. Han certainly was willing but he lacked both the resources and the time to implement a broader province-wide program.

Although there is not sufficient space to evaluate Liang Sou-ming's rural reconstruction program in detail, it should be noted that the program was an important conservative alternative in the debate over how China should deal with her rural crisis. In contrast to the plans tried by the

Kuomintang, Liang's approach did not attempt to insert a new entity, the political party, as the major element in the local political process. This is the great difference between rural reconstruction in Shantung and efforts directed by the Kuomintang in Kiangsi and Chekiang.[31] Both Liang's program and that of the Kuomintang sought to build on the traditional socio-economic relationships in the countryside. The Kuomintang tried to harness those forces in its own service; Liang was content to see them reorganized and functioning once again. The third approach, and the one that was ultimately applied throughout China, was that of Mao Tse-tung, which destroyed the existing socio-political leadership in the countryside and substituted a new leadership under the guidance of the Chinese Communist party.

Liang Sou-ming's program contributed to Han Fu-ch'ü's reputation as a successful reform governor whose efforts at rural reconstruction could compare favorably with those of anyone in China, including Chiang Kai-shek. Han won the support of many Chinese leaders, especially those conservatives from North China who distrusted Chiang Kai-shek as a radical militarist innovator operating under the mantle of Sun Yat-sen's inadequate political philosophy.

In other aspects of internal administration Han also stressed reestablishing old networks and then improving them, by undertaking road construction, canal building, and telegraph and telephone line extensions. For example, he supported the reopening and modernization of the Hsiao-ch'ing Canal, which had been one of the first modernization projects undertaken in Shantung. Here he was acting to revitalize an established transportation link important to many of the powerful Ch'i region commercial interests. Yet he opposed too-rapid industrialization.[32]

The overall direction of Han Fu-ch'ü's plans for Shantung was not highly favorable to commercial and industrial interests. Reliance on traditional land taxes reduced the opportunities for tax farming, and Han's banking arrangements placed fiscal soundness far above any considerations of the profitability of trade and industry for the Chinese bourgeoise. By the standards of the late nineteenth century, Han's approach was liberal; but by the standards of the 1930s, with the rapidly growing commercial and industrial power of Chinese interests in other large Chinese cities, it was decidedly conservative. A true Chinese conservative, Han feared the adverse social effects of industrialization and hoped to return Chinese society to its old pathways.

Even Han's own administration did not uniformly follow his predilection for improving the rural infrastructure and reasserting traditional rural leadership. For example, Han's educational commissioner was young, American-educated Ho Ssu-yuan, a member of the

Kuomintang. Ho's record as head of the school system reveals that he favored education in the large urban areas. Tsinan retained its place as the center of modern education, with the best schools, teachers, and facilities in the province. Ho made great efforts to improve the city's elementary and secondary schools, staffing them with graduates of modern normal schools. Tsinan schools also had a large number of teachers who were members of the Kuomintang.[33]

These apparent inroads by the Kuomintang did not seem to bother Han Fu-ch'ü; he trusted his young commissioner because Ho always balanced adherence to Kuomintang policy with careful cultivation of equally strong ties among the conservative gentry leadership in Shantung. Han also was more tolerant of such new ideas in cities like Tsinan, but in the countryside he followed Liang Sou-ming, who looked askance at the Kuomintang's urban bias as inadequate to the task of transforming China's rural masses. Ho Ssu-yuan followed Han's wishes by not insisting on implementing the modern, Kuomintang-shaped new curricula in Shantung's rural schools.[34]

Han Fu-ch'ü's differences with Chiang Kai-shek were not confined to the ideological issues but extended to practical political questions as well. These differences ultimately led to Han's death, but in the first rounds, Han frequently bettered Chiang. Han Fu-ch'ü's Third Group Army, composed of three divisions and a brigade commanded and staffed by loyal officers, was not the only army in Shantung. Two former subordinates of Feng Yü-hsiang—Ma Hung-k'uei and Sun Lien-chung—also remained in the province with large numbers of troops, while Liu Chen-nien, a former subordinate of Chang Tsung-ch'ang, continued to garrison the Shantung peninsula after 1930.[35]

Chiang Kai-shek had reason to fear three former armies of Feng Yü-hsiang—led by Han Fu-ch'ü, Ma Hung-k'uei, and Sun Lien-chung—all operating in the same area; they were too much of an invitation to Feng to resume his meddling in North China. Consequently, Han Fu-ch'ü received Nanking's support in an effort to have Ma Hung-k'uei's Fifteenth Route Army and Sun Lien-chung's Twenty-sixth Route Army transferred outside Shantung. The problem of Liu Chen-nien was different, however, for Liu had gone over to the Nanking side during the 1928 campaign and had been promised continuing support for his independent satrapy on the Shantung peninsula. Initially, Liu Chen-nien controlled the Chefoo region without interference from the Kuomintang, but in the fall of 1929 he permitted representatives of Nanking to take over tax administration and to establish party offices.[36]

Han Fu-ch'ü objected to Liu's independence and hoped to extend his own power into the peninsula area. Nanking's policies seemed to offer him no openings, but in 1932 a dispute over finances gave Han an opportunity.

169

Even though Han Fu-ch'ü had resumed tax remittances from Shantung to Nanking as a result of his financial program, he was startled to find that Nanking no longer gave his Third Route Army its full former monthly subsidies.[37] Han protested against this reduction in his budget, but Nanking would not restore the cuts. From evidence at the time and later, this action by Nanking authorities sealed Han's disenchantment with Chiang Kai-shek. Han finally worked out a deal with Nanking whereby he received about 80 percent of his former allotments, but he was still unhappy. He felt he could right these wrongs if he withheld funds from Liu Chen-nien. When Liu objected, Han set in motion a confrontation that he used to destroy Liu Chen-nien's power in eastern Shantung.

In the fall of 1932 Han Fu-ch'ü's armies suddenly took the field against Liu Chen-nien. Chiang Kai-shek sent Chiang Po-ch'eng, a Chekiang man who handled Chiang's personal liasion with Han, to see if the assault on Liu could be stopped. Han refused, and sent his own favorite go-between, Chang Yüeh, back to explain the situation to Chiang. As the offensive developed, Nanking tried to transfer out of Tsinan all munitions available in the local arsenal. Han managed to stop the munitions train and continue his campaign but was profoundly angered by this effort to stop his offensive. Finally a truce was arranged and Chiang Kai-shek agreed to remove Liu Chen-nien's troops to Chekiang. The vacated area came under the control of Han Fu-ch'ü's administration, giving Han complete control of the province.*

The significance of the incident, however, lies in the altered character of the relationship between Han and Chiang. Han Fu-ch'ü felt he had reached understandings with Chiang on revenue matters and learned only after resuming remittances to Nanking that Chiang's commitments to others took precedence over these understandings. In other words, a deal with Chiang Kai-shek was no better than what Chiang's deals with others would allow. Chiang often used this technique of making contradictory arrangements with two or more parties and living up to the terms most advantageous to his own position. Later, when Han Fu-ch'ü found himself caught between the demands of Nanking and the Japanese, his distrust of Chiang Kai-shek was a major element in formulating his position.

TSINAN UNDER HAN FU-CH'Ü

Today, the times of Liu E [who wrote *The Travels of Lao Ts'an*] are several decades past. Tsinan has been colored by modernization and has progressed a great deal. Nevertheless, the basic character has not changed much from Liu E's

---

*In Chekiang, Liu's army was first stationed at Wenchou. One unit went over to Communist forces in the area, and Liu himself was executed after a trial in Nanch'ang during 1935.

description: a festive city that is both a commercial center and political pillar, which in its vanity has not yet cast off the air of the late Ch'ing.[38]

The author of this characterization was expressing more than a nostalgia for Tsinan's past. The new foreign trade, the foreign-style buildings, the factories, the telephones, newspapers, state-operated schools, and new-style armies still did not add up to a modern urban community. Beneath the many evidences of change, older forces, only somewhat altered, continued to operate.

The mandarins in long gowns were largely gone from the yamens, for Han Fu-ch'ü decreed that his officials wear the simple, unadorned Chung-shan-style uniforms. Yet even Han himself often dressed in long gowns of the traditional scholar-official. The air of the yamen was much the same as in the late Ch'ing. Han ruled in the manner of a traditional benevolent autocratic official. He consulted with men of substance and learning in forming his policies, but once policies were formed, allowed no dispute of them. The hand of the government was not light but it did attempt to be just. In legal matters Han favored simple, clear laws rigorously applied.[39]

The population of Tsinan had grown to 427,000 by 1933, a growth rate of better than 3 percent since 1919 (Appendix B). There were about three hundred Europeans and some two thousand Japanese residents of the city—not even enough to dominate the character of the settlement district. The larger buildings and biggest firms in the settlement were run on foreign lines, but most of the people living in the settlement were Chinese. Most of their dwellings and their businesses were run along traditional lines. The typical residence of the city dweller still was dark, with a dirt floor, a straw roof, no running water, and outside communal toilet facilities.[40]

Visitors remarked that Tsinan, even though it was the most important city between Nanking and Tientsin, still had the air of a market town about it. Country people, selling their handicraft wares and buying necessities, filled the streets. Crowds of poor refugees camped around the city after floods or in late winter after a poor fall harvest. A few large international transactions in wheat or cotton might take place in the high-ceilinged office of a foreign-style bank, but Tsinan's crowded streets and dirty barrowmen still left in visitors' minds the impression of a medieval or country market town.[41]

Edgar Snow called Tsinan "barrow city" because of the thousands of traditional transport workers who swarmed around the railroad yards and warehouses in 1929. Motor transport could not compete with the low charges, long hours of service, and almost infinite flexibility the thousands of carters and barrowmen provided. In 1933 there were no trucks and only twenty-five buses operating around Tsinan. Each bus—consisting of a body constructed in Tsinan shops placed on an American truck chassis—held fifteen passengers.[42]

Still, Tsinan did continue to adopt modern forms and make them workable, as it had during other periods of tranquility. The most important innovation was the establishment of a regular city administration, under Wen Cheng-lieh as mayor. Wen was assisted by a chief of police, a public works officer, a financial officer, and an educational officer. Each of these men ran departments staffed by regularly paid public servants. The police remained the major arm of the civil administration, with a wide range of duties. In the more traditional lines of police control, they licensed gambling and prostitution, although they could not completely eradicate those social problems. Drugs were even more difficult to control, partly because so many of the people involved in the trade were Japanese and Koreans not under Chinese legal jurisdiction.[43] Han Fu-ch'ü, however, supported suppression of the opium and morphia trade, in spite of Japanese pressure against over-zealous anti-opium policies.

The most noticeable success in public works was the removal of the city gates damaged in the Tsinan incident. Paved motor roads running through the gate openings improved access to the city, and all the main through-fares in the walled city were paved. Most side streets and lanes, however, could still accommodate only carts and barrows. The main city wall was left intact and extensively repaired. Atop the wall was built a pathway suitable for pedestrians, and wide enough for a touring car.

The city's public works department also took over the private Tsinan Electric Company when it failed in 1934 after several years of unsatisfactory service. Since the company operated an unregulated monopoly, it is not clear why the management could not establish a profitable rate structure or obtain the necessary bank financing to replace their ancient generators. The troubles in the electric company had gone on for several years, and it seems obvious that private capital wanted little part of such investments in the 1930s. Consequently, the city's public works office acquired the company and bought new equipment from the Japanese. Another public works project that had originally been proposed as a privately owned monopoly was a water system using the flow from the Leaping Springs. This, too, became a government-owned project in the 1930s, and work began in 1936, again with Japanese engineering help and equipment.[44]

These two examples of the Tsinan city administration taking over public service industries reveals the beginning of an important shift in Tsinan. In the previous quarter-century new public facilities had been constructed, either through cooperation between officials and Chinese comprador capital or by bureaucratic capitalists. After 1930 large capital investment projects were no longer undertaken by comprador capitalists or by bureaucratic capitalists, but came instead into the hands of the government in Tsinan. This trend toward state capitalism began under Han Fu-ch'ü, accelerated under the Japanese, and was not reversed during the short postwar rule of the Kuomintang. Consequently, in 1949 the Communists, in establishing their rule in Tsinan, found practically all of the public service facilities plus many of the industrial factories in the city already in official hands.

Under the vigorous leadership of Ho Ssu-yuan the Tsinan educational system enlarged and improved. Since the best primary and secondary schools in the province were located in the city, many wealthy families from rural areas sent their children into the city for their schooling. Cheloo University remained in operation, although it suffered some administrative difficulties when Nanking required that all missionary schools be headed by Chinese.[45]

The pace of change in Tsinan remained slow, in part because Han Fu-ch'ü, as already mentioned, opposed rapid industrialization. A good measure of the restricted pace of change at Tsinan can be obtained by contrasting that city with Tsingtao. Tsingtao emerged in the 1930s as a center of light industry, with manufactures including cotton textiles, grain milling, tanning, chemicals, and food processing. Its population grew from 275,000 in 1925 to 452,000 in 1934.[46]

At Tsingtao Japanese investment became dominant,* especially the cotton textile business. The 15,000 Japanese residing in the city worked for Japanese banks, shipping firms, and factories. The harbor was filled with Japanese vessels. Japanese owned only 48 of the 181 factories in Tsingtao in 1931, but these 48 firms employed two-thirds of the industrial labor force. Many visitors felt that Tsingtao was still a Japanese city, even though it had been returned to China in 1923.

A Chinese naval officer named Shen Hung-lieh served as mayor of Tsingtao. Shen was able to maintain excellent relations with the Japanese, the northern warlord elements, and Nanking, all at once. Under his administration Tsingtao contributed more to Nanking's finances than it cost to maintain, and consequently Shen's stock remained high in Nanking throughout the 1930s.[47]

Tsingtao was also regarded as a demilitarized city, which meant that neither the Chinese nor the Japanese stationed any significant military

---

*Chinese capital, with bureaucratic and warlord connections, played a secondary role in Tsingtao. A primary source of such investment was the retired warlords and bureaucrats who favored treaty-port life because they found a safe, well-ordered existence beyond the control of their Chinese enemies. A pleasant coastal climate added to Tsingtao's attractions.

forces there. Thus the Japanese could move their troops ashore at Tsingtao at any time without major opposition. This knowledge encouraged additional Japanese industrial investments and reassured Tokyo about the safety of the Tsingtao-Tsinan railroad.

Han Fu-ch'ü kept his military units scattered around the province, with one division in the Wei *hsien* area, but no closer to Tsingtao. Some of the best units were kept in Tsinan, where they helped maintain civil order. Because Han was a military man, he assigned to military officers and troop units many functions usually carried out by civilians. Han's army had its own newspaper, *Kung-yen t'ung-hsün pao* (The Public Information Report), available to the troops and to the public.[48]

The army also was the major force behind Han Fu-ch'ü's personal program for improving public morality. In 1932 Han Fu-ch'ü created the *Chin-te hui* (Improve Virtue Society) and required both civilian officials and military officers to attend its meetings. The society promoted such practices as regular calisthenics for all government workers. The most prominent of the *Chin-te hui*'s efforts was a public park in the settlement district, offering harmless amusements or character-building events in contrast to the various forms of relaxation found in the nearby *ta-kuan-yuan* (High Officials Garden), a center of teahouses and theatre.[49]

The *Chin-te hui* was similar in conception and organization to the New Life Movement later established by Nanking, which predictably never gained official or popular support in Shantung. Han Fu-ch'ü obviously resented Nanking's attempt to exercise leadership in this area, as he did in so many others.

Tsinan had eight newspapers in the 1930s. Table 7.1 gives information on their circulation and their editorial views. During several periods they contained no editorials, Han Fu-ch'ü fearing that open expression of opinion would encourage the anti-Japanese and nationalistic sentiments aroused by the Manchurian incident.

The political alignment of the newspapers is of some interest. Clearly the Kuomintang, although heavily involved in several newspapers, was not able to control any of them without the interference of Han Fu-ch'ü. Consequently, Nanking lacked an organ to attack Han on his own ground. The pro-Japanese *Chi-nan jih-pao* (Tsinan Daily) had the greatest editorial freedom of any of Tsinan's papers. It often printed stories damaging to either Han Fu-ch'ü or the Kuomintang, stories that were never answered by the other papers because of Han's ban on editorializing.

Not only was public opinion tightly controlled in those years, but no real representative institutions existed. The provincial assembly of the early Republic was never revived. Han went ahead with the plans for

174

Table 7.1
Tsinan's Newspapers in the 1930s

Name	Circulation	Editor	Ownership and Editorial Views
Shan-tung min-kuo jih-pao (Shantung Republican Daily)	4,000	Wang Yu-min	Founded in 1929. Officially owned by Shantung Kuomintang, but financed by both the party and the provincial government. Anti-Japanese; pro-American
Chi-nan jih-pao (Tsinan Daily)	1,000	Pi Hsueh-ch'en	Founded in 1919 by pro-Japanese interests. Subsidized by the Japanese. Anti-U.S.; anti-Kuomintang; pro-Japanese
Li-hsia hsin-wen (Tsinan News)	1,000	Wang Shu-t'ien	Founded in 1931 and owned by the Tsinan Kuomintang. Anti-Japanese; pro-Kuomintang
P'ing-min jih-pao (The Masses' Daily)	1,000	Wang Kung-ch'en	Founded in early 1920s. A conservative, pro-Han Fu-ch'ü paper. Seldom opposed Kuomintang
Hsin-she-hui jih-pao (New Society Daily)	800	Ho Ping-ju	Founded 1930. Pro-foreign, but anti-Japanese. Ho Ping-ju also owner. Subsidized by cotton merchants
T'ung-su jih-pao (Popular Daily)	800	—	Founded in 1930 by Lo Ya-min. Pro-Han Fu-ch'ü; anti-Japanese
Chi-nan wan-pao (Tsinan Evening News)	750	—	Founded 1931 and subsidized by Liu Chen-nien when he controlled Chefoo. Pro-American; anti-Japanese. Fond of scandal
Kung-yen t'ung-hsin pao (Public Information Report)	—	—	Founded in 1930 and owned by Third Route Army. Subsidized by Han Fu-ch'ü

Source: U.S. National Archives, Department of State, China, Tsinan Consulate, File 800/Political Affairs, 1931.

village-level assemblies that were compatible with his conception of rural reconstruction, yet nothing of this sort was tried in Tsinan itself. The American consul remarked in 1932 that the Shantung chamber of commerce was the "only example in the city of an organization of even semi-public character voicing public opinion."[50]

TSINAN'S ECONOMY IN THE 1930s

Since Tsinan was a "commercial center" as well as a "political pillar," its history must take into account the economic changes occurring in the city and its rural hinterland. By the mid-1920s, as a result of the flowering of Chinese capitalism, the area near Tsinan had become considerably commercialized. Peasants in the trading area connected with Tsinan had begun to produce cotton, peanuts, and cattle for market; scholars have correlated this shift with the availability of cheap, modern transportation.[51] Ideally, under the terms of the Western-derived model of economic development, this increased commercialization would produce more commercial, and then more industrial, opportunities in Tsinan. The city would respond with an expansion of commerce, followed by a build-up of the industrial sector.

The benefits of this process of commercialization and industrialization would be significant to both the rural and the urban residents. The rural peasants and the newly arrived urban commercial and industrial work force were both dependent upon maintaining and increasing the levels of commercialization. The forces of the market might turn against the peasants, leaving them unable to sell their agricultural products at a profit and at the same time not having produced what they needed to be self-sufficient. The commercial and industrial work force in cities like Tsinan would also be directly affected by a decline in trade, and the workers would typically be forced to return to their rural relatives who would help them over the difficult times.

In Tsinan, the peasants and the urban work force first faced adversity not from the impersonal forces of the marketplace but from warlord disputes. Under Chang Tsung-ch'ang and then under Kuomintang control through 1930, trade was interrupted by the presence of rival armies, their control over the railroads, and the general disorder prevailing in the absence of a stable provincial administration. Many peasants, urban workers, and rural craftsmen were forced to emigrate or to return to subsistence agriculture in the late 1920s. Thus, political disruption had already weakened Tsinan's industrial sector as well as handicraft production and commercial agriculture before Han Fu-ch'ü took office.[52]

Then in 1932 the effects of the world depression began to be felt in Shantung. Demand for some of the major handicraft lines completely disappeared. For example, all twenty of the silk filatures in Tsinan were closed. According to a British government trade report,

... during the years 1929 to 1931, while the depression was at its height in other countries, China was, on account of the depreciation of the Chinese dollar in terms of gold currencies and rising prices internally, experiencing a comparative boom in trade. Since the beginning of 1932, China's foreign trade has undergone a progressive decline, internal prices have sagged and a period of severe deflation has set in.[53]

In this situation Han Fu-ch'ü's administration could not revive the agricultural economy of the province even by restoring internal peace. The economic situation in rural Shantung was no longer chaotic, but the larger domestic and world situations—to which commercialization had linked the peasants—were unfavorable to substantive economic advances.

The falling prices of the mid-1930s favored Tsinan's residents over the rural masses. The many government employees, including all the petty officials, teachers, clerks, soldiers, and yamen helpers, benefited from the falling cost of living and the regularity of their own incomes under Han Fu-ch'ü's stable and financially sound administration. Other sectors of the Tsinan economy that fared well in the mid-1930s were the railroads and other forms of transporation, for both the Shantung and the Tientsin-Pukow railroads operated at a profit and suffered few of the interruptions in service that had plagued them during the 1920s. The provincial administration also helped Tsinan's economy by purchasing public service industries such as telephone and electric light companies, as well as financing new public service investments such as water lines and sewers in addition to public works, efforts in wall repair, road construction, and canal improvement. Consequently, the government-supported sector of Tsinan's economy was vigorous in these years, matching an overall pattern of increasing Chinese state capitalism in the 1930s.[54]

The picture in the private commercial and industrial sectors of Tsinan was not bright, but surprisingly shows some areas of improvement. In discussing the economy during earlier periods, attention has been concentrated upon banking and industry, especially flour milling. In order to explain the economic forces at work, these areas will be reviewed briefly for the 1930s. In addition, the cotton trade, which shows the increased Japanese power, will be briefly described.

Industry in Tsinan during the 1930s was not booming; nevertheless, a survey conducted in 1936 by Shantung officials revealed that Chinese interests started two new cotton-spinning plants and three new match factories. In the meantime, however, Japanese capital had built six new match factories in Tsingtao and the Japanese had won control of more

177

than half the Shantung market for matches in the mid-1930s.[55] Japanese inroads into the Chinese cotton-thread industry by means of large new plants at Tsingtao were almost as great.

Four of Tsinan's ten flour mills closed during the general interruption of trade in 1925-1930. After 1930 two closed mills were reorganized and reopened. The seven mills remaining were all larger and better equipped than they had been in the 1920s. Significantly, the mills with connections in the Ch'i trading area—and thus with native-bank connections in Tsinan—were the ones that managed to survive into the 1930s. The Lu millers, lacking such connections in Tsinan, also lacked credit to get them through difficult times and had greater difficulty reopening.[56] Tsinan did get three new brick kilns in the 1930s, reflecting the building boom in the city and its suburbs. The bricks were used to build more permanent structures in the settlement district and to build residences for the many peasants forced into Tsinan's surrounding villages by flood, famine, or other loss of livelihood.[57]

In banking, the situation in Tsinan underwent a major change in the 1930s. Ever since Chang Tsung-ch'ang's ruinous currency policies in the mid-1920s, people had not had full confidence in Chinese banknotes of any kind. Even the notes of the central government's banks were suspect, and many Shantungese depended instead on Japanese currency. This situation ended abruptly with the Japanese devaluation of 1931, when all Chinese with any significant part of their capital in Japanese currency or bank deposits were severely hurt. Many Tsinan businessmen suffered heavy losses.[58]

Because of their domestic problems most Japanese banks were less active in Tsinan and Shantung after 1931. The large trading banks with official connections, however, such as the Yokohama Specie Bank or the Bank of Korea, remained important both in Tsingtao and in Tsinan. Chinese banks, especially those associated with the central government, benefited from the decline of Japanese bank activities. The Bank of China, the Bank of Communications, the Central Bank, and the Chinese Commercial Bank became the leading Chinese banks in Tsinan in the 1930s. Bank officers began to appear as community leaders.

Since these newly powerful banks were based in Shanghai, this development can be seen as evidence of the fact that Tsinan was beginning to be incorporated into a sphere of Shanghai's economic influence. The links between Shantung and Shanghai grew stronger and more complex throughout the 1930s, reflecting the growing integration of the Chinese national economy and the importance of the modern financial and commercial institutions based there. Even as Shanghai banking and trading interests expanded in Tsinan, Shantungese interests became

178

stronger in Shanghai. One crude measure of this strength is the fact that 35,000 Shantungese lived in Shanghai, making up the sixth largest element from the eighteen provinces.[59]

Still, local commercial and political interests at Tsinan kept control over a sizable portion of the banking industry. In 1931 Han Fu-ch'ü created his own bank, Shantung People's Livelihood Bank, to serve as the central banking authority for his administration in Shantung. Like his other financial operations, Han's bank was run well and honestly. It controlled a considerable amount of the Tsinan banking business, handled the province's tax monies, and issued paper notes that were widely circulated. Han had asked Shantungese merchants to participate in the bank, but after their experience with previous warlords they invested only modestly.[60]

The Shantungese commercial elements had retreated from the field of modern banking to the so-called native banks, or *ch'ien chuang*. Fifty-two of these operated in the 1930s, having survived the difficult times of the late 1920s which caused several dozen native banks to close their doors. Over half represented the Chang-ch'iu banking elements, and another large group was run by people from Wei *hsien*. A few banks based in Shansi still survived, but the Lu region of Shantung, as already mentioned, had little power in native banking. [61] The failure of Shantung commercial interests to create modern banks and the decline of the traditional banks both point toward the decreasing importance of the Chinese bourgeoisie in Tsinan during the 1930s. Part of this decline can be attributed to the poor commercial conditions overall, but Han Fu-ch'ü's traditionalist approach did not emphasize programs to stimulate Chinese commerce and industry. Thus, his administration contributed in part to the weakness of Tsinan's commercial class in the 1930s.

In another sector of the banking world there had been a strange turn. During Chang Tsung-ch'ang's rule in Shantung, all the Chinese-owned pawnshops—including firms a century old—closed. In their place appeared Japanese-owned and -operated pawnshops. Only the Japanese, by virtue of their extraterritorial status, could promise real security for the people's goods, another indication of how pervasive Japanese influence was becoming at Tsinan in the 1930s. The situation continued throughout Han Fu-ch'ü's rule, in spite of efforts by Han's subordinates to establish Chinese pawnshops.[62]

A forward glance at the situation in Tsinan after 1937 reveals the real power of Japanese banking and the weakness of the Shantung commercial forces. Japanese rule beginning in January 1938 naturally ended the operation of the Nanking government banks. In addition, thirty-six of the fifty-two native banks closed permanently during the lunar New Year in

1938. The defeat of the local Shantung commercial interests in banking was so thorough that by the end of the 1930s their power, which had seemed in the early 1920s to be the dominant force in Shantungese banking, had all but disappeared.[63]

In the 1930s the supply of cotton in China increased, not because yields per acre were higher, but because more acres were devoted to cotton. During the same period, handicraft yarn and cloth production declined, while machine production of cotton cloth increased.[64] Without becoming drawn into the wider question of the impact of these changes on peasant life, we can predict that this situation should have had two effects in Tsinan. First, the cotton trade should have increased as more cotton was grown and worked on power looms. Second, the Chinese yarn and textile industry at Tsinan should have grown.

In fact, the cotton trade did increase in Tsinan. New baling operations appeared in the city to prepare the cotton for transshipment to Tsingtao, where it was ginned, spun, and woven in the Tsingtao mills. The fourteen large firms that came to dominate the raw cotton trade formed an association that acted like a combine and controlled prices. The leaders of these firms became powerful in Tsinan commercial circles.[65]

The cotton yarn and textile industry in Tsinan also prospered. The full financial background of the two new cotton-spinning plants is not known, but at least one of these new mills, the Jen-feng, was primarily Japanese-financed. In contrast, Tsingtao had increased its capacity to nine large modern mills, seven of which were owned and controlled by the Japanese. These Tsingtao mills produced over 80 percent of the power-loomed cotton cloth made in Shantung. As in the match industry, Japanese elements moved in and then expanded their production in China for the China market. Chinese industry was able to survive, but clearly was losing ground to the Japanese.[66]

This brief sketch of the cotton industry in Shantung indicates that Tsinan was losing its position as a manufacturing center to Tsingtao in the 1930s. Belatedly—and by another power—the conception of Tsingtao's economic role originally held by the Germans began to be fulfilled. The main difference between the situations in Tsinan and Tsingtao is found in the Japanese cotton manufacturers' willingness to invest capital in Tsingtao, whereas both Chinese and Japanese capital were less interested in such investments in Tsinan.

The overall pattern of economic power in Tsinan during the 1930s saw the decline of the real power of the Shantungese commercial interests. In particular, the Tsinan and Ch'i trading system merchants who had increased their power in Tsinan until the mid-1920s never really got back on their feet again in the 1930s. Both the Japanese and the Shanghai commercial interests, however, increased in importance at Tsinan.

Shanghai was able to influence Tsinan through banking and domestic commercial ties, but the Japanese exerted even greater influence. The large Japanese industrial investment at Tsingtao and the continuing expansion of Japanese-backed trade and industry in the province meant that Tsinan was being drawn further and further into the economic orbit of the Japanese.

The absence of a strong Chinese momentum toward industrialization in Tsinan in the 1927-1937 decade marks a critical failure in the city's modernization. In order to meet the contemporary canons of progress, Tsinan would have had to continue to move toward the Western model of an industrial city. Beginnings had been made after 1900, and during the "golden age" of Chinese capitalism a brief spurt of industrial development had occurred after the start of World War I. Yet, that momentum did not carry through the 1920s, nor was it revived in the 1930s. In this account we have looked closely at the political and economic situation in Tsinan all during those years, and it is clear that the failure to industrialize cannot be attributed to any social class or to a single cause—either foreign or domestic. Instead, it was tied in with the world economic crisis of the 1930s, the policies of the warlords, the effects of economic imperialism, and the shortcomings and weaknesses of Chinese entreprenuerial elements. Still, we can clearly fix the time of this failure: it came in the mid-1920s with the disruptive warlord rule of Chang Tsung-ch'ang and was not reversed in the subsequent period of tranquil warlord rule under Han Fu-ch'ü. Thus, Tsinan had passed the critical point in her potential for industrialization when the processes begun in the 1900 to 1925 years could not continue to mature.

Intimately related to this failure of industrialization was the structure of the political system in Tsinan, for the wealthy and privileged elements in Tsinan would have needed much greater control over the city's political life to be willing to risk large investments in new industry. Some investors tried to achieve such control by aligning themselves with the government to obtain monopoly rights for public service industries, but they all found that the warlords had too strong a grip on the political system. In fact, the Shantungese merchant and gentry interests steadily lost political power from their great period of influence after the 1911 revolution until the 1930s, when the autocratic and anti-industrial Han Fu-ch'ü ruled Tsinan. As their political power ebbed, so did the hope of industrialization and urban transformation after the Western model.

THE FALL OF HAN FU-CH'Ü

In late 1937 a curious situation developed in Shantung. Following the Marco Polo Bridge incident outside Peking in July 1937, Japanese armies began a general offensive in China that included a North China front with

181

units moving southward from Peking, as well as a second front involving Shanghai and the Lower Yangtze River Valley. Literally in the midst of this undeclared war, Shantung remained undisturbed and rather calm. While the Japanese blockaded the China coast, the port of Tsingtao remained open, and Japanese land forces did not cross the Yellow River in their North China operations.

Han Fu-ch'ü mobilized his regular armies and began to improve his militia's preparations for war. He spoke out against Japanese aggression and told newspapermen, "Even if the Japanese are at the gates of Tsinan, I will lead my men to defend it to the last." At the same time, Han Fu-ch'ü maintained regular contact with Japanese military commanders as part of an understanding he had worked out with the Japanese to keep Tsinan and most of Shantung free from the fighting. In 1937 Han also had some hope that he might become head of a Japanese-sponsored North China regional government.[67]

Then in December 1937, after the fall of Nanking and the beginning of the Kuomintang withdrawal toward Szechwan, Han Fu-ch'ü left Tsinan without offering any resistance to the advancing Japanese troops. Han's dream of a larger role in a Japanese-controlled North China had evaporated, and his withdrawal spared Tsinan from the possibility of another terrible assault such as had occurred in Nanking, while also preserving his 100,000-man army intact. Although Chiang Kai-shek had himself recently undertaken a strategic withdrawal very much like Han's, he did not sanction such retreats by others, and he had Han arrested on 4 January 1938. A court-martial convicted Han of failing to defend Tsinan and Shantung, and he was executed on 24 January 1938, less than a month after leaving Tsinan.[68]

The long train of events involving dealings among Han Fu-ch'ü, Chiang Kai-shek, and the Japanese for control of Shantung make complex and intriguing political history. Here, because the focus of our attention is the city of Tsinan, only those portions relevant to the theme of the effects of warlord rule on the city will be related.

Han Fu-ch'ü was the last in the line of militarist governors in Shantung that began in the late nineteenth century when several commanders in the antirebel armies achieved the position of governor. He faced the same set of strategic problems that had confronted all his predecessors. As governors and military commanders, these militarists needed firm control over the province's revenues, a bureaucracy staffed with trustworthy subordinates, and insurance that their armies would remain strong, well-paid, and loyal. Han had done extremely well at all of these.

Another critical element in a governor's survival in Tsinan lay in his relations with the chief powerholders in North China. Thus, we have discussed how the late-nineteenth-century governors fitted into Li Hung-chang's dominion over North China, how Yüan Shih-k'ai controlled the province down to 1916, and how Tsinan experienced serious problems after 1916 as the stability of political leadership in North China deteriorated.

In the 1930s Han Fu-ch'ü in Shantung, and other warlords in Shansi, Honan, and Hopei as well, found themselves caught between the Nanking government of Chiang Kai-shek and the Japanese. It was impossible for Han Fu-ch'ü and others in similar positions to come to terms with Chiang Kai-shek, for Chiang's government worked to destroy warlordism and establish administrations subordinate to Nanking wherever possible.[69] The Japanese, on the other hand, wanted to pull the North China region away from the control of Nanking because they believed that Chiang Kai-shek and the Kuomintang represented a regional power that would always mean less than national government for China.

Previous governors at Tsinan had shifted their loyalties as the power in North China had changed configuration. For example, T'ien Chung-yü managed to remain governor when power in Peking shifted from the Anfu to the Chihli clique. In the 1930s Han Fu-ch'ü did the same thing by accommodating himself to the rising Japanese power in North China.

We have already discussed the economic aspects of this rising Japanese power, which meant for Shantung increased Japanese commercial activity throughout the province and, in particular, the rapid growth of Tsingtao as a center of Japanese industrial investment. On the political side the creation of Manchuko in 1932 was only the first step in a series of Japanese moves, led by elements in the Imperial Army, which increased Japanese power in North China.

In January 1933 the Japanese Kwantung Army had occupied the province of Jehol, bordering on Hopei. At Nanking, Chiang Kai-shek was forced to seek a new agreement with the Japanese concerning North China, and in May 1933 the Tangku Truce was signed, creating a special Political Affairs Council in Peking to deal directly with the Japanese authorities in North China, independent of the regular diplomatic channels controlled by Nanking.

The Tangku Truce was widely regarded at the time as evidence that Chiang Kai-shek was following a policy of appeasement toward the Japanese. The new Political Affairs Council at Peking was interpreted as a means by which Chiang hoped to avoid direct confrontation between Nanking and Tokyo and thus keep the Nanking government from having to openly oppose the Japanese encroachments on China's sovereignty. Yet, paradoxically, the Tangku Truce increased Chiang Kai-shek's power in North China because his men—Ho Ying-ch'in, a close military

183

subordinate from the Whampoa clique, and Huang Fu, a trusted inter-
mediary in Sino-Japanese affairs—controlled the Political Affairs
Council, while the independent generals of the north, such as Han Fu-ch'ü
or Yen Hsi-shan, were regulated to consultant roles.

Han Fu-ch'ü's distrust of Chiang Kai-shek was already well established
because Nanking had proved unwilling to provide him with agreed-upon
military allotments and because Chiang Kai-shek had given assistance to
Liu Chen-nien when Han tried to drive Liu out of eastern Shantung.
When, in 1933, it appeared that Chiang's new arrangements with the
Japanese might weaken Han's power, Han quickly moved to ingratiate
himself with the rising Japanese power in North China.

In April 1933, a month before the signing of the Tangku Truce, the
American consul in Tsinan reported,

> An unconfirmed rumor [is circulating] that General Han and the local Japanese
> consul [Nishida Kōichi] had come to a mutual understanding over maintenance
> of peace and order in Shantung in case the Japanese find it necessary to occupy
> the Peking-Tientsin area and other territory in North China. That rumor has it
> that Japan would not send forces to Shantung, if Shantung troops remained
> neutral to happenings in other parts.[70]

Han Fu-ch'ü himself frequently hinted that such an arrangement existed,
and the rumors persisted. Han granted a number of interviews to reporters
and foreign diplomatic officials from the time of the Tangku Truce until
his fall in 1937. Throughout all of these statements runs the common
thread of Han's distrust of Chiang Kai-shek. On several different
occasions Han charged that Chiang Kai-shek had no fixed policies, did not
live up to his promises, and slighted requests for needed support. For all
these reasons, Han told his visitors, cooperating with Chiang would be
political suicide.[71] Thus Han seemed to blame Chiang Kai-shek for any
arrangements between Han himself and the Japanese.

In the mid-1930s Han also took a number of steps to placate the feelings
of the Japanese, which can be seen as indications of an understanding with
them. Among these were stricter censorship of Tsinan's newspapers to
prevent publication of anti-Japanese news and editorials, bans on student
demonstrations against Japan, cutbacks in the provincial funds available
to Kuomintang operations in Tsinan, and dismissal of anti-Japanese
officials, including the mayor and chief of police in Tsinan.

Once war came to North China in the wake of the Marco Polo Bridge
incident, the situation in Tsinan conformed to the outlines of the agreement reported by the American consul. Although no written agreement
has ever been found, in the fall of 1937, Han Fu-ch'ü himself confirmed to
Frank Dorn, an American military attaché in Tsinan, that such an
agreement had existed.[72]

As the Japanese became more open about their designs on North China in 1936 and 1937, Han Fu-ch'ü hoped to be able to retain his position at Tsinan and possibly even to enlarge upon his existing power by playing a more important role in the new North China regional government the Japanese would create. Han's grounds for hope seem to have been rather weak, for the Japanese favored a figurehead with less real power than Han, who had both a large army and an established reputation as a conservative administrator. The most plausible role Han could have played was that of a buffer between the Japanese and Chiang Kai-shek, but such a position was inherently a dangerous one, considering the level of anti-Japanese feeling that was continuing to build up in China.[73]

As the Japanese units moved into Shantung in late 1937, Shen Hung-lieh, the Kuomintang-backed governor of Tsingtao, sanctioned the destruction of much Japanese industrial property and part of the city's port and public service facilities in order to deny them to the Japanese.[74] At Tsinan, Han Fu-ch'ü finally decided to throw in his lot with Chiang Kai-shek against the Japanese but did not carry out a similar policy of destruction of assets to keep them out of the hands of the Japanese. Given his difficulties with Chiang Kai-shek and his rather open policy of accommodation with the Japanese in 1937, it is difficult to imagine why Han felt Chiang might accept him as an ally, and, in fact, Han did misjudge Chiang's willingness to overlook his transgressions.

The fascinating and somewhat mysterious story of Han Fu-ch'ü's efforts to maintain his own power through a shifting pattern of alliances and loyalties in the 1930s indicates the essentially destructive nature of warlordism in Chinese politics. While certain aspects of Han's rule were constructive—for example, his efforts at rural reconstruction and his program of road building in the province—as long as he or any other governor was concerned with the problems of preserving an army and playing off the interests of the various extra-provincial forces controlling North China, that warlord was incapable of responding to local Shantungese interests. As a result, the political order in Tsinan during the 1930s under Han Fu-ch'ü failed—as, except for a short period from 1911 to 1913, it had always failed—to be shaped by the interests of Shantungese. The men of local importance, the representatives of the important Ch'i and Lu areas within the province, regularly came to Tsinan in hopes of obtaining a voice in the affairs of the province, but warlords holding the top administrative posts remained essentially free of the influence of these local elements.

Warlords frequently followed policies which helped the wealthy and powerful Shantungese who came to Tsinan, but only incidentally to their own fundamental power interests, and when those interests were at stake the warlords abandoned the local interests. In Tsinan, as elsewhere in China, this split between the interests of the ruling warlords based in some of China's important cities and the wealthy and important urban residents was most serious from 1916 to 1928, but as the case of Han Fu-ch'ü reveals, this divergence carried over into the Nanking decade. Thus, even in the Chinese-controlled cities there existed a basic split between the interests of the governors and the governed. This was clearly the case in the treaty ports, where Chinese sovereignty was limited by the treaty privileges and by the thousands of administrative and legal practices which made it impossible for the urban Chinese bourgeoisie to manage the administration of the city so that it fully served their interests. In the non-treaty-port cities of China like Tsinan, where Chinese political power was concentrated, the same contradiction existed wherever a city was under the rule of warlords.

SUMMARY

In evaluating power and progress in Tsinan during the Nationalist decade, we find that the clearest change is the great decrease in the influence of wealthy and landed interests. Such interests—both those with traditional gentry leanings and those with the modern background of commercial or industrial bourgeoisie—lost power in Tsinan. In politics they no longer had a provincial legislature as a forum and a source of power, and they never regained the influence they had had before 1925. Han Fu-ch'ü's autocratic style further blocked their political aspirations. In the economic realm, they lost out to other interests: sometimes to the new power of the Shanghai-Nanking financial groups; in other cases to the Japanese firms producing or trading for the China market.

The principal powerholder in Tsinan during this decade was Han Fu-ch'ü, who showed a remarkable ability in building a strong position for himself from tentative beginnings. Han preferred to function as an autocrat, like many other Chinese in the 1930s. The political style of China had turned away from democracy and representative government in those years, and it had become common to praise the success of fascism in Europe and decry the weaknesses of democracy. Han Fu-ch'ü fit the style of the times fully as well as Chiang Kai-shek, for both came from a military backgrounds, and both emphasized their upright moral characters, their authoritarian attitudes and antidemocratic preferences. Chiang, however, won the mantle of national leadership in 1936 and 1937, while Han Fu-ch'ü made critical miscalculations in his efforts to save his power in the face of the new war in North China.[75]

Han Fu-ch'ü's autonomy gives further proof of the limited authority of the Nanking regime in the 1927-1937 period. In Shantung this situation goes back to the Kuomintang weakness in Shantung (and all of North China), which in turn goes back to the days of the Revolutionary alliance before the 1911 revolution. This past history not only plagued the Kuomintang and Chiang Kai-shek in the period from 1927 to 1937 but also decidedly influenced the events the following decade, which saw the Communist party gain strength during the years of Japanese occupation and the Kuomintang fail in an attempt to take over North China from the Japanese after 1945.

The biggest gainers of this decade of Kuomintang rule were the Japanese, for their influence in the province continued to expand. Japanese power in Shantung was never checked after 1914, even though the pace of Japanese penetration slowed under the Shidehara policies in the early 1920s. Tanaka's more aggressive policies stirred up renewed Chinese nationalistic resistance, which became more obvious in Shantung after 1928. But Han Fu-ch'ü refused to support the politics of mass nationalism and suppressed most nationalistic protest. In that atmosphere Japanese power steadily increased in Shantung and Tsinan during the 1930s: Japanese capital became increasingly important in Shantung's industrialization and commerce, and Shantung was drawn more closely into the orbit of Japanese imperialism.

Japanese interest, however, centered on Tsingtao rather than on Tsinan. Consequently, during the Nanking decade the pace of modernization in Tsinan for the first time seemed to lag behind that in Tsingtao. The Germans had hoped that Tsingtao would be the first city of Shantung, and the Japanese made that dream a reality in the 1930s, with the combination of Nanking's political authority and Japanese investment.

187

8

Tsinan in War, 1938-1948

AFTER HAN FU-CH'Ü LEFT TSINAN in December 1937, the city lost its importance as the center of Chinese political power in Shantung. The Japanese controlled Tsinan as they did Tsingtao and the rest of Shantung's principal cities, as well as the railroads. Yet they could never extend their power from the cities and the railways to rule the rural hinterlands of North China because of rural-based guerrilla resistance. The Kuomintang regime of Chiang Kai-shek showed only moderate interest in supporting anti-Japanese military units within Shantung until late 1938, when the Communists began to show interest. Then the Chinese Communist party (CCP) and the Kuomintang began to vie for control of the anti-Japanese movement in the province. The CCP won and largely dominated the struggle against the Japanese, especially in 1944 and 1945.[1] With a border-region government located in the vastness of the Shantung mountains, the CCP-led resistance movement sharply limited the extent of Japanese control. The effect in Shantung, as elsewhere in North China, was to create a division of political and economic power, with the Japanese ruling only the railroads, the cities, and the immediately adjacent agricultural areas.

With the city's economy, politics, and culture dominated by a foreign power and armed resistance growing in its hinterland, Tsinan could make no further real progress toward modernization. This chapter sketches the main outlines of the Japanese occupation and the ensuing Kuomintang effort to establish power in the city after 1945.

THE JAPANESE ADMINISTRATION IN TSINAN, 1938-1945

Ever since the Japanese had begun to dream of an independent or semi-autonomous North China in the early 1930s, they had talked of various programs for realizing the dream. Most envisioned some kind of close economic cooperation among Japan, Manchuria, and North China. North China would supply agricultural products and industrial raw materials and receive Japanese capital investments or exports. The exact formula varied, but there were basically two different plans—a military plan and a civilian plan.[2] The long-standing differences between Japanese military and civilian economic interests in the development of Korea and Manchuria were extended to North China, the chief point of contention being control of economic development. In 1938, with the Japanese Imperial Army already deeply involved in North China, there was really no contest, and the military plan prevailed.

It is worth noting, however, that both the civilian and the military programs looked toward a new North China—encompassing Shantung, Hopei, Honan, Shansi, and parts of Jehol and Suiyuan—as an autonomous but Japanese-dominated region carved from the poorly functioning body of China. The Japanese vision was based on some hard realities: the failure of the Kuomintang to establish political control over North China and the still incomplete economic integration of North China with Central China.

The Japanese North China Area Army was following this policy of regionalization when in late 1937 it created a Provisional Government of the Republic of China in Peking, to coordinate the political and economic potential of North China. General Kita Seiichi controlled the administration as the head of the special civil and political affairs units (*tokumu-bu*) of the North China Area Army. In effect General Kita served as officer in charge of the Japanese Army's civil affairs command in North China, and Wang Mao-k'un followed his direction as head of the Peking Provisional Government.[3] The presence of such a new level of central political authority—below the nation and above the province—clearly indicates that provincial cities such as Tsinan were no longer intended to be the chief centers of political power below the national level.

When the Japanese armies arrived in Tsinan after Han Fu-ch'ü's withdrawal they were ready to make the city and the province of Shantung part of this North China regional government. The Japanese takeover of Tsinan was not entirely bloodless, even though the city escaped the fate of Nanking. The Japanese reported 120 casualites in four days of fighting in and around Tsinan, and retreating Chinese troops destroyed several buildings in the city, among them the Japanese consulate, a Japanese hospital, Japanese schools, and Han Fu-ch'ü's headquarters. None of the Japanese-associated businesses in Tsinan suffered as they had in Tsingtao, where the seven Japanese-owned cotton mills were destroyed on 18 December.[4]

In Tsinan, as elsewhere in North China, the Japanese Army upon its arrival established a Peace Preservation Committee (*pao-an hui*) headed by whatever prominent local figures would agree to work with the Japanese. In Tsinan the Japanese found some businessmen who had stayed on to

Figure 6. The southwestern portion of Tsinan's walled area is shown in this aerial photograph. The two walls stand out quite clearly, as does the moat. The large open area in the upper right is the governor's yamen. The widening of main thoroughfares and removal of some gates after the Japanese bombardment of 1928 can also be detected. The area in the upper left originally was not part of the settlement district, but had become fully occupied by urban structures in the 1940s. The grounds of Cheloo University are outside the outer wall in the lower part of the photograph. The regular, newly developed area to the left of Cheloo University is probably a military encampment. (Aerial photograph 23 March 1945, unclassified; U.S. Department of Defense, Defense Intelligence Agency.)

operate their firms after the departure of Han Fu-ch'ü. The Peace Preservation Committee was only temporary, serving until March 1938, when General Kita's civil affairs units established a Provincial Council under the

Figure 7. The northeastern corner of Tsinan's outer wall protrudes into the left center of this aerial photograph. The low, wet, and marshy ground along the north city wall, above Ta-ming Lake, is clearly visible. The main tracks of the Tsingtao-Tsinan railroad cross the upper portion of the photograph, with a branch line curving off toward Huang-tai. The higher and drier land in the center is much more sparsely populated. The large village along the righthand side is part of Hung-chia-lou, and some of the large buildings of the Catholic archdiocese are clearly visible. (Aerial photograph, 23 March 1945, unclassified; U.S. Department of Defense, Defense Intelligence Agency.)

chairmanship of Ma Liang. Ma was an old Anfu adherent who had not been active in politics since the May Fourth movement. His high-handed actions against nationalistic students in 1919 had led to his dismissal as Tsinan's defense commissioner. Since that time Ma Liang had lived in

191

Tsingtao and taken part in a number of pro-Japanese enterprises, both political and economic. Ma was representative of the kind of unpopular and distrusted men the Japanese enlisted in their new puppet regimes in North China. Ma took his direction from Nishida Kōichi, the former Japanese consul in Tsinan (1927-1936), who returned as a special advisor to the Provisional Government.[5]

Tax receipts fell to $9,000,000 in 1939-1940 from levels of $30,000,000 during the Han Fu-ch'ü era. This situation simply reflects the limited territorial authority of the Provisional Government: the land, which ordinarily provided two-thirds of Shantung's provincial tax revenues, was not under its control. The 1939-1940 budget figures in Shantung show an excess of receipts over expenditures, but this would not have been the case without Japanese subsidies.[6]

Under this new regional administration, Tsinan's economy became increasingly subordinated to Japan and more tightly integrated into the North China regional economy. In December 1939, the North China Development Company, a Japanese creation, took over the Tsinan Electric Company. The former provincial Min-sheng Bank, created by Han Fu-ch'ü, was replaced by a branch of the Japanese-backed Federated Bank of China. The Federated Bank, a regional institution headquartered in Peking, redeemed the Min-sheng's paper currency at 40 percent of face value in 1938. The Lu-feng Cotton Mill also was taken over by the Japanese Toyo Cotton Spinning and Weaving Company in 1939.[7]

The reorganization of these three large businesses in Tsinan indicates the total collapse of Chinese bureaucratic capitalism after 1937. These men had been the primary support for large industrial innovations in Tsinan, in both the private and the public sector, since 1911. Most of their enterprises had encountered difficulties during the 1930s—both the Electric Company and the Lu-feng mills were taken over by the Shantung Commissioner for Redevelopment in the mid-1930s—but now control passed into Japanese hands. The closure of many of Tsinan's traditional banks reveals that a similar loss of power occurred within the ranks of Tsinan's leading merchants. Thus after 1938 Japanese economic interests increasingly supplanted both bureaucratic and merchant capital in Tsinan.

Many Japanese commercial adventurers now came to North China to enter all kinds of small businesses, from exporting to restaurants to narcotics. In Tsinan these new arrivals found a Japanese community already established, with its own chamber of commerce, newspaper, schools, hospitals, and bank. There were also several thousand Japanese troops stationed in the city.

As the war wore on in North China after 1940, the Japanese began to despair of a North China integrated economically with Japan and

Manchuria. First, they had to contend with an armed resistance movement that hindered all their economic plans. Second, as the war came to involve all of East Asia, they found themselves overextended and thus unable to maintain the flow of investment and trade upon which their dream rested.

In Shantung the effects of the bifurcation of the economy into a Japanese sector and a largely self-sufficient rural sector under guerrilla control was not completely ruinous to Tsinan. The rural areas which were controlled by the Japanese were already heavily commercialized because they lay so close to the cities and the railways. They provided Tsinan with enough grain, other foodstuffs, and cotton to maintain life, but only with rationing. But there was no possibility of expanding industry or increasing trade.[8]

Instead, as the war dragged on, the level of trade fell and the larger modern factories in Tsinan shut down. In their place appeared small marginal producers using sweated labor and one or two pieces of modern spinning or weaving equipment. The economy of Tsinan was atrophying for lack of contact with its own hinterland, and for lack of a regular export market.[9]

As commerce and industry declined, Tsinan suffered from the general wartime inflation in China. By 1942 wholesale prices in Tsinan were already five time what they had been in 1936. The real force of the inflation, however, was felt in 1944, when wholesale prices were more than twenty times as high as in 1936. Inflation at these rates further constricted commerce and generally reduced constructive economic activity at Tsinan.[10]

In the city the Japanese quickly assumed control over education and established their own curriculum, including the Japanese language. Education at the elementary level was maintained, but the flight of educated Chinese to the anti-Japanese cause led to real difficulties in staffing the secondary schools. The Japanese also installed their own political apparatus, the *Hsin-min hui* (New People's Association) headed by the Chinese mayor Chu Kuei-shan. This organization attacked both the Kuomintang and the Communists. Because of the weakness of both parties in Tsinan before 1937, and the lack of local sympathy for Sun Yat-sen's Three Principles of the People, the Japanese criticisms were moderately well received. Still, the clear Japanese violation of Chinese sovereignty and the prospects of permanent subordination to the Japanese were so distasteful that the *Hsin-min hui* failed to turn the Tsinan dislike of the Kuomintang and the CCP into favor for Japanese imperialism.[11]

Under Japanese control the population of Tsinan swelled to 575,000. Most of the newcomers arrived as refugees from battle areas in the province. The civilian Japanese population numbered more than 20,000,

193

and there were at least as many Japanese military troops in Tsinan or its immediate vicinity during the war years. Fearing an attack on the city, the Japanese military ringed its unprotected commercial district, as well as the walled city and its suburbs, with barbed wire. People could enter the city only through two check points that were open from 8 A.M. to 6 P.M. Between 1938 and 1945, Tsinan was no longer the province's economic and political center, as it had been from 1890 to 1937, but a city under siege.[12]

TSINAN UNDER KUOMINTANG RULE, 1945-1948

At the time of the Japanese surrender in August 1945 the Communists had an estimated 85,000 troops in Shantung under the command of Ch'en Yi. Since 1944 General Ch'en had controlled an area that encompassed central and southern Shantung as well as parts of Honan, Kiangsu, and Anhwei. After soundly defeating the Kuomintang troops in Honan, the Communist armies had grown rapidly to exercise effective control over much of rural Honan, and Shantung.[13]

In the first weeks after surrender the Communist armies in the northeast and in North China seemed capable of occupying many of the Japanese-held cities. To forestall such a move, Chiang Kai-shek sought and received American help in transporting troops to the large urban centers north of the Yangtze River. In addition, under arrangements worked out with the Japanese, the Japanese troops continued to run skeleton urban administrations until the Kuomintang armies arrived. At Tsinan there was some fear that the returning Kuomintang generals might take revenge on those Chinese who had stayed on and collaborated with the Japanese. Except for a few cases, however, the Kuomintang commanders ignored the past and concentrated instead of the immediate task of denying the city to the Communists.[14]

Initially Kuomintang troops moved into Tsinan by air and landed at the two large airfields maintained by the Japanese. The Kuomintang position in Shantung improved markedly when the United States Navy and Marines garrisoned Tsingtao and made it their chief North China port and base. The Kuomintang reinforced its own troops in Shantung by landing its Eighth Army at Tsingtao in December 1945 and reinforced the Tsinan garrison by overland marches. These moves kept Ch'en Yi from launching an offensive on the two cities but did not deal with the problem of the rural areas. For instance, rail service between Tsingtao and Tsinan could not be reopened.[15]

Wang Yao-wu, a Shantungese from T'ai-an who had attended the Whampoa Military Academy, became the Kuomintang commander at Tsinan. A relatively young general of only forty, Wang had a reputation as

194

an able field commander. Given a series of commands in Honan during the war against the Japanese, he had steadily risen in rank. He arrived in Tsinan in January 1946 to relieve the officer who had accepted the Japanese surrender of the city and quickly bolstered his command with two divisions that had served under him in Honan. Wang remained in Tsinan as the chief military commander, and later as the civil governor, until Tsinan fell to the Communists in late September 1948.[16]

Ho Ssu-yuan, the provincial educational commissioner from the 1930s, had left Tsinan in 1937 and had spent the eight years with the Kuomintang in Chungking, first as head of Shantung civil affairs in the exile administration and then after 1944 as governor (officially his title became chairman of the Shantung provincial government). He had a good reputation in Tsinan and was a loyal Kuomintang member. Apparently Ho Ssu-yuan did not get on well with Wang Yao-wu and was consequently transferred to other duties.* Wang then received the concurrent post of provincial governor, and with it, clear civil as well as military authority in Tsinan.[17]

In some ways Tsinan appeared to have returned to normal. The foreign missionaries returned to run their churches, schools, and hospitals. A Chinese provincial governor once again made Tsinan his capital city, and a new Shantung provincial legislature was elected, the first in over twenty-five years. The electorate eligible to participate in the voting was quite limited, given the general state of administration, but the election was an attempt to revive representative institutions.

Wang Yao-wu's administration at Tsinan was responsible for the whole province but naturally could administer only those parts the Kuomintang actually controlled. The top provincial administrators were for the most part military officers, many of them Shantungese who had previously been serving with Wang Yao-wu. The official administrative records of Wang's years show the large bureaucracy in Tsinan receiving an unending series of directives from Nanking, covering everything from the rules for labor unions to the dimensions of fishing grounds in the Gulf of Chihli. The Shantung bureaucracy always responded to these paper calls for action with appropriate paper answers, an accommodation which masked an administration largely ineffective and unable to govern.[18]

The Tsinan city administration was headed by Wang Tsung-wu, another Shantungese who served as mayor. As in earlier periods, the police in Tsinan performed an unusually large number of civil administrative functions. Among their responsibilities were efforts to stop Communist infiltration in the city, and the whole tone of life in Tsinan during these

---

*Ho initially went to Tsinan to assume his duties as chairman in 1946, but was shifted in November 1946 to mayor of Peking, where he served until an assassination attempt against him in January 1949.

years was marked by efforts to resist the Communists. Newspapers were more tightly controlled than during the 1930s. Wang Tsung-wu's city administration did return the public service industries to operation, repair streets and bridges, and perform other housekeeping functions necessary to make the city livable. The traditional gruel kitchens were opened in February 1946 to help the rural poor who came into the city, as they had for centuries, when their supplies of grain failed in the latter part of the winter.[19]

Yet, the situation was not the same as in the 1920s or the 1930s, for the Kuomintang government in Tsinan, like the Japanese before them, had lost touch with most of rural Shantung. The gap between Tsinan and its hinterland now widened into a civil war in which the Communists steadily increased their military strength and their ability to govern the Shantung countryside. Three years after the Japanese surrender, the Communists felt that their control in the North China countryside was strong enough to establish their own formal government, even though they did not yet control all the major cities, such as Tsinan. A North China People's Provisional Representative Congress met in August 1948 and created a new North China People's Government that began on 1 September 1948.[20]

Wang Yao-wu's administration in Tsinan had a distinctly martial tone, and improving the defense works became a primary concern. Although Wang was counted among the more progressive Kuomintang generals, his plans called for a static siege defense of the city against Communist forces. Wang had pillboxes constructed around the city and improved the Japanese barbed wire perimeter defense works connecting these strongpoints. Since the city relied on air transportation for munitions and other critical supplies, the defense plan depended on the two airfields. To protect them Wang Yao-wu's troops had to dig into the hills that overlook the city from the south.[21]

Living conditions did not improve in Tsinan under Wang Yao-wu's rule: food and fuel still had to be rationed, and trade and commerce remained at almost a standstill. Tsinan also suffered from the disastrous inflation that everywhere plagued the postwar rule of the Kuomintang. The Chinese authorities could do little to revive Tsinan's economy, primarily because they could never reestablish Tsinan's railroad connections to Tientsin, Tsingtao and the Lower Yangtze River Valley. The Communist armies kept the Tsingtao-Tsinan link closed from 1945 through 1948. At one point in mid-1947 American reconnaissance pilots reported that most of the bridges and more than half the track between Tsingtao and Tsinan had been destroyed. The situation on the Tientsin-Pukow railroad was slightly better; the Pukow Hsu-chou segment at least was kept open into 1948. The line between Hsu-chou and Tsinan, however, was usually closed to traffic from 1946 onward. North of Tsinan the Communist armies held Te-chou and blocked any hope of rail connections with Tientsin.[22]

In 1947 the Kuomintang armies undertook two separate offensives in North China in an effort to clear out Ch'en Yi's forces and open land communications with Tsinan. The first started from Hsu-chou and attempted to move northward along the Tientsin-Pukow railroad through Yen-chou to link up with Wang Yao-wu's armies at T'ai-an. The offensive began well, but bold generalship by Liu Po-ch'eng, who moved to threaten the Kuomintang base at Hsu-chou, ended the offensive before it could secure the railroad. The second offensive was an amphibious assault on Chefoo that was intended to develop into a drive across the Shantung peninsula and throught the plains portion of the Ch'i region, relieving first a Kuomintang garrison at Wei-hsien, and then Tsinan. This second attempt turned out to be an even greater setback, for the Kuomintang suffered heavy losses to the armies of General Su Yü, the Communist commander.[23]

Encircled more tightly every week, Wang Yao-wu found himself in a situation reminiscent of Han Fu-ch'ü's in 1937. Both men were considered vigorous, able military officers, and both had promised to hold the city at all costs in the face of a strong enemy who was clearly preparing to take it. But both Wang and Han had grown disenchanted with Chiang Kai-shek and the Nanking regime. Like Han, Wang complained that Chiang refused to supply the men and the materials needed to win military victories in his area. In this situation both men turned for help to the most powerful foreign presence in Shantung. For Han Fu-ch'ü that had meant dealing with the Japanese; Wang Yao-wu began to explore the possibilities of direct American aid.

In May 1948 Wang Yao-wu had a discussion with Robert C. Strong, the United States consul from Tsingtao, who was visiting Tsinan. After their official meeting was over, Wang sent a trusted subordinate, Hsu Ching-yu, to lay before Strong a plan of resistance. After discussing Wang's distrust of Chiang Kai-shek and his conclusion that the Nanking regime was rotten and would collapse, Hsu outlined Wang's plans for Shantung—a stable, secure anti-Communist regime based on good government, a strong militia, and a healthy economy. Hsu stated Wang would have nothing to do with third-party efforts that might compromise with the Communists.* In view of all this, would the United States provide

---

*This was a reference to the efforts by the Revolutionary Committee of the Kuomintang and the Democratic League to reach some kind of accommodation with the Communists in a coalition government.

him direct military aid? If so, Wang could prevent Tsinan from falling into Communist hands.[24]

Although United States Ambassador John Leighton Stuart endorsed this idea, it never came to fruition, because by the spring of 1948 Communist armies in Shantung had already taken Wei-hsien, closing the land corridor for resupply of Tsinan from the secure American base at Tsingtao. Then in July 1948 Ch'en Yi's armies took Yen-chou, a major garrison city in southern Shantung, without serious resistance. The American missionaries who ran Shantung Christian University had begun to leave. Robert Strong expressed the feeling that "the prospects of a successful defense of Tsinan is [sic] rather slight."[25]

At that point, Wang Yao-wu's 80,000 troops and the 575,000 inhabitants of Tsinan were completely encircled by Communist armies, and Wang continued his static defense posture, depending on supplies ferried in by Civil Air Transport and Chinese Air Force planes. The situation remained quiet in Shantung for nearly two months after the fall of Yen-chou, but then the Communist armies, under the command of Su Yü, launched a frontal assault on the city.

The eight-day battle was marked by large-scale defections from the ranks of Wang's troops. The Communist armies took up positions on the mountains south of Tsinan early in the battle and forced the closing of the city's airfields. Wu Hua-wen, a Kuomintang commander who had served in Shantung and North China since 1937, was commanding the Eighty-fourth Division, charged with defending the southwestern sector of the city's defense perimeter. Wu and part of his division, the largest single unit at Tsinan, defected to the Communists early in the battle, and by 24 September the Communist troops had penetrated into the walled city and captured Wang Yao-wu, ending the Kuomintang rule of Tsinan and thus of Shantung.[26] Wu Hua-wen had survived during the long years of the anti-Japanese war through his ability to avoid battles and to reach understandings with the Japanese, Kuomintang, and Communist commanders; consequently, it should have been no surprise when he again decided not to fight.

The Kuomintang-controlled press played up the defection of Wu Hua-wen as the cause of the Kuomintang defeat, but the American consul-general at Tsingtao, William Turner, saw the situation differently:

Defection of Wu Hua-wen was merely the manifestation of a general phenomenon. His treason was not of itself the cause of defeat. . . . Prime cause for swift loss of city is psychological rather than material or military. Nationalist garrison had been isolated for 2 months with no possibility [of] ground support. Previous Nationalist defeats in which Nationalist troops failed [to] fight known to Tsinan garrison and people. Commie victory at Tsinan felt [to be] inevitable in view [of] record of failure of Nationalists. . . . Nationalist soldiers and population in

Shantung in general no longer consider Nationalist Government merits continued support in civil war, loss of lives and economic chaos.[27]

The report continued, in this staccato telegraphic style, to describe how Wang's troops had come from Honan and had little interest in defending a strange city. Moreover, the defense strategy consisted of simply falling back into the walled city when Communist armies began launching attacks. Once inside the walls, the defenders were helpless before Communist artillery and mortar attacks, even though they had enough food and ammunition. Chinese Air Force planes bombed and strafed around the city, but without ground coordination they were no real help to the defenders.

Before entering Tsinan the forces of Su Yü announced a seven-point policy that stated the attacking armies would

1) undertake to protect the life and property of all classes . . . [and] 2) to protect all native industry, business and private capital, [while] 3) all publicly owned commercial, industrial and financial enterprises will be taken over by the democratic government if found to be of a bureaucratic nature. [In addition] 4) the principal officials and the employees of public utilities and educational, religious and cultural institutions shall be protected by the liberation army and will not be molested . . . ; 5) [other] provincial, municipal and *hsien* government officials and *paochia* personnel shall not be arrested unless they offer armed resistance. 6) The life and property of foreign Consulates and their personnel as well as other foreign residents will be protected, provided they observe the regulations of the democratic government. . . . [Finally] 7) all public organizations and people of all classes should take joint responsibility in maintaining peace and order. Rewards and punishments will be made accordingly.[28]

The first reports from Tsinan after its fall indicate that the Communist armies lived up to their word rather well and were favorably received by the city's populace. The American missionaries were reportedly well treated and urged to continue their medical, educational, and religious work. Wu Hua-wen was regarded as a hero rather than a traitor in Tsinan, for the city's populace had become disenchanted with Kuomintang corruption and excesses. About one-third of the city had been damaged by a combination of Communist assaults and Kuomintang air attacks, but only two of the city's seven large flour mills were destroyed. Electric power and water service were soon restored, public transport was running, and market prices quickly stabilized.[29] The new era had begun in Tsinan, as it was soon to begin for most of China.

THE IMPACT OF THE WAR YEARS ON TSINAN

It is clear Tsinan had never regained its pre-1937 political and economic dominance. As a result of the Japanese invasion and the ensuing anti-Japanese struggle, the city had ceased to be the dominant center of

Shantung political power. In addition, Tsinan's economy, which after 1925 had lost its momentum toward modernization was severely damaged by the severing of its ties with the hinterland, the decline in trade, and the runaway inflation, all of which occurred in the last stage of the war against Japan. Even the end of the anti-Japanese war brought no real improvement to Tsinan, for the returning Kuomintang was no better prepared to govern Tsinan in 1945 than it had been in 1928. Indeed, it was less well prepared, because it faced an armed enemy in the rural areas. Again it relied on a Shantungese military officer, but Wang Yao-wu lacked the style and ambition of Han Fu-ch'ü and, more important, faced skilled and stubborn domestic opponents in the Communists. Under Wang's rule Tsinan merely limped along as an outpost of Kuomintang power and never again became the focal point of economic and political power in Shantung.

In Chapter 1 we considered Mao Tse-tung's views of the cities as citadels of imperialism and reactionary feudalism hampering China's progress. Mao Tse-tung did not indicate precisely the period to which this characterization applied, but generally he has been interpreted to mean that the whole treaty-port era (1842-1949) saw the existence of that kind of city. In the history of Tsinan it is clear that foreign individuals and foreign influences established themselves in the city, while both the traditional Chinese gentry and the new Chinese commercial elements also congregated there. What is not so obvious, however, is that the changes that took place hampered or prevented the development of Chinese society in a modern form. In Tsinan the record reveals that while "development" in its Western form did not succeed, it would nevertheless be unfair to say that changes in the city hampered progress. It is more a story of attempted, but arrested, development.

Only in 1937, with the long-term Japanese military occupation and administration of Tsinan, did the split between Tsinan and its hinterland become both irreversible and truly reactionary. During the period from 1937 to 1949, then, Tsinan does fulfill the role Mao Tse-tung assigned to cities in the treaty-port era. This judgment about the impact of the anti-Japanese war period is similar to the conclusions that Ramon Myers reached in his study of Chinese agricultural development in Shantung and Chihli. Myers maintains that before 1938 no serious deterioration in rural living standards, no dramatic increase in the inequality of land distribution, and no enslavement of the Shantung peasantry by unfair credit arrangements occurred. He does, however, see a serious decline after 1937. First, under the impact of the anti-Japanese war, the trend toward increasing commercialization of agriculture that had been underway since the 1890s was reversed. Second, the Chinese civil war put more strain on

200

the changing rural economies of Hopei and Shantung, resulting in a collapse that spelled bankruptcy and destitution to millions of North China peasants.[30]

The effects of these reversals were also felt in Tsinan. Tsinan's economy had become geared to a greatly expanded level of internal trade, processing for export, and some light industrial production for Shantungese consumption. After 1937 not enough peasants and urban residents had the monetary incomes necessary to continue the former levels of trade and industry at Tsinan. This was especially true after 1943, when the Japanese stopped subsidizing urban residents in their chief North China garrisons and the city's residents had to rely on the limited levels of economic activity or on their savings in order to live.

These disastrous economic conditions came upon Tsinan after her critical momentum toward economic modernization had been disrupted, and never fully reestablished, in the period from 1925 to 1937. Thus in the case of Tsinan, Myers' conclusion about the decisive nature of the war years must be somewhat modified. In that particular city the economic constriction of the war years simply added a final measure of certainty to a situation where it had proved impossible to sustain the model pattern of economic development.

Politically and economically, Tsinan after 1937 could not be said to have made any real progress toward modernization. In the third area of our concern, cultural modernization, Tsinan did not suffer so much, because all the modern-style cultural forms in education, entertainment, public information, public services, and health continued to function even though they were under direct Japanese control. In the discussion of Tsinan in the 1930s, we have seen how many thoughtful Chinese worried about the growing cultural gap between the city and the countryside that was an inevitable result of Tsinan's cultural modernization. These men had undertaken a program, during a period of domestic tranquillity and strong leadership, to reestablish the cultural links between the city and the countryside. After 1937 politics and economics combined to make such efforts impossible, and the existing links became even weaker.

The Japanese surrender brought no real change to the underlying forces in Tsinan's urban life. Political power reverted to the hands of militarists while the economy remained stagnant. The city's culture continued to function along the lines of foreign and bourgeois influence that had been growing steadily since 1900. When the Communist forces entered Tsinan they came as enemies of military power not firmly subordinated to ideological control and as opponents, as well, of the kind of economic and cultural changes that had been occurring in Tsinan for the past sixty years.

9

Politics and Development in Tsinan, 1890-1949

THE FALL OF TSINAN to the Communist armies in late 1948 ended one era of the city's history and began another. The idea that Chinese cities would follow the same path of maturation as Western cities was rejected, and Chinese political leaders began slowly, step by step, to build their nation according to an entirely different model, in which the cities would not dominate as centers of political, economic, and cultural advancement.[1] A detailed account of Tsinan's history since 1949 would require another book-length study to examine this new plan and to show how its various components have been applied in the city. Nevertheless, a brief indication of the general direction in which Tsinan has developed since 1949 should be provided in order to put the sixty years we have just studied in better perspective.

TSINAN'S DEVELOPMENT SINCE 1949

In March 1949, Mao Tse-tung made a major statement on the problems awaiting the Communists in the cities. He began by noting that the experience of both the party and the army had been limited to the countryside for the past twenty years and might not be fully applicable to the cities. He gave special attention to two aspects in the administration of the cities: the party's relationship to urban classes and the need to restore production. Basically Mao said—following formulas of New Democracy—that the CCP should rely on the working class but should work for unity with the rest of the "laboring masses" (*lao-tung ch'ün-chung*) and try to win over those intellectuals and members of the national bourgeoisie who could cooperate with the party.

The issue of production, however, stood out as the central problem in the cities in 1949. Mao Tse-tung put the seriousness of this issue in no uncertain terms:

> Other work in the cities, for example, in Party organization, in organs of political power, in trade unions and other people's organizations, in culture and education . . .—all this work revolves around and serves the central task,

production and construction. If we know nothing about production and do not master it quickly, if we cannot restore and develop production as speedily as possible and achieve solid successes so that the livelihood of the workers, first of all, and that of the people in general is improved, we shall be unable to maintain our political power, we shall be unable to stand on our feet, we shall fail.[2]

It was in this context that Mao Tse-tung referred to transforming consumer cities(*hsiao-fei ch'eng-shih*) into producer cities (*sheng-ch'an ch'eng-shih*) as the goal of Communist urban policy. The reference was a passing one, but before the end of the year it had been picked up as a slogan to characterize the basic direction of CCP urban policy. As early as September 1949, the Tientsin City Communist Party's General Study Committee used the concept and even the phrase, "changing consumer cities into producer cities," when drawing up its plans and programs.[3]

The same goal served as the unifying theme of a special collection of articles on urban progress published in 1959 on the tenth anniversary of the People's Republic of China. At that time the Urban Construction Bureau of Shanghai stated the principle in a straightforward manner: ". . . it is only through the transforming of consuming cities into producing ones that the people's livelihood can be assured and also that urban construction can look forward to a bright future. This also represents the difference between socialist urban construction and imperialist urban construction."[4] Creating producer cities has remained the most durable of Communist urban goals and still in the mid-1970s is often mentioned as the unifying theme of urban policy.

Unfortunately, Chinese theorists have encountered practical problems in defining exactly what kind of production, and how much, is required in this type of city. The description always imply that "producer cities" should have an economy based on the production of goods, both through industrial and handicraft methods, for use by all segments of the society. In these new-style cities the majority of the urban population is assumed to be engaged in production. The contrast is drawn with the "consumer city" in which a combination of the feudal gentry, the modernizing Chinese bourgeoisie, and sojourning foreigners shaped urban life before 1949 so that the major characteristic of city life became the consumption of the wealth produced by Chinese peasants and workers. Since 1949, the Chinese have not railed overlong against the administrative and commercial functions in urban life. In fact, it seems probable that, in terms of numbers of people involved, the combination of government administration, warehousing, and exchange of goods, along with service functions such as education, medicine, and other social institutions, is the dominant element in the life of most Chinese cities. Still, the concept of the "producer city" requires that these administrative, commercial, and

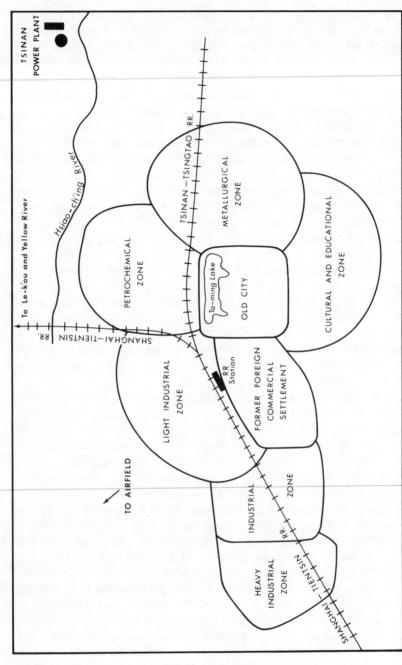

Map 5. Tsinan functional zones, 1974, schematic drawing. (Based on remarks of Wang Shan-chih, Tsinan Urban Construction Bureau, November 1974. Reprinted from David D. Buck, "Directions in Chinese Urban Planning," *Urbanism Past and Present* No. 1 [Winter 1975-76].)

204

service activities should never be granted priority over production. Thus, Chinese descriptions of urban life since 1949 always emphasize the importance of production in the new socialist era.[5]

In November 1974 when I visited Tsinan for the first time and talked with members of the Urban Construction Bureau in the city, they stressed that this goal remains a real one in their plans for the city. In the past twenty-five years, Tsinan has greatly expanded its industrial capacity, largely by developing the smaller repair shops that had been situated in the city before 1949 into larger production facilities. The city has been divided into various functional zones, several of which are classified on the basis of the types of industry they contain. The city now boasts heavy-machine-tool plants, a truck-manufacturing plant, an entire district that specializes in metallurgical industry, textile mills, and a new petrochemical area linked to the new Sheng-li oil fields along the Gulf of Chihli. This stress on the development of industry is typical of China's cities in the past quarter-century.

There are many ways in which the post-1949 society in Chinese cities differs radically from the historical experience described for 1890 to 1949 in Tsinan. Most notably, the Chinese, once having established the control over the cities Mao sought in early 1949, redirected their attention toward the countryside to carry out a thorough rural revolution starting with land reform was being carried out, Communist policy in Chinese cities, true to the direction laid down by Mao Tse-tung, worked to restore production while establishing control over administration, education, and other facets of urban life. In this situation, which lasted beyond 1952, the urban industrial and commercial enterprises experienced no major changes. Many of the large industrial enterprises, expecially the public service sector, had already come into the hands of the state—either the Japanese or the Kuomintang—sometime between the 1930s and 1949. Consequently, little more remained to be done after 1949 to gain control of the type of industries then considered appropriate to the state-owned sector.

The major changes in urban economic life did not occur until the last half of 1955, when a nation-wide campaign led to the transformation of formerly privately owned industrial and commercial concerns into joint state-private companies. Before 1955 the transformation had been taking place on a factory-by-factory basis, but, following a call for a speed-up by Mao Tse-tung in October 1955, the movement turned toward amalgamating all the concerns in a given line of business (e.g., grain millers, shoe stores) into a single specialized company (*chuan-men kung-ssu*). This rapid and radical transformation of commerce and industry came six years after the founding of the People's Republic of China, and it

205

Figure 8. Former settlement district of Tsinan in 1974: a busy Tsinan street on a chilly November morning. Many of the buildings date from the pre-1949 era, but the many trees, pedestrians, and bicycles and the occasional automobiles are very much a reflection of Chinese city life in the 1970s. (Photographed by Trev Sue-A-Quan.)

thoroughly altered the basis of private ownership of commercial and industrial operations.[6]

Another form of organization based on cooperative ownership by a group of individuals, including both former owners and employees, was also used in transforming privately owned businesses in Chinese cities. It appears, however, to be of considerably less significance because it involved only tiny handicraft manufacturing arrangements or the smallest commercial shops, stalls, or pushcarts.

During the Great Leap Forward (1958-1960) urban communes were tried, but generally the complexities of urban commercial, industrial, and residential patterns lent themselves poorly to the communal concept.[7] Nonetheless, the urban commune movement, even though it failed to achieve its original goals further altered urban living by doing away with urban landlordism. After this great redistribution of urban property, private ownership of individual residences was possible, but all other urban residential property belonged to the state. These two major changes in the ownership of property in the cities during the late 1950s swept away the chief characteristics of economic power and social advantage in urban life as they were known in Tsinan prior to 1949.

The Chinese policy toward industrialization has undergone several major shifts in the past twenty-five years. The various phases have included imitation at first of Soviet emphasis on heavy industry; shifts back to the wartime experience in Yenan, which stressed local self-reliance; modifications of Soviet highly centralized planning in order to avoid serious deficiencies in basic consumer goods; and attempts to marshal the work potential of women for production in neighborhood factories. Tsinan experienced all these various policy changes, but we need not trace each one here. The basic intent of all these efforts was to turn Tsinan from a place of residence or consumption into a place of production. And indeed the great majority of the population in cities like Tsinan had been drawn into periodic participation in production and construction by means of a comprehensive network of organizations which operate both in places of work and places of residence. Residential organizations have taken on increasingly important roles in the production process since the late 1950s, when large numbers of neighborhood workshops and small factories employing underemployed persons—especially women—made their first appearance. Along with these neighborhood organizations, factories, schools, and offices arrange the details of seasonal participation in rural agricultural work and contribute labor to civic construction tasks. Such short-term diversion of a small portion of an organization's labor force to special work became a regular feature of Chinese urban life in the 1960s and 1970s. Some urban residents, notably middle-school graduates,

207

have been resettled in rural areas for periods of several years. Occasionally such out-migrants from the cities become permanent residents of rural communes.

Since 1970 increased emphasis has been placed on relating industrial production to agricultural needs. A 1975 article about the industrial city of Changchow in Kiangsu stressed a new effort to gear industrial production to the needs of agriculture. The situation before 1949 in that city was characterized as one in which Changchow's industry was intended to provide profit to the Chinese entrepreneurs and not to help agricultural development. This constituted an antagonistic relationship, while the 1970s pattern is described as mutually beneficial because the city's factories now produce the kinds of motors, tractors, electrical equipment, and chemicals needed in local agriculture.[8]

The direction emphasized at Changchow formed part of a current national campaign in China and naturally affected Tsinan. Also, the characterization of Changchow's pre-1949 relationship with its hinterland is valid for Tsinan. At Tsinan, in addition to the class antagonism between urban merchants and rural peasants, we would have to take into account the factor that industry at Tsinan primarily served either the foreigners, through export processing, or the taste and convenience of its own urban residents. Industry to help transform Chinese agriculture was lacking at Tsinan, as elsewhere in Chinese treaty ports.

Ramon Myers in his account of the North China rural economy has laid special emphasis on the failure of the cities to transmit technological change into the countryside: ". . . agriculture could not develop more rapidly and introduce technological change to the peasant economy."[9] But it should be noted that an emphasis on relating urban industrial production to rural development needs was not a key element in the nineteenth-century Western model of the industrial city dominant in China until 1949. Moreover, urban handicraft production in late traditional China served urban rather than rural demand. Thus since 1949 Chinese cities have had to change the direction of both their traditional and modern industrial production to achieve a complete reorientation of their industrial goals. That adjustment itself has required more than twenty years to achieve.

At the same time, Tsinan has now regained its position as the leading political and administrative center of the province. Within a few months of the Kuomintang surrender, K'ang Sheng, a Shantungese who was a major figure within the top rank of CCP leadership, until his death in 1975, came to Tsinan as governor. Under K'ang Sheng and his successor, Chao Chien-min, another Shantungese, who served as governor from

1953 to 1958, Tsinan continued its historical role as the chief seat of civil administration and political power.

In addition Tsinan retained its importance as an educational and military center. In 1958, Shantung University was transferred from Tsingtao to new grounds in Tsinan's southwestern educational district, which already contained the Shantung Teachers' College, the Shantung Hospital (formerly the heart of the missionary Cheloo University), and the Shantung Engineering Institute. In military affairs, Tsinan has served as the headquarters for the Shantung Military District since 1949 and thus has been a major element in the command structure of the People's Liberation Army. In these four important sectors, then, Tsinan after 1949 continued to dominate the province along lines discussed in the earlier chapters of this book.

Political power in Tsinan after 1949, however, had a much different structure than before. The groups of military men, traditional gentry, and modernizing bureaucrats, new professionals and liberal commercial elements who had struggled for control in Tsinan, had disappeared with the economic and social reforms of the 1950s. In their place were officials of the Communist party, bureaucrats, and officers from the People's Liberation Army. In marked contrast to the failure of political parties in the pre-1949 era, there is reason to believe that the Communist party in Tsinan, as elsewhere in China, has succeeded in establishing itself as a critical element that permeates the whole society. Moreover, a network of representative bodies functioning from the neighborhoods up to the provincial level has been established to make the concept of representative government meaningful, although, again in this area of representative government, the principles of operation and expectation are quite different from those prevailing in the earlier Chinese experiments at Tsinan.

The cultural life of Tsinan has also undergone major changes since 1949. As the political and economic bases of the old culture were altered in the 1950s, the old cultural practices and attitudes lost much of their vitality. The Cultural Revolution of the late 1960s, however, marked an important watershed. In general the Cultural Revolution offered a challenge to cultural styles of the pre-1949 era, both those of a bourgeois character and those based on traditional Chinese culture, and was largely successful in replacing them with forms compatible to the proletarian and socialist character of the new era.

The foreign presence in Tsinan has completely disappeared in the mid-1970s, and the chief legacy of the various groups of foreigners who lived in the city from the late nineteenth century onward is found in the city's architecture. Various buildings around the city show the unmistakable architectural styles of their German, Japanese, British, American, and Russian designers. Today's new construction is based on a highly functional architectural style that seems suitable to a city with a socialist political and economic system and a proletarian culture.

THE FAILURE TO MODERNIZE

In this account of Tsinan's history, the city's modernization has been measured against the Western-derived standards that both Chinese and foreigners accepted until 1949. Rather than deal with a highly formalized and structured model of modernization, I have used the term "development" as a convenient reference for the aggregate elements from Western urban-industrial life—including some of the more ephemeral phenomena usually omitted from the highly abstract models of social scientists—that made up Tsinan's goals before 1949. To make this concept of development somewhat more manageable while describing the city's history, I have broken it into three facets—economic, political, and cultural. In each of these areas I have selected cases to illustrate how foreign influence, economic change, and political power—especially that wielded by the militarists, the traditional gentry, and the more modern commercial elements—worked to promote or block modernization.

Rather than comparing what was occurring in Tsinan with the situation in Shanghai, Tientsin, Wuhan, or other Chinese cities, in this account of Chinese urban change I have concentrated on the events in that particular city. The case of Tsinan, I believe, reveals quite clearly the overall pattern of Chinese urban development down to 1949. Although significant beginnings were made, Chinese cities failed to reach the levels of economic and political modernization necessary to achieve success along the lines of the Western model; in the areas of culture and technology, however, they assimilated Western practices that set them apart from their rural hinterlands, which remained largely traditional in those respects.

ECONOMIC MODERNIZATION

Throughout this account great importance has been attached to Tsinan's economic modernization, especially in considering, first, how the city changed from traditional commercial patterns to more modern ones, and then how its industrial capacities were developed.[10] We have seen how Tsinan underwent considerable economic change from 1890 to 1949, initially with an expanded commercial role as a result of canal and railroad construction, followed by the beginnings of modern industry. Surveys of Tsinan (Appendix A) reveal a slowly increasing level of industry, but much of that development was connected with transportation, public service functions, or export processing. Moreover, the numbers of industrial workers, both in absolute terms and as a percentage of Tsinan's work force, remained very low. In Tsinan, as in most other Chinese cities, industry clearly remained secondary to commerce. This one element itself meant that Tsinan, and other Chinese cities, could not achieve the Western urban industrial pattern of modernization.

Although there are no dependable trade figures for internal Chinese commerce, it is clear that Tsinan's commercial growth owes more to shifts and increases in the level of Chinese domestic commerce than to the expansion of foreign trade. This fact is of considerable importance because it undermines the argument of critics of the capitalist world economic system who relate the "underdevelopment" of Third World economics to the control of finance and commerce in coastal entrepôt cities by foreigners who come to dominate entire native economic systems. While this was the case in parts of Latin America and Africa, it was not in China.[11] We have seen how the fear of foreign economic dominance at Tsingtao drew Chinese officials and commercial interests together in Tsinan. Also, in spite of the increasing importance from the early 1900s onward of Japanese economic interests in Shantung, Tsinan remained, until 1937, free of true foreign domination. Accordingly, the term "semi-colonial" applies very aptly to Tsinan's economy, for Tsinan was strongly influenced, but still never completely dominated, by foreign economic interests.

In a number of specific cases we have traced the influence of foreign interests, Chinese commercial interests, and general economic conditions upon the development of Tsinan's economy. In particular, the kinds of economic modernization undertaken by Chinese at Tsinan have been detailed and described in terms of local commercial interests that modernized traditional lines such as banking and grain milling, as well as in terms of more innovative lines of industrialization undertaken by officials and merchants in cooperation. The most important factor in Tsinan's failure to achieve economic modernization, however, was the influence of the Chinese militarists.

In the period of Yüan Shih-k'ai's political domination, from 1900 to 1916, officially backed programs helped start Tsinan's industrialization, but Yüan's successful efforts to strictly limit the political power of local Shantungese interests helped preserve and transmit into the Republican era the traditional subordination of wealth to officialdom that prevailed in the Ch'ing period. The Chinese commercial and industrial interests at Tsinan proved to be politically weak, unable to control the province on their own terms. They remained subordinate to a series of militarist officials who took over after 1911. After 1916 these militarists damaged

Tsinan's efforts at commercial and industrial modernization through their excessive taxation and disruptive warfare. So baleful was their influence that Tsinan's real hopes for economic modernization were effectively crippled by 1925.

Tsinan's failure to achieve economic modernization antedated the great world depression and the ensuing war which was so damaging to the overall Chinese economy. The treaty ports like Shanghai, Tientsin, and Tsingtao did not suffer the same kind of disruptions Tsinan did in the mid-1920s, and the decisive moments in their own patterns of economic development came later, in the 1930s, with the world depression and the Sino-Japanese War.

The damage that Chinese warlordism did to economic modernization was not peculiar to Tsinan. Examples of similar maladministration and disruption attributable to warlords can be found in the history to Chinese-administered portions of the treaty ports, also. Still, the treaty ports, such as Shanghai and Tientsin, through their foreign-controlled enclaves, offered zones of safe refuge where Chinese industry and capital could retreat to avoid the effects of warlordism. Initially, I had hypothesized that Tsinan's freedom from the divided sovereignty which prevailed in the treaty ports constituted an advantage for the city. With a stable administration committed to economic modernization, that might have been the case. In fact, the deleterious effects of warlordism were so pervasive that Tsinan's status as a Chinese-governed city down to 1937 turned out to be a detriment to its economic modernization.

Comparison with Shenyang (Mukden), a similar inland political and administrative center in the northeast, shows that, in economic terms, less political independence and more foreign control meant more economic modernization. Shenyang was transformed primarily as a result of Japanese investment and control, and that city was well along the path to achieving the shape of a Western industrial-urban center by 1949.[12] The same could be said of Tsingtao, closer to Tsinan, which also developed under Japanese control a capacity for light industry that made it correspond more nearly to the economic aspect of Western modernization.

POLITICAL MODERNIZATION

The primary criterion of political modernization is the establishment of a stable, efficient, and rational bureaucracy that serves a representative political regime. Tsinan did acquire a bureaucracy that was—if not stable, efficient, and rational—at least usually Western-trained; but the other half of the requirement was definitely not fulfilled. Tsinan never had a truly representative government in the entire period from 1890 to 1949.

Instead, as we have just detailed, a series of strong military men dominated Tsinan from 1900 through 1949. The strongest and most effective of these praetorian leaders, Yüan Shih-k'ai, accomplished a great deal in terms of economic and cultural modernization, as well as in promoting modern bureaucracy in Tsinan. Yet Yüan had no taste for representative institutions, and can be blamed for destroying the prospect for representative government in the whole of China.

The success of militarist leadership in Tsinan—in men such as Yüan Shih-k'ai and Han Fu-ch'ü—depended in considerable measure upon their attention to traditional styles in administration, personal relations, and social practices. Yüan achieved much of his success through a group of officials bound to him by traditional loyalties of the Chinese bureaucracy and working from traditional Chinese assumptions about the nature of politics. Han Fu-ch'ü clearly sought to emulate the model traditional official in his administrative style, which stressed frugality, hard work, honesty, and stern administration of justice.

Tsinan had as many years of incompetent and unenlightened rule by other men in the praetorian mode. Chang Tsung-ch'ang was the worst of them, but most of the other warlord governors contributed little to Tsinan's progress. Tsinan's experience shows that warlord rule could be either ruinous or mildly progressive, but there was nothing in the system to protect the people from the installation of an undesirable warlord. Consequently the praetorian control of Tsinan's politics must be judged one of the main causes of the city's failure to modernize politically, as well as economically.

The warlord governments that ruled Tsinan during most of the years from 1890 to 1949 also affected efforts to create a professional and modern bureaucracy in the provincial administration. In particular, the various governors after 1916 found it difficult to extend their rule beyond the chief cities into the entire province, aggravating the already troublesome separation between Tsinan and the rural hinterlands. At other times the corrupt and self-seeking practices of various warlords demoralized the bureaucracy or caused an outright breakdown in the regular operation of major administrative bodies such as the financial department or the schools in Tsinan.

Under governors like Yüan and Han, the modernizing bureaucracy fared much better. Han's traditional political style was compatible with such a bureaucracy, and under his aegis during the 1930s the Shantung provincial bureaucracy began reestablishing administrative, political, and cultural links between the city and the rural areas of the province. Moreover, Tsinan for the first time established a true urban municipal administration that worked rather well.

The failure of representative institutions in Shantung is one of the obvious shortcomings of the pre-1949 years. The last elected Shantung provincial assembly from the late 1940s was a belated effort to revive the representative institutions destroyed by Yüan Shih-k'ai in 1913 and 1914. It is noteworthy that representative institutions flourished only for a very short period during the late Ch'ing reforms and the first years of the Republic—at the most, eight years. During the rest of the period, formal governmental representative bodies were either nonexistent or operated without any real substance.

The degree of political involvement, especially for the educated members of Tsinan's society, increased markedly in the 1890 to 1949 period. The acceptance of representative institutions after 1900, the growth of newspapers, the anti-Japanese nationalistic demonstrations of the May Fourth period and afterwards, make Tsinan fit the general pattern of increased politicization that marked all of Chinese urban life in the years before 1949.

Another political institution often associated with Western-style modernization is the political party. We have seen that in Tsinan political parties never became firmly rooted in the polity. Before 1911 the Revolutionary Alliance attracted considerable support from dissatisfied young men pursuing both civilian and military careers, but after the fall of the Manchus political parties never flourished in Tsinan. Predictably for this period, the Communist party suffered from the same kinds of conservative pressure that drove it out of other Chinese cities. The inability of the Kuomintang ever to establish itself in the city of Tsinan is somewhat more surprising. One explanation is that during the 1930s the Kuomintang preferred Tsingtao, which was administered directly by Nanking, to Tsinan, which was administered by a warlord. Thus Tsinan remained the political stronghold of Han Fu-ch'ü and those Shantungese who were opposed to modern political parties.

CULTURAL MODERNIZATION

Although various visitors to Tsinan throughout the 1930s referred to the persistence of traditional cultural values and practices, there can be little doubt that the greatest changes in Tsinan occurred in this realm of life.

The area of most marked change was education, in which new state-supported schools employed a Western-derived curriculum with a strong nationalistic tone. The teaching staffs in these schools were frankly modern and professional in outlook. They assimilated the cultural aims of Western education in a very thorough fashion and succeeded best in cities like Tsinan where the money, the interested students, and the necessary facilities all came together. One crude measure of the pervasiveness of the switch to Western educational modes and goals is that fifteen years after

214

the founding of the People's Republic of China, a major reform process—the Cultural Revolution of the 1960s—took as one of its chief goals ridding the educational establishment of these "bourgeois" influences.

Foreign culture penetrated other areas of Tsinan's life, from entertainment and style of dress to the layout of new streets and the appearance and design of new buildings. Hospitals, newspapers, the cinema, automobiles, radios, electricity, and all the other trappings of urban-industrial society in the West functioned best in cities such as Tsinan and thoroughly affected the lives of the people who lived there. In the countryside, by contrast, most of these technological innovations were seldom part of daily life. Thus these changes divorced the urban residents from the realities of life confronting the vast majority of Chinese who continued to live in the countryside. Cultural modernization without economic and political development proved to be not a blessing but a curse, for it robbed those who acquired modern culture of their grasp of the traditional culture without providing a firm economic and political base on which all China could change.

Reference Matter

Appendix A
Tsinan's Industry, 1900-1936

The tables in this appendix present as much detailed information on Tsinan's industry as is available through the late 1930s. The first two tables concern the organization and control of Tsinan's Western-style industry during the early years of the twentieth century when Western technology was first being imported into the city. Unfortunately, the later surveys do not contain as much information about the always fascinating question of ownership and control of the city's industrial plants.

Tables A.3 and A.4 are true surveys of industry which cover most lines of industrial production in the city. Although not strictly comparable, the two surveys do provide fairly adequate information on the numbers of firms in various lines, the capital investments, and the numbers of employees. These surveys show that Tsinan continued to develop as an industrial center in the 1930s under Han Fu-ch'ü, especially in textiles and machinery. Yet it should be noted that development along these lines at Tsinan was much slower than it was at Tsingtao, where Japanese investments backed larger and more advanced plants.

Some general information is available about Tsinan's industry after the Japanese occupation in 1938, but the accounts list only the larger industries and therefore are much less complete than the surveys made in the 1920s and 1930s. These Japanese surveys show that the number of flour mills had increased to ten by 1938, but they do not provide adequate information to judge how the textile and machinery lines, which had been expanding in the 1920s and 1930s, fared under Japanese management. Most of these firms, in fact, came under Japanese control after 1938 and probably did rather well for a few years before the general contraction of the North China economy in the later stages of the war.*

*See Manabe Gorō, *Hokushi chihō toshi gaikan* (Osaka: Ajia shuppanksha, 1940) and Basho Shotaro, *Hokushi hashō no shigen* (Tokyo: Tokyo shigyo nihonsha, 1939). For the conditions in the Tsinan textile industry in the later stages of the war see Kahoku sōgō chōsa kenkyūjō, ed., *Sainan shokufugyō chōsa hōkokusho* (Peking: Kahoku sōgō chōsa kenkyūjō, 1945)

Table A.1
Large Industrial Concerns in Tsinan, 1901-1911

Name	Date Founded	Operating and Financial Information
China Merchants Electric Company	1906	Headed by Liu En-chu. More than 200,000 *taels* capital. Official connections and linked to another electric power company in Chefoo. Started operation in 1906 with used German equipment from Tsingtao. Employed 130 men.[a, b, c]
Le-yuan Paper Mill	1906	Joint official-merchant undertaking. 250,000 *taels* capital. Located in building constructed for Shantung provincial mint. Closed in 1909 because of peculation by manager of its subsidiary printing plant.[b, d]
Official Dyeing and Weaving Works	1903	Began as project of a new provincial handicraft bureau (*kung-i chü*) started by Yüan Shih-k'ai. At first had wooden cotton looms, later obtained metal frame looms. Main importance was as a training ground for weavers and dyers. By 1918 Tsinan had six large private firms engaged in this handicraft industry.[c]
I-hua Weaving and Dyeing Plant	1911	A branch of a Tientsin cotton textile manufacturer. 5000 *yuan* capital. No known official connections. Employed 27 workers; used wooden looms.[b, c]
Tsinan Telephone Company	1908	Originally started as an official enterprise in 1902. Became a joint stock company in 1908. Reorganized in 1915. Service very restricted prior to 1911.[a, c]
Chi-ho Machine Company	190-?	A small machine shop founded by Chou Ch'ing-yu. Not as large or complex as other Chinese machine shops at Wei-hsien, Chefoo, and Tsingtao. Closed prior to 1911.[f]
Chih-ch'eng Brick Factory	1904	Begun to meet demand for bricks to be used in new construction in the Tsinan settlement. This firm did not survive, but Hsi-nan liang-chia-chuang village in the settlement area became a center for brick manufacture.[f]
Ch'uan-chi-t'ai Iron Works	1903?	A factory involved in the construction of the Tientsin-Pukow railroad. Headed by Wang Chuan-hsun. Capital of 20,000 *taels*, 80 workmen. Closed around 1911.[e]
Hsing-shun-fu Oil Pressing Plant	1911?	Used German equipment to process peanuts and soybeans. First Chinese operation in Tsinan to give competition to foreign oil presses operating at Tsingtao and Chefoo.[c, f]

Sources:

[a]Ch'en Chen, comp., *Chung-kuo chin-tai kung-yeh shih tzu-liao, ti-erh chi* (Peking: San-lien shu-tien, 1958), 1:38-53.

[b]"New Industry at Tsinan," *Chinese Economic Monthly* 2.4 (January 1925): 13-26.

[c]Oka Itaro, *Santō keizai jijō, Sainan o chū to shite* (Osaka: n.p., 1918), pp. 73-79.

[d]Ho Ping-yin, ed., *Chung-kuo shih-yeh chih, Shan-tung sheng* (Shanghai: Shih-yeh pu, kuo-chi mao-i chü, 1934), 6:636-40, 7:36.

[e]P'eng Tse-i, comp., *Chung-kuo chin-tai shou kung-yeh shih tzu-liao, 1840-1949,* 4 vols. (Peking: San-lien shu-tien, 1957), 2:655-56.

[f]Shan-tung ta-hsüeh, li-shih hsi, *Shan-tung ti-fang shih chiang-shou t'i-kang* (Tsinan: Jen-min ch'u-pan she, 1959), p. 58.

Table A.2
Major Industrial Operations in Tsinan, 1914

Name	Ownership	Background
Tsinan Electric Light Company	Liu En-chu	Had moved from original plant to larger quarters in a developing industrial section within the inter-wall area. Served 5,000 subscribers and employed over 40 workmen.
Tsinan Telephone Company	Joint official merchant relationship. Ma Kuan-ho most prominent Chinese associated with telephone company.	Purchased new equipment in in 1913 from the Germans. Had 600 subscribers.
Hsing-shun-fu Machine Flour Milling Factory	Unknown	Developed from bean-and-peanut-oil pressing operations begun in 1911. Used German milling equipment. Sold flour locally, and in Tsingtao and Tientsin as well. About half of the peanut oil production in 1913 was exported to Germany and Japan.
Che-yeh Match Company	Ts'ung Liang-pi	Ts'ung had lived in Osaka for twenty years, where he worked in a match factory. He returned to Shantung after the Revolution and raised $250,000, with the assistance of Chou Tzu-ch'i and P'an Fu, in order to start his match factory. In later years the Che-yeh Company opened two other factories in Shantung.
Tai-pei Model Weaving & Dyeing Works	Ma Kuan-ho	Had more than twenty mechanized looms. Produced cloth both for domestic consumption and export. Capital of $10,000.
Chang-feng Weaving & Dyeing Works	Kao Hsiang-p'u	Had more than twenty advanced model handicraft looms. Employed 50 workers. Capital of $10,000.

Sources: Yeh Ch'un-ch'ih, ed., *Chi-nan chih-nan* (Tsinan: Ta-tung jih-pao, 1914), pp. 54-57; *Chinese Economic Bulletin* 148 (22 December 1923): 2.

Table A.3
Survey of Tsinan Industry, 1926

Type	Number of Firms	Capital (yuan)	Workforce	Founded	Location
Food processing					
Flour mills	9	5,100,000	810	1916-1923	Walled city; settlement
Sugar refining	1	5,000,000	130	1920	Suburb
Oil pressing plants	4	284,000	198	1908-1924	Settlement
Noodle manufacture	2	7,000	39	1916-1918	Walled city
Subtotal	16	10,391,000	1,177		
Clothing					
Cotton spinning	1	2,300,000	2,500	1919	Suburbs
Toweling	8	11,000	220	1911-1924	Walled city
Cotton cloth	10	21,000	180	1913-1925	Walled city
Cotton hosiery	6	110,000	90	1921-1923	Walled city
Dye makers	1	100,000	54	1919	Walled city
Cap & glove maker	2	3,000	19	1923	Walled city
Silk filatures	20	42,000	360	1904-1925	Villages
Silk cloth	12	18,000	121	1917-1925	Villages
Subtotal	60	2,605,000	3,544		
Machinery & metal					
Machine works	4	250,000	530	1913-1921	Settlement
Flour mill equipment	4	15,000	160	1917-1921	Settlement; walled city

222

	No.	Capital	Workers	Years	Location
Machinery repair	3	8,000	152	1917-1920	Settlement
Cotton looms	2	7,000	90	1913-1914	Settlement
Needle manufacture	1	100,000	69	1921	Settlement
Ironware	7	11,000	88	1913-1925	Walled city
Subtotal	21	391,000	1,089		
Construction					
Brick kilns	4	80,000	670	1919-1923	Settlement
Cement plant	1	15,000	21	1923	Settlement
Subtotal	5	95,000	691		
Miscellaneous					
Match manufacture	1	500,000	800	1914	Walled city
Paper manufacture	1	1,000,000	80	1919	Walled city
Tanneries	3	14,000	155	1914-1921	Settlement; walled city
Rug weaving	4	190,000	390	1913-1921	Settlement; walled city
Glass light fixture	1	30,000	50	1917	Settlement
Glassware	2	47,000	110	1918-1922	Settlement
Soap	3	50,000	105	1920-1923	Settlement; walled city
Perfume	3	9,000	30	1899-1911	Walled city
Subtotal	18	1,840,000	1,720		
Total	120	15,322,000	8,221		

Source: Sun Pao-sheng, comp., *Li-ch'eng hsien hsiang-t'u tiao-ch'a lu* (Tsinan: Li-ch'eng hsien shih-yeh chü, 1928), pp. 152-61.
Note: Wholly Japanese-owned industry, public utilities, and the Fifth Division arsenal are not included.

223

Table A.4
Survey of Tsinan Industry, 1933

Type	Number of Firms	Capital (yuan)	Workforce	Founded
Food processing				
Four mills	7	910,000	662	1915-1932
Sugar refining[a]				
Oil pressing[b]				
Noodles[b]				
Soybean products	131	173,000	675	1850s-1932
Wine	2	9,000	20	1913, 1926
Canned food	1	150,000	35	1914
Subtotal	141	1,242,000	1,392	
Textiles & clothing				
Cotton spinning	3	4,800,000	3,500	1919, 1932, 1933
Cotton weaving & dyeing	38	228,000	980	1913-1932
Cotton weaving	29	70,000	1,195	1913-1932
Dyeing	8	18,300	220	1890s-1932
Calendaring	3	12,300	55	1930-1933
Cotton baling	1	300,000	100	1931
Silk filatures[a]				
Silk weaving[a]				
Silk ribbons	4	24,000	393	1924-1931
Toweling	4	5,100	59	1908-1930
Embroidery	4	1,800	75	1928-1933
Dyestuff manufacture	1	100,000	75	1921
Subtotal	95	5,559,500	6,652	
Machinery & metal				
Machine works	5	15,400	307	1917-1931
Machinery repair	6	12,700	211	1920-1932
Textile machinery	5	13,300	90	1924-1931

Flour milling machinery[b]				
Brass	21	35,300	329	1877-1918
Ironware	2	6,200	63	1923-1928
Needle manufacture	1	50,000	90	1921
Subtotal	40	132,900	1,090	
Construction				
Brick kilns	9	155,500	995	1919-1932
Traditional brick making	11	31,700	227	1916-1929
Subtotal	20	187,200	1,222	
Public service				
Electricity	1	720,000	225	1906
Telephone	1	—	150	1908
Subtotal	2	720,000	375	
Miscellaneous				
Match manufacture	4	520,000	1,275	1913, 1930, 1931, 1932
Paper manufacture[c]	1	1,000,000	75	1919
Tanneries	20	53,000	—	1918-1937
Rug weaving	6	5,600	50	1913-1918
Soap	6	44,000	130	1919-1933
Printing	20	64,800	395	1921-1932
Medicine	5	5,600	—	1905-1918
Cigarettes	1	20,000	143	1931
Subtotal	63	1,713,000	2,068+	
Total	362	9,554,600+	12,799+	

Source: Ho Ping-yin, ed., *Chung-kuo shih-yeh chih, Shan-tung sheng.*

Note: Wholly Japanese-owned industry, railroad shops, or military arsenals are not included. However, the 1933 survey does include many industrial enterprises, such as soybean products firms or brass foundries, which were overlooked in the 1926 summary.

[a]Closed.

[b]None listed, survey oversight.

[c]Paper mill only working sporadically because of financial problems and Japanese competition.

Appendix B
Tsinan's Population, 1770-1975

In the text, information on Tsinan's population has been mentioned only in passing, but the subject is important enough to warrant a more detailed discussion. It seemed best for two reasons to put this discussion into an appendix. First, segregation of the population data makes it easier for the reader to appraise critically the information and the conclusions I have drawn. Second, there are serious problems with the reliability of various kinds of population statistics, and they are best presented in an appendix rather than in a series of notes scattered through the text.

In the course of my research about Tsinan, I found several different sets of population figures for the city, from three different political periods. First, there are two sets of population figures for Tsinan from the middle Ch'ing. Second, I have found four sets of population data from the Republican era, and finally, five separate population totals for the years 1949 to 1974.

Each set has its own peculiar limitations and weaknesses. The middle Ch'ing figures have been criticized by Ho Ping-ti because of serious lacunae in the system of houshold registration.* Nevertheless, the Japanese scholar Nakamura Jihei has made a careful evaluation of some of the best *pao-chia* registers (*ch'ing-tse*) from the North China region, including Tsinan. The middle Ch'ing figures are questionable because of problems of under-registration and the fact that registration practices leave us in doubt about how servants, refugees, and long-term sojourners were dealt with by the registrars. This information would seem to affect the computation of household size most seriously, and yet the registers give a fair indication of the general size of the city and its overall growth pattern.

The most significant deficiency in the Ch'ing population data is the fact that no figures at all are available for Tsinan's population from 1837 to 1911. The fact that no population registration figures could be found for Tsinan for more than three-quarters of a century in the late Ch'ing surely indicates that some of the underlying control mechanisms of the late traditional Chinese state were never reestablished after the great rebellions. This was a period in which the city's population certainly grew, for we know that the city's walls were extended to surround the two bustling commercial areas at the northeastern and southwestern gates. It also was a time

*Ho Ping-ti, *Studies on the Population of China, 1368-1953* (Cambridge: Harvard University Press, 1959), pp. 47-53.

when the city's population was temporarily swelled by refugees fleeing internal rebellion, foreign invasion, flood disasters, and famine. Unfortunately, we have no information on how many people came to Tsinan, or when and why they did or did not return to their original homes. The only information on Tsinan's population from the late nineteenth century that I located consisted of a number of estimates by foreign residents and visitors. These have been quoted in Table B.3 but are only a kind of guess at the very best. Their chief value would seem to be that the wide variation shows how carefully one must use such estimates.

Four different sets of figures about Tsinan are available from the Republican era, and although scholars have always treated Republican era figures with the greatest caution, for Tsinan there is good reason to accord these statistics more credibility than usual. Much of the criticism of Republican-period population figures is directed to various estimates of urban, provincial, and national population as developed by the Chinese Post Office or other organs of the Chinese central government. At best these were estimates and in some instances were outright guesses. The Tsinan figures, based on a system of household registration, are much sounder.

At the times of the 1914, 1919, 1933, and 1942 registration reports Tsinan had a modern police force, modeled on Japanese practices. The Japanese developed excellent census and household registration procedures and some of them were followed by the Chinese police force in Tsinan. Unfortunately, the rules by which the registrations were carried out are not included with the figures, so again we do not know exactly how children, servants, refugees, and sojourners from outlying communities were treated. The figures from the Republican era do provide totals for households, sexes, and districts within the city. The extent of these districts was indicated on accompanying maps and showed that there was considerable redefinition of the area referred to as the suburbs (*hsiang-ch'ü*). The changing size and definition of that area makes that component of the population figures the least reliable and significant. Therefore, I have not computed growth rates for the suburbs. On the other hand, the other three sections of the city, the old walled area (pre-1860s), the new walled area (post-1860s), and the settlement district (post-1905), remained almost constant in size. Given the general principles of the Japanese model and the fact that one such set of population figures actually dates from a period of Japanese administration (1942), these data should be given much more credence that the Post Office estimates.

The third set of population information, that from the period of the People's Republic, is probably the least satisfactory, for only population totals are provided, with no indication of household size, sex ratios, or dimensions of the urban area. Yet given the character of the administration under the People's Republic and the fact that a genuine census was conducted in 1953, there seems to me to be little reason to doubt the totals are more than guesses and to accept them generally as being based on a sound household registration system.

With the various kinds of data available, it has been possible to plot the overall pattern of increase in Tsinan's population from the late eighteenth century until the mid-1970s. In addition, some of the information has permitted the computation of sex ratios (male/female), household size, and rate of increase within

227

various sections of the city. When possible, I have compared the growth of Tsinan with what we know about the overall population of Shantung, in spite of the fact that the Shantung estimates are likely to be much less accurate than the Tsinan figures. Finally, I have tried to relate the rate of Tsinan's increase in population to what one might expect for a Western-style, rapidly industrializing city of the nineteenth century.

Let us begin with the figures from the late eighteenth century, as presented by Nakamura, which make Tsinan a city of 50,000 (Table B.1). At that time Tsinan's commercial importance was much lower than it was in the late nineteenth century, for the chief trading avenues still lay westward along the Grand Canal, and cities such as Lin-ch'ing and Chi-ning remained the large commercial centers in western Shantung.

Table B.1
Population of Tsinan, 1772

	Households	Population	Average Household Size
Within city walls	6,117	25,946	4.24
Suburbs	6,394	23,188	3.63
Total	12,511	49,134	3.93

Source: Nakamura Jihei, "Shintai kahoku no tōshi no kokō ni kansuru ichi kōsatsu," *Shien* 100 (March 1968), pp. 169-80.

The second set of population data comes from household registers of 1837 (Table B.2). These figures indicate that Tsinan had more than doubled its population in the sixty-five years since 1772, a growth rate of 1.5% per annum. The 1837 figures also provide us a glimpse into the population of Tsinan's immediate hinterland, Li-ch'eng *hsien*. This territory south of the city included mountainous land unsuitable for most farming, while east, west, and north of Tsinan, Li-ch'eng *hsien* comprised part of the flat North China plain that was rather thickly settled with small rural villages and trading communities. The northern boundary lay along the banks and dikes of the Yellow River. These 1837 figures show that the rural population of Li-ch'eng was five times as great as the urban concentration in Tsinan, so in spite of Tsinan's increasing population, the city was still located within a predominately rural district. Unfortunately, we have no figures for Li-ch'eng *hsien* in the late eighteenth century, so it cannot be determined if Tsinan was growing faster than its hinterland. The only available way of gauging Tsinan's growth is to compare it with the overall growth in Shantung's population. Because of the many sources of possible inaccuracies in the Shantung totals, such comparisons are only capable of indicating general trends. Shantung's population from 1787 to 1850 grew at a rate of 0.6% (see Table B.8), while my computations for Tsinan indicate a somewhat higher rate (1.5% down to 1837 and 0.9% after that date). Thus we can conclude that Tsinan was growing slightly faster than the overall increase in Shantung population, but certainly was not serving as a powerful magnet to draw rural residents in large numbers into a traditional Chinese urban environment.

Table B.2
Population of Tsinan, 1837

	Households	Population	Average Household Size	Growth Rate (1772-1837)[a]
Li-ch'eng *hsien*	144,520	603,177	4.17	—
Tsinan	25,374	127,717	5.04	1.5%

Source: Wang Tseng-fang, comp., *Chi-nan fu-chih* (1840), ch. 15/10b-11a.

[a]Growth rates were calculated using the formula $r = \dfrac{\ln (Yo/Yt)}{T}$ where r is the rate of growth, Yt is the population in first observation, Yo is the population in the second instance, $\ln$ is the natural log, and T is the number of years between the two observations.

After 1837, the growth rate of Tsinan declined. The best available figures after 1837 are the 1914 and 1919 household register figures (Tables B.4 and B.5). The increase to a population of 245,990 in 1914 yields a growth rate of 0.9%, while the lower 1919 population totals of 202,316—a result from a reduction in size of the suburb area—give a 0.7% growth rate. This again is a larger rate of increase than the comparable increase in Shantung's population from 33,127,000 in 1850 to 37,826,000 in 1930, with the quite low growth rate of 0.2%. The Shantung total for 1930 was not based on sound demographic procedures and it seems best to limit any inference drawn from these data to the conclusion that Tsinan was still growing slowly, at a slightly faster rate than the general increase in Shantung's population. The estimates of foreigners from the late nineteenth century (Table B.3) are not much help, but their reports and the scanty photographic evidence from the early twentieth century indicate that, although certain commercial and administrative areas in the city were crowded with throngs of people, much of the inner walled section retained an uncrowded, park-like atmosphere.

In 1914 the first of the four reproductions of police registers was printed (Table B.4). The 1914 data are divided by districts within the city and we see that a great deal of the city's increased population had come to reside in sections which first

Table B.3
Late Nineteenth-Century Estimates of Tsinan's Population

Date	Source	Estimate
1860s	Williamson	100,000
1880s	Armstrong	515,000
	Coltman	200,000-300,000
1898	von Hesse Wartegg	250,000-500,000
1906	Neal	250,000

Sources: Alexander Williamson, *Journeys in North China, Manchuria and Eastern Mongolia with some account of Korea*, 2 vols. (London: Smith and Elder: 1870), 1:102-4; Alexander Armstrong, *In a Mule Litter to the Tomb of Confucius* (London:Nisbet, 1886), pp. 61-62; Robert Coltman, *The Chinese, Their Present and Future: Medical, Political and Social* (London: F. A. Davis, 1891), p. 58; Ernst von Hesse Wartegg, *Schantung und Deutsch:China im Jahre 1898* (Leipzig: J. J. Weber, 1898), p. 124; James Boyd Neal, "Tsinanfu, Capital of Shantung," *East of Asia Magazine* 5 (1906):334.

were protected by walls in the 1860s. The new settlement district, which already had a sizable population, was still only in its infancy and would grow much more rapidly in the coming years.

Table B.4

Population of Tsinan, 1914

	Households	Population	Average Household Size	Sex Ratios (Males/Females)	Growth Rate 1837-1914
Within old city walls	12,990	56,574	4.36	1.91	
Within outer city walls	17,806	70,186	3.94	1.45	
Settlement district	2,556	11,159	4.37	2.44	
Suburbs	28,829	108,071	3.75	1.22	
Total	62,181	245,990	3.96	1.47	0.9%

Source: Yeh Ch'un-ch'ih, ed., *Chi-nan chih-nan* (Tsinan: Ta-tung jih-pao, 1914), p. 417.

The rapid growth of the settlement district becomes obvious in the 1919 statistics, which show that the district had tripled its population in just five years (Table B.5). The new walled section continued to grow, but much less rapidly. The 1919 figures also show quite unmistakably how the redefinition of the suburbs strongly affected the overall population totals for the city. On the basis of travelers' descriptions there seems to be good reason to think that these areas outside or adjacent to the city were also rapidly increasing in population, but statistical evidence of this was lost when the urban area was redefined. There was less regulation in those villages, and although economic opportunity was not readily available, many refugees and poor immigrants who came to Tsinan may have been forced to live in what formerly had been small rural villages only a few kilometers from the city. Unfortunately, the statistical data and maps only alert us to the possibility of such development and contain no real information that might indicate what was occurring.

Although the totals from Table B.5 indicate that Tsinan was declining in population, this is clearly an incorrect picture. When we exclude the fluctuating suburbs from our information, and consider only the two walled areas and the settlement district, Tsinan's population increased at a 4.4% rate.

The next set of data from the 1930s, when the Kuomintang was in control of Tsinan, shows that the suburban area had been enlarged again, possibly to take into the urban administration some of these closely related suburban settlements (Table B.6). The data for the walled sections and the settlement district show that all continued to grow and that more and more people were living in the older sections of the city as well as in the fast-growing and somewhat enlarged settlement district. Photographs of Tsinan from these years show that many two-story residences were constructed in walled sections, while the settlement district also contained two- and three-story buildings which combined commercial, storage, and residential functions.

230

Table B.5
Population of Tsinan, 1919

	Households	Population	Average Household Size	Sex Ratio (Males/Females)	Growth Rate (1914-1919)
Within old city walls	12,666	54,804	4.33	1.80	- 0.6%
Within outer city walls	17,722	84,769	4.79	2.00	3.8%
Settlement district	8,356	32,304	3.87	2.60	21.3%
Suburbs	7,535	30,439	4.04	1.40	—
Total	46,279	202,316	4.37	1.94	- 3.9%
Tsinan less suburbs	38,744	171,877	4.4	2.02	4.4%

Source: Mao Ch'eng-lin, comp., *Hsü-hsiu Li-ch'eng hsien-chih* (1924), ch. 4/la-3a.

Table B.6
Population of Tsinan, 1933

	Households	Population	Average Household Size	Sex Ratio (Males/Females)	Growth Rate (1919-1933)
Within old city walls	14,493	71,543	4.94	1.71	1.9%
Within outer city walls	21,108	105,618	5.00	1.61	1.6%
Settlement district	14,957	80,233	5.36	2.36	6.5%
Suburbs	46,310	170,378	3.68	1.32	—
Total	96,868	427,772	4.42	1.60	5.3%

Source: Ho Ping-yin, ed., *Chung-kuo shih-yeh chih, Shan-tung sheng* (Shanghai: Shih-yeh pu, kuo-chi mao-i chü, 1934), 4, *chia*/7-10.

These figures from the period of Chinese rule in the early twentieth century (Tables B.4, B.5, and B.6) show an interesting variation in average household size and sex ratios in the different sections of the city. There clearly is a distinction between the old walled city, which has an average household size of 4.3 or better all during these years, and the suburban areas, which have a smaller average household size. This probably reflects the fact that wealthier households seemed to have favored the old walled city or other parts of the city proper rather than the suburbs, which were much more the domain of the poor and less well established people.

In sex ratio figures the great number of men in the settlement district stands out quite clearly. This probably reflects the newness of the district and the choice of that area for residence by large numbers of men working in Tsinan who either did not have families or chose not to reside with their families in the city. It is also worth mentioning that throughout the city of Tsinan, the city proper had a much higher ratio of men to women than prevailed in the suburban areas.

231

When we turn to the question of growth rates in the early twentieth century, we find that the comparison between the 1914 and 1942 figures yields a growth rate of 3.0 percent. The rate of growth shown by comparing the 1919 and 1933 figures is much higher, 5.9 percent, but part of that can be attributed to distortions in the totals, introduced by the redefinition of the suburban districts in each of the sets of figures. If we recompute the yearly percentage of growth between 1919 and 1933 using the three essentially fixed areas within Tsinan (old and new walled sections together with the settlement district) the growth rate comes out at 2.9 percent. This figure is quite close to the growth rate indicated between 1933 and 1942 (3.3 percent). Taken together, these figures reveal that Tsinan was growing at roughly 3 percent in the the Republican period, three times as fast as during the years from 1837 to 1914.

It would be possible to compare Tsinan's rate of growth with some of the Post Office estimates from the early twentieth century to show that Tsinan's population was growing much faster than the province overall. Given the weakness of the Shantung totals this procedure is somewhat doubtful, but the same conclusion can be reached simply by applying Tsinan's twentieth-century growth rate of 3.0 percent to any figure for Shantung's total population. For instance a 3.0 percent growth rate applied to Shantung's population of 37,821,000 for 1930 would have produced a population of 50 million for Shantung by 1940. Clearly Shantung's population was growing at a much lower rate, probably around 1 percent as indicated by the computation of a growth rate between the 1937 total of 37.8 million and the 1953 total of 48.9 million.

Table B.7
Population of Tsinan, 1942

	Households	Population	Average Household Size	Sex Ratio (Males/Females)	Growth Rate (1933-1942)
Within old city walls	13,356	81,253	6.08	1.47	1.4%
Within outer city walls	25,010	130,053	5.20	1.54	2.3%
Settlement district	32,510	164,056	5.05	1.69	5.1%
Suburbs	42,626	200,459	4.70	1.35	—
Total	113,502	575,821	5.07	1.50	3.3%

Source: *Chi-nan shih-cheng kung-pao* 3.3 (December 1942): 44-45.

There are two possible explanations for the upturn in Tsinan's growth rate in the twentieth century. First, and probably foremost, was the increase in migration to the city as wealthier families were drawn into Tsinan because of its relative security, its better schools, and its increased political and economic opportunities. More ordinary folk, seeking employment in Tsinan's transportation, commercial, and industrial functions, also flocked to the city, as did refugees from the peasantry or working classes in other parts of Shantung, who came in flight from natural or manmade disasters. This increase continued even during the Japanese occupation (Table B.7).

The other explanation for Tsinan's increasing rate of growth is the improvement in public health. The introduction of Western medical practices and Western industrial standards of nutrition, the construction of hospitals by missionaries and Japanese and Chinese interests, the growth of public sanitation work under police supervision, and the development of better sewage disposal and water supply facilities by the city's public works office all certainly made the city a healthier place to live in than it was in the late eighteenth century. We have no information on death rates in Tsinan, but the kind of improvements Tsinan experienced in medicine and public health after 1900 are those associated with a rapid decline in infant mortality and a general improvement in life expectancy for adults. Both migration and declining death rates obviously contributed to Tsinan's growth: although it is impossible from the data to determine which was the more important, my own choice would be to emphasize increased migration to the city.

Table B.8
Shantung's Population, 1787-1970

Year	Total Population	Growth Rate	
1787	22,565,000[a]		
1850	33,127,000[a]	1787-1850	0.6%
1930	37,826,000[b]	1850-1930	0.2%
1953	48,877,000[a]	1930-1953	1.1%
1970	57,000,000[c]	1953-1970	0.8%

Sources:

[a]Ho Ping-ti, *Studies on the Population of China, 1368-1953,* Appendix II.

[b]Ho Ping-yin, ed., *Chung-kuo shih-yeh chih, Shan-tung sheng,* chia/58.

[c]R. M. Field, "Chinese Provincial Population Data," *China Quarterly* 44 (October-December 1970): 195-202.

The best way to understand this question is to approach it indirectly by investigating the ratio of Tsinan's population to the total population of Shantung in the nineteenth and twentieth centuries (Table B.9). While the overall total of population in China remained rather stable, at 430 to 480 millions, according to the available estimates, from 1850 to the 1930s, the North China region in which Tsinan is located continued to grow. The province of Shantung officially increased from 33,127,000 in 1850 to 48,877,000 in 1953, or 47 percent, in spite of regular large-scale emigration to the Northeast (Manchuria). The growth of Tsinan's population should reflect this general increase in the population of its hinterland, but the city should also have grown at an even higher rate because of its increasing economic and political importance. In fact, Tsinan grew from a city of 149,000 in 1850 to 680,000 in 1953, a 456 percent increase. As we have concluded earlier, Tsinan grew at a slightly faster rate than its hinterland down to the first decade of the twentieth century, when it began growing at about three times the overall growth rate of the province (Table B.8).

Yet, as dramatic as Tsinan's growth was in the century from 1850 to 1950, the city never had 1.5 percent of the province's total population. To fulfill the model of a Western industrial city, Tsinan should have pulled residents of smaller cities, towns, and rural villages into its population at an even higher rate to work in new factories, offices, and transportation operations. Ideally, to fit the model of a

Table B.9
Tsinan's Population as a Percentage
of Shantung's Total Population

Year	Tsinan	Shantung	Column A as a % of Column B
1787	61,429	22,565,000	0.27
1850	149,000	33,127,000	0.45
1930	385,000	37,826,000	1.02
1953	680,000	48,877,000	1.39
1970	1,100,000	57,000,000	1.93

Sources: Derived from Fig. B.1 Tsinan Population; Shantung figures same as Table B.8.

Western industrial city, Tsinan should have come to have about 5 to 10 percent of its economic hinterland's total population. Tsinan's economic hinterland in the twentieth century included most of northern and western Shantung north of Chi-ning. Tsinan also dominated Shantung eastward to Wei-hsien, an important city in its own right, which was falling under the increasing domination of Tsingtao, a rapidly growing port city which, on the basis of its industrial development financed largely by Japanese capital as well as its trade and tourist importance, passed Tsinan in the 1930s as the province's single largest city. Table B.9 gives Tsinan's population as a ratio of the overall provincial population, and even if Tsinan is considered to have split the total Shantung population with Tsingtao, the city of Tsinan never came close to having 5 or 10 percent of the total population of its economic hinterland. The failure of Tsinan's population to increase at a more rapid rate is a reflection of the general pattern of failure to achieve the kind of modernization which both foreigners and Chinese envisioned for Tsinan and other Chinese cities in the early twentieth century.

Population figures for Tsinan after the founding of the PRC in 1949 reveal that the city remained, as before, among the twenty largest urban places in China. Within the province of Shantung, however, Tsinan was second in total population, a situation which first developed in the 1930s, when Tsingtao grew more rapidly.

For the post-1949 period we are able only to compare population totals (Table B.10), and these show that Tsinan grew at a rather slower rate (1.5 percent) during the eleven years from 1942 to 1953. In the 1950s, however, Tsinan experienced another spurt of growth and continued to grow at about 3-4 percent per annum to the mid-1960s. The figures available from 1966 to 1974 indicate no growth or even a decline in the total population of Tsinan. These conclusions are admittedly based on comments which are only passing references to the size of Tsinan's population in a general description of the city, but which must, I believe, be taken at their face value to mean that the urban administration has intended that the city not grow in recent years.

Yet, on the basis of my 1974 visit to Tsinan, I find it rather hard to believe that the city has not grown since the mid-1960s. All around there was evidence of increased productive capacities in heavy industry, including petroleum processing, and in light industry. Surely these new productive facilities required some importation of new workers. In these circumstances the only way in which Tsinan

Table B.10
Population of Tsinan Since 1949

Year	Population	Growth Rate	
1953	680,000[a]	1942-1953	1.5%
1957	862,000[a]	1953-1957	5.9%
1958	882,000[a]	1957-1958	2.3%
1966	1,100,000[b]	1958-1966	2.8%
	1,200,000[c]	1958-1966	3.9%
1974	1,100,000[d]	1966-1974	0.0%
		1953-1966	3.7%

Sources:
[a]Morris B. Ullman, *Cities of Mainland China, 1953 and 1958* (Washington, D.C., 1961).
[b]Rewi Alley, *Travels in China, 1966-1971* (Peking: Foreign Languages Press, 1973), p. 227.
[c]*Nagel's China* (New York, 1968), p. 704.
[d]Remarks of Wang Shan-chih of Tsinan Urban Construction Bureau in interview with author on November 22, 1974.

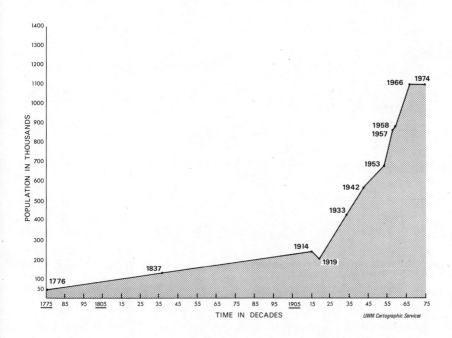

Figure B.1. Population of Tsinan, 1776-1974

235

could have maintained a steady population total is to have resettled a considerable number of people in other parts of the province to offset both the natural increase in population and the new workers brought in to the community. Explanations given to me in 1974 stressed that young people had been resettled in the countryside and that many of the new workers required in the city were either taken from the underemployed residents of the city or represented the return of a small proportion of the resettled youth.

While it is not possible to explore fully the various issues involved in the limitation of Tsinan's population at the levels of the mid-1960s, the preceding discussion of Tsinan's long-term growth since the late eighteenth century and the clear indication of the increased growth rate in the twentieth century, not only under the Kuomintang but during the first fifteen years of the PRC rule as well, do show how dramatically different the current approach is both from Tsinan's own past and from what we know of other urban places in the developing world.

Appendix C

Demands of the Shantung Provincial Assembly, November 1911

ADOPTED 5 NOVEMBER 1911 FOR SUBMISSION TO THE CENTRAL GOVERNMENT IN PEKING. IF NOT ACCEPTED IN THREE DAYS, THE PROVINCE WILL DECLARE ITS INDEPENDENCE.

1. The Government should not borrow foreign monies to kill our fellow countrymen.
2. The Government must quickly declare a cease-fire and accede to the demands of the Southern Army, no matter what those demands are.
3. Elements of the New Army now stationed in Shantung are not to be transferred outside the province.
4. For the time being, stop remission of funds [to the Central Treasury] and the payment of relief to other provinces in order to provide for the training of troops and for relief within this province.
5. The Constitution of China must take a federal form.
6. The provinces themselves should decide on the rule of avoidance and land taxes, and the Government must not interfere.
7. The right to revise the regulations governing the Provincial Assembly should belong to the Assembly since these are the constitution of the provinces.
8. This province has the right to maintain troops to protect its own territory.

Source: Translated from telegram of 5 November 1911 from Sun Pao-ch'i to Grand Secretariat. "Sun Pao-ch'i tsui-yen," *STCTSTL,* 2: 72-73.

Notes

ABBREVIATIONS USED IN NOTES

CFMA   Chinese Foreign Ministry Archives, 1906-27, Academia Sinica, Institute of Modern History, Nankang, Taiwan.

CKSYC:STS Ho Ping-yin, ed., *Chung-kuo shih-yeh chih: Shan-tung sheng* [Industrial gazetteer of China: Shantung Province] (Shanghai: Shih-yeh pu, kuo-chi mao-i chü, 1934).

CNFC   Wang Tseng-fang, comp., *Chi-nan fu-chih* [Gazetteer of Tsinan Prefecture] (1840).

CYB   H. G. H. Woodhead, ed., *China Yearbook* (Tientsin: Tientsin Times, various dates).

FRUS   *Foreign Relations of the United States* (Washington, D.C.: Government Printing Office, various dates).

JPRS   Joint Publication Research Service, Washington, D.C.

LCHC   Mao Ch'eng-lin, comp., *Hsü-hsiu Li-ch'eng hsien-chih* [New edition of the Li-ch'eng County gazetteer] (1924).

NCH   *North China Herald and Supreme Court and Consular Gazetteer*, Shanghai.

SSZ   Kogawa Heichi, ed., *Shina shōbetsu zenshi: Santō-shō* [Gazetteer of the Chinese provinces: Shantung], vol. 4 (Tokyo: Tōa dōbunkai, 1917).

STCTSTL Chung-kuo shih-hsüeh hui, Chi-nan fen-hui, comp., *Shantung chin-tai shih tzu-liao* [Materials on Shantung modern history], 3 vols. (Tsinan: Shan-tung jen-min ch'u-pan she, 1957-58).

STTC   Sun Pao-t'ien, comp., *Shan-tung t'ung-chih* [Shantung provincial gazetteer] (1915).

TIR   Tsinan Intelligence Reports, 1909-30, British Foreign Office, Consular Archives, China, F.O. 228, Public Record Office, London.

Translations of Chinese- and Japanese-language titles are given in the notes (at the first citation) for items not included in the Selected Bibliography.

CHAPTER 1: TSINAN AND THE QUESTION OF THE CITY IN MODERN CHINESE HISTORY

1 The classical study is A. F. Weber, *The Growth of Cities in the Nineteenth Century* (New York: Macmillan, 1899). An excellent study is Asa Briggs, *Victorian Cities* (London: Oldhams, 1963).

2 See Brian J. L. Berry, *The Human Consequences of Urbanization* (New York: St. Martin's Press, 1973), pp. 27-73; and James H. Johnson, *Urban Geography: An Introductory Analysis* (London: Pergamon Press, 1967).

3 In the United States, Louis Wirth summed up the conclusion that cities brought specific social ills in his important article "Urbanism as a Way of Life," *American Journal of Sociology* 44 (1938): 1-24.

4 Samuel Huntington, *Political Order in Changing Societies* (New Haven: Yale University Press, 1968), pp. 397 ff.

5 Rhoads Murphey, "The Treaty Ports and China's Modernization," in Mark Elvin and G. William Skinner, *The Chinese City Between Two Worlds* (Stanford: Stanford University Press, 1974), p. 67.

6 Hu Shih, *The Chinese Renaissance* (Chicago: University of Chicago Press, 1934), p. 96.

7 Ibid., pp. 96-97.

8 Feng Yu-lan, "P'an hsiang-ch'eng" [Distinguishing between the city and the countryside], *Hsin-shih lun* (Shanghai: Shang-wu yin-shu kuan, 1940); and Fei Hsiao-t'ung, *China's Gentry* (Chicago: University of Chicago Press, 1953), pp. 95 ff.

9 The phrase is that of E. R. Hughes, *The Invasion of China by the Western World* (London: Black, 1938), p. 268.

10 See Philip Hauser, *Handbook for Social Research in Urban Areas* (Ghent: UNESCO, 1965), p. 101; and T. G. McGee, *The Southeast Asian City: A Social Geography of the Primate Cities of Southeast Asia* (New York: Praeger, 1967), pp. 52-75.

11 H. B. Morse, *The Trade and Administration of China* (London: Longmans, Green, 1913), pp. 226-28.

12 See McGee, *Southeast Asian City*, pp. 15-28; Andre Gundar Frank, *Capitalism and Underdevelopment in Latin America* (New York: Monthly Review Press, 1967), pp. 3-14; and Gerald Breeze, *Urbanization in Newly Developing Countries* (Englewood Cliffs, N.J.: Prentice-Hall, 1966).

13 "The Chinese Revolution and the Chinese Communist Party" (December 1939), *Selected Works of Mao Tse-tung*, 4 vols. (Peking: Foreign Languages Press, 1965), 2:316-17.

14 See Joint Publication Research Service (hereafter JPRS) 5258, *Urban Construction in Communist China*, part 2 (August 1960), for a translation of articles from *Ch'eng-shih chien-she* [Urban construction] 10 (October 1959) reflecting this view.

15 Rhoads Murphey, *Shanghai: Key to Modern China* (Cambridge: Harvard University Press, 1953), p. 9.

16 Murphey, "Treaty Ports," in Elvin and Skinner, eds., *The Chinese City Between Two Worlds*, p. 57.

17 Ibid., pp. 67-68.
18 In particular see Mark Elvin, *The Pattern of the Chinese Past* (Stanford: Stanford University Press, 1972); Ramon Myers, *The Chinese Peasant Economy: Agricultural Development in Hopei and Shantung, 1890-1949* (Cambridge: Harvard University Press, 1970); Evelyn Sakakida Rawski, *Agricultural Change and the Peasant Economy of South China* (Cambridge: Harvard University Press, 1972); Gilbert Rozman, *Urban Networks in Ch'ing China and Tokugawa Japan* (Princeton: Princeton University Press, 1973); W. E. Willmont, ed., *Economic Organization of Chinese Society* (Stanford: Stanford University Press, 1972); and G. William Skinner, ed., *The City in Late Imperial China* (Stanford: Stanford University Press, 1977).
19 Berry, *The Human Consequences of Urbanization;* Walter B. Stohr, *Interurban Systems and Regional Economic Development* (Washington, D.C.: Association of American Geographers, 1974); and Anthony R. de Souza and Philip W. Porter, *The Underdevelopment and Modernization of the Third World* (Washington, D.C.: Association of American Geographers, 1974).
20 Dwight Perkins, *Agricultural Development in China, 1368-1968* (Chicago: Aldine, 1969), Appendix E: "Urban Population Statistics, 1900-1958," pp. 290-96.
21 Lucian W. Pye, *Warlord Politics: Conflict and Coalition in the Modernization of Republican China* (New York: Praeger, 1971); Donald Gillin, *Warlord: Yen Hsi-shan in Shansi Province, 1911-1949* (Princeton: Princeton University Press, 1967); and James Sheridan, *Chinese Warlord: The Career of Feng Yü-hsiang* (Stanford: Stanford University Press, 1966).
22 This discussion of bureaucratic capitalism draws heavily on Lloyd Eastman's paper "Bureaucratic Capitalism Under the Nationalists" delivered at the annual meeting of the Association for Asian Studies in 1973. Eastman's recapitulation of these arguments as well as discussions at the working conference on business and politics in Republican China, held at Cornell in October 1975 and sponsored by the Joint Committee on Contemporary China on the ACLS and SSRC, have been most helpful to me in developing this line of analysis.

CHAPTER 2: TSINAN IN THE LATE NINETEENTH CENTURY

1 James Boyd Neal, "Tsinanfu, Capital of Shantung," *East of Asia Magazine* 5 (1906): 324-34. This view of Chinese cities as the chief seats of resistance to the West even found its way into the writings of Karl Marx. See C. Wright Mills *The Marxists* (New York: Dell, 1962), p. 50.
2 Ernst von Hesse Wartegg, *Schantung und Deutsch: China im Jahre 1898* (Leipzig: J. J. Weber, 1898), pp. 131-32.
3 The descriptions of Tsinan in the nineteenth century have been drawn from the works of several foreign observers, supplemented by local gazetteers. The most important foreigners' descriptions are Alexander Armstrong, *In a Mule Litter to the Tomb of Confucius* (London: Nisbet, 1886); Robert Coltman, *The Chinese, Their Present and Future: Medical, Political and Social* (London: F. A. Davis, 1891); and Alexander Williamson, *Journeys in North China, Manchuria and Eastern Mongolia with some account of Korea,* 2 vols.

(London: Smith and Elder, 1870). The three chief gazetteers are Mao Ch'eng-lin, comp., *Hsü-hsiu Li-ch'eng hsien-chih* (hereafter *LCHC*), 1924; Wang Tseng-fang, comp., *Chi-nan fu-chih* (hereafter *CNFC*), 1840; and Sun Pao-t'ien, comp., *Shan-tung t'ung-chih* (hereafter *STTC*), 1915. The basic reference on all administrative matters for the pre-1911 years has been *Ta-ch'ing hui-tien,* 1899 edition. Other important materials are Frederic de Garis, ed., *Guide to China* (Tokyo: Japanese National Railways, 1st ed., 1915, 2d ed., 1923); Ho Ping-yin, ed., *Chung-kuo shih-yeh chih: Shan-tung sheng* (hereafter *CKSYC:STS*) (Shanghai: Shih-yeh pu, kuo-chi mao-i chü, 1934), and Kogawa Heichi, ed., *Shina shōbetsu zenshi: Santō-shō* (hereafter *SSZ*), vol. 4 (Tokyo: Tōa dōbunkai, 1917).

4 Coltman, *The Chinese,* pp. 47-53.

5 Teng Ssu-yü, *The Nien Army and Their Guerrilla Warfare, 1851-1868* (Paris: Mouton, 1961); Cheng T'ien-t'ing, et al., eds., *Sung Ching-shih ch'i-i shih-liao* [Historical materials on the uprising of Sung Ching-shih] (Peking: Chung-hua shu-chü, 1954); and Ma Chen-wen, "Yüeh-fei hsien Lin-ch'ing chi-lüeh" [A brief account of the Taiping assault on Lin-ch'ing], in Chung-kuo shih-hsüeh hui, Chi-nan fen-hui, comp., *Shan-tung chin-tai shih tzu-liao* (Hereafter *STCTSTL*), 3 vols. (Tsinan: Shan-tung jen-min ch'u-pan she, 1957-58) 1:25-29.

6 *STTC*, ch. 102/1a-4b, 119/7a-9a; O. J. Todd, "The Yellow River Reharnessed," *Geographical Review* 39.1 (January 1949): 38-56.

7 The books of Armstrong and Williamson are especially valuable records of the economic and social change in the Wei-hsien area. Also see Isabelle Williamson, *Old Highways in China* (New York: American Tract Society, n.d. [ca. 1895]).

8 Huang Tse-ts'ang, *Shan-tung* (Shanghai: Chung-hua shu-chü, 1936), pp. 103-14; Ho Ping-ti, *Studies on the Population of China 1368-1953* (Cambridge: Harvard University Press, 1959), pp. 158-63; and Seitō shubigun minseibu [Civil Government Bureau of the Tsingtao Garrison Command], *Santō no rōdōsha* [The workers of Shantung] (Tsingtao: Seitō shubigun, 1921), pp. 232-59.

9 *LCHC*, ch. 14/27-33, contains the basic data on the monuments. See also David D. Buck, "Public Monuments as a Guide to Political Leadership," *Ch'ing-shih wen-t'i* [Bulletin of the Society for Ch'ing Studies] 3.1 (1974): 62-70.

10 *LCHC*, ch. 13/4a-5b. These efforts were at the scale of multiplex *t'uan* described by Philip Kuhn, *Rebellion and Its Enemies in Late Imperial China* (Cambridge: Harvard University Press, 1970), pp. 69-76.

11 *LCHC*, ch. 40/15a-15b, 35a-37a.

12 For a discussion of this case see *North China Herald and Supreme Court and Consular Gazette* (hereafter *NCH*), 18 December 1891, p. 840, 31 December 1891, p. 898, 7 October 1910, p. 19; and Philip West, "The Tsinan Property Disputes (1887-1891): Gentry Loss and Missionary 'Victory,'" *Harvard Papers on China* 20 (1966): 119-43.

13 *STTC*, ch. 119/7a-8a, ch. 122/1a.

14 For biographies of local Tsinan flood relief donors see *LCHC*, ch. 44.

15 Shantung merchants by the same token were not major influences in trade else-where, although they were involved both at Shanghai and Tientsin. The overall situation in Shantung commerce has been summarized in Chang Peng, "The Distribution and Relative Strength of the Provincial Merchant Groups in China, 1842-1911" (Ph.D. diss., University of Washington, 1957), pp. 125 ff. For provincial associations in Tsinan see SSZ 4:986 ff., and "Sainanfu bōeki jijō" [Trading conditions in Tsinan], *Shina* 4.22 (November 1913): 23-27, and 4.23 (November 1913): 13-16.

16 J. H. Lockhart, *Confidential Report of a Journey in Shantung* (Hong Kong: Government Printing Office, 1903), pp. 49-53.

17 Vitalis Lange, *Das Apostolisch Vikariat Tsinanfu* (Werl: Societas Divine Verbas, 1929); and John Thauren, *The Missions in Shantung China* (Techny, Illinois: S.D.V. Mission Press, 1932), pp. 28-38.

18 R. C. Forsyth, ed., *Shantung, Sacred Province of China* (Shanghai: Christian Literature Society, 1912), pp. 184-90.

19 Wang Erh-min, *Ch'ing-chi ping-kung-yeh te hsing-ch'i* (Taipei: Chung-yang yen-chiu yuan, chin-tai shih yen-chiu so, 1963), pp. 113-14; *NCH*, 12 August 1893, p. 225, and 11 December 1901, p. 1123.

20 Kuo T'ing-i, ed., *Hai-fang tang* (Taipei: Chung-yang yen-chiu yuan, chin-tai shih yen-chiu so, 1957), 1:262, 294; 2:1142. For restricted use of telegraph, see von Hesse Wartegg, *Schantung*, p. 202.

21 *STTC*, ch. 88.

22 See Harold Shadick's translation, *The Travels of Lao Ts'an* (Ithaca: Cornell University Press, 1952), p. 27.

23 *LCHC*, ch. 1/3b-8a.

24 See Rozman, *Urban Networks*, pp. 172-75, for a description of Tientsin during these years, based on the work of the Japanese scholar Momose Hiromu.

25 *CNFC*, ch. 12/2a.

26 Armstrong, *Tomb of Confucius*, pp. 61-62; Coltman, *The Chinese,* pp. 95 ff.; *NCH*, 9 April 1897, p. 632.

27 See Ching Su and Lo Lun, *Ch'ing-tai Shan-tung ching-ying ti-chu te she-hui hsing-chih* (Tsinan: Shan-tung jen-min ch'u-pan she, 1959).

28 Coltman, *The Chinese*, pp. 95 ff.

29 John Murray, "Mohammedanism in Shantung," in Forsyth, ed., *Shantung*, pp. 287-92.

30 This brief characterization of the Boxer uprising departs from the main lines of of historical debate about that dramatic antiforeign uprising, summarizing evidence presented in considerable detail in my Ph.D. dissertation, "Tsinan, Shantung: Political and Social History of a Chinese City, 1900-1925" (Stanford University, 1971), pp. 108-26.

CHAPTER 3: TSINAN DURING THE LATE CH'ING REFORMS, 1901-1911

1 Quoted in Teng Ssu-yü and John K. Fairbank, *China's Response to the West* (Cambridge: Harvard University Press, 1954), p. 196.

2 Liu Feng-han, *Hsin-chien lu-chün* (Taipei: Chung-yang yen-chiu yuan, chin-tai shih yen-chiu so, 1966), p. 313; John E. Schrecker, *Imperialism and Chinese*

Nationalism: Germany in Shantung (Cambridge: Harvard University Press, 1971), pp. 111-13.

3 *NCH*, 17 April 1901, pp. 735-36.

4 For excellent appraisals of Chou Fu see Lockhart, *Confidential Report*, p. 3; *NCH*, 11 November 1904, p. 1073; Schrecker, *Imperialism*, p. 151. Chou Fu's memorials are found in *Chou ch'üeh-shen-kung ch'üan-chi* [Collected works of Chou Fu] (1922).

5 Arthur W. Hummel, ed., *Eminent Chinese of the Ch'ing Period*, 2 vols. (Washington, D.C.: U.S. Government Printing Office, 1943-44), 2:872; *NCH*, 11 October 1907, p. 92; Schrecker, *Imperialism*, pp. 151-52.

6 Bertram Giles, Tsinan Intelligence Report (hereafter TIR), 4th Quarter 1908, F.O. 371/632 China, political; *NCH*, 30 October 1908, p. 15, 10 July 1909, p. 80.

7 H. G. H. Woodhead, ed., *China Yearbook, 1924* (hereafter *CYB*) (Tientsin: Tientsin Times, 1925), p. 1038; Howard L. Boorman, ed., *Biographical Dictionary of Republican China*, 4 vols. (New York: Columbia University Press, 1967-71), 3:169-70.

8 John V. A. MacMurray, comp., *Treaties and Agreements with and Concerning China, 1894-1919*, 2 vols. (Washington, D.C.: Carnegie Endowment for International Peace, 1922), 1:115.

9 Ibid., 1:236. At the end of 1908 an officially sponsored attempt to have Shantung gentry purchase one million taels of Tientsin-Pukow railroad stock was unsuccessful. Bertram Giles, TIR, 4th Quarter 1908, F.O. 371/632 China, political.

10 See materials concerning the activities of Sun Wen and others at Kao-mi in *STCTSTL* 2:91-98; see also Schrecker, *Imperialism,* pp. 111-24, for an account of the problems at Kao-mi. For the reaction in Tung-ch'ang, see *NCH*, 24 July 1903, p. 186.

11 Schrecker, *Imperialism*, pp. 176-78; *NCH*, 14 August 1903, p. 346.

12 "Sainan bōeki jijō," *Shina* 4.22 (November 1913): 23-24; see also 4.23 (December 1913): 13-16.

13 MacMurray, comp., *Treaties and Agreements,* 1:266-67; Percy Kent, *Railway Enterprise in China* (London: Arnold, 1907), pp. 148-51; Bertram Giles, TIR, 4th Quarter 1908, F.O. 371/632 China, political.

14 *NCH*, 4 November 1910, p. 271, 26 October 1912, p. 245.

15 MacMurray, *Treaties and Agreements,* 1:116.

16 See Schrecker, *Imperialism,* pp. 179-91.

17 Liu Chieh-ch'ung, Liu ts'an shih Chieh-ch'ung tiao-ch'a pao-kao chi-tsa lu [Investigative report and miscellaneous records of Advisor Liu Chieh-ch'ung], Chinese Foreign Ministry Archives (hereafter CFMA) R-1670.19, April 1920; *CKSYC:STS* 7:37-38.

18 Schrecker, *Imperialism*, pp. 229-30.

19 Oka Itaro, *Santō keizai jijō, Sainan o chū to shite* (Osaka: n.p., 1918), pp. 21-22; *Shina* 3.18 (September 1912): 5-10.

20 Schrecker, *Imperialism*, pp. 228-30.

21 Chu Shou-p'eng, comp., *Tung-hua hsü-lu, Kuang-hsü ch'ao* (Peking, n.d.), ch. 187/12a.
22 Ibid.
23 J. T. Pratt, TIR, 4th Quarter 1914, F.O. 228/1913; B. G. Tours, TIR, 2d Quarter 1924, F.O. 228/3277.
24 *NCH*, 2 February 1906, p. 213.
25 Land and Building Regulations for Tsinanfu Commercial Settlement. Police Regulations for Commercial Settlement at Tsinanfu, F.O. 228/2165 Tsinanfu Settlement.
26 H. B. Morse, *The International Relations of the Chinese Empire,* 3 vols. (London: Longmans, Green, 1918), 2:148-50; 3:370.
27 Report on Tsinan Settlement, 1911, F.O. 228/2165 Tsinanfu Settlement.
28 *NCH*, 31 July 1901, p. 206-7; 26 May 1905, p. 430; 10 April 1909, p. 75. For German plans to expand their postal service in Shantung, see Schrecker, *Imperialism,* pp. 171-73.
29 *NCH*, 26 November 1902, p. 1110; 15 June 1906, p. 572.
30 Ch'en Chen, comp., *Chung-kuo chin-tai kung-yeh shih tzu-liao, ti-erh chi* (Peking: San-lien shu-tien, 1958), 1:38-53; 4:872.
31 *NCH*, 20 April 1907, p. 132. Later editions went under the names of *Shan-tung kung-pao* [Shantung Gazette] and *Shan-tung cheng-fu kung-pao* [Shantung Government Gazette].
32 Ko Kung-chen, *Chung-kuo pao-hsüeh shih* (Shanghai: Shang-wu yin-shu kuan 1927), p. 146; *NCH*, 8 December 1905, p. 536.
33 *NCH*, 30 October 1901, p. 827; 20 November 1901, p. 964; 27 November 1901, pp. 1018-19; 7 May 1902, p. 887.
34 Yüan Shih-k'ai, *Yang-shou-yuan tsou-i chi-yao* (1937), ch. 10/4a-7b.
35 *STTC,* ch. 88.; and R. W. Luce, "Education in Shantung," in Forsyth, ed., *Shantung,* p. 302.
36 Liu Feng-han, *Hsin-chien lu-chün,* p. 313; Lieutenant Colonel Pereira, Report of Visit to Chinanfu, F.O. 371/41 China, political, 1908.
37 Ch'in Te-ch'un, *Ch'in Te-ch'un hui-i lu* (Taipei: Chuan-chi wen-hsüeh ch'u-pan she, 1967), pp. 9-11; Yeh Ch'un-ch'ih, ed., *Chi-nan chih-nan* (Tsinan: Ta-tung jih-pao, 1914), pp. 32-33.
38 Wang Erh-min, *Ch'ing-chi ping-kung-yeh te hsing-ch'i,* pp. 113-14.
39 Pereira Report, F.O. 371/41 China, political, 1908.
40 Ibid.; although not identified by name, Mr. Quincy, an Anglo-Chinese who headed the Settlement District Police for a time, was the source of this information.
41 Neal, "Tsinanfu, Capital of Shantung," *East of Asia Magazine* 5 (1906): 324-34; interview with Sister Sira, a Catholic nun born in Hung-chia-lou in 1920, Milwaukee, Wis., 13 December 1970.
42 H. Balme, "Union Medical College at Tsinanfu," *Chinese Recorder and Missionary Journal* 46.11 (November 1915): 692-95; Chiao-yü pu, ed., *Ti-i-tz'u Chung-kuo chiao-yü nien-chien* (Peking: Chiao-yü pu, 1934), 3:119-20.
43 W. L. Garnett, *Journey Through the Provinces of Shantung and Kiangsu* (A

Report Submitted to Parliament) China, no. 1 (London: His Majesty's Stationery Office, 1907), pp. 8-9; also the obituary of Mrs. Whitewright, *NCH*, 23 February 1924, p. 283.

44 *Shina* 3.18 (September 1912): 5-10.

45 Bertram Giles, TIR, 4th Quarter 1908, F.O. 371/632 China, political.

46 Liu Tung-hou, comp., *Wei-hsien chih* (1937), ch. 27/27a.

47 Wang Lin-k'o "Hsin-hai ch'ien chih ko-ming yun-tung" [The revolutionary movement prior to 1911], *STCTSTL* 2:67-69; and "Lü Tzu-jen hsien-sheng fang-wen chi-lu" [Transcript of an interview with Mr. Lü Tzu-jen], *STCTSTL* 2:221-27.

48 Ch'in Te-ch'un, *Ch'in Te-ch'un hui-i lu*, pp.6-7.

49 Compare with Mary Backus Rankin's study of the situation in Chekiang, "The Revolutionary Movement in Chekiang: A Study in the Tenacity of Tradition," in Mary Wright, ed., *China in Revolution: The First Phase, 1900-1913* (New Haven: Yale University Press, 1968), pp. 321-61.

50 See John Fincher, "Political Provincialism and the National Revolution," in Wright, ed., *China in Revolution*, p. 201.

51 Ch'en Ch'i-t'ien, *Tsui-chin san-shih-nien Chung-kuo chiao-yü shih* [A history of Chinese education during the past thirty years] (Shanghai: Chung-hua shu-tien, 1930), pp. 71-73; Shu Hsin-ch'eng, *Chin-tai Chung-kuo chiao-yü shih-liao* [Materials on the history of modern Chinese education], 4 vols. (Shanghai: Shang-wu yin-shu kuan, 1928), 2:131-35.

52 Bertram Giles, TIR 4th Quarter 1909, F.O. 371/632 China, political.

53 Based on information in the author's file of Shantung personalities. The information was compiled primarily from English-, Chinese- and Japanese-language biographical dictionaries, supplemented by biographies from local gazetteers.

54 Ichiko Chūzō, "The Role of the Gentry: A Hypothesis," in Wright, ed., *China in Revolution*, pp. 308-9.

55 Ho Ping-ti, *The Ladder of Success in Imperial China* (New York: Columbia University Press, 1962), pp. 48-50; Chang Chung-li, *The Chinese Gentry: Studies on Their Role in Nineteenth Century Chinese Society* (Seattle: University of Washington Press, 1955), pp. 137-41.

56 *STCTSTL* 2:58-60, 221-27.

57 *LCHC*, ch. 40/41a-43a.

58 "Huang-hsien ko-ming shih-shih" [The real history of the revolution in Huang-hsien], *STCTSTL* 2:156.

59 Materials concerning the Lai-yang case have been collected in *STCTSTL* 2:1-64. I have relied upon "Shan-tung lu-ching t'ung-hsiang Lai-yang hsien shih-pien-shih te tiao-ch'a pao-kao shu" [Investigative report by the Shan-tungese residing in Peking on the facts in the Lai-yang incident]; a draft account by Shang Ching-han, "Shan-tung ts'an-i chu i-yuan Wang Chih-hsun, Ting Shih-i, Chou Shu-piao, Chang Chieh-li, Shang Ching-han t'i-chih yüan yu pao-kao shu" [Report of the reasons for the resignations of the Shantung Provincial Assemblymen Wang Chih-hsun, etc.]; and an account from *Lai-yang hsien-chih* [Gazetteer of Lai-yang County] (1935).

60 "Report on Tsinanfu Settlement," 1911, F.O. 228/2165 Tsinanfu Settlement; Oka, *Santō keizai jijō*, pp. 32-37.
61 *Shina* 3.18 (September 1912): 5-10; Oka, *Santō keizai jijō*, pp. 32-35.
62 *CKSYC:STS* 2:128-37.
63 Kuo Jung-sheng, ed., *Chung-kuo sheng yin-hang shih-lüeh* (Taipei: Chung-kuo yin-hang, 1967), pp. 97-98; Schrecker, *Imperialism*, pp. 10-11.
64 "Banking and Currency in Tsinan," *Chinese Economic Monthly* 3.4 (April 1925): 68-76; Oka, *Santō keizai jijō*, pp. 33-35, 93-95, 103-10.

CHAPTER 4: TSINAN DURING THE EARLY REPUBLIC, 1912-1916

1 Wang Hsiang-ts'en, "Kuan-yü Shan-tung tu-li ti jih-chi" [A diary concerning Shantung's independence], *STCTSTL* 2:113. There are over two dozen accounts of events in Tsinan during the period from November 1911 through June 1912. The most complete collection of these is available in *STCTSTL* 2:70-277. The only foreign observations readily available are those from the correspondents of the *North China Herald*. See also Shan-tung ta-hsüeh, li-shih hsi, *Shan-tung ti-fang shih shih chiang-shou t'i-kang* (Tsinan: Jen-min ch'u-pan she, 1959), pp. 58-60.
2 *Ch'i-lu kung-pao* [Gazette of Ch'i and Lu], 15 and 16 November 1911, *STCTSTL* 2:87-97; *NCH*, 11 November 1911, p. 361.
3 Memorial of Li Chia-ch'u of 8 November 1911, contained in Ku-kung tang-an kuan [Records Office of the Palace Museum], comp., "Shan-tung ch'i-i ch'ing-fang tang-an" [Corrected records of the Shantung uprising], *STCTSTL* 2:263-64.
4 Wang Na, "Hsin-hai Shan-tung tu-li chi" [Record of Shantung's independence in 1911], *STCTSTL* 2:82; Kuo Hsiao-ch'eng, "Shan-tung tu-li ch'üan-k'uang" (The circumstances of Shantung's independence], *STCTSTL* 2:250-51.
5 Ku-kung tang-an kuan, comp., "Shan-tung ch'i-i ch'ing-fang tang-an," *STCTSTL* 2:267; "Sun Pao-ch'i tsui-yen" [The false statements of Sun Pao-ch'i], *STCTSTL* 2:74-75; *NCH*, 16 December 1911, p. 726.
6 *Ch'i-lu kung-pao*, 15 December 1911, *STCTSTL* 2:103-4.
7 *NCH*, 27 January 1912, p. 241, 3 February 1912, p. 296; "Huang-hsien ko-ming shih-shih" [The history of the revolution in Huang-hsien], *STCTSTL* 2:136-47.
8 Wang Na, "Yüan Shih-k'ai p'an-pien ko-ming yü min wu-t'ao Yüan" [Yüan Shih-k'ai's overthrow of the revolution and the people's five charges against Yüan], *STCTSTL* 2:285-86; *NCH*, 22 June 1912, p. 851, 29 June 1912, p. 915, 13 July 1912, p. 102.
9 Wang Na, "Hsin-hai Shan-tung tu-li chi," *STCTSTL* 2:87.
10 *NCH*, 25 January 1913, p. 232.
11 Li Chien-nung, *The Political History of China, 1840-1928* (New York: Van Nostrand, 1956), pp. 277-79; George Yu, *Party Politics in Republican China: The Kuomintang, 1912-1914* (Berkeley and Los Angeles: University of California Press, 1966), pp. 91-92, 103-4.
12 Wang Na, "Hsin-hai Shan-tung tu-li chi," *STCTSTL* 2:86.

13 J. T. Pratt, TIR, 4th Quarter 1913, F.O. 228/1913; and biographical data on the eighteen Shantung members of the 1913 national parliament as recorded in Satō Sanjirō, ed., *Min-kuo chih ching-hua* (Peking: Pei-ching hsien-chen t'ung-hsin she, 1916).

14 Yeh Ch'un-ch'ih, ed., *Chi-nan chih-nan,* p. 44; Gaimushō Jōhōbū, *Gendai Chūka minkoku jinmeikan* (Tokyo: Gaimushō, 1924), p. 643.

15 *NCH,* 5 July 1913, pp. 22-23; J. T. Pratt, TIR 4th Quarter 1913, F.O. 228/1913.

16 *NCH,* 5 July 1913, p. 22.

17 See Li Chien-nung, *The Political History of China,* pp. 288-90; Jerome Ch'en, *Yüan Shih-k'ai, 1859-1916* (rev. ed., Stanford: Stanford University Press, 1972), pp. 156-59, 181.

18 J. T. Pratt, TIR, 4th Quarter 1913, F.O. 228/1913.

19 David D. Buck, "Educational Modernization in Tsinan, 1899-1937," in Elvin and Skinner, eds., *The Chinese City Between Two Worlds*, pp. 189-90.

20 J. T. Pratt, TIR, 4th Quarter 1913, 1st Quarter 1914, F.O. 228/1913.

21 J. T. Pratt, TIR, 3d and 4th Quarters 1914, F.O. 228/1913.

22 Ibid.

23 This characterization of German policy is drawn from Schrecker, *Imperialism,* pp. 210-11.

24 "Economic Development of Shantung Province, China, 1912-1921," Excerpts from Decennial Report of Tsingtau Customs, U.S. Department of Commerce, Trade Information Bulletin 70 (9 October 1922), p. 3. See also Schrecker, *Imperialism,* pp. 233-38, for a different statement of the same general conclusions.

25 The most extensive account in English of this campaign is Jefferson Jones, *The Fall of Tsingtau* (New York: Houghton Mifflin, 1915).

26 In addition to establishing military barracks at several points, the Japanese put into operation Japanese-controlled civil governments at Wei-hsien, Fang-tzu, and Tsingtao. Shan-tung ta-hsüeh, li-shih hsi, *Shan-tung ti-fang shih chiang-shou t'i-kang,* p. 63.

27 Huang Chia-mu, "Chung-kuo tui Ou-chan te ch'u-pu fan-ying," *Chung-yang yen-chiu yuan, chin-tai shih yen-chiu so chi-k'an* 1 (1969): 3-18.

28 Telegrams of J. T. Pratt at Tsinan to John Jordan in Peking, 13, 14, and 15 August 1914, F.O. 228/1913.

29 Telegrams of J. T. Pratt at Tsinan to John Jordan in Peking, 18, 22, and 24 August, F.O. 228/1913.

30 Masaru Ikei, "Japan's Response to the Chinese Revolution of 1911," *Journal of Asian Studies* 25.2 (February 1966): 225-26.

31 James B. Crowley, *Japan's Quest for Autonomy: National Security and Foreign Policy, 1930-1938* (Princeton: Princeton University Press, 1966), p. 12.

32 Li Yü-shu in his book on the Twenty-One Demands has examined several drafts of the demands in the Japanese Foreign Office archives, but does not claim that the military dominated the original drafting process. *Chung-Jih erh-*

shih-i t'iao chiao-she (*shang*) (Taipei: Chung-yang yen-chiu yuan, chin-tai shih yen-chiu so, 1966), pp. 169-81.

33 Kao Yin-tsu, comp., *Chung-hua min-kuo ta-shih chi* (Taipei: Shih-chieh she, 1957), pp. 27-28.

34 For the full text of the Sino-Japanese Treaty of 25 May 1915, concerning Shantung, see MacMurray, comp., *Treaties and Agreements,* 1:1216-17.

35 J. T. Pratt, TIR, 1st Quarter 1915, F.O. 228/1913.

36 Telegram of J. T. Pratt at Tsinan to John Jordan in Peking, 22 March 1915, F.O. 228/1953; also *NCH*, 10 April 1915, p. 79, 24 April 1915, pp. 276-77.

37 Telegrams and letters of J. T. Pratt at Tsinan to John Jordan in Peking, 5, 7, and 10 May 1915, F.O. 228/1953.

38 Report of R. T. Eckfort, March 1915, F.O. 228/2707.

39 This story is best told in Edward Friedman, *Backward Toward Revolution: The Chinese Revolutionary Party* (Berkeley and Los Angeles: University of California Press, 1974).

40 The principal sources for the account of the 1916 uprising are Chü Cheng's own papers, *Chü Chueh-sheng hsien-sheng ch'üan-chi* (Taipei: n.p., 1963), pp. 337-59; Wang Na, "Yüan Shih-k'ai p'an-pien ko-ming yü min wu-tao Yüan," *STCTSTL* 2:279-97; Shen Yin-nan, "Min-kuo wu-nien Wu Ta-chou tsai Chou-ts'un tu-li kai-lüeh" [A brief account of Wu Ta-chou's uprising at Chou-ts'un in 1916], *STCTSTL* 2:341-42; Wang Sui-shan, "Ku-yü hsien-t'ung ting-ssu [Foolish and lofty thoughts], *STCTSTL* 2:342-80; J. T. Pratt, TIR, 1915-16, F.O. 228/1953, and the *North China Herald*.

41 Satō, ed., *Min-kuo chih ching-hua,* p. 243; *CYB, 1924,* p. 977.

42 "Lü Tzu-jen hsien-sheng fang-wen chi-lu," *STCTSTL* 2:228. Lü's account of his role is borne out by the other sources, including Chü Cheng's.

43 Wang Shui-shan, "Ku-yü hsien-t'ung ting-ssu," *STCTSTL* 2:345.

44 J. T. Pratt described Japanese support for the 1916 uprising as "open and notorious." In Tsinan he observed Japanese troops taking over the settlement district and denying access to Chin Yun-p'eng's troops from May through early July 1916. TIR, 2d Quarter 1916, F.O. 228/1983; *NCH*, 22 July 1916, p. 135.

45 Wang K'o-lin, "Yüan Shih-k'ai p'an-pien ko-ming yü min wu-tao Yüan," *STCTSTL* 2:284ff.

46 Kao Yin-tsu, comp., *Chung-hua min-kuo ta-shih chi,* pp. 35-36.

47 Shen Yin-nan, "Min-kuo wu-nien Wu-Ta-chou tsai Chou-ts'un tu-li kai lüeh," *STCTSTL* 2:341-42.

48 *NCH*, 25 November 1916, pp. 417-18, 9 December 1916, p. 525, 17 February 1917, p. 327.

49 J. T. Pratt, TIR, 3d Quarter 1918, F.O. 228/1953.

50 Ko Kung-chen, *Chung-kuo pao-hsüeh shih,* p. 148; Letter of J. T. Pratt at Tsinan to John Jordan in Peking, 11 March 1915, F.O. 228/1953.

51 S. Wyatt-Smith, TIR, 2d Quarter 1918, F.O. 228/1983.

52 *SSZ* 4:79-80; Yeh Ch'un-ch'ih, ed., *Chi-nan chih-nan,* p. 146; Letter of J. T. Pratt at Tsinan to John Jordan in Peking, 11 March 1915, F.O. 228/1953. Among the papers published in Tsinan from 1911 through 1915 with clear po-

litical orientations were *Tung-lu jih-pao* [East Shantung Daily], edited by Wang Shih-p'eng and associated with the parliamentary Nationalist party; *Hsin Shan-tung jih-pao* [The New Shantung Daily], edited by Wang Sung-t'ing, a Shantung assemblyman associated with the Progressive party; and the *Min-te pao* [People's Virtue], which was associated with the Huang *hsien* trading group in Tsinan. All of these papers had circulations of 300 to 400.

53 Yeh Ch'un-ch'ih, ed., *Chi-nan chih-nan*, pp. 7 ff.
54 Oka, *Santō keizai jijō*, charts 1 and 2.
55 Yeh Ch'un-ch'ih, ed., *Chi-nan chih-nan*, pp. 102, 116-17.
56 Ibid., pp. 137-41.
57 Ibid., pp. 62, 143, 145.
58 Balme, "Union Medical College at Tsinanfu," *Chinese Recorder and Missionary Journal* 46.11 (November 1915): 692-95.
59 Yeh Ch'un-ch'ih, ed., *Chi-nan chih-nan,* pp. 24-42.
60 Ibid., p. 86.
61 Ibid., pp. 141-44.
62 Ibid., p. 145.

CHAPTER 5: POLITICAL POWER IN TSINAN
DURING THE WARLORD ERA, 1916-1927

1 *Kuo-wen chou-pao* [Kuo-wen Weekly, Illustrated] 3.13 (11 April 1926): 46; American International Corporation and China, Agreement for the Grand Canal of Shantung Province, 7% Improvement Loan, in MacMurray, comp., *Treaties and Agreements,* 1:1287-93; *NCH,* 14 October 1916, p. 13.
2 *Shina* 10.1 (January 1919): 102-4, 10.10 (October 1919): 7; Bertram Giles, TIR, 1st Quarter 1922, F.O. 228/3277.
3 S. Wyatt-Smith, TIR, 4th Quarter 1918, F.O. 228/3277.
4 Peter Duus, *Party Rivalry and Political Change in Taisho Japan* (Cambridge: Harvard University Press, 1968), chapter 4; Tatsuji Takeuchi, *War and Diplomacy in the Japanese Empire* (New York: Doubleday, 1935), p. 191.
5 W. L. Godshall, *Tsingtau under Three Flags* (New York: Macmillan, 1929), pp. 229-32, 499-502; W. W. Lockwood, *The Economic Development of Japan* (Princeton: Princeton University Press, 1968), p. 517.
6 MacMurray, comp., *Treaties and Agreements* 1: 1450-53; Niida Noboru, et al., eds., *Ajia rekishi jiten,* 10 vols. (Tokyo: Heibonsha, 1961) 8:235-36.
7 Sino-Japanese Agreement of 24 September 1918. CFMA R-1605.
8 Lockwood, *Economic Development of Japan,* pp. 50-52; Kungtu Sun and Ralph Huenemann, *The Economic Development of Manchuria in the First Half of the Twentieth Century* (Cambridge: Harvard East Asian Monographs, 1969), pp. 19-41.
9 Craig Canning, "The Japanese Occupation of Shantung in World War I" (Ph.D. diss. Stanford University, 1975), chapter 5.
10 Lockwood, *Economic Development of Japan,* pp. 50-52.
11 The Japanese population of Tsingtao reached its high point in 1922 at 24,100 and thereafter declined with the prospect of Chinese administrative control. See "Economic Development of Shantung Province, China, 1912-1921," U.S.

Commerce Reports, Trade Information Bulletin 70 (9 October 1922); de Garis, ed., *Guide to China* (1923 edition), pp. 170-78; Godshall, *Tsingtau under Three Flags,* pp. 190-246.

12 Lockwood, *Economic Development of Japan,* pp. 386.

13 I am indebted to Craig Canning again for this insight into Japanese policy.

14 Shih Lu-pen, "Shan-tung pei Jih-chün chan-ling ch'üan-lu" [Complete record of Shantung's occupation by the Japanese army] (hereafter Shih Report A), contained in CFMA file entitled "Shan-tung wen-t'i ch'ao-tang" [Selected archival materials on the Shantung question], but not listed in Kuo T'ing-i, ed., *Sino-Japanese Relations, 1867-1927: A Checklist of the Foreign Ministry Archives* (New York: Columbia University, East Asian Center, 1965).

15 Shih Report A, Part 1, railroads.

16 In 1921 the railroad supposedly returned a profit of 7.5 percent. Shih Report A, Part 1, railroads.

17 Shih Report A, Part 4, posts and telegraphs.

18 Shih Report A, Part 2, mining; *Far Eastern Review* 17.2 (February 1921): 145-48.

19 Shih Lu-pen, "Shan-tung pei Jih-chün shou-hai ch'üan-lu" [Complete record of damages suffered in Shantung from the Japanese army] (hereafter Shih Report B), contained in CFMA file, "Shan-tung wen-t'i ch'ao-tang."

20 Report from A. Archer at Tsingtao to John Jordan in Peking, 16 October 1919, F.O. 228/3803.

21 Oka, *Santō keizai jijō,* pp. xv-xvi.

22 Bertram Giles, TIR, 4th Quarter 1918, F.O. 228/3277.

23 Oka, *Santō keizai jijō,* Appendix A.

24 Shih Report B.

25 S. Wyatt-Smith, TIR, 4th Quarter 1917, F.O. 228/1983.

26 S. Wyatt-Smith, TIR, 1st Quarter 1918, F.O. 228/3277.

27 Telegrams dated 22 and 26 February 1919, in file The Paris Peace Conference and the Shantung Question, CFMA R-1606.

28 Letter of J. T. Pratt at Tsinan to John Jordan in Peking, 2 July 1919, F.O. 228/3256.

29 Lu Cheng-hsiang telegraphed these instructions to Peking on 28 March 1919. The replies from Peking were sent in April. CFMA file "Shan-tung wen-t'i ch'ao-tang," items 31-42.

30 Ibid., items 38-42, dated 26, 27 April 1919.

31 Chang Kung-chih (Chih-lieh) et al., "Kuan-yu Shan-tung hsüeh-sheng wu-ssu yun-tung te hui-i" [Recollections of the Shantung student movement of the May Fourth period], *Shan-tung sheng-chih tzu-liao* (1959): 20-29.

32 Li Teng-chih, "Hui-i wu-ssu yun-tung tsai Chi-nan" [Recalling the May Fourth movement in Tsinan], *Shan-tung sheng-chih tzu-liao* 2 (1959): 1-19.

33 *NCH,* 7 July 1919, p. 628; Letter of J. T. Pratt at Tsinan to John Jordan in Peking, 2 July 1919, F.O. 228/3256.

34 Letter of J. T. Pratt at Tsinan to John Jordan in Peking, 17 June 1919, F. O. 228/3256.

35 Pratt described the crowd as "consisting almost entirely of respectable

people." Letter from Tsinan of 2 July 1919 to John Jordan in Peking, F.O. 228/3256.

36 Fang Ch'uan-kuei, "T'ung *Ch'ang-yen* pao-kuan shih-mo" [Complete account of the smashing of the newspaper *Plaindealer*], *Shan-tung sheng-chih tzu-liao* 2 (1959): 74-89; Report of J. T. Pratt, 5 August 1919, F.O. 228/3256.

37 *NCH*, 23 August 1919, pp. 474-75.

38 Letter of J. T. Pratt at Tsinan to John Jordan in Peking, 29 July 1919, F.O. 228/3543.

39 Letter of A. Archer at Tsingtao to John Jordan in Peking, 17 October 1919, F.O. 228/3257; Fang Ch'uan-kuei, "T'ung *Ch'ang-yen* pao-kuan shih-mo," *Shan-tung sheng-chih tzu-liao* 2 (1959): 83-84.

40 Li Teng-chih, "Hui-i wu-ssu yun-tung tsai Chi-nan," *Shan-tung sheng-chih tzu-liao* 2 (1959): 18-19; Chow Tse-tung, *Research Guide to the May Fourth Movement* (Cambridge: Harvard University Press, 1963), items 382, 461, 462. *Ta min-chu pao* [The Democrat] had some backing from American missionaries and was considered by the Japanese to be pro-American.

41 Bertram Giles, TIR, 1st Quarter 1922, F.O. 228/3277.

42 Chang Wen-ch'iu, "Liu Chien-ch'u lieh-shih sheng-ping lüeh-li" [Brief account of the life of the martyr Liu Chien-ch'u], *Shan-tung sheng-chih tzu-liao* 3 (1960): 68-70; Li Hsu-chi and Ts'ao Chen-tung, "Wu-ssu tsai Shan-tung" [May Fourth in Shantung], *Shan-tung sheng-chih tzu-liao* 2 (1959): 58-60.

43 Translations of anti-British and anti-American articles from the *Seitō Shimpo* [Tsingtao News], of 29 and 30 May 1919 in letter of J. T. Pratt at Tsinan to John Jordan in Peking, 5 June 1919, F.O. 228/3256; H. King, TIR, 1st Quarter 1924, F.O. 228/3277.

44 W. W. Willoughby, *Foreign Rights and Interests in China,* 2 vols. (Washington, D.C.: Johns Hopkins University Press, 1927), 1:277-78.

45 Ibid., 1:279-80.

46 Telegrams of January, February, and April 1920, CFMA R-1608; *NCH*, 31 January 1920, p. 280.

47 Bertram Giles, TIR, 3d Quarter 1921, F.O. 228/3277.

48 Li Hsu-chi and Ts'ao Chen-tung, "Wu-ssu tsai Shan-tung," *Shan-tung sheng-chih tzu-liao* 2 (1959): 62-63; see also descriptions of these two groups' publications, Chow, *Research Guide,* items 382, 383; and Bertram Giles, TIR, 4th Quarter 1921, and 1st Quarter 1922, F.O. 228/3277.

49 Bertram Giles, TIR, 1st and 2d Quarters 1922, F.O. 228/3277.

50 Willoughby, *Foreign Rights and Interests in China,* 1:297-302.

51 Yu Wu-huan, "Lu-ta Kung-ssu chih li-shih" [History of the Lu-ta Company] originally appeared in *K'uang-yeh chou-pao* [Mining Industry Weekly], 1928, reprinted in Wang Ching-yü, comp., *Chung-kuo chin-tai kung-yeh shih tzu-liao, ti-i chi, 1895-1914 nien* (Peking: K'o-hsüeh ch'u-pan she, 1957), vol. 1; *NCH*, 22 August 1922, p. 590; Bertram Giles, TIR, 2d Quarter 1922, F.O. 228/3277.

52 "Chiao-chi t'ieh-lu ku-fen yü-hsien kung-ssu chou-pei-chü ti-i tz'u hsuan-kao" [First report of the planning section of the Shantung Railroad Company,

Ltd.], Peking 1924, CFMA R-110108; Bertram Giles, TIR, 1st Quarter 1922, F.O. 228/3277; Willoughby, *Foreign Rights and Interests in China,* 1:304-16; *NCH,* 4 February 1922, pp. 287-88.

53 J. Brown Scott, comp., *Treaties and Agreements with and Concerning China, 1919-1929* (Washington, D.C.: Carnegie Endowment for International Peace, 1929), pp. 89-129.

54 *NCH,* 23 December 1922, p. 780.

55 In Tsingtao new Japanese cotton mills were only the most visible signs of the continuing Japanese influence. "Tsingtao Today," *Chinese Economic Journal* 1.1 (January 1927): 48-52.

56 S. Wyatt-Smith, TIR, 2d Quarter 1918, F.O. 228/3277; Bertram Giles, TIR, 3d Quarter 1921, F.O. 228/3277.

57 Bertram Giles and A. H. George, TIR, 3d Quarter 1921 through 1st Quarter 1923, F.O. 228/3277; *NCH,* 4 February 1922, p. 290.

58 Boorman, ed., *Biographical Dictionary of Republican China* 1:122-27; TIR, 1920-22, F.O. 228/3277.

59 H. King, TIR, Semi-annual, October 1924—March 1925, F.O. 228/3277.

60 H. King, TIR, Semi-annual, March-October 1925, F.O. 228/3277.

61 *NCH,* 15 October 1927, p. 99.

62 H. King, TIR, March-September 1928, F.O. 228/3824.

63 J. N. Affleck, TIR, October 1927—March 1928, F.O. 228/3824.

64 J. N. Affleck, TIR, September 1927—March 1928, F.O. 228/3824; *NCH,* 24 December 1927, p. 527.

65 Tai Hsüan-chih, *Hung-ch'iang hui, 1916-1949* (Taipei: Shih-huo ch'u-pan she, 1973); Roman Slawinski, "The Red Spears in the late 1920s," and Lucien Bianco, "Secret Societies and Peasant Self-Defense, 1921-1933," in Jean Chesneaux, ed., *Popular Movements and Secret Societies in China, 1840-1950* (Stanford: Stanford University Press, 1972), pp. 201-24.

CHAPTER 6: ECONOMIC AND SOCIAL LIFE IN TSINAN DURING THE WARLORD ERA

1 A. G. Parker, *Social Glimpses of Tsinan* (Tsinan: Shantung Christian University, 1924), p.1.

2 For a general description of this period see Hu-pei ta-hsüeh, comp., *Chung-kuo chin-tai kuo-min ching-chi-shih chiang-i* (Peking: Kao-teng chiao-yü ch'u-pan she, 1958), pp. 301-52; also M. C. Bergère, "La bourgeoisie chinoise et les problèmes de dévelopment économique (1917-1923)," *Revue d'histoire moderne et contemporaine* 16.2 (April-June 1969): 246-67.

3 Harry A. Franck, *Wandering in North China* (New York: Century, 1923), p. 226.

4 "Tsingtao Today," *Chinese Economic Review* 1.1 (January 1927): 48-52.

5 Oka, *Santō keizai jijō,* pp. 149-55, 230-45.

6 Sun Pao-sheng, comp., *Li-ch'eng hsien hsiang-t'u tiao-ch'a lu* (Tsinan: Li-ch'eng hsien shih-yeh chü, 1928), p. 101. For the situation in Canton see Edward J. M. Rhoads, "Merchant Associations in Canton, 1895-1911," in Elvin and Skinner, eds., *The Chinese City Between Two Worlds,* pp. 97-108.

7 Oka, *Santō keizai jijō*, pp. 32-33; Mishina Yoritada, *Kahoku minzoku kōgyō no hatten* [The development of China's national industry] (Tokyo: Chuō koran, 1942), quoted in Ch'en Chen, comp., *Chung-kuo chin-tai kung-yeh shih tzu-liao, ti-erh chi,* 1:300-307.

8 For a detailed description of the operation of traditional banks, see Susan Mann Jones, "Finance in Ningpo: The 'Ch'ien Chuang,' 1750-1880," in Willmont, ed., *Economic Organization in Chinese Society*, pp. 47-48; and the same author's "The Ningpo Pang and Financial Power at Shanghai," in Elvin and Skinner, eds., *The Chinese City Between Two Worlds,* pp. 73-98.

9 *Shina* 10.1 (January 1919): 87-104.

10 *CKSYC:STS* 8:7; "Banking and Currency in Tsinan," *Chinese Economic Monthly* 1.8 (August 1925): 25.

11 S. Wyatt-Smith, TIR, 1st Quarter 1918; Bertram Giles, TIR, 3d Quarter 1921 and 2d Quarter 1922, F.O. 228/3277.

12 Bertram Giles, TIR, 3d Quarter 1921, F.O. 228/3277; "Banking and Currency in Tsinan," *Chinese Economic Monthly* 1.8 (August 1925): 27.

13 Gaimushō Jōhōbū, *Chūka minkoku Manshūko jinmeikan* (Tokyo: Gaimushō, 1933), p. 8; *CKSYC:STS* 8:6.

14 Mishina, *Kahoku minzoku kōgyō no hatten*, in Ch'en Chen, comp., *Chung-kuo chin-tai kung-yeh shih tzu-liao, ti-erh chi,* pp. 301-5.

15 "Banking and Currency in Tsinan," *Chinese Economic Monthly* 1.8 (August 1925): 27-28.

16 Sun Pao-sheng, comp., *Li-ch'eng hsien hsiang-t'u tiao-ch'a lu,* pp. 148-52; "Banking and Currency in Tsinan," *Chinese Economic Monthly* 1.8 (August 1925): 23-28.

17 "New Industry at Tsinan," *Chinese Economic Monthly* 2.4 (January 1925): 12; Bertram Giles, TIR, 3d Quarter 1921, F.O. 228/3277; *NCH*, 15 March 1907, p. 548.

18 "New Industry at Tsinan," *Chinese Economic Monthly* 2.4 (January 1925): 14 ff.; Oka, *Santō keizai jijō,* pp. 73-74.

19 "Flour Industry in Tientsin," *Chinese Economic Journal* 6.4 (October 1932): pp. 290-99; "Advance in Flour Milling in China," *Far Eastern Review* 21.1 (January 1925): 75-79.

20 *Chinese Economic Bulletin* 227 (27 June 1925): 373.

21 "New Industry at Tsinan," *Chinese Economic Monthly* 2.4 (January 1925): 13 ff.; Oka, *Santō keizai jijō,* pp. 84-85; Sun Pao-sheng, comp., *Li-ch'eng hsien hsiang-t'u tiao-ch'a lu,* pp. 152-61.

22 C. Walter Young, "Chinese Labor Migration to Manchuria," *Chinese Economic Journal* 1.7 (July 1927): 613-33.

23 Based on the estimates given in *CKSYC:STS* 1:61-64.

24 Bertram Giles, TIR, 3d Quarter 1921, F.O. 228/3277.

25 J. T. Pratt, TIR, 2d Quarter 1916, F.O. 228/3277. Letter of F. J. Griffith at Tsinan to Bishop Illiff in London, 23 February 1917. Archives of the Society for the Propagation of the Gospel (London).

26 Parker, *Social Glimpses of Tsinan,* pp. 18-20.

27 Ibid.

28 Bertram Giles, TIR, 4th Quarter 1921 and 2d Quarter 1922, F.O. 228/3277.
29 B. G. Tours, TIR, 1st and 3d Quarters 1923, F.O. 228/3277.
30 B. G. Tours, TIR, 3d Quarter 1923, F.O. 228/3277; Jean Chesneaux, *The Chinese Labor Movement, 1919-1927* (Stanford: Stanford University Press, 1968), pp. 119-23.
31 Ibid., pp. 187-201; H. King, TIR, Semi-annual, October 1924—March 1925, F.O. 228/3277; *NCH*, 4 February 1925, p. 258.
32 Sun Pao-sheng, comp., *Li-ch'eng hsien hsiang-t'u tiao-ch'a lu,* pp. 24-29.
33 Ibid., pp. 25-27.
34 S. Wyatt-Smith, TIR, 1st Quarter 1918, F.O. 228/3277.
35 Bertram Giles, TIR, 3d and 4th Quarters 1921, F.O. 228/3277.
36 A. H. George, TIR, 4th Quarter 1922, F.O. 228/3277.
37 "Educational Modernization in Tsinan, 1899-1937," in Elvin and Skinner, eds., *The Chinese City Between Two Worlds,* pp. 192-98.
38 Sun Pao-sheng, comp., *Li-ch'eng hsien hsiang-t'u tiao-ch'a lu,* pp. 30-31; Parker, *Social Glimpses of Tsinan,* pp. 22-24.
39 For conditions in other parts of China, see Taga Akigorō, *Sō fu no kenkyū* [A study of clan genealogies] (Tokyo: Tōyō Bunko, 1960), pp. 578-580.
40 Parker, *Social Glimpses of Tsinan* pp. 8-9.
41 Ibid., pp. 6-7.
42 Mao Tse-tung, *Selected Works* 2:220-22, 316-17.
43 Liao T'ai-ch'u, "Rural Education in Transition: A Study of Old Fashioned Chinese Schools (*ssu-shu*) in Shantung and Szechuan," *Yenching Journal of Social Studies* 4.1 (August 1948): 19-67; B. G. Tours, TIR, 3d Quarter 1923, F.O. 228/3140; Kuhn, *Rebellion and Its Enemies in Late Imperial China,* pp. 211-25; and Tai Hsüan-chih, *Hung-ch'iang hui, 1916-1949.*
44 Myers, *The Chinese Peasant Economy,* pp. 55-60, 288-91.
45 Oka, *Santō keizai jijō,* pp. 104-5.
46 Sun Pao-sheng, comp., *Li-ch'eng hsien hsiang-t'u tiao-ch'a lu,* pp. 185-93; Parker, *Social Glimpses of Tsinan,* p. 15.
47 Sun Pao-sheng, comp., *Li-ch'eng hsien hsiang-t'u tiao-ch'a lu,* pp. 50-53; Parker, *Social Glimpses of Tsinan,* pp. 24-27.
48 Report of H. L. Milbourne, United States Vice Consul, in Julean Arnold, ed., *China: A Commercial and Industrial Handbook* (Washington, D.C.: U.S. Government Printing Office, 1926), p. 733.
49 Charles Corbett, *Shantung Christian University (Cheloo)* (New York: United Board for Christian Colleges in China, 1955), pp. 145 ff.; B. A. Garside, *One Increasing Purpose: The Life of Henry Winters Luce* (Taipei: Mei-ya Publications, 1967), pp. 121-23, 247; W. A. Swanberg, *Luce and His Empire* (New York: Scribners, 1972), pp. 46-48.
50 *NCH*, 23 August 1914, p. 292; B. G. Tours, TIR, Semi-annual, March-October 1924, F.O. 228/3277.
51 Bertram Giles, TIR, 2d Quarter 1922, F.O. 228/3277.
52 Illegal Sale of Arms and Munitions by the Mihara Company, September 1917, CFMA R-0710; Illegal Sale of Arms by Nanike Saichi and others, September 1925, CFMA R-0714.

53 *NCH*, 5 January 1924, p. 8; S. Wyatt-Smith, TIR, 1st Quarter 1918, F.O. 228/3277.

54 J. T. Pratt, TIR, 4th Quarter 1918, F.O. 228/3277; B. G. Tours, TIR, 3d Quarter 1923, F.O. 228/3277; Chung Hua-min and Arthur C. Miller, *Madame Mao: A Profile of Chiang Ch'ing* (Hong Kong: Union Research Institute, 1968), p. 14.

55 S. Wyatt-Smith, TIR, 2d Quarter 1918; Bertram Giles, TIR, 3d Quarter 1921, F.O. 228/3277.

56 B. G. Tours, TIR, 3d Quarter 1923 and 2d Quarter 1924, F.O. 228/3277.

57 Parker, *Social Glimpses of Tsinan*, pp. 14-15.

58 Bertram Giles, TIR, 3d Quarter 1921 and 2d Quarter 1922, F.O. 228/3277; O. J. Todd, "Taming 'Flood Dragons' Along China's Hwang Ho," *National Geographic* 81.2 (February 1942): 205-34.

59 Andrew J. Nathan, *A History of the China International Famine Relief Commission* (Cambridge: Harvard East Asian Monographs, 1967).

60 Ronald A. Keith, "Tsinan, A Chinese City," *Canadian Geographical Journal* 12.3 (March 1936): 153-60; *Chinese Economic Bulletin* 18 (10 June 1922): 7.

61 *Chinese Economic Bulletin* 20 (8 July 1921): 4; *NCH*, 14 February 1920, p. 419.

62 Parker, *Social Glimpses of Tsinan*, pp. 21-22.

CHAPTER 7: TSINAN IN THE DECADE OF KUOMINTANG RULE, 1927-1937

1 Nobuya Bamba, *Japanese Diplomacy in a Dilemma: New Light on Japan's China Policy, 1924-1929* (Vancouver: University of British Columbia Press, 1973).

2 See Chang Hsü-hsin, "The Kuomintang's Foreign Policy, 1925-1928" (Ph.D. diss., University of Wisconsin, 1967).

3 See John H. Boyle, *China and Japan at War, 1937-1945: The Politics of Collaboration* (Stanford: Stanford University Press, 1972), pp. 44-82.

4 *CYB 1929-30* (1931), pp. 727-28; also Akira Iriye, *After Imperialism: The Search for a New Order in the Far East, 1921-1931* (Cambridge: Harvard University Press, 1965), pp. 192-205.

5 Rodney Gilbert, "The Military Situation in Shantung," *NCH*, 28 January 1928, p. 216, and "Northern Prospect for War," *NCH*, 3 March 1928, p. 333-34; Tsinan Political Summary, 1st Quarter 1928, F.O. 228/3824.

6 *NCH*, 28 April 1928, pp. 132-33, 5 May 1928, pp. 175-78.

7 *NCH*, 28 January 1928, p. 130.

8 *NCH*, 21 April 1928, pp. 172-75, 26 May 1928, p. 325; *CYB* 1929-30, pp. 878-79.

9 *The Tsinanfu Crisis* (Peking: n.p., May 1928), pp. 6-7. This pamphlet was compiled by students of Tsinghua University who opposed Japanese intervention at Tsinan. The translation of the Japanese original into English is inelegant, but there is no reason to doubt that the Japanese wanted the railroad left alone.

10 *NCH*, 5 May 1928, pp. 172-75, 26 May 1928, p. 325.

11 Ch'en Hsun-cheng, "Wu-san shih-pien" [The May Third affair], Lo Chia-lun, ed., *Ko-ming wen-hsien* (Taipei, n.p., 1957), 19:3504-37; *NCH*, 5 May 1928, pp. 175-78, 12 May 1928, pp. 213-15.

12 Statement of Chinese Foreign Minister (Nanking), Huang Fu, 9 May 1928, *CYB 1929-30,* p. 881.

13 "Kuan-yü Chi-nan shih-chien te hsi chiao-shih jih-chi," [Diary of a Western professor concerning the Tsinan incident], "Jih-pen cheng-ch'ao yü tsui-chin Chung-Jih wai-chiao hsing-shih te ch'uan-pien" [The Japanese domestic political scene and the latest turn in Sino-Japanese relations], Lo Chia-lun, ed., *Ko-ming wen-hsien* 19: 3591-92, 19:3621-24; *NCH*, 5 May 1928, p. 175, 26 May 1928, pp. 314-15, 17 March 1929, p. 342.

14 "Kuan-yü Chi-nan shih-pien chi chiao-she ching-kuo te yen-lun" [Statement concerning the Tsinan incident and the process of negotiations], Lo Chia-lun, ed., *Ko-ming wen-hsien* 19: 3639-40; *NCH*, 12 May 1928, pp. 215-17; Tsinan Political Summary, 2d Quarter 1928, F.O. 228/3824.

15 Chiang Kai-shek, "Shih-hsüeh wu-san kuo-chih" [Lessons from the national shame of May Third], a speech given on 3 May 1929, Lo Chia-lun, ed., *Ko-ming wen-hsien* 19:3626-39.

16 Iriye, *After Imperialism,* pp. 201-5; "Chan-ti cheng-wu wei-yuan Lo Chia-lun pao-kao tsai Chi-nan shih-pien chung chih ching-li" [Report of Lo Chia-lun, member of the warzone government, on what occurred in Tsinan during the incident], Lo Chia-lun, ed., *Ko-ming wen-hsien* 19:3595-3609.

17 "Chi-nan wei-fu fu-tzu-ling Su Tsung-che pao-kao Chi-nan shih-pien ching-kuo (i)" [First report of Su Tsung-che, vice-commander of the Tsinan garrison, about what occurred during the Tsinan incident], and "Su Tsung-che pao-kao Chi-nan shih-pien ching-kuo (erh)" [Second report of Su Tsung-che concerning the Tsinan incident], Lo Chia-lun, ed., *Ko-ming wen-hsien* 19: 3611-19.

18 *NCH*, 9 February 1929, p. 221, 20 April 1929, p. 91.

19 "Ts'an-an chi-shih" [Record of the grievous case], Lo Chia-lun, ed., *Ko-ming wen-hsien* 19:3555-83; *NCH*, 2 June 1928, p. 360, 9 June 1928, p. 410, 16 June 1928, p. 456, 30 June 1928, p. 546, 18 August 1928, p. 272, 25 August 1928, p. 310, 1 September 1928, p. 360.

20 "Shantung Pawn of Politics—Land of Famine," *China Weekly Review,* 6 October 1928, pp. 190-91.

21 Sheridan, *Chinese Warlord,* p. 261.

22 Henry Handley-Derry, TIR, March-September 1930, F.O. 228/4205.

23 Tien Hung-mao, *Government and Politics in Kuomintang China, 1927-1937* (Stanford: Stanford University Press, 1972), pp. 132-33, 143.

24 U.S. National Archives, Record Group 84/Records of Foreign Service Posts of the Department of State, Tsinan Consular Archives, File 800/Political Affairs, Political Reports, October 1932, February 1934, and January 1935. Reports from the Tsinan Consular Archives are hereafter cited as (U.S.) Tsinan Consulate, File number, report title, and date.

25 (U.S.) Tsinan Consulate, File 800, Political Report, June 1933, quoting the

Shan-tung min-kuo jih-pao [Shantung Republican Daily], 20 June 1933.
26 *NCH*, 15 February 1933, p. 249; Paul H. Whang, "Shantung Medley," *China Weekly Review*, 10 October 1932, p. 187.
27 Swanberg, *Luce and His Empire*, p. 142.
28 (U.S.) Tsinan Consulate, File 800, Political Reports, December 1930, January 1932, and May 1932.
29 Tien, *Government and Politics in Kuomintang China*, Appendix C, Provincial Revenues, 1930-36, pp. 189-91.
30 Lyman P. Van Slyke, "Liang Sou-ming and the Rural Reconstruction Movement," *Journal of Asian Studies* 17.4 (August 1959): 457-74; Guy S. Alitto, "Rural Reconstruction During the Nanking Decade: Confucian Collectivism in Shantung," *China Quarterly* 66 (June 1976): 213-46; (U.S.) Tsinan Consulate, File 800, Political Report, May 1931.
31 Noel R. Miner, "Chekiang: The Nationalist Efforts at Agrarian Reform and Construction" (Ph.D. diss., Stanford University, 1973).
32 For a summary on reconstruction efforts, see *Shan-tung sheng chien-she pan-yüeh k'an* 1.14 (November 1936): 159-64; also *NCH*, 13 December 1933, pp. 497-98.
33 *Biographical Sketches of Kuomintang Leaders* (Yenan: n.p., 1945), p. 104, and *China Weekly Review*, 25 July 1931, p. 323.
34 Buck, "Educational Modernization in Tsinan," in Elvin and Skinner, eds., *The Chinese City Between Two Worlds*, pp. 198-201.
35 (U.S.) Tsinan Consulate, File 800, Political Reports, December 1930, February and November 1931.
36 R. P. Shaw, Chefoo Political Summaries, 2d and 3d Quarters 1929, F.O. 228/4005; *NCH*, 10 May 1929, p. 260, 25 May 1929, p. 298.
37 (U.S.) Tsinan Consulate, File 800, Political Reports, January and May 1932.
38 Ni Hsi-ying, *Chi-nan*, Tu-shih ti-li hsiao ts'ung-shu (Shanghai: Chung-hua shu-chü, 1936), p. 2.
39 *NCH*, 13 December 1933, pp. 497-98; *CKSYC:STS* 4:7-10.
40 Keith, "Tsinan, A Chinese City," *Canadian Geographical Journal* 12.3 (March 1936): 153-60; (U.S.) Tsinan Consulate, File 800, Political Report, May 1931.
41 *NCH,* 28 April 1931, p. 119.
42 Edgar Snow and S. Y. Hu, "Through China's Holy Land," *China Weekly Review*, 9 November 1929; (U.S.) Tsinan Consulate, File 866.16/Automobiles, Report on Automobiles in Tsinan Consular District, 1932.
43 *Chi-nan shih-cheng yüeh-k'an* 4.1 (August 1931), appendix pp. 3-4; 4.2 (November 1931) Public Notices, pp. 1-2, Reports, pp. 1-9.
44 (U.S.) Tsinan Consulate, File 800, Political Reports, December 1934 and May 1935.
45 Corbett, *Shantung Christian University*, pp. 251 ff.
46 C. Y. W. Meng, "Tsingtao Still Under Japanese Domination," *China Weekly Review,* 17 February 1934, p. 448; *NCH*, 13 December 1933, pp. 407-8; Chao Ch'i, ed., *Ch'ing-tao t'e-pieh-shih shih-kung-shu hsing-cheng nien-chien* (Tsingtao: n.p., 1939), p. 10.

47 Gaimushō Jōhōbū, *Gendai Chūka minkoku Manshū teikoku jinmeikan* (Tokyo: Gaimushō, 1937), p. 253.
48 (U.S.) Tsinan Consulate, File 800, Political Report, January 1933.
49 Ibid., March 1933.
50 Ibid., May 1932.
51 Myers, *The Chinese Peasant Economy,* pp. 187-94.
52 *CKSYC:STS* 4:19-20; *Shih-shih yüeh-pao* 4.2 (February 1931): 58, 4.6 (June 1931): 226.
53 Great Britain, Department of Overseas Trade, *Trade and Economic Conditions in China, 1933-1935* (London: His Majesty's Stationery Office, 1935), p. 75.
54 For an excellent summary of the provincial administration's economic efforts, see the speech of the Shantung Commissioner for Reconstruction, Chang Hung-lieh, *Shan-tung sheng chien-she pan-yüeh k'an* 1.14 (November 1936): 159-64; also 2.3 (February 1937): 1-9, and 2.4 (February 1937): 12-14. For the affairs of Tsingtao-Tsinan and Tientsin-Pukow railroads, see the annual summaries in *China Yearbook* for the 1930s.
55 *Shan-tung sheng chien-she pan-yüeh k'an* 1.2 (May 1936): 175-77.
56 *CKSYC:STS* 4:435-36.
57 *Shan-tung sheng chien-she pan-yüeh k'an* 1.2 (May 1936): 175-77.
58 "Sainan no kin-yū jijō," *Hokushi nōgyō chōsa shiryō* (Dairen: Mantetsu Chōsabu, December 1937), pp. 493-524. The field work was conducted in Tsinan during April 1937.
59 *Shih-shih yüeh-pao* 4.3 (March 1931): 88.
60 *China Annual, 1944* (Shanghai: Commercial Press, 1944), pp. 286-87.
61 Matsuzaki Yūjirō, *Hokushi keizai kaihatsu ron* (Tokyo: Daiyamondosha, 1940), pp. 581-82.
62 Li Te, "Tsung ch'ü-ti wai-shang tang-tien t'an-tao chiu-chi p'in-min" [Taking control of foreign-owned pawnshops and helping the poor], *Chi-nan shih-cheng yüeh-k'an* 4.2 (November 1931), Essays, pp. 1-23.
63 Matsuzaki, *Hokushi keizai kaihatsu ron,* pp. 581-82.
64 Richard A. Kraus, "Cotton and Cotton Goods in China, 1918-1936: The Impact of Modernization on the Traditional Sector" (Ph.D. diss., Harvard University, 1968). Kraus is an excellent guide to the complex questions of cotton supply and use in the early twentieth century.
65 Kahoku sōgō chōsa kenkyūjō, ed., *Sainan shokufugyō chōsa hōkokushu* (Peking: Kahoku sōgō chōsa kenkyūjō, 1945). The field work was conducted in Tsinan in 1943.
66 For the situation in Tsingtao see Manabe Gorō, *Hokushi chihō toshi gaikan* (Osaka: Ajia shuppansha, 1940), pp. 48-65, and *CYB* 1939, pp. 109-12
67 *China Weekly Review,* 25 September 1937, p. 35, 2 October 1937, p. 76.
68 Boorman, ed., *Biographical Dictionary of Republican China* 2:51-54; Frank A. Dorn, *The Sino-Japanese War, 1937-1941* (New York: Macmillan, 1974), pp. 144-45.
69 Lloyd Eastman, *The Abortive Revolution: China Under Nationalist Rule* (Cambridge: Harvard University Press, 1974), p. 85.

70 (U.S.) Tsinan Consulate, File 800, Political Report, May 1933.
71 (U.S.) Tsinan Consulate, File 800, Correspondence 1936, Dispatches of Horace H. Smith at Tsinan, 15 January 1936 and 4 April 1936; also *NCH*, 6 October 1937, p. 2.
72 Dorn, *The Sino-Japanese War, 1937-1941*, pp. 80-85.
73 (U.S.) Tsinan Consulate, File 800, Dispatch of H. T. Chen at Tsinan, 15 December 1937; Dorn, *The Sino-Japanese War, 1937-1941*, p. 84; Boyle, *China and Japan at War*, pp. 119-22, 243-49.
74 Eastman, *The Abortive Revolution*, pp. 140-58; *China Weekly Review*, 25 December 1937, p. 98; Dorn, *The Sino-Japanese War, 1937-41*, pp. 136-44.
75 To a large extent, Han Fu-ch'ü's role in Shantung is comparable to what Eastman has attributed to Chiang Kai-shek; see *The Abortive Revolution*, pp. 278-82.

CHAPTER 8: TSINAN IN WAR, 1938-1948

1 Wang Yu-chuan, "Organization of a Typical Guerrilla Area in Southern Shantung," an appendix to Evans F. Carlson, *The Chinese Army, Its Organization and Military Efficiency* (New York: Institute of Pacific Relations, 1940); Chalmers Johnson, *Peasant Nationalism and Communist Power: The Emergence of Revolutionary China, 1937-1945* (Stanford: Stanford University Press, 1962), pp. 109-13; *K'ang-jih chan-cheng shih-chi chieh-fang ch'ü kai-k'uang* [An overview of the liberated areas during the period of the war to resist Japan] (Peking: Jen-min ch'u-pan she, 1953), pp. 78-93; Laurance Tipton, *Chinese Escapade* (London: Macmillan, 1949), pp. 87-247.
2 For an example of the differences in various Japanese spokesmen's formulations see the statements of Ambassador Kawagoe on economic development. (U.S.) Tsinan Consulate, File 800, Political Report, August 1936. Kawagoe's approach was too strongly favorable to the Japanese capitalists for the taste of the Japanese army. For their approach, which emphasized maintaining established Confucian virtues and contributing to Japan's overall military strength, see *Chi-nan jih-pao* articles of November 1935 as reported in (U.S.) Tsinan Consulate, File 800, Dispatches of 19 and 27 November 1935.
3 Boyle, *China and Japan at War*, pp. 83-107; George E. Taylor, *The Struggle for North China* (New York: Institute for Pacific Relations, 1940), pp. 17-34.
4 *China Weekly Review*, 27 December 1937, p. 134, 22 January 1938, p. 215.
5 "China's Sacred Province Like Gaul of Old Divided into Three Parts," *China Weekly Review*, 8 July 1939, pp. 54-55; Shan-tung shih-fan ta-hsüeh, li-shih hsi [History Department of Shantung Normal University], "K'ang-Jih chan-cheng shih Shan-tung jen-min fan-ti tou-cheng" [The anti-imperialist struggle of the Shantung people during the war against Japan], *Shan-tung sheng-chih tzu-liao* 1 (1959): 12-27.
6 *China Weekly Review*, 8 July 1939, pp. 54-55.
7 Ibid.; *China Annual, 1944*, pp. 286-87, 948; Manabe, *Hokushi chihō toshi gaikan*, pp. 30-34.
8 *Chi-nan shih-cheng kung-pao* 3.3 (December 1942). For conditions in a rural village in the immediate vicinity of Tsinan see Niida Noboru, ed., *Chugoku*

nōson chōsakanko 6 vols. (Tokyo: Iwanami shoten, 1952-58), vol. 4. For an English summary of the main findings see Myers, *The Chinese Peasant Economy,* pp. 88-104.

9 Kahoku sōgō chōsa kenkyūjō, ed., *Sainan shokufugyō chōsa hōkokushu,* p. 81.

10 See Myers, *The Chinese Peasant Economy,* Table 56, Wholesale Price Indices for Three Major North China Cities, 1936-1944, p. 284.

11 Taylor, *Struggle for North China,* Appendix 9, "Education under the Provisional Government," 221-32; and *Chi-nan shih-cheng kung-pao* 3.3 (December 1942).

12 *Chi-nan shih-cheng kung-pao* 3.3 (December 1942): 44-45; Taylor, *Struggle for North China,* pp. 70-76, 82.

13 Second Secretary of (U.S.) Embassy in China (Rice) at Nanking to Secretary of State in Washington, D.C., 9 February 1945, *Foreign Relations of the United States* (hereafter *FRUS*), 1945, 7:167.

14 Ambassador Hurley at Nanking to Secretary of State in Washington, D.C., 9 September 1945, *FRUS* 1945, 7:552-53.

15 Commanding General U.S. Forces, China Theatre (Wedemeyer) at Nanking to Chief of Staff, U.S. Army (Eisenhower) in Washington, D.C., 20 November 1945; Chargé of Embassy in China (Robertson) at Nanking to Secretary of State in Washington, D.C., 16 December 1945, *FRUS* 1945, 7:655, 692.

16 *China Handbook, 1937-1945* (New York: Macmillan, 1947), p. 698; Hsu Long-hsuen and Chang Ming-kai, *History of the Sino-Japanese War, 1937-1945,* 2 vols. (Taipei, Chung-wu: 1971), 1:510, 945-46.

17 *FRUS* 1947, 7:1414; Lionel Max Chassin, *The Communist Conquest of China: A History of the Civil War, 1945-1949* (Cambridge: Harvard University Press, 1965), p. 211.

18 *Shan-tung sheng cheng-fu kung-pao* 31 (15 December 1946) through 111 (27 June 1948).

19 *Shan-tung sheng cheng-fu kung-pao* 38 (2 February 1947).

20 Ch'i Wu, *I-ko ko-ming ken-chü ti te ch'eng-ch'ang* [The growth of a revolutionary base area], (Peking: Jen-min ch'u-pan she, 1958), pp. 220 ff.; Ambassador to China (Stuart) at Nanking to Secretary of State in Washington, D.C., 3 September 1948, *FRUS* 1948, 7:449-50.

21 Consul General at Tsingtao (Turner) to Secretary of State in Washington, D.C., 5 June 1948, *FRUS* 1949, 7:276-78.

22 Record of Report by J. P. Lake to General Marshall, Tsinan, 2 March 1946, *FRUS* 1946, 9:468-69; Ambassador to China (Stuart) at Nanking to Secretary of State in Washington, D.C., 21 March 1947; Consul General at Tsingtao (Spiker) to Secretary of State in Washington, D.C., 22 August 1947; Ambassador to China (Stuart) at Nanking to Secretary of State in Washington, D.C., 18 November 1947; *FRUS* 1947, 7:72-73, 261-62, 365-66.

23. Chassin, *The Communist Conquest of China,* pp. 121-26, 141.

24 Consul General at Tsingtao (Turner) to Secretary of State, 5 April 1948, *FRUS* 1948, 7:180-81.

25 Ambassador to China (Stuart) at Nanking to Secretary of State in Washington,

D.C., 5 April 1948; Consul General at Tsingtao (Turner) to Secretary of State in Washington, D.C., 5 June 1948, Memorandum by Consul at Tsingtao (Strong), 30 July 1948, *FRUS* 1948, 7:182, 276-78, 391-95.

26 See dispatches of Henry Lieberman from Nanking, *New York Times,* 19, 22, 23, 24, and 26 September 1948.

27 Consul General at Tsingtao (Turner) to Secretary of State in Washington, D.C., 1 October 1948, *FRUS* 1948, 7:480.

28 Consul at Peiping (Touchette) to Secretary of State in Washington, D.C., 22 September 1948, *FRUS* 1948, 7:468-69.

29 Consul General at Tsingtao (Turner) to Secretary of State in Washington, D.C., 11 October 1948, *FRUS* 1948, 8:847.

30 Myers, *The Chinese Peasant Economy*, pp. 273 ff. Also see my review of Myers' book in *China Quarterly* 48 (October-December 1971): 766-68.

CHAPTER 9: POLITICS AND DEVELOPMENT IN TSINAN, 1890-1949

1 See Joseph Whitney, *China: Area, Administration and Nation Building* (Chicago: University of Chicago Press, 1970); and Rhoads Murphey, "Aspects of Urbanization in Contemporary China: A Revolutionary Model," paper delivered at the Seventy-first Annual Meeting of Association of American Geographers, 20-23 April 1975, Milwaukee, Wisconsin.

2 Mao Tse-tung, "Report to the Second Plenary Session of the Seventh Central Committee of the Communist Party of China" (5 March 1949) in *Selected Works* 4:365.

3 *Tien-chin jih-pao* [Tientsin Times], editorial of May-June, 1949, entitled "Pa hsiao-fei ch'eng-shih pien-ch'eng sheng-ch'an ch'eng-shih" [Turn consumer cities into producer cities], in Liu Shao-ch'i, et al., *Hsin min-chu chu-i ch'eng-shih cheng-tse* (Hong Kong: Hsin-min-chu ch'u-pan-she, 1949), pp. 32-36.

4 "The New Shanghai in Socialist Construction," *Ch'eng-shih chien-she* 10 (October 1959): 28-31, as translated in JPRS 5258, *Urban Construction in Communist China*, part 2 (August 1960), p. 42.

5 David D. Buck, "Directions in Chinese Urban Planning," *Urbanism Past and Present* 1.1 (Winter 1976): 24-35; and Rewi Alley, *Travels in China, 1966-1971* (Peking: Foreign Languages Press, 1973), pp. 227-35.

6 Based on Ezra Vogel, *Canton Under Communism: Programs and Policies in a Provincial Capital, 1949-1968* (Cambridge: Harvard University Press, 1969) pp. 156-73.

7 See Franz Schurmann, *Ideology and Organization in Communist China* (Berkeley and Los Angeles: University of California Press, 1968), pp. 380-403; and Janet Salaff, "The Urban Communes and Anti-city Experiments in Communist China," *China Quarterly* 29 (January-March 1967): 82-110.

8 "How an Industrial City Grows," *China Reconstructs* 24.8 (August 1975): 6.

9 Myers, *The Chinese Peasant Economy*, p. 293.

10 I have drawn these definitions of political, economic, and social modernization from a treatment by Berry, *The Human Consequences of Urbanization.*

11 Frank, *Capitalism and Underdevelopment,* pp. 3-14.

12 No adequate history of Shenyang exists, but see Frank Leeming, "Reconstructing Late Ch'ing Feng-t'ien" (Mukden, Liaoning), *Modern Asian Studies* 4.4 (October 1970): 305-24; Hōten shōkōkaigisho, ed., *Hōten keizai sanjūnenshi* (Mukden: Hōten shōkō kokai, 1940); and Shen Chi, "Shenyang— Socialist Industrial City," *China Reconstructs* 22.1 (January 1975): 16-22.

Selected Bibliography

Works listed in the Bibliography are arranged under the following headings: Government Archives; Gazetteers and Local Surveys; Handbooks, Guides, and Encyclopedias; Newspapers and Magazines; Collected Documents; Autobiographies, Diaries, and Travelers' Accounts; Biographies, Monographs, and Special Studies; Fiction

GOVERNMENT ARCHIVES

Great Britain. Foreign Office. Consular Archives. China. Tsinan Intelligence Reports, 1909-30. Tsinan Correspondence, 1904-30. F.O. 228. Public Record Office, London.

Republic of China. Ministry of Foreign Affairs. Archives, 1906-27. Academia Sinica, Institute of Modern History, Nankang, Taiwan. All items except *Shantung wen-t'i chao-tang* 山 東 問 題 照 檔 [Selected archival materials on the Shantung question] are cited by the file numbers used in Kuo T'ing-i, ed., *Sino-Japanese Relations, 1867-1927: A Checklist of the Foreign Ministry Archives*. New York: Columbia University, East Asian Institute, 1965.

United States. Department of State. Tsinan Consulate Archives, 1930-38. United States National Archives, Washington, D.C.

GAZETTEERS AND LOCAL SURVEYS

Chang Chen-sheng 張 振 聲 , comp. *Fan hsien chih* 范 縣 志· [Gazetteer of Fan County]. 1935.

Chao Ch'i 趙 琪 , comp. *Chiao-ao chih* 膠 奧 志· [Gazetteer of Chiao-chou Bay]. 1928.

Ch'en Ch'ing-fan 陳 慶 藩 , comp. *Liao-ch'eng hsien chih* 聊 城 縣 志 [Gazetteer of Liao-ch'eng County]. 1910.

Ho Ping-yin 何 炳 賢 , ed. *Chung-kuo shih-yeh chih: Shan-tung sheng* 中

國寶業志 山東省 [Industrial gazetteer of China: Shantung Province]. Shanghai: Shih-yeh pu, kuo-chi mao-i chü 寶業部國際貿易局, 1934.

Hu Te-lin 胡德琳, comp. *Li-ch'eng hsien chih* 歷城縣志 [Gazetteer of Li-ch'eng County]. 1772.

Kahoku sōgō chōsa kenkyūjō 華北總合調查研究所 [Research Institute of the North China General Survey], ed. *Sainan shokufugyō chōsa hōkokushu* 濟南織布業調查報告書 [Report of investigation of the Tsinan textile industry]. Peking: n.p., 1945.

Kogawa Heichi 小川平吉, ed. *Shina shōbetsu zenshi* 支那省別全誌 [Gazetteer of the Chinese Provinces]. 18 vols. Vol. 4 山東省 *Santō-shō* [Shantung Province]. Tokyo: Tōa dōbunkai 東亞同文會, 1917.

Li Shu-te 李德樹, comp. *Te-hsien chih* 德縣志 [Gazetteer of Te County]. 1935.

Liao T'ai-ch'u 廖泰初. "Rural Education in Transition: A Study of Old Fashioned Chinese Schools (*ssu-shu*) in Shantung and Szechuan." *Yenching Journal of Social Studies* 4.1 (August 1948):19-67.

Liu Tung-hou 劉東侯, comp. *Wei-hsien chih* 濰縣志 [Gazetteer of Wei County]. 1937.

Mantetsu shiryōya 滿鐵資料課 [Data section of the South Manchurian Railway]. *Hokushi jijō sōran* 北支事情總覽 [Survey of conditions in North China]. Dairen: Mantetsu 滿鐵, 1935.

Mao Ch'eng-lin 毛承霖, comp. *Hsü-hsiu Li-ch'eng hsien-chih* 續修歷城縣志 [New edition of the Li-ch'eng County gazetteer]. 1924.

Matsuzaki Yūjirō 松崎雄二郎. *Hokushi keizai kaihatsu ron* 北支經濟開發論 [North China's economic development]. Tokyo: Daiyamondosha ダイヤモンド社, 1940.

Niida Noboru 仁井田陞, ed. *Chugoku nōson kanko chōsa* 中國農村慣行調查 [Investigations of conditions in Chinese villages] 6 vols. Tokyo: Iwanami shoten 岩波書店, 1952-58.

266

Oka Itarō 岡 尹 大 郎 . *Santō keizai jijō, Sainan o chū to shite* 山 東 經 濟 事 情, 濟 南 を 中 と し て [Economic conditions in Shantung with special reference to Tsinan]. Osaka: n.p., 1918.

Parker, A. G. *Social Glimpses of Tsinan.* Tsinan: Shantung Christian University, 1924.

P'an Shou-chang 潘 守 章 , comp. *Chi-ning chih-li chou hsü-chih* 濟 寧 直 隸 州 續 志 [Continuation of the Chi-ning independent department gazetteer]. 1926.

"Sainan no kin-yū jijō" 濟 南 の 金 融 事 情 [Conditions in the Tsinan money market]. *Hokushina nōgyō chōsa shiryō* 北 支 那 農 業 調 查 資 料 [Field reports on North China agriculture].

Dairen: Mantetsu chōsabu 滿 鐵 調 查 部 , 1937.

Shu Hsiao-hsien 舒 孝 先 , comp. *Lin-tzu hsien chih* 臨 淄 縣 志 [Gazetteer of Lin-tzu County]. 1920.

Sun Pao-sheng 孫 寶 生 , comp. *Li-ch'eng hsien hsiang-t'u tiao-ch'a lu* 歷 城 縣 鄉 土 調 查 錄 [A survey of Li-ch'eng County]. Tsinan: Li-ch'eng hsien shih-yeh chü 歷 城 縣 實 業 局 , 1928.

Sun Pao-t'ien 孫 葆 田 , comp. *Shan-tung t'ung-chih* 山 東 通 志 [Shantung provincial gazetteer]. 1915.

Ts'ao Meng-chiu 曹 夢 九 , comp. *Kao-mi hsien chih* 高 密 縣 志 [Gazetteer of Kao-mi County]. 1935

Wang Tseng-fang 王 贈 芳 , comp. *Chi-nan fu-chih* 濟 南 府 志 [Gazetteer of Tsinan Prefecture]. 1840.

Wang Yin-kuei 王 蔭 桂 , comp. *Po-shan hsien chih* 博 山 縣 志 [Gazetteer of Po-shan County]. 1937.

Yang, Martin C. *A Chinese Village: Taitou, Shantung Province.* New York: Columbia University Press, 1945.

Yang Ching-kun. *A North China Local Market Economy, A Summary of a Study of Periodic Markets in Chowping Hsien, Shantung.* New York: Institute of Pacific Relations, 1944.

HANDBOOKS, GUIDES, AND ENCYCLOPEDIAS

Arnold, Julean, ed. *China: A Commercial and Industrial Handbook.* Washington, D.C.: U.S. Government Printing Office, 1926.

Behme, Dr. F., and Krieger, Dr. M. *Guide to Tsingtao*. Wolfenbuttel: H. Wessel, 1910.

Boorman, Howard L., ed. *Biographical Dictionary of Republican China*. 4 vols. New York: Columbia University Press, 1967-71.

Brunnert, H. S., and Hagelstrom, V. V. *Present-Day Political Organization of China*. Shanghai: Kelly and Walsh, 1911.

Chao Ch'i 趙琪 , ed., *Ch'ing-tao te-pieh shih shih-kung-shu hsing-cheng nien-chien* 青島特別市市公署行政年鑑 [Yearbook of municipal administration for the City of Tsingtao]. Tsingtao: n.p., 1939.

Cheng I-ch'iao 鄭亦橋 . *Chi-nan* 濟南 [Tsinan]. Tsinan: Shan-tung jen-min ch'u-pan she 山東人民出版社 , 1964.

Chiao-yü pu 教育部 [Ministry of Education], comp. *Ti-i-tzu Chung-kuo chiao-yü nien-chien* 第一次中國教育年鑑 [First education yearbook for China]. Peking: Chiao-yü pu, 1934.

China Annual, 1944. Shanghai: Commercial Press, 1944.

China Handbook, 1937-1945. New York: Macmillan, 1947.

Chow Tse-tsung. *Research Guide to the May Fourth Movement*. Cambridge: Harvard University Press, 1963.

de Garis, Frederic, ed. *Guide to China*. Tokyo: Japanese National Railways, 1915 (1st ed.), 1923 (2d ed.).

Forsyth, R. C., ed. *Shantung, Sacred Province of China*. Shanghai: Christian Literature Society, 1912.

Gaimushō Jōhōbū 外務省情報部 [Japanese Foreign Ministry, Intelligence Bureau]. *Gendai Chūka minkoku Manshū teikoku jinmeikan* 現代中華民國滿州帝國人名鑑 [Biographical dictionary of the present-day Republic of China and the Empire of Manchuria]. Tokyo: Gaimushō, 1937. Earlier editions of the same reference work cited under the titles, *Gendai Chūka minkoku jinmeikan* 現代中華民國人名鑑 [Biographical dictionary of the present-day Republic of China], 1924; and *Chūka minkoku Manshūko jinmeikan* 中華民國滿州國人名鑑 [Biographical dictionary of the Republic of China and the State of Manchuria], 1933.

Hauser, Philip, ed. *Handbook for Social Research in Urban Areas*. Ghent: UNESCO, 1965.

Huang Tse-ts'ang 黃澤蒼 . *Shan-tung* 山東 [Shantung]. Shanghai: Chung-hua shu-chü 中華書局 , 1936.

268

Hummel, Arthur W., ed. *Eminent Chinese of the Ch'ing Period, 1644-1912.* 2 vols. Washington, D.C.: U.S. Government Printing Office, 1943-44.

Kao Yin-tsu 高蔭祖, comp. *Chung-hua min-kuo ta-shih chi* 中華民國大事記 [Chronology of the Republican period]. Taipei: Shih-chieh she 世界社, 1957.

Kuo T'ing-i 郭廷以. *Chin-tai Chung-kuo shih-shih jih-chi* 近代中國史事日記 [Chronology of modern Chinese history]. 2 vols. Taipei: Chung-yang yen-chiu yüan, Chin-tai shih yen-chiu so 中央研究院近代史研究所, 1962.

Nagel's Encyclopedia-Guide: China. Paris: Nagel, 1968.

Ni Hsi-ying 倪錫英. *Chi-nan* 濟南 [Tsinan]. Tu-shih ti-li hsiao ts'ung-shu 都市地理小叢書 [Collection of urban geography]. Shanghai: Chung-hua shu-chü, 1936.

Niida Noboru 仁井田陞 et al., eds. *Ajia rekishi jiten* アジア歴史辞典 [Encyclopedia of Asian history]. 10 Vols. Tokyo: Heibonsha 平凡社, 1960.

Satō Sanjirō 佐藤三郎, ed. *Min-kuo chih ching-hua* 民國之精華 [Leaders of the Republic]. Peking: Pei-ching hsien-chen t'ung-hsin she 北京寫真通信社, 1916.

Sonoda Kazuki 園田一亀. *Hsin-chung-kuo fen-sheng jen-wu chih* 新中國分省人物誌 [Who's who in the provinces of China]. Translated by Huang Hui-ch'uan 黃惠泉. Shanghai: n.p., 1930.

Who's Who in China, 1925. Shanghai: Millard's Review, 1925.

Woodhead, H. G. H., ed. *China Yearbook.* London and Tientsin: Tientsin Times. Issued annually (sometimes biennially) between 1912 and 1939.

Yeh Ch'un-ch'ih 葉春墀, ed. *Chi-nan chih-nan* 濟南指南 [Guide to Tsinan]. Tsinan: Ta-tung jih-pao 大東日報, 1914.

Young, John. *The Research Activities of the South Manchurian Railway Company, 1907-1945.* New York: Columbia University, East Asian Institute, 1966.

NEWSPAPERS AND MAGAZINES

Chi-nan shih-cheng kung-pao 濟南市政公報 [Tsinan city government gazette]. Tsinan, 1942. Monthly.

Chi-nan shih-cheng yüeh-k'an 濟南市政月刊 [Tsinan city government monthly]. Tsinan, 1929-33.

China Review. Peking, 1920-24. Weekly

China Weekly Review. Shanghai, 1925-39.

Chinese Economic Bulletin. Peking, 1919-26. Weekly.

Chinese Economic Journal. Peking, 1927-28. Nanking, 1929-37. Formerly the *Chinese Economic Monthly*; also absorbed the *Chinese Economic Bulletin*.

Chinese Economic Monthly. Peking, 1924-26.

Chinese Recorder and Missionary Journal. Shanghai, 1881-1925. Monthly.

Far Eastern Review. Shanghai, 1914-30. Monthly.

Kuo-wen chou-pao 國文周報 [Kuo-wen weekly, illustrated]. Shanghai, 1928-30.

North China Herald and Supreme Court and Consular Gazette. Shanghai, 1888-1939. Weekly.

Shan-tung chiao-yü yüeh-k'an 山東教育月刊 [Shantung educational monthly]. Tsinan, 1922-24.

Shan-tung sheng cheng-fu kung-pao 山東省政府公報 [Shantung provincial government gazette]. Tsinan, May 1946-July 1948.

Shan-tung sheng chien-she pan-yüeh k'an 山東省建設半月刊 [Shantung provincial development bimonthly]. Tsinan, May 1936—February 1937.

Shih-shih yüeh-pao 時事月報 [Current affairs monthly]. Shanghai, 1930-35.

Shina 支那 [China]. Shanghai. 1910-16. Bimonthly.

Tung-fang tsa-chih 東方雜誌 [Eastern Miscellany]. Shanghai. 1904-25. Monthly.

COLLECTED DOCUMENTS

Ch'en Chen 陳真 , comp. *Chung-kuo chin-tai kung-yeh shih tzu-liao, ti-erh chi, Ti kuo chu-i tui Chung-kuo kung k'uang shih-yeh ti ch'in-lüeh ho lung-tuan* 中國近代工業史資料第二集帝國主義對中國工礦實業的侵略和壟斷 Materials on China's modern industrial history, second collection, imperialist aggression against and monopolization of China's industries and mines]. Peking: San-lien shu-tien 三聯書店, 1958.

Chu Shou-p'eng 朱壽朋 , comp. *Tung-hua hsü-lu, Kuang-hsü*

ch'ao 東 華 續 錄 光 緒 朝 [Records from the Eastern Gate (district in Peking where the State Historical Office was located) for the reign of the Kuang-hsü emperor (r. 1875-1908)]. Peking: n.p., n.d.

Chü Cheng 居 正 . *Chü Chueh-sheng hsien-sheng ch'üan chi* 居 覺 生 先 生 全 集 [Collected papers of Chü Cheng]. Taipei: n.p., 1963.

Chung-kuo shih-hsüeh hui, Chi-nan fen-hui 中 國 史 學 會 濟 南 分 會 [Chinese Historical Association, Tsinan Branch], comp. *Shan-tung chin-tai shih tzu-liao* 山 東 近 代 史 資 料 [Materials on Shantung modern history]. 3 vols. Tsinan: Shan-tung jen-min ch'u-pan she, 1957-58.

Chung-kuo shih-hsüeh hui, Shan-tung fen-hui 中 國 史 學 會 山 東 分 會 [Chinese Historical Association, Shantung Branch], comp. *Shan-tung sheng-chih tzu-liao* 山 東 省 志 資 料 [Materials for the Shantung gazetteer]. Tsinan: Shan-tung jen-min ch'u-pan she, 1959-60. Quarterly.

Great Britain. Department of Overseas Trade. *Report on Conditions and Prospects for Trade with China*. London: His Majesty's Stationery Office, 1919-37. Biennial.

Kuo T'ing-i 郭 廷 以 , ed. *Hai-fang tang* 海 防 檔 [Archives on maritime defense]. Taipei: Chung-yang yen-chiu-yuan, chin-tai shih yen-chiu so, 1957.

Liu Shao-ch'i, et al. *Hsin-min-chu chu-i ch'eng-shih cheng-tse* 新 民 主 主 義 城 市 政 策 [Urban policy for the new democracy]. Hong Kong: Hsin-min-chu ch'u-pan-she 新 民 主 出 版 社 , 1949.

Lo Chia-lun 羅 家 倫 , ed., *Ko-ming wen-hsien* 革 命 文 獻 [Documents on the Revolution]. Vol. 19. Taipei: n.p., 1957.

Lu-an Chung-Jih lien-ho wei-yuan-hui hui-i lu 魯 案 中 日 聯 合 委 員 會 會 議 錄 [Minutes of the Sino-Japanese joint conference on the Shantung case]. 11 vols. Peking: n.p., 1923.

MacMurray, John V. A., comp. *Treaties and Agreements with and Concerning China, 1894-1919*. 2 vols. Washington, D.C.: Carnegie Endowment for International Peace, 1922.

P'eng Tse-i 彭 澤 益 , comp. *Chung-kuo chin-tai shou kung-yeh shih tzu-liao, 1840-1949* 中 國 近 代 手 工 業 史 資 料 [Materials on the history of handicraft industry in modern China]. 4 vols. Peking: San-lien shu-tien, 1957.

Scott, J. Brown, comp. *Treaties and Agreements with and Concerning China, 1919-1929*. Washington, D.C.: Carnegie Endowment for International Peace, 1929.

Ta-ch'ing hui-tien 大 清 會 典 [Collected Statutes of the Ch'ing Dynasty]. Peking: n.p., 1899 ed.

The Tsinan Affair. Shanghai: International Relations Committee, 1928.

Ting Wei-fen 丁 惟 芬 , comp. *Shan-tung ko-ming-tang shih-kao* 山 東 革 命 黨 史 稿 [Draft history of the Shantung Revolutionary Party]. Taipei: n.p., 1970.

Tu-pan lu-an shan-hou shih-i kung-shu 督 辦 魯 案 善 後 事 宜 公 署 [Office for supervision of the settlement of the Shantung question], ed. *Lu-an shan-hou yüeh-pao t'e-k'an* 魯 案 善 後 月 報 特 刊 [Special monthly bulletin on the reconstruction of Shantung]. 5 vols. Tsinan: Tu-pan lu-an shan-hou shih-i kung-shu, 1923-24.

U.S. Department of State. *Foreign Relations of the United States*. 1945-48. Washington, D.C.: U.S. Government Printing Office, 1970-73.

U.S. Department of State. *United States Relations with China*. Washington, D.C.: U.S. Government Printing Office, 1949.

Wang Ching-yü 王 敬 虞 , comp. *Chung-kuo chin-tai kung-yeh tzu-liao, ti-i chi, 1895-1914 nien* 中 國 近 代 工 業 第 一 集 1895- 1954 年 [Materials on the history of modern industry in China, first collection, 1895-1914]. Peking: K'o-hsüeh ch'u-pan she 科 學 出 版 社 , 1957.

Yüan Shih-k'ai 袁 世 凱 . *Yang-shou-yuan tsou-i chi-yao* 養 壽 園 奏 議 輯 要 [Selected memorials from the Garden of Cultivating Longevity]. n.p., 1937.

AUTOBIOGRAPHIES, DIARIES, AND TRAVELERS' ACCOUNTS

Alley, Rewi. *Travels in China, 1966-1971*. Peking: Foreign Languages Press, 1973.

Armstrong, Alexander. *In a Mule Litter to the Tomb of Confucius*. London: Nisbet, 1886.

Ch'in Te-ch'un 秦 德 純 . *Ch'in Te-ch'un hui-i lu* 秦 德 純 回 憶 錄 [Recollections of Ch'in Te-ch'un]. Taipei: Chuan-chi wen-hsüeh ch'u-pan she 傳 記 文 學 出 版 社 , 1967.

Coltman, Robert. *The Chinese, Their Present and Future: Medical, Political and Social*. London: F. A. Davis, 1891.

Davis, John Francis. *Sketches of China*. London: Charles Knight, 1841.

Dewey, John. "Shantung as Seen from Within." *New Republic* 22.274 (3 March 1920): 12-16.

Edmunds, C. K. "Shantung: China's Holy Land." *National Geographic Magazine* 36.3 (September 1919): 245-51.

Fauvel, A. "The Province of Shantung" *China Review* 3 (1874-75): 364-77.

Forsyth, R. C. "Tsinanfu, Capital of Shantung." *Chinese Recorder* 14.5 (May 1914): 304-10.

Franck, Harry A. *Wandering in North China*. New York: Century, 1923.

Garnett, W. L. *Journey Through the Provinces of Shantung and Kiangsu*. A report Submitted to Parliament, China, no. 1. London: His Majesty's Stationery Office, 1907.

Grosier, J. B. *A General Description of China*. London: Robinson, 1788.

Heeren, J. J. "On the Famine Front of Shantung." *Asia* 21.6 (June 1922); 541-42.

Heeren, J. J. *On the Shantung Front: A History of the Shantung Mission of the Presbyterian Church of the U.S.A., 1861-1940*. New York: Board of Foreign Missions, 1940.

Hsu Ying 徐盈 et al. *Lu-min feng-yun* 魯閩風雲 [Letters from Shantung and Fukien]. Shanghai: Sheng-huo shu-tien 生活書店, 1938.

Huang Yen-p'ei 黃炎培. *Huang Yen-p'ei kao-ch'a chiao-yü jih-chi, ti-erh chi* 黃炎培考查教育日記，第二集 [Diary of Huang Yen-p'ei's educational investigations. second collection]. Shanghai: Shang-wu yin-shu kuan 商務印書館, 1916.

Keith, Ronald A. "Tsinan, A Chinese City." *Canadian Geographical Journal* 12.3 (March 1936): 153-60.

Kemp, E. G. *The Face of China*. New York: Duffield, 1909.

Lin Lin. "Tsinan of Shantung Today." *Chung-kuo hsin-wen* 中國新聞 [China news], 19 October 1963; Canton. Joint Publication Research Service Translation 23,835 (24 March 1964): 28-31.

Lockhart, J. H. *Confidential Report of a Journey in Shantung*. Hong Kong: Government Printing Office, 1903.

Neal, James Boyd. "Tsinanfu, Capital of Shantung." *East of Asia Magazine* 5 (1906): 324-34.

Richard, Timothy. *Forty-five Years in China*. London: Unwin, 1916.

von Hesse Wartegg, Ernst. *Schantung und Deutsch: China im Jahre 1898*. Leipzig: J. J. Weber, 1898.

Wang I-chien 王 意 監 [Chiang Kuei 姜 貴]. *Wu-wei chi* 無 違
集 [Collected writings of an apolitical man]. Taipei: Yu-shih wen-i ch'u-pan
she 幼 獅 文 藝 出 版 社, 1974.
Williams, Maynard Owen. "The Descendants of Confucius." *National Geo-graphical Magazine* 36.3 (September 1919): 252-65.
Williamson, Alexander. *Journeys in North China, Manchuria and Eastern Mon-golia with some account of Korea.* 2 vols. London: Smith and Elder, 1870.
Williamson, Isabelle. *Old Highways in China.* New York: American Tract Soci-ety, n.d. [ca. 1895].

BIOGRAPHIES, MONOGRAPHS, AND SPECIAL STUDIES

Bamba, Nobuya. *Japanese Diplomacy in a Dilemma: New Light on Japan's China Policy, 1924-1929.* Vancouver: University of British Columbia Press, 1973.
Barbour, George B. "The Springs of Tsinanfu." *Journal of the North China Branch of the Royal Asiatic Society* 56 (1925): 70-75.
Basho, Shotarō 馬 場 鍬 大 郎 . *Hokushi hashō no shigen* 北 支
八 省 の 資 源 [Resources of the eight provinces of North China].
Tokyo: Tokyo shigyō nihonsha 東 京 實 業 日 本 社 , 1939.
Bergère, M.C. "La bourgeoisie chinoise et les problèmes de dévelopment écono-mique (1917-1923)." *Revue d'histoire moderne et contemporaine* 16.2 (April-June 1969): 246-67.
Berry, Brian J. L. *The Human Consequences of Urbanization.* New York: St. Martin's Press, 1973.
Boyle, John H. *China and Japan at War, 1937-1945: The Politics of Collabora-tion.* Stanford: Stanford University Press, 1972.
Britton, Roswell. *The Chinese Periodical Press, 1800-1912.* Hong Kong: Kelly and Walsh, 1933.
Buck, David D. "Directions in Chinese Urban Planning." *Urbanism Past and Present* 1.1 (1976): 24-35.
Buck, David D. "Educational Modernization in Tsinan, 1899-1937." In *The Chinese City Between Two Worlds,* edited by Mark Elvin and G. William Skinner, pp. 171-212. Stanford: Stanford University Press, 1974.
Canning, Craig. "The Japanese Occupation of Shantung During World War I." Ph.D. dissertation, Stanford University, 1975.
Chang Chung-li. *The Chinese Gentry: Studies on Their Role in Nineteenth Cen-tury Chinese Society.* Seattle: University of Washington Press, 1955.
Chang Hsü-hsin. "The Kuomintang Foreign Policy, 1925-1928." Ph. D. disserta-tion, University of Wisconsin, 1967.
Chang Peng. "The Distribution and Relative Strength of Provincial Merchant

Groups in China, 1842-1911. Ph.D. dissertation, University of Washington, 1957.

Chassin, Lionel Max. *The Communist Conquest of China: A History of the Civil War, 1945-1949*. Cambridge: Harvard University Press, 1965.

Ch'en, Jerome. *Yuan Shih-k'ai, 1859-1916*. Rev. ed. Stanford: Stanford University Press, 1972.

Chesneaux, Jean. *The Chinese Labor Movement, 1919-1927*. Stanford: Stanford University Press, 1968.

Chiang Shen-wu 蔣 慎 吾 . *Chin-tai chung-kuo shih-cheng* 近 代 中 國 市 政 [Modern China's urban administration]. Shanghai: Chung-hua shu-chü, 1937.

Ch'ien Tuan-sheng. *The Government and Politics of China, 1912-1949*. Cambridge: Harvard University Press, 1950.

Ching Su 景 甦 and Lo Lun 羅 崙 . *Ch'ing-tai Shan-tung ching-ying ti-chu te she-hui hsing-chih* 清 代 山 東 經 營 地 主 的 社 會 性 質 [The social character of entrepreneurial landlords in Shan-tung during the Ch'ing]. Tsinan: Shan-tung jen-min ch'u-pan she, 1959.

Chow Tse-tsung. *The May Fourth Movement*. Cambridge: Harvard University Press, 1960.

Ch'u T'ung-tsu. *Local Government in China under the Ch'ing*. Cambridge: Harvard University Press, 1962.

Cohen, Paul. *China and Christianity*. Cambridge: Harvard University Press, 1963.

Corbett, Charles. *Shantung Christian University (Cheloo)*. New York: United Board for Christian Colleges in China, 1955.

Crowley, James B. *Japan's Quest for Autonomy: National Security and Foreign Policy, 1930-1938*. Princeton: Princeton University Press, 1966.

Dorn, Frank A. *The Sino-Japanese War, 1937-1941*. New York: Macmillan, 1974.

Eastman, Lloyd. *The Abortive Revolution: China Under Nationalist Rule*. Cambridge: Harvard University Press, 1974.

Elvin, Mark, and Skinner, G. William, eds. *The Chinese City Between Two Worlds*. Stanford: Stanford University Press, 1974.

Feng Yu-lan 馮 友 蘭 . *Hsin-shih lun* 新 社 論 [Essays on contemporary affairs]. Shanghai: Shang-wu yin-shu kuan, 1940.

Frank, Andre Gundar. *Capitalism and Underdevelopment in Latin America*. New York: Monthly Review Press, 1967.

Friedman, Edward. *Backward Toward Revolution: The Chinese Revolutionary Party*. Berkeley and Los Angeles: University of California Press, 1974.

Garside, B. A. *One Increasing Purpose: The Life of Henry Winters Luce*. Taipei: Mei-ya Publications, 1967.

Geil, William E. *Eighteen Capitals of China*. Philadelphia: Lippincott, 1911.

Himeno Tokuichi 姫野徳一 . *Hokushi no seijō* 北支 の 政 情 [Political conditions in North China]. Tokyo: Nichi-shi mondai kenkyū-kai 日支問題研究會 , 1936.

Ho Ping-ti 何炳棣 . *Chung-kuo hui-kuan shih-lun* 中國會館 史論 [An historical survey of *Landsmannschaften* in China]. Taipei: Hsüeh-sheng shu-chü 學生書局 , 1966.

Ho Ping-ti. *The Ladder of Success in Imperial China*. New York: Columbia University Press, 1962.

Hokushi goshō kōgyō gaiyō 北支五省礦業概要 [Essentials of the mining industry in five provinces of North China]. Tokyo: Nichi-man jitsugyō kyokai 日滿實業合會 , 1937.

Hosack, Robert E. "Shantung: An Interpretation of a Chinese Province." Ph.D. dissertation, Duke University, 1951.

Hōten shōkō kaigishō 奉天商工會議所 [Mukden Chamber of Commerce]. *Hōten keizai sanjūnenshi* 奉天經濟三十年 史 [Mukden's economic history during the last thirty years]. Mukden: Hōten shōkō kokai, 1940.

Hou Chi-ming. *Foreign Investment and Economic Development in China, 1840-1937*. Cambridge: Harvard University Press, 1965.

Hsiao Kung-chuan. *Rural China: Imperial Control in the Nineteenth Century*. Seattle: University of Washington Press, 1960.

Hsu Long-hsuen and Chang Ming-kai. *History of the Sino-Japanese War, 1937-1945*. 2 vols. Taipei: Chung-wu, 1971.

Hu Shih. *The Chinese Renaissance*. Chicago: University of Chicago Press, 1934.

Hu-pei ta-hsüeh 湖北大學 [Hupei University], comp. *Chung-kuo chin-tai kuo-min ching-chi-shih chiang-i* 中國近代國民經 濟史講議 [Lectures on China's modern national economic history]. Peking: Kao-teng chiao-yü ch'u-pan she 高等教育出版 社 , 1958.

Huang Chia-mu 黃嘉謨 . "Chung-kuo tui Ou-chan te ch'u-pu fan-ying" 中國對歐戰的初步反映 [China's initial reaction to World War I]. *Chung-yang yen-chiu yuan, chin-tai shih yen-chiu so chi-k'an* 中央研究院近代史研究所集刊 [Bulletin of the Institute of Modern History, Academia Sinica] 1 (1969): 3-18.

Huang Ch'un-hai 黃春海 "The Springs of Tsinan." *Ti-li hsüeh*

tzu-liao 地理學資料 [Geographical materials] 4 (1959): 67-69. Joint Publication Research Service Translation 38,917 (1 December 1966): 115-38.

Hughes, E. R. *The Invasion of China by the Western World*. London: Black, 1938.

Ikei, Masaru. "Japan's Response to the Chinese Revolution of 1911." *Journal of Asian Studies* 25.2 (February 1966): 213-24.

Iriye, Akira. *After Imperialism: The Search for a New Order in the Far East, 1921-1931*. Cambridge: Harvard University Press, 1965.

Israel, John. *Student Nationalism in China, 1927-1937*. Stanford: Stanford University Press, 1966.

Jacobs, Joseph E. *Investigation of Likin and Other Forms of Internal Taxation in China*. U.S. Department of State, Series D.82 China 39 (June 1925). Washington, D.C.: U.S. Government Printing Office, 1925.

Johnson, Chalmers. *Peasant Nationalism and Communist Power: The Emergence of Revolutionary China, 1937-1945*. Stanford, Stanford University Press, 1962.

Kapp, Robert A. *Szechwan and the Chinese Republic: Provincial Militarism and Central Power, 1911-1938*. New Haven: Yale University Press, 1973.

Ko Kung-chen 戈公振 *Chung-kuo pao-hsüeh shih* 中國報學史 [A history of Chinese journalism]. Shanghai: Shang-wu yin-shu kuan, 1927.

Kraus, Richard A. "Cotton and Cotton Goods in China, 1918-1936: The Impact of Modernization on the Traditional Sector." Ph.D. dissertation, Harvard University, 1968.

Ku Tun-jou 辜敦柔. *Chung-kuo i-hui shih* 中國議會史 [History of Chinese parliaments]. T'ai-chung: Tung-hai ta-hsüeh 東海大學 , 1962. Originally published 1931.

Kuo Jung-sheng 郭榮生 , ed. *Chung-kuo sheng yin-hang shih-lüeh* 中國省銀行史略 [A brief history of Chinese provincial banks]. Taipei: Chung-yang yin-hang, 1967.

Lange, Vitalis. *Das Apostolisch Vikariat Tsinanfu*. Werl: Societas Divine Verbas, 1929.

Li Chien-nung. *The Political History of China, 1840-1928*. New York: Van Nostrand, 1956.

Li Kuo-ch'i 李國祁 . "San-kuo kan-she huan liao hou, Chung-Te tsu-chieh kang-wan te ho shan yu te-tsui-lin shang te cheng-fu chien-i-shu" 三國干涉還遼後中德租借港灣的洽商與德璀琳上德政府建議書 [Sino-German negotiations concerning the lease of harbors after the triple intervention and Detring's recommendations to the German government]. *Chung-yang yen-chiu yuan, chin-tai shih yen-chiu so chi-k'an* 中央研究院, 近代史研究所集刊 [Bulletin of the Institute of Modern History, Academia Sinica] 1 (1969): 83-112.

Li Yü-shu 李毓澍. *Chung-Jih erh-shih-i t'iao chiao-she shang* 中日二十一條交涉 (上) [Sino-Japanese negotiations on the Twenty-One Demands, first part]. Taipei: Chung-yang yen-chiu yuan, chin-tai shih yen-chiu so, 1966.

Liu Feng-han 劉鳳翰. *Hsin-chien lu-chün* 新建陸軍 [The new army]. Taipei: Chung-yang yen-chiu yuan, chin-tai shih yen-chiu so, 1966.

Lockwood, W. W. *The Economic Development of Japan*. Princeton: Princeton University Press, 1968.

Manabe Gorō 眞鍋五郎 *Hokushi chihō toshi gaikan* 北支地方都市概 [An overview of North China cities]. Osaka: Ajia Shuppansha アジア出版會, 1940.

Mao Tse-tung. *Selected Works of Mao Tse-Tung*. 4 vols. 2d ed. Peking: Foreign Languages Press, 1965.

Miner, Noel. "Chekiang: The Nationalist Effort at Agrarian Reform and Construction." Ph.D. dissertation, Stanford University, 1973.

Morse, H. B. *The International Relations of the Chinese Empire*. 3 vols. London: Longmans, Green, 1918.

Morse, H. B. *The Trade and Administration of China*. London: Longmans, Green, 1913.

Murphey, Rhoads. *Shanghai: Key to Modern China*. Cambridge: Harvard University Press, 1953.

Murphey, Rhoads. *The Outsiders: Western Experience in India and China*. Ann Arbor: University of Michigan Press, 1976.

Myers, Ramon. "Commercialization, Agricultural Development and Landlord Behavior in Shantung during the Late Ch'ing Period." *Ch'ing-shih wen-t'i* [Bulletin of the Society for Ch'ing Studies]. 2.8 (May 1972): 31-55.

Myers, Ramon. *The Chinese Peasant Economy: Agricultural Development in Hopei and Shantung, 1890-1949*. Cambridge: Harvard University Press, 1970.

Nakamura Jihei 中村治兵. "Shintai kahoku no tōshi no kokō ni kansuru ichi kōsatsu" 清代華北の都市の戶口に關する一考察 [An investigation of the household enumeration of North China cities in the Ch'ing period]. *Shien* 史源 100 (March 1968): 169-80.

Perkins, Dwight. *Agricultural Development in China, 1368-1968*. Chicago: Aldine, 1969.

Ross, Timothy. *Chiang Kuei*. New York: Twayne, 1974.

Rozman, Gilbert. *Urban Networks in Ch'ing China and Tokugawa Japan*. Princeton: Princeton University Press, 1973.

Schrecker, John E. *Imperialism and Chinese Nationalism: Germany in Shantung*. Cambridge: Harvard University Press, 1971.

Schurmann, Franz. *Ideology and Organization in Communist China*. Berkeley and Los Angeles: University of California Press, 1968.

Seitō shubigun minseibu 青島守備軍民政部 [Civil Government of the Tsingtao Garrison Command]. *Santō no rōdōsha* 山東の労働者 [Shantung workers]. Tsingtao: Seitō shubigun, 1921.

Shan-tung ta-hsüeh, li-shih hsi 山東大學歷史系 [Shantung University, History Department]. *Shan-tung ti-fang shih chiang-shou t'i-kang* 山東地方史講授提綱 [Lecture notes on Shantung modern history]. Tsinan: Jen-min ch'u-pan she, 1959.

Sheridan, James. *Chinese Warlord: The Career of Feng Yü-hsiang*. Stanford: Stanford University Press, 1966.

Shih-cheng ch'üan-shu 市政全書 [The complete book of urban administration]. Shanghai: Tao-lu yüeh-k'an she 道路月刊社, 1928.

Skinner, G. William, ed. *The City in Late Imperial China*. Stanford: Stanford University Press, 1977.

Skinner, G. William. "Marketing and Social Structure in Rural China." *Journal of Asian Studies* 24.1 (November 1964): 3-43; 24.2 (February 1965): 195-228; 24.3 (June 1965): 363-99.

Sun, E-tu Zen. "The Pattern of Railway Development in China." *Far Eastern Quarterly* 14.2 (February 1955): 179-99.

Sun Kungtu and Heunemann, Ralph. *The Economic Development of Manchuria in the First Half of the Twentieth Century*. Cambridge: Harvard East Asian Monographs, 1969.

Tai Hsüan-chih 戴玄之. *Hung-ch'iang hui, 1916-1949*. 紅槍會 [The Red Spears, 1916-1949]. Taipei: Shih-huo ch'u-pan she 食貨出版社, 1973.

Takeuchi, Tatsuji. *War and Diplomacy in the Japanese Empire*. New York: Doubleday, 1935.

T'an T'ien-k'ai 譚天凱. *Shan-tung wen-t'i shih-mo* 山東問題史末 [A complete account of the Shantung question]. Shanghai: Shang-wu yin-shu kuan, 1925.

Tanaka Kazuhide 田中一英. *Santō tetsudō oyobi kosan* 山東鐵

道與 礦山 [Shantung railways and mines]. Tokyo: Nichi-chu jitsugyō kabushiki kaisha, 1917.

Teng Ssu-yü. *The Nien Army and Their Guerrilla Warfare, 1851-1868.* Paris: Mouton, 1961.

Thauren, John. *The Missions in Shantung China.* Techny, Ill.: S.D.V. Mission Press, 1932.

Tien Hung-mao. *Government and Politics in Kuomintang China, 1927-1937.* Stanford: Stanford University Press, 1972.

Todd, O. J. "Taming 'Flood Dragons' Along China's Hwang Ho." *National Geographic Magazine.* 81.2 (February 1942): 205-34.

Todd, O. J. "The Yellow River Reharnessed." *Geographical Review* 39.1 (January 1949): 38-56.

Van Slyke, Lyman P. "Liang Sou-ming and the Rural Reconstruction Movement." *Journal of Asian Studies* 17.4 (August 1959): pp. 457-74.

Vogel, Ezra. *Canton Under Communism: Programs and Policies in a Provincial Capital, 1948-1968.* Cambridge: Harvard University Press, 1969.

Wang Erh-min 王 爾 敏 . Ch'ing-chi ping-kung-yeh te hsing-ch'i 清 季 兵 工 業 的 興 起 [The rise of the arms industry in the Late Ch'ing]. Taipei: Chung-yang yen-chiu yuan, chin-tai shih yen-chiu so, 1963.

Wei Hsin-chen 魏 心 鎮 and Chu Yun-ch'eng 朱 雲 成 T'ang-shan ching-chi ti-li 唐 山 經 濟 地 理 [An economic geography of Tangshan]. Peking: San-lien shu-tien, 1960.

Whitney, Joseph. *China: Area, Administration and Nation Building.* Chicago: University of Chicago Press, 1970.

Willoughby, W. W. *Foreign Rights and Interests in China.* 2 vols. Washington, D.C.: Johns Hopkins University Press, 1927.

Wood, Ge-Zay. *The Shantung Question: A Study in Diplomacy and World Politics.* New York: Revell, 1922.

Wright, Mary C., ed. *China in Revolution: The First Phase, 1900-1913.* New Haven: Yale University Press, 1968.

FICTION

Wang I-chien 王 彝 墅 [Chiang Kuei 姜 貴]. *Hsuan-feng* 旋 風 [Whirlwind]. Taipei: Ming-hua ch'u-pan she 明 華 出 版 社 , 1959.

I-hsien 衣 仙 [pseud.]. *Ch'eng-hsien chih-hou* 城 陷 之 後 [After the fall of the city]. Shanghai: n.p., 1933.

280

Liu E. [alt. T'ieh-yun] 劉鶚 （鐵雲）. *The Travels of Lao Ts'an.* Translated by Harold Shadick. Ithaca: Cornell University Press, 1952. Original title: *Lao-ts'an yu-chi* 老殘遊記 . A portion also translated by Lin Yu-t'ang, *The Nun of T'ai-shan and Other Stories.* New York: John Day, 1938.

Shu Ch'ing-ch'un 舒慶春 [Lao She （老舍）]. *Cat Country.* Translated by William Lyell. Columbus: Ohio University Press, 1970. Original title: *Mao-ch'eng chi* 貓城記 .

Character List

Characters are provided for terms used in the text, and for many places and individuals as well. Shantung *hsien* and place names outside Shantung have been excluded from the glossary if they are available in the standard reference work, *Chung-kuo ti-ming ta-tzu tien* [A dictionary of Chinese place names]. Those individuals who are dealt with by any of the three standard biographical dictionaries—*Eminent Chinese of the Ch'ing Period, Biographical Dictionary of Republican China,* and *Biographical Dictionary of Chinese Communism, 1921-1965*—have also been omitted. There were a few individuals mentioned in Western-language materials for whom the characters are not available.

Ai Ch'ing-yung
艾慶鏞

ai-kuo pu
愛國布

ch'a-yuan
茶園

Chang Chao-ch'üan
張肇銓

Chang Chih-lieh
張制烈

Chang Kuang-chien
張廣建

Chang Jen-chün
張人駿

Chang Lu-ch'üan
張魯泉

Chang Lung-ts'ai
張龍采

Chang Wei-ts'un
張葦村

Chang-feng jan-chih kung-ch'ang
長豐染織工廠

Ch'ang Mien-chai
常勉斎

Ch'ang-ch'un-chen
長春鎮

Ch'ang-yen pao
昌言報

Che-yeh huo-ch'ai kung-ssu
振業火柴公司

Cheng Shih-ch'i
鄭士琦

Cheng-li-hou mien-fen kung-ch'ang
正利厚麵粉工廠

cheng-shou chü

徵收局

Ch'eng-feng mien-fen kung-ssu

咸豐麵粉公司

Chi-feng mien-fen kung-ssu

濟豐麵粉公司

Chi-ho chi-ch'i kung-ch'ang

濟和機器工廠

Chi-nan Hua-shang tien-tung kung-ssu

濟南華商電燈公司

Chi-nan jih-pao

濟南日報

Chi-nan lao-tung chou-k'an

濟南勞動周刊

Chi-nan tien-hua kung-ssu

濟南電話公司

Chi-nan wan-pao

濟南晚報

Ch'i

齊

Ch'i Yao-shan

齊耀珊

Ch'i-lu kung-pao

齊魯公報

Ch'i-lu yin-hang

齊魯銀行

Chia Ping-ch'ing

賈賓卿

Chiang Po-ch'eng

蔣伯誠

Chiao-t'ung yin-hang

交通銀行

Chien-pao

簡報

chien-sheng

監生

ch'ien-chuang

錢莊

Ch'ien Neng-hsun

錢能訓

Ch'ien-fo shan

千佛山

Ch'ien-yeh kung-hui

錢業公會

Chih-ch'ün hsüeh-hui

智群學會

Chin Kung

靳翠

Chin-ling-chen

金嶺鎮

Chin-pu-tang

進步黨

chin-shih

進士

Chin-te hui

進德會

ch'ing-ts'e

清冊

Chou Shu-piao

周樹標

Chuan-men kung-ssu

專門公司

chü-jen

舉人

Ch'ü Cho-hsin

曲卓新

Ch'ü Ying-kuang

屈映光

284

ch'üan-hsüeh so
勸學所

Chuang Kai-lan
莊諧蘭

Chung-hua ko-ming chün
中華革命軍

Chung-kuo shih-yeh yin-hang
中國實業銀行

Chung-kuo yin-hang
中國銀行

Fang-tzu
坊子

Feng-nien mien-fen kung-ssu
豐年麵粉公司

Feng-shan
鳳山

fou-lin hui-she
阜林會社

fu
府

fu-fei
幅匪

fu-sheng
附生

Fu-te hui-kuan
福德會館

Han-chuang
翰莊

hang
行

Heng-hsing mien-fen kung-ssu
恆興麵粉公司

Ho Ssu-yuan
何思源

ho-fang chü
河防局

Hsia Chi-ch'üan
夏繼泉

hsiang-ch'ü
鄉區

Hsiao-ch'ing ho
小清河

hsiao-fei ch'eng-shih
消費城市

Hsin-chia-chuang
辛家莊

Hsin-chuang
辛莊

Hsin-min hui
新民會

Hsin-she-hui wan-pao
新社會晚報

Hsing-shun-fu chi-ch'i cha-yu ch'ang
興順福機器榨油廠

Hsing-shun-fu mien-fen kung-ssu
興順福麵粉公司

Hsiung Ping-ch'i
熊炳琦

Hsu Chung-hsin
徐鐘心

hsün-fang-ying
巡防營

Hu T'ing-kan
胡廷幹

Hu-kuo chün
護國軍

Hua-ch'ing mien-fen kung-ch'ang
華慶麵粉工廠

Hui-feng mien-fen kung-ch'ang
惠豐麵粉工廠

hui-kuan
會館

Hung-chia-lou
洪家樓

I-hua jan-chih kung-ch'ang
益華染織工廠

Jen-feng sha-ch'ang
仁豐紗廠

jen-la ch'e
人拉車

Kao Ching-ch'i
高景祺

Ko-ming-tang
革命黨

kuan
關

kuan-ch'ien chü
官錢局

kuan-tu shang-pan
官督商辦

Kuang-jen shan-chü
廣仁善局

K'uang-yeh chou-pao
礦業周報

kun-fei
棍匪

Kung Chi-ping
龔積炳

kung-ch'eng-ch'u
工程處

Kung-ho-tang
共和黨

kung-i chü
工藝局

Kung-min-tang
公民黨

kung-sheng
貢生

Kung-yen t'ung-hsün pao
公言通訊報

Kuo-min-tang
國民黨

Kuo-hui
國會

lao-tung ch'ün-chung
勞動群眾

Le-k'ou
濼口

Le-yuan
濼源

Li Shih-wei
李士偉

Li Yen-nien
李延年

286

Li-ch'eng

歷城

Li-ching

利津

Li-hsia

歷下

Li-hsia hsin-wen

歷下新聞

lin-shih ts'an-i hui

臨時參議會

ling-sheng

廩生

Liu Chen-nien

劉珍年

Liu En-chu

劉恩駐

Liu Kuan-san

劉冠三

Lu

魯

Lu Cheng-hsiang

陸徵祥

Lu-feng sha-ch'ang

魯豐紗廠

Lu-ta kung-ssu

魯大公司

Lü Tzu-jen

呂子人

Ma Hung-k'uei

馬鴻逵

Ma Kuan-ching

馬官菔

Ma Kuan-ho

馬官和

Ma Liang

馬良

Mao-hsin mien-fen kung-ch'ang

茂新麵粉公司

Miao Chi-ts'un

苗吉村

Min-an mien-fen kung-ch'ang

民安麵粉公司

Ming-hua yin-hang

明華銀行

Mo Po-jen

穆伯仁

Nichi-chu jitsugyō kabushi kaisha

日中實業株式會社

pa-p'i

扒皮

P'an Fu

潘復

pang

邦

pao-an-hui

保安會

pao-chia

保甲

P'ao-t'u-ch'üan

跑突泉

Pei-yang-chia

北楊家

287

P'ing-min jih-pao

平民日報

Po-hai jih-pao

渤海日報

P'u-i chih-t'ang kung-ch'ang

溥益製糖工廠

Sainan ginkō

濟南銀行

Santō Shimbun

山東新聞

Shan-tso kung-hsüeh

山左公學

Shan-tso yin-hang

山左銀行

Shan-tung jih-pao

山東日報

Shan-tung kuan-pao

山東官報

Shan-tung kuan yin-hang

山東官銀行

Shan-tung kung-pao

山東公報

Shan-tung min-kuo jih-pao

山東民國日報

Shan-tung shang-wu yin-hang

山東商務銀行

Shan-tung shih-yeh yin-hang

山東實業銀行

Shan-tung tzu-chih chün

山東自治軍

Shang Ch'i-heng

尚其亨

shang-pu

商埠

shang-pu tsung-chü

商埠總局

Shen Hung-lieh

沈鴻烈

sheng-ch'an ch'eng-shih

生產城市

sheng-i-hui

省議會

sheng-yüan

生員

Shih Yu-san

石友三

shih-jen t'uan

十人團

shu-yuan

書院

So-chen

索鎮

Ssu-fang

四方

sui-k'ao

歲考

Sun Lien-chung

孫連仲

Ta min-chu pao

大民主報

Ta-ch'ing ho

大清河

Ta-ch'ing yin-hang

大清銀行

ta-hsüeh
大學

ta-ku shu
大鼓書

ta-kuan-yuan
大官園

Ta-lu yin-hang
大陸銀行

Ta-ming hu
大明湖

Ta-tung jih-pao
大東日報

Tai-pei jan-chih kung-ch'ang
岱北染織工廠

T'ai-feng yin-hang
泰豐銀行

Tang-yeh yin-hang
當業銀行

T'ang K'o-san
唐柯三

Tao-sheng yin-hang
道生銀行

tao-t'ai
道台

tao-yin
道尹

Te-chun
德凖

t'i-hsüeh shih
提學使

T'ien Wen-lieh
田文烈

Ting Shih-i
丁世嶧

tokumu-bu
特務部

Tsao-chuang
棗莊

tseng-sheng
增生

Ts'ung Liang-pi
叢良弼

Tu O
杜鍔

tu-chün
督軍

tu-tu
都督

t'uan-lien
團練

Tung-lai yin-hang
東萊銀行

Tung-lu jih-pao
東魯日報

Tung-pei chün
東北軍

T'ung-hai yin-hang
通海銀行

t'ung-hsiang hui
通鄉會

T'ung-hui yin-hang
通惠銀行

T'ung-feng mien-fen kung-ch'ang
同豐麵粉工廠

T'ung-meng-hui
同盟會

T'ung-su jih-pao
通俗日報

T'ung-wa-hsiang

銅瓦鄉

tzu-chih

自治

Wai-wu pu

外務部

Wang Chih-hsiang

王治薌

Wang Chin-mei

王盡美

Wang Hsiang-ch'ien

王湘岑

Wang Hsiang-jung

王向榮

Wang Hu

王瑚

Wang Hung-i

王鴻一

Wang I-chien

王彝堅

Wang Le-p'ing

王樂平

Wang Mao-k'un

王懋琨

Wang Na

王訥

Wang Tsung-wu

王崇五

Wang Yao-wu

王耀武

Wen Cheng-lieh

聞承烈

Wu Hua-wen

吳華文

Wu Ping-hsiang

吳炳湘

Wu Ta-chou

吳大洲

wu-wei yu-chün

武衛右軍

ya-hang

牙行

ya-shui

牙稅

Yang Shih-ch'i

楊士騎

Yang Shih-hsiang

楊士驤

Yang-chiao-kou

羊角溝

Yeh Ch'un-ch'ih

葉春墀

Yü P'u-yüan

于普源

Yü Yüeh-hsi

于耀西

Yü-hsing yen-liao kung-ssu

裕興顏料公司

Yüan Shih-tun

袁世敦

Yüan Shu-hsun

袁樹勛

Yüan Ta-ch'i

袁大啟

290

Index

Academies (*shu-yuan*), 33, 34, 55-56
Administration, 21, 28-29, 81, 91, 144-45, 171, 208-209. *See also* Bureaucracy; Governors; Urban administration
Agriculture, 23, 35-36, 94, 131, 139n, 176, 193, 200-201, 208
Akiyama Masanosuke (Tsingtao administrator), 109-10
Anfu clique, 105, 113, 123, 144, 146, 155. *See also* Chin Yun-p'eng; Tuan Ch'i-jui
Architecture, 19-20, 155, 172, 178, 210
Armstrong, Alexander (missionary), 36-37, 149-51
Artisans, 36-37, 143. *See also* Handicraft production
Automobiles, 55, 94-95. *See also* Transportation

Banditry, 25, 35, 106, 128, 152, 164
Bank of China, 70, 135, 178
Bank of Communication, 70, 178
Banking, 32, 69-70, 73, 95, 126-27, 133-37, 178-80, 192
Beggars, 37, 151
Benevolence Bureau (*Kuang-jen shan-chü*), 30, 33, 147. *See also* Philanthropy
Bureaucracy, 28-29, 36-37, 52-55, 81-82, 91-92, 98-102, 117-18, 124, 144-47, 149, 164, 172, 177, 188-92, 195-96, 212, 213. *See also* Administration; Official-merchant relations; Taxation
Bureaucratic capitalism, 13-14, 54-55, 70, 104-105, 112, 138, 173, 192. *See also* Kuan-tu shang-pan

Capitalism. *See* Bureaucratic capitalism; Chinese capitalism

Chamber of Commerce, 67, 114, 122, 149, 163-64
Chang Chao-ch'üan (Tsinan banker), 80, 114n, 122, 124, 126-27, 135, 136, 154
Chang Huai-chih (warlord and governor), 56, 57, 90, 99, 106, 114
Chang Shu-yuan (military governor), 89, 103, 106, 117, 126n
Chang Tso-lin (warlord of Manchuria), 107, 125, 159
Chang Tsung-ch'ang (warlord and governor), 105, 107, 123, 125, 128, 152, 160, 163, 213
Chang Yao (late-Ch'ing governor), 29-30
Chang-ch'iu, 23, 49, 69-70, 135, 179
Chao Chien-min (1950s governor), 208-209
Charity. *See* Philanthropy
Chefoo (Yen-t'ai), 27, 34, 72, 77
Cheloo University. *See* Shantung Christian University
Ch'en Yi (Communist general), 194, 197, 198
Chi-ning, 22-23, 25-26, 34, 94, 103-104, 160
Ch'i region: defined, 26-28, 105; role in modernization, 61; economic activity in, 70, 80, 133-34, 178, 180-81; political activity in, 77, 90-91, 119-20, 125; mentioned, 92, 97, 167, 185, 197
Chiang Kai-shek: during Northern Expedition, 156, 157, 160; policies concerning Japan, 157, 158, 160n, 161-62, 182-84, 191; involvement in Tsinan incident, 161-63; dispute with Han Fu-ch'ü, 169-70; mentioned, 89n, 97, 182, 185
Chin Yun-p'eng (Anfu clique politician),

81, 84, 86, 103-104, 106, 113, 121, 122, 137, 138. *See also* P'an Fu
Chin-te hui (Improve Virtue Society), 174
Chinese bourgeoisie, 155, 179
Chinese capitalism: types of, 13-14, 138, 173; preferences of, 45, 54, 131, 139-40, 141, 143; attitudes toward railroads, 46; cooperation with Japanese, 112; flowering of, 130-32; monopoly privileges of, 138; political power of, 148, 191; shift to state capitalism, 172-73, 177; evaluated, 181, 200; warlords and, 186; failures in 1930s, 192. *See also* Banking; Industry; *Kuan-tu shang-pan*
Chinese cities: views of, 7-10, 17; post-1949 developments in, 9, 202-203, 205, 207-10; class structure of, 36-37: mentioned, 12, 19, 150. *See also* Shanghai; Tientsin; Treaty ports; Tsingtao; Western cities
Chinese Communist Party (CCP): efforts in 1920s, 119-20, 143-44; during anti-Japanese war, 188, 194, 196; takeover of Tsinan, 198-99; program for cities, 201-203
Chinese Imperial Maritime Customs, 7, 52, 83
Chinese merchants: monopoly privileges of, 13, 54, 138, 139; and the railroads, 68; struggles for political power, 82, 91, 124-25; mentioned, 49-50, 60, 70-71, 118, 131-33, 137, 155, 179
Chou Fu (late-Ch'ing governor), 43, 45, 50, 56, 105
Chou Tzu-ch'i (post-1911 governor), 77-78, 79-80, 87
Chü Cheng (leader of 1916 anti-Yüan expedition), 88-89
Cities. *See* Chinese cities; Urbanization; Western cities
City government. *See* Urban administration
City planning, 44, 52, 148, 172, 195-96
Coal, 49, 50, 111, 122-23, 136
Commerce: impact of war upon, 93, 164, 193, 201; state control over in 1950s, 205-206; mentioned, 93, 127, 210-12. *See also* Banking; Economy; Foreign Trade
Commercial district (at Tsinan), 44, 50-51, 53, 93, 96, 142, 155, 206

Compradors. *See* Chinese capitalism
Construction. *See* Architecture
Coolies, 140
Corruption, 124-25, 146
Cotton, 94, 137-38, 143, 164, 177-78, 180, 192
Crime, 128, 152-53. *See also* Banditry
Cultural modernization, 151, 201, 209, 214-15. *See also* Education; Medicine; Modernization; Newspapers; Technology
Cultural revolution, 209

Dairen (Ta-lien), 27, 88, 109
Demography, 226-36. *See also* Population
Deutsch-Asiatische Bank, 53, 69
Development: defined, 5; theories of, 6, 11, 211; evaluated, 200, 210. *See also* Modernization
Dewey, John (American educator), 119
Drugs, 153, 172

Economy: nineteenth-century form, 10-11, 16; urban-rural links of, 128; impact of World War I on, 131; effects of warlordism upon, 156, 201; effects of world depression upon, 176-77; under the Japanese, 188, 192, 193; under the Kuomintang, 196, 199-200; changes evaluated, 210-12. *See also* Banking; Chinese capitalism; Chinese merchants; Commerce; Imperialism; Industry; Japan
Education, 55-57, 60-63, 126, 147, 151, 168-69, 193, 209, 214-15. *See also* Cultural modernization; Missionaries
Elections, 63-65, 124, 195. *See also* Provincial assembly; Representative institutions
Electricity, 54, 172. *See also* Technology
Employment, 35, 140-44, 207
Entertainment, 34, 37, 53, 96, 153-54
Examination system, 34, 61
Extraterritoriality, 7, 51, 52, 153

Famine, 127, 139n, 154, 164
Feng Yü-hsiang (warlord), 126, 156, 159, 160, 163-64, 165, 169
Fifth Division (of Peiyang Army), 41, 56, 72, 74-75, 77, 84-86, 99, 105, 107, 126. *See also* Peiyang Army

Fire, 35, 77, 148

Flood, 31, 35, 127, 154

Flour milling, 138-40, 178

Foreign trade, 7, 33, 52-53, 60, 83, 87, 94, 105, 110, 112, 113, 128, 131, 164, 176-77, 193, 201

Foreigners: influence of, 33, 59-60, 83-87, 151, 152-53, 155, 209, 215. *See also* Education; Medicine; Missionaries; Technology

Fukuda Hikosuke (Japanese general in Tsinan incident), 162-63

Gentry: changes in, 29-30, 36, 38-39, 40, 60-61, 69-71, 96, 125; described, 36, 66-67; anti-imperialism of, 42, 114-16, 121; role in 1909 assembly, 65-67; rejection of Yüan Shih-k'ai, 78-83; evaluated, 124-25, 150, 186, 200. *See also* Chinese bourgeoisie, Chinese merchants

Germany, 40, 42, 46, 83, 84, 95. *See also* Imperialism, German

Giles, Bertram (British consul at Tsinan), 60, 119

Governors, 43, 76, 98-99, 102, 103, 105

Grand Canal, 23, 25, 32-33, 46, 154

Great Britain, 46, 47, 51, 97

Great Leap Forward, 207

Guilds, 37, 143. *See also* Hui-kuan (provincial associations)

Han Fu-ch'ü: compared with Yüan Shih-k'ai, 165, 213; relations with Chiang Kai-shek, 165-66, 169-70, 184; governing style of, 165-70; economic policies of, 168, 176-77, 179; relations with Japan, 182, 184-85; as warlord, 182-83, 185-86, 213-14; mentioned, 137, 191, 200

Handicraft production, 94, 141-42, 164, 180, 208. *See also* Employment; Industry; Urban-rural relations

Health, 35, 148. *See also* Medicine

Ho Ssu-yuan (educational commissioner in 1930s), 168-69, 173, 195

Hospitals. *See* Medicine

Hsia Chi-ch'uan (president of Shantung assembly), 74, 78, 91

Hsiao-ch'ing canal, 32, 51

Hu Shih, 6-7, 119n

Hui-kuan (provincial associations), 32, 68n, 132-33, 135

Hung-chia-lou, 33, 59, 189

Ichiko Chūzō, 65-66

Imperialism: as an element in modern Chinese history, 9-10, 40-42, 87, 127, 128, 210, 214-15; German, 44-50, 83-84, 113-14; Japanese, 83-84, 107-14, 123, 157, 160, 180-81. *See also* Germany; Great Britain; Japan, economic imperialism of; United States

Independence. *See* Self-rule

Industry, 3, 54-55, 70, 137-40, 168, 172-73, 193, 205-206, 207-208, 219-25. *See also* Chinese capitalism; Handicraft production

Japan: economic imperialism of, 53, 83, 105, 110-11, 131, 140, 177-78, 180, 183-84, 193; involvement in 1911 revolution at Tsinan, 74n; policy toward China, 83-85, 108, 157, 159, 187-89, 191; role in 1916 anti-Yuan expedition, 89, 90-91; policy in Shantung, 98, 107-14, 120-24, 143, 157, 160-61, 185, 188-94; Chinese demonstrations against, 114, 116, 126; mentioned, 47, 51. *See also* May Fourth

Japanese: residing in Tsinan, 53, 55, 59-60, 92, 112, 151, 178, 179, 191-92; residing in Tsingtao, 83-84, 110, 122-23, 173-74, 177-78, 180, 189

Japanese Imperial Army, 83-84, 86, 109, 111, 159, 181-82, 188-91, 194

K'ang Sheng (Communist leader), 208

Kato Komei (Japanese Foreign Minister), 84-85

Kita Seiichi (Japanese military officer), 189-90

Ko-ming-tang. *See* Revolutionary Party

Kuan-tu shang-pan (official supervision and merchant management), 13, 54. *See also* Bureaucratic capitalism; Official-merchant relations

Kuomintang (Nationalist party): in Shantung, 91, 164-66, 194, 197, 200, 214; as a political party, 156, 159, 164, 187, 191; mentioned, 156, 168, 174, 188, 199, 205

Labor, 35, 140-44, 207
Lai-yang case (1910), 67
Le-k'ou, 23, 31, 33, 54, 57
Lenin, V. I., 8
Li Hung-chang, 29-30, 32, 38, 43, 183
Li Ping-heng (governor who supported Boxers), 33, 38
Li-ch'eng district (surrounding Tsinan city), 35-36, 52, 145, 146-47
Liang Sou-ming (conservative reformer), 167-68, 169
Likin (transit taxes), 7, 52-53, 113. *See also* Provincial finances; Taxation
Lin-ch'ing, 22, 23, 25, 45
Liu Chen-nien (warlord on Shantung peninsula), 169-70, 184
Liu E (novelist), 34, 170
Liu En-chu (Tsinan capitalist), 54, 136, 138
Lu region: defined, 26-28; economic activities in, 80, 104-105, 178; political activity in, 90-91, 115, 125; mentioned, 92, 97, 185
Lu-ta Company, 122-23, 136
Lü Tzu-jen (supporter of 1911 revolution), 89

Ma Kuan-ho (Chinese capitalist), 92, 136, 138
Ma Liang (Tsinan defense commissioner), 103, 117, 126n, 191-92
Manchuria, 27, 108-10, 127, 144, 158, 183, 189
Mao Tse-tung, 8-9, 150, 168, 200, 202-203, 205
Marco Polo Bridge incident, 181, 184
Marxist groups. *See* Chinese Communist Party
May Fourth, 107-109, 114-15, 151
Medicine, 35, 59, 95, 112, 148, 151
Merchant groups (*pang*), 49, 68-69, 131-34, 150. *See also Hui-kuan*
Miao Chi-ts'un (Tsinan merchant), 137
Militarization of China, 16, 72, 75, 98-9, 145-46, 174. *See also* Warlords
Military engagements, 25, 38-39, 84-85, 88-90, 157-60, 170, 181-82, 185, 191, 198-99, 212. *See also* Tsinan, military engagements at
Militia, 26, 29-30, 38

Mining, 45, 47-50, 111, 122-23, 136
Missionaries, 31, 33, 55, 59-60, 120, 151, 195, 198. *See also* Cultural modernization; Education; Medicine
Mitsui Trading Company, 53, 112, 122
Mo Po-jen (Tsinan merchant), 137
Modernization: officials' role in, 55; missionaries' role in, 59-60, 214-15; warlords' role in, 176-77; failure of, 210-15. *See also* Cultural modernization; Representative institutions
Moslems, 37, 103, 117-18
Mukden. *See* Shen-yang
Murphey, Rhoads, 6, 9
Myers, Ramon, 150, 200, 201, 208

Nationalism, 41-42, 114-19, 123-24. *See also* May Fourth
Nationalists. *See* Kuomintang
New Life Movement, 174
Newspapers, 92, 117, 174, 184, 196, 214. *See also* Cultural modernization
Nien. *See* Taipings
1909 assembly, 65-71
1911 revolution, 57, 72-78, 239. *See also* Revolutionary Alliance
Nishida Kōichi (Japanese consul at Tsinan), 162, 184, 192
Nishihara Kamezo (Japanese representative in China), 108
Northern Expedition (1926-28), 156, 157
Northwest Shantung, 22, 23, 25, 45

Official-merchant relations, 27-28, 32-33, 50, 60, 62, 65-66, 68, 148-49

P'an Fu (Anfu clique politican), 81, 90, 103-104, 122, 137-38, 160
Pang. See Merchant groups
Parker, A. G. (American sociologist at Tsinan), 130, 147-48, 153-54
Pawnshops, 95, 179
Peiyang Army, 41, 56-57, 88, 98. *See also* Fifth Division; Military engagements
Peiyang clique, 90, 98-99, 108
Philanthropy, 30-31, 33, 95, 147, 154
Po-shan, 23, 26, 49, 68, 93, 110, 111, 143, 147
Police, 44, 52, 148, 172, 195-96
Political parties, 79-80, 214. *See also*

Chinese Communist Party; Kuomintang; Revolutionary Alliance; Revolutionary Party
Political power: urban forms of, 5-9, 12-13, 150, 209; alignments in Tsinan, 21-22, 28-31, 48, 51-52, 75-76, 96, 114, 121, 164, 186-87, 194-95, 209; alignments in Shantung, 26-28, 38-39, 41-44, 57, 71-72, 78, 80, 82, 91, 96-97, 99, 124-25, 126, 156-57, 164-66, 196; alignments in Peking, 38-39, 40, 41, 57, 73, 87-88, 98-99, 107, 121. *See also* Chinese capitalism, political power of; Ch'i region; Gentry; Lu region, political activity in; Political parties
Population, 22, 34-35, 149, 171, 193, 226-36
Postal services, 53-54, 111, 144, 155
Poverty, 26, 37, 127, 140, 149, 151, 154
Pratt, J. T. (British consul in Tsinan), 115, 116-17, 118
Prostitution, 37, 153-54
Provincial assembly, 79-80, 106, 114, 115, 124, 125, 135-36, 140, 149, 174-75, 195. *See also* Ch'i region
Provincial associations. *See Hui-kuan*
Provincial finances, 74-80-82, 145, 146, 166-67, 169-70

Railroads, 44-47, 69, 94, 210. *See also* Tsingtao-Tsinan railway; Tientsin-Pukow railway
Representative institutions, 5, 62-65, 78-79, 149, 174-76, 209, 212-14. *See also* Chamber of Commerce; Provincial assembly
Revolutionary Alliance (*t'ung-meng-hui*), 55, 57, 61-62, 66, 73, 77
Revolutionary Party (*ko-ming-tang*), 87-88, 90-91
Riots, 45, 77-78, 119n, 117-18, 126

Salt merchants, 31-32, 68, 144
Schantung Bergbau Gesellschaft (SBG), 47, 49-50. *See also* Mining
Schantung Eisenbahn Gesellschaft (SEG), 44-45, 104-105. *See also* Railroads; Tsingtao-Tsinan railway
Self-rule (*tzu-chih*), 73-75, 82, 126, 237
Semi-colonialism, 8, 211
Settlement district. *See* Commercial district

Shanghai, 9, 11-12, 44, 45-46, 88, 178-79, 180-81, 203
Shansi bankers, 32, 69, 135
Shantung Bank, 126, 135
Shantung Christian University (Cheloo), 59, 95, 130, 152, 209
Shen Hung-lieh (mayor of Tsingtao), 173, 185
Shen-yang (Mukden), 111, 212
Shu-yuan. See Academies
Sino-German Convention of 1898, 44, 47
Soldiers, 37, 77, 140, 151, 162. *See also* Fifth Division; Militia
Soviet influence, 8, 207
Strikes, 143-44
Students, 116-20, 122, 151
Sü Yu (Communist general), 197, 199
Sun Pao-ch'i (governor in 1911 revolution), 44, 75
Sun Yat-sen, 166, 168, 193. *See also* Kuomintang; Revolutionary Party
Sung Ching-shih (nineteenth-century rebel), 25

Ta-ch'ing River, 26. *See also* Flood; Yellow River
Taipings, 16, 25
Tanaka Giichi (Japanese premier), 157, 159, 160-61
T'ang K'o-san (Tsinan official), 103, 126n
Tangku truce, 183-84
Taxation, 5, 81-82, 127-28, 145, 147-48, 166-67, 192, 212. *See also* Likin; Provincial finances
Technology, 3, 4-5, 10, 33-34, 53-54, 55, 57, 58-59, 111, 138-39, 159, 172-73, 208. *See also* Automobiles; Electricity; Industry
Telegraph, 33-34, 53, 111
Telephone, 54, 154
Terauchi Seiki (Japanese premier), 107
Theatre, 34, 37, 53, 153-54
T'ien Chung-yü (civil governor), 106-107, 136, 184
Tientsin, 11, 30, 45, 196, 203
Tientsin-Pukow railway, 46-47, 143, 165, 177, 196-97
Ting Pao-chen (late nineteenth-century governor), 29, 33
Ting Shih-i (1911 revolution leader in Shantung), 73-75
Trading systems, 22-23, 32

Transportation, 14-15, 68-69, 94-95, 171-72, 210-12. *See also* Automobiles; Railroads; Technology

Treaty ports, 7-12, 40-41, 212. *See also* Mao Tse-tung; Murphey, Rhoads; Western cities

Tsinan: comparison with other Chinese cities, 11-13, 111, 173, 200-201, 210, 212; descriptions of, 17-21, 35-36, 56, 95-96, 151-53, 170-72, 205; centralizing influences at, 21-22, 28-29, 56, 61-62, 68-69, 150-51; military engagements at, 30, 77-78, 89, 161-64, 184-86, 188-89, 191, 198-99; population of, 36-37, 94, 140-41, 171, 193, 226-35; railroads at, 45-47, 95, 196-97

—economy of, 12-14, 19-21, 93-94, 130-33, 168-69, 193-94, 201, 210-12; and trade of, 31-32, 45-46, 69-70, 127, 137, 164, 176-81; and industry at, 53-54, 137-39, 172-73, 193-94, 219-25

—foreigners at, 33, 40-41, 59-60, 209-10, 210-12; missionaries at, 37-38, 152, 159. *See also* Japanese, residing at Tsinan

—modernization of, 12-15, 40-41, 42-43, 47, 91-92, 170-71, 210-15; and education, 33-34, 55-56, 61-63, 95, 150, 169, 173, 209

Tsingtao, 44, 46, 68, 83, 157, 167, 182, 194, 196, 198, 211, 212-14. *See also* Germany

Tsingtao-Tsinan railway: described, 45; Japanese control of, 84, 112, 126, 160-61, 163, 167; mentioned, 32-33, 44-45, 46-47, 104-105, 118, 143, 160, 177, 196

Ts'ung Liang-pi (Tsinan capitalist), 138n

Tu O (militia organizer), 29

Tuan Ch'i-jui (leader of Anfu clique), 99, 103, 108, 113, 117, 121, 124, 137

T'ung-meng-hui. See Revolutionary Alliance

Twenty-one Demands, 85-86

United States, 5, 47, 125, 152, 194, 197-98

Urban administration, 4-5, 21, 50-53, 89, 144-49, 172-73, 195, 198-99. *See also* Bureaucracy; Commercial district; Police

Urban communes, 207

Urban-rural relations, 128, 192-93, 196, 200-201, 207-208

Urbanization: defined, 3-4. *See also* Mao Tse-tung

Wages, 141-42

Wang Hung-i (gentry reformer), 116, 124

Wang Mao-k'un (late Ch'ing official), 46, 66, 67, 74

Wang Yao-wu (post-1945 governor), 194-95, 196, 197, 200

Warlords, 13, 105-106, 107, 124, 128, 148, 181-83, 185-86, 201, 211-12. *See also* Governors; Militarization of China

Washington Conference, 121-22, 157

Wei-hsien, 22, 26, 34, 94

Western cities, 3-5, 11, 154, 176, 208. *See also* Treaty ports

Whitewright Museum, 59, 112

Wu Hua-wen (Kuomintang general at Tsinan, 1948), 198-99

Wu P'ei-fu (North China warlord), 107-108

Wu Ta-chou (revolutionary in 1911, 1916), 89, 90, 91

Yeh Ch'un-ch'ih (newspaper editor), 92-93

Yellow River, 23, 25-26, 31-33, 46, 160-61

Yen-t'ai. *See* Chefoo

Yokohama Specie Bank, 53, 112, 135, 178

Young Men's Christian Association (YMCA), 152

Yüan Shih-k'ai: plans for Tsinan, 40, 42; compared with warlords, 41-42, 128; educational policy of, 55-56; economic policies of, 69, 70-71, 80-82; political programs of, 72-73, 75, 78, 79-80, 81-82; relations with Japan, 85-86; mentioned, 16, 38-39, 44, 47, 50-51, 55, 57, 60, 68, 96-97, 113, 136, 165, 183, 211, 213, 214

Yüan Shu-hsun (late Ch'ing governor), 43-44, 51

DESIGNED BY ROBERT JACOBSON
COMPOSED BY DUARTE COMPANY, LEWISTON, MAINE
MANUFACTURED BY THOMSON-SHORE, INC., DEXTER, MICHIGAN
TEXT IS SET IN ENGLISH TIMES, DISPLAY LINES IN WEISS

Library of Congress Cataloging in Publication Data
Buck, David D   1936-
Urban Change in China.
Bibliography: p.
Includes index.
1. Tsinan, China—History. I. Title.
DS796.T68B8   309.1'51'14   76-11309
ISBN 0-299-07110-3

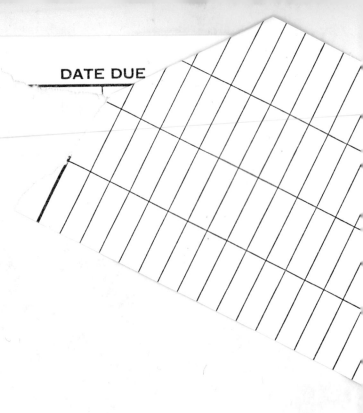